WHEREABOUTS
·UNKNOWN·

M ARGARET R EESON

WHEREABOUTS ·UNKNOWN·

AN ALBATROSS BOOK

© Margaret Reeson 1993

Published in Australia and New Zealand by
Albatross Books Pty Ltd
PO Box 320, Sutherland
NSW 2232, Australia
in the United States of America by
Albatross Books
PO Box 131, Claremont
CA 91711, USA
and in the United Kingdom by
Lion Publishing plc
Peter's Way, Sandy Lane West
Oxford OX4 5HG, England

First edition 1993

National Library of Australia
Cataloguing-in-Publication data

Reeson, Margaret
Whereabouts Unknown

ISBN 0 7324 1003 7 (Albatross)
ISBN 0 7459 2426 3 (Lion)

1. Montevideo Maru (Ship). 2. World War, 1939–1945 — Prisons and
   prisoners, Japanese. 3. Missionaries' wives — Australia.
4. Missionaries — Pacific Area. 5. Missionaries — Asia. I. Title

940.547252

Cover illustration: Michael Mucci
Printed and bound in Australia by McPherson's Printing Group, Victoria

Contents

Acknowledgements

To tell a story such as this, with the interconnected strands of private human experience weaving through the broader theme of nations at war, it has been necessary to spend time talking with people who experienced it, as well as exploring collections of archives. Because such a large number of people were affected by the fall of Rabaul in 1942, I have chosen to focus my storytelling on the close-knit group who were working with Methodist Overseas Missions in the islands immediately before the war. They formed an identifiable community within the wider community and their experiences are representative.

In the process of research, I have been welcomed and honoured with the confidences of some very special people and I thank them all most sincerely. They have become friends whom I value. My gratitude goes to the women who were willing to be interviewed on the theme of their experience of losing their husband in the sinking of the *Montevideo Maru*: Jean Mannering (Poole), Mel Walker (Trevitt), Jean Stuart (Shelton) and Nellie Thirkettle (Simpson).

My thanks goes to the following family members who shared the stories of the other mission widows: Malcolm and Gloria McArthur, Bill and Carolyn Linggood, Loloma (Linggood) Puls, George and Edna Oakes, Parker Oakes, Keith Pearson, Russell and

Winifred (Shelton) Playford, Clem Christopher, Janet (Wayne) Gambrill and Margaret (Simpson) Henderson.

Mavis Green and Dora (Wilson) Dunn were willing to talk about their experiences as prisoners of the Japanese and offered diary material as well as various mementoes of that time. Rodger and Kath Brown have been generous with their time and interest as they have offered detailed memories of pre-war, evacuation, escape and post-war experiences. It was a special pleasure to meet Elsie Wilson, who had been known to me by name for many years because of her later work in the Highlands of Papua New Guinea, and to hear her story of the war years.

Contemporaries of the missionary team, Netta (Allsop) Gamble, Jessie March, Hazel Jones and Gordon and Grace Young also offered helpful memories of that period. Ping Hui kindly gave his time to describe the situation for the Rabaul Chinese community during those years. Bishop William To Kilala contributed his memories as a young New Guinean who witnessed the impact of war on his own people.

Of great value in the research was the long years of gathering material on this theme by the Rev. Arthur Brawn and his wife Jean. Because the Brawns remembered the lost mission staff as friends and former colleagues, and persisted in keeping their memory alive over fifty years, they were able to collect a range of information: this they kindly passed on to me. It is a sadness that Arthur and Jean Brawn, as well as a number of other people who were willing to be interviewed for this book, have died during 1992–1993. It is my hope that the fruit of their efforts will be that the friends and family members who meant so much to them all will not be forgotten.

The many writings on Rabaul and the work of the Methodist/United Church in New Guinea Islands by Neville Threlfall have been particularly useful. My thanks to Neville for his willingness to give me access to his major manuscript on the history of Rabaul before it was published, with special reference to the appendix on the debate about the *Montevideo Maru*.

It has also been very helpful to correspond with men who were serving in Rabaul with the 2/22nd in 1941–1942. My thanks to

C.O. (Bill) Harry and Canon John May, as well as to Ben Dawson, for a thought-provoking phone conversation. Hank Nelson of the Research School of Pacific Studies, ANU, an authority on this subject, has been generous with guidance and this is greatly appreciated.

A number of people have contacted me to share something of their own family stories about the fall of Rabaul. As this event touched so many, it is hoped that this book will be seen as representing and respecting the experience of all the families, even though many are not named. Thankyou to you all.

Once again it has been a pleasure to work with the people of Albatross Books. My thanks go to John Waterhouse for encouraging me to write another book and to Ken Goodlet for his friendship and skills as editor.

A long writing project can become a lonely and discouraging process. To those special friends who continue to ask real questions about the work, to the people of Weston Creek Uniting Church and Kippax Uniting Church (Canberra) who are great encouragers, to Jessie Byrne-Hoffman who was a helpful critic and Averill Edwards and Chris Oyston with advice: thankyou all. The staffs of several collections of archives have been very helpful and I would like to record a particular thanks for the courtesy and helpfulness of the Australian War Memorial Research Centre over several years.

Most of all I want to record how much my own family means in the long process of creating a book. To my husband, Ron, and to Ruth and Glen Powell, Jenni and Colin Hudson, and David: you six know that your encouragement, teasing, questioning, stirring, interest and love are at the heart of the matter.

Margaret Reeson
Canberra
September 1993

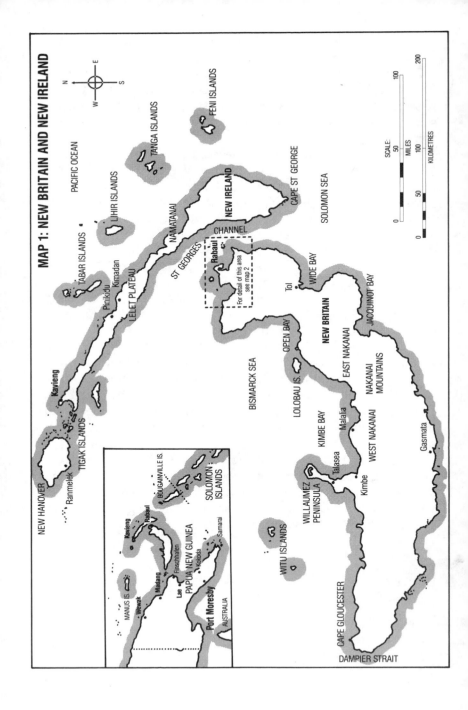

MAP 1: NEW BRITAIN AND NEW IRELAND

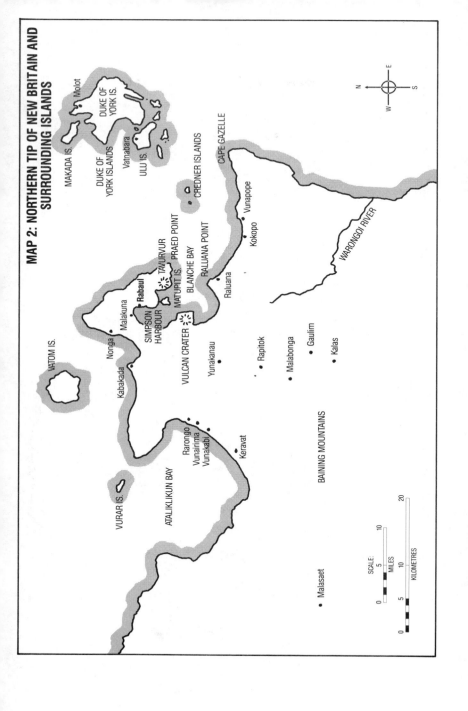

MAP 2: NORTHERN TIP OF NEW BRITAIN AND SURROUNDING ISLANDS

1

December 1939– December 1940

THE CLOCKFACE GLEAMED IN THE LAMPLIGHT, time silently passing while she worked. Ten minutes, he had said. No, it was not time yet.

The night was warm and pungent with the odour of chemicals, silent but for the wind in the rainforest. A moth, velvet-winged and mesmerised by the flame, lunged against the glass of the lamp, casting new shadows that flickered and ran.

It still seemed strange to be in this place and with this man. Only months earlier it would have seemed unlikely. This time last year, just before Christmas 1939, Jean thought, it seemed an impossibility. Yet now, here she was, watching the clock for John.

He was close, just beyond a shut door, locked away in the total darkness of the windowless storeroom to perform his magic. It was still all an experiment, a new experience. It was like everything else they were doing these days. Everything — marriage, moving to a foreign country, coming to a newly-built house to pioneer new work, learning another language — everything was changing around her. Every day there were new demands, new challenges, new astonishments — and Jean, sitting beside the ticking clock, was delighted.

As for this latest experiment, John's attempt to develop his own negatives, they had been warned that in the extreme humidity of the tropics their film would grow mould in the camera if they left it too long, so this was yet another new thing to try.

Time was up. Jean banged on the door. 'John? John, that's ten minutes!'

There was the sound of movement and the door opened. John emerged from among the shadowed shelves of flour, rice and tinned fish with strips of film negative suspended.

'Let's hope we've got something this time,' he said. Their first attempt had failed and the film of their honeymoon, such as it was, had turned completely black.

He held the insubstantial strip to the light. She watched his face, the square profile that even now sometimes still seemed the outline of a stranger, a face she loved but needed to learn.

There was a sigh of relief. 'This is better. It looks as if we have some good ones of the bush patrol, and the meetings with our new friends — here's you sitting by the river. . . Have a look.'

Very gingerly, Jean held the narrow strip of film. Images were there, though they were tiny and unclear. But nothing was as she remembered it. Everything seemed altered, mysterious, back-to-front. Black was white, light was dark, vivid colour had become shades of grey. The colours, the smells, the music had gone. Tiny figures were just discernible; rows of white people black and black ones white, the shape of a picnic, a hint of village dancers, the curve of a beach, everything in reverse.

'I think they may be very good, once they are printed,' she said.

She moved the dark translucent strip in front of the lamp. For a moment it seemed that the lamp flame darted among the shadowy figures, as if they walked through fire. . .

A year earlier — it had been December 1939 — everything was about to change. The classroom was heavy with heat. Children fidgeted and drooped, too hot to be bothered with serious lessons and only half-interested in the rehearsal for the school concert. Jean was thankful that the school year was nearly over. In a week or so, the children would be free to spend the long summer days on

1. *Staff at Methodist synod, New Britain, 1939*
l. to r. *Carl Vasey, Bill Huntley, Laurie Linggood, Helen Pearson, Howard Pearson, Nellie Simpson, Jean Christopher, Mary Jenkins, Laurie McArthur, Jessie March, Tom Simpson, Dorothy Beale, Margaret Harris, Ben Chenoweth, Con Mannering, Herbert Shelton, Syd Beazley, Dan Oakes, Percy Clark*

2. *Afternoon tea at Raluana, synod 1940*

holidays in their small New South Wales country town, Murrurundi in the Hunter Valley, and she could go home to her family in Sydney for Christmas. There was only the end-of-year concert with prize-giving, and the final tidying of the classroom still to be done — and the farewells. The farewells. The young teacher had been trying all day, unsuccessfully, not to think about the farewells.

'John Poole's not the only one leaving,' she said to herself sternly. 'Think of the men who are enlisting. He is only a good friend, anyway.'

It was true enough that others from their rural community were leaving, too. It was only a few months since she had heard the Australian Prime Minister speak to the nation through the crackle of static on the wireless: 'It is my melancholy duty to inform you officially that, in consequence of a persistence by Germany in her invasion of Poland, Great Britain has declared war upon her and that, as a result, Australia is also at war.' Young men from the district were joining up and they were to be farewelled, too. At least John was not going off to war. She knew that she had no choice but to say goodbye with grace. He was going and she was not going with him. That was that.

That afternoon after the last of the children had gone home, trailing schoolbags behind them, he came to the school.

'Come out for a last ride later,' he said, 'when it's not so hot.'

They saddled their horses together in the paddock when the sun was dropping and the dusk brought some coolness. This was where they had first had time to talk together nearly two years earlier, when they had both arrived in the community early in 1938. Jean Colditz had come to teach at the local school and John Poole was to be the new Methodist minister. Both newcomers were in their early twenties, strangers to Murrurundi and, when they discovered that each of them had a horse grazing in the same paddock, it was natural to begin riding together.

Now they rode out along the road and Jean knew that it was for the last time. Soon there would be the formal farewell from the community, a final service in the church, the Scout troop he had begun would be handed over to another leader — and when she came back for the 1940 school year, he would not be there.

She watched the back of his smooth head as he rode ahead along a narrow track through bushland, erect and compact on horseback. If he turned his head, she would see the lively sparkle in his eyes, and hear his voice speaking with enthusiasm about his work and his faith in God.

'Have you heard where they'll be sending you yet?'

'Not yet. The mission board probably won't decide till we candidates are part way through our missionary training.' John brought his horse to a halt and waited for her. 'It could be North Australia with an Aboriginal community, or Fiji, or maybe New Guinea. Wherever the church wants to send me, I guess. This is something that I've been thinking about for years — I'm really excited about it.'

He talked on as they rode back through the last shreds of sunset, painting a word picture of challenges of the future. Jean listened carefully but a little wistfully. John Poole's plans for the future had no place for her.

Months flowed by after that, school holidays, Christmas, John's farewell from Murrurundi, and then the new school year. Jean returned to the school and church in Murrurundi, picking up again the threads of life in that community. School work, riding, church choir, leading the Cub troop ('John encouraged me to start this with the small boys,' she remembered), community social events; everything went on as always, but a new Methodist minister stood in the church pulpit and he was not John. Sometimes she received a letter with his familiar handwriting, telling tales of his studies at George Brown Missionary Training College in Sydney, and of the other young men and women who were there with him. In time he wrote that he had been appointed to New Guinea and would be travelling to Rabaul in August, 1940.

The next letter included a curious request. 'Please be at the public phone box outside the post office,' John wrote, and he gave a date and a time.

She went and waited by the phone box that evening, puzzled, nervous. Why had he not written what he wanted to say? People only made trunk calls from long distances when something was very wrong, in emergencies, or. . .?

The phone jangled into alarming life. It was hard to lift the receiver. Then she heard his voice. When she replaced the telephone with a hand that shook a little, she knew that John Poole had asked her to marry him and travel with him to New Guinea. And she had said 'Yes'.

(John did not tell her at that time that he had an audience for his phone call. A few fellow students who had suspected what he was up to had lurked around the front foyer near the public phone, taking uncharacteristic interest in the glass case of stuffed tropical birds there. At intervals the eavesdroppers offered whispered encouragement and distracting comments to the young man who clutched the phone against his ear and did his best to screen out their intrusions. The diminutive girl in Murrurundi with the curly brown hair and beautiful smile could not see the wicked grins of his mates, or hear their cheers when he stepped out of the phone booth and said, 'She says yes!')

They planned to marry in August, days before sailing for New Guinea. Jean resigned from teaching to return to her parents' home in Sydney to prepare for the wedding. She became a frequent visitor at the missionary college, sometimes sitting in on lectures on anthropology or missionary principles, or joining the students, destined for a range of Pacific and north Australian locations, for meals.

Over dinner in the college dining room of the elegant Federation house in Haberfield, Jean began to make new friends. Dora Wilson was a tall slim nurse from Newcastle, NSW, and Rodger and Kath Brown were newly-weds from Adelaide, South Australia. The three of them came to sit with Jean and John.

'It's good to meet you, Jean. We've been telling John here that he needs a wife,' Rodger said. 'Now we five will all be travelling to New Guinea together.' Like John Poole, Rodger Brown was a Methodist minister and the two men had already discovered many mutual enthusiasms. All of them were in their twenties, fit, trained and eager to begin work; each of them told stories of the influences which had brought them to this time and place.

Jean, Kath and Dora found themselves talking weddings.

3. *Methodist mission families' picnic in botanical gardens, Rabaul, November 1940*

4. *Rodger and Kath Brown, guests at Poole wedding, 9 August 1940*

Kath had been married just before they left their home state to travel to missionary college in Sydney a few months earlier and they enjoyed talk of bridal tulle and lace and glory boxes. Kath was concerned to find that Jean seemed to have no skills in domesticity. Jean's interests were in science and teaching, specially in botany, but she could not cook. Kath had deliberately left work during her engagement to study cookery, sewing and household management.

'You'll never have any money, you know, if you marry a missionary minister! How will you survive in New Guinea?' Kath asked.

On the day before John Poole and Jean Colditz were married in Rockdale Methodist Church on 9 August 1940, on the far side of the globe a desperate struggle was beginning. One day people would call it the Battle of Britain. It seemed very distant from the security and simplicity of that Sydney suburban church, where John waited solemnly in dark suit and clerical collar, even more neat than his usual precision.

Jean walked up the aisle towards him on her father's arm, through cascades of flowers, and pews filled with family and friends. Dora and the Browns were beaming at her as she passed, and then came her mother, watching her bridal daughter with eyes filled with tears. She and John made their promises to love each other 'till death us do part'. Death seemed very far away, yet another kind of parting and separation was very close.

Later, catching her parents' eyes over the elaborate icing filigree and silver leaves of the wedding cake, Jean recognised a little of their feelings as they watched her beside her bridegroom. Within days she would be leaving Australia and it would be years before she came home again, she expected. Her parents had asked many questions about her future; 'pioneering work' and 'living out in the bush' was all anyone could tell them.

Saying goodbye to their guests after the wedding reception was hard. They were not leaving for a lighthearted honeymoon, but for two days of last minute packing before they left their home city and friends for an unknown future.

Of all their guests, only three would be travelling with them into their life together: Dora, Kath and Rodger.

As the last guests waved goodbye to the bridal couple, Rodger Brown shouted after them, 'Don't forget to be at the wharf on Monday! Dora and Kath and I will be waiting for you on board the ship.'

It hardly counted as a real honeymoon, Jean thought later. The excitement and delight of the wedding was on Friday; by Sunday her beautiful lace wedding gown was put away and the final packing of wedding gifts and personal things into boxes for travel had to be complete.

'I won't be needing my winter clothes again for years!' she told her sisters. 'You can have them — next time we are home in Sydney in winter all these things will be very old-fashioned.'

The last hours were a rush of packing and farewells, hugs and some tears. There was little time to spend with John. By Monday they were on board the ship, the farewell streamers tightening in their hands as the ship drew slowly away from the wharf, and the slight, papery ties between her and her family at home snapped.

If Jean had dreamed of an idyllic sea voyage to the tropics to begin married life with John, the dream soon evaporated. The ship was scarcely beyond Sydney Heads when she discovered how bad a sailor she was. Miserably seasick she lay on her bunk, uncomforted by John's announcement that Rodger was in his cabin as sick as she was, but that Dora, Kath and he were all feeling fine and would keep each other company till they reached dry land again in nine days.

For most of the time she felt too miserable to be disappointed but, as the ship sailed at last in sight of the island of New Britain where they were to work, she stood beside John on deck. The rounded greens of the volcanic caldera which formed the harbour came nearer, and the iron roofs of the government tropical town of Rabaul reflected the sun.

'I'm sorry. It's not been much of a honeymoon,' she said.

'Don't worry. Once we're ashore you'll soon feel better. Anyway, we have the rest of our lives together.'

Under the shade of an umbrella, the woman stood beside her husband on the wharf waiting for the gangway to be lowered. High above, Daisy McArthur could see the faces of passengers lined along the ship's railing waiting to disembark. Among them were five new staff, come to Rabaul to join them as workers with the Methodist mission.

'Can you see them?' she asked her husband. Laurie McArthur was chairman of the district, and had been corresponding with their head office in Sydney for some time about the new young missionaries.

'I can recognise Rodger Brown. The others I don't know, but they are sure to be together.'

Passengers began to file down the slope of the gangway and Daisy and Laurie McArthur moved forward. Daisy was looking for two brides and a single lady. Laurie would take care of the two men. She remembered so well that time ten years earlier when she, too, had been a bride arriving in the islands for the first time, wedding gifts packed in the glory box Laurie had made for her, wondering what life would bring them both. She had never forgotten that sensation of being overwhelmed by the torrent of the new.

In some ways the flood of the unfamiliar had been exciting, exhilarating, yet there were times when she felt she was almost drowning in it. It would be the same for these three girls arriving today, she knew. They would each have to face a strange country and people, with colleagues who were still strangers; they would hear an unfamiliar language and live in a climate unlike anything they had known. Two of them were new brides, operating in the foreign landscape of marriages they had barely begun to explore.

The five arrived on the wharf together, young, hopeful, a little anxious about their first meeting with the chairman and his wife. Hands reached out in formal greeting: 'Mr McArthur. . . Mrs McArthur. . .' Daisy remembered the chairman in those days when she and Laurie were new, a revered senior man with nearly thirty years of experience in the islands. Perhaps she and Laurie, in their mid-thirties, would not seem quite so awe-inspiring to the newcomers and Laurie might even seem young to be chairman.

With a smile, she escorted them through the glare of the wharf to the waiting vehicle.

Sitting in her living room, some of them looked a little shy and ill at ease on the edge of their cane armchairs. Kath and Rodger Brown, Jean and John Poole and Dora Wilson began to introduce themselves over morning tea. Daisy listened and observed. Tall Dora, the nurse, seemed a gentle girl, not as outspoken as some of the others. To Jean, the little one, Daisy said, 'I met my husband when I was a teacher and he came to be Methodist minister in the same town, just as you did.'

Kath was a sportswoman, though she would have little opportunity for sport now she was in New Britain. Daisy was pleased to find that Kath also knew many of the South Australian places and people known to her, and it was good to catch up with home news. Laurie was talking with the men, asking about the church at home and discussing the latest war news, though war seemed impossibly remote from the safety of the islands.

'We have arranged for your appointments,' Laurie said. 'Miss Dora Wilson is to go out to the health centre at Malabonga, inland on the border of the Baining Mountains, working with Miss Mavis Green. I believe you and Miss Green know each other from your nurse training at Newcastle General Hospital. Is that right?'

Dora nodded. She knew Mavis well from their training years and was pleased to think that she would begin her work with a friend from home.

'The Browns will spend the first months until synod in a nearby circuit, and then will go out to our most isolated station along the north coast of New Britain. The Pooles are appointed to Kalas, in hill country beyond Malabonga where Dora Wilson is going. They will be our first appointment of an Australian missionary to the people of the Baining mountains. But not yet, of course,' Laurie McArthur explained. 'Later today I'll drive you all out to Vunairima, where our major schools and educational institutions are, and you will spend two weeks making a start on learning the local language.'

Laurie spread a map and they crowded around it, following his finger as he pointed out the locations of mission circuits, schools and hospitals. The litany of foreign names would be meaningless, Daisy knew. Laurie was listing names of places — Malaguna, Raluana, Vunairima — and staff, teachers, nurses, accountant, ministers, as well as local leadership, in a rapid procession of words. The newcomers were listening intently, but she knew that it would be weeks and even months before the blur of information came into clear focus for them.

They were still leaning over the map when the table began to shake. Not very much, just a minor earth tremor, but the new arrivals stepped back in alarm. Teacups rattled daintily in saucers and the hanging light in the centre of the room swung in an elegant curve.

'It's nothing. Don't worry about it.' Laurie was reassuring. 'Earth tremors, large and small, are normal here around Rabaul. The town has been built within a circle of volcanoes and not all of them are extinct. It's a place with an exciting past — some time you might like to ask the people at Vunairima about the time a volcano erupted in the middle of a mission staff wedding! But, for now, this lovely part of the world is a great deal safer than Europe. You will probably see nothing more worrying than an occasional earth tremor.'

The sea of brown faces rippled as three hundred students stood. A single voice sounded a note and then the whole assembly burst into harmony. Jean Poole watched and listened, enchanted. She loved to sing in choirs, but this was a massed choir unlike any she had known.

The students and staff of the various schools on the mission education campus at Vunairima had gathered to welcome the new staff: the District Girls' School; George Brown College for the training of local pastor-teachers; six men preparing for the ordained ministry; and the staff of Stewart Hospital. There had been speeches and songs, and she had sat in front of them all with John and the others, fascinated. Now the song came to an end and the students filed out in procession, passing by the cluster of new missionaries with hands outstretched for a ceremonial handshake, some smiling broadly and many with faces shyly averted. There were so many of them and somehow they all looked alike to her.

The last hand was shaken and Jean followed John and the others along a path between lawns, flowers and towering tropical trees. Laurie McArthur introduced them to the other Australian staff. For Rodger and Kath, this was something of a reunion.

'John, Jean, come and meet our old friends from South Australia, Howard and Helen Pearson and Elsie Wilson. We've all been part of the Adelaide network and I trained for the ministry with Howard.'

The Browns went off happily with the Pearsons while Dora Wilson was welcomed by namesake, teacher Elsie Wilson and nurse Dorothy Beale. Jean and John were given hospitality by Jack and Mel Trevitt from NSW; Jack was headmaster of George Brown College. Like almost everyone they had met that day, they were or had been schoolteachers.

That evening over a meal at the Trevitts' table, Jean and John began to learn more of the place where they had come. Though they had not known them well previously, the Trevitts and the Pooles were from the same network of young Methodists in NSW and were familiar with many of the same places and people. Jean discovered that Mel Trevitt was a graduate in earth sciences and Jack in languages, both of them teachers and both independently offering for missionary work before their marriage; she was going to enjoy talking to them, she knew. Mel showed her the sole photograph that had survived of the Trevitt wedding; the story of their wedding had become a legend.

'A volcano erupted in the harbour on the day Jack and I were married, just as we were saying "I do" — and no-one stayed for our wedding reception, not even Jack or me!'

It was not from lack of interest — everything she was hearing was fascinating — but as the evening went on Jean began to find it hard to absorb anything more. Perhaps it was the heat, perhaps it was because it had been a very long day since she had woken on board the ship. Jack Trevitt was talking to John about the school which was clearly his pride and joy.

'Our college has become one of the most respected in the country,' she heard: '. . .innovative educational philosophy. . .

Laurie McArthur was headmaster before me and had a wide vision for education among the New Guinean youth. . . broad impact. . . introduction of basic English as well as education in vernacular. . . education for girls and women. . . fine new buildings specially designed for climate and purpose in the past ten years. . .'

By the time the Trevitt baby woke and the conversation broke up, Jean was overwhelmed with impressions and information. When she finally climbed in under the mosquito net to bed that night, Jean was weary but very excited. The people, the names, the language, the amazing vegetation, the heat, erupting volcanoes — everything circled in her mind in a great confusion. In time she would sort it all out, she hoped.

Out of all the lists and processions, the only person she had known more than six months was John and even this relationship was new: bride and groom were still discovering new things about each other every day. Jack Trevitt had explained that in the morning he would begin language classes with them. As she fell asleep beside John, she was thinking that tomorrow she would like to explore Vunairima.

The young teacher looked up. A shadow had fallen across the doorway into her classroom. Hesitating at the door was one of the new married couples who had just arrived at Vunairima. Elsie Wilson stepped forward to invite them in, motioning to the room full of schoolgirls to stand in welcome. The small Australian woman and her husband stepped inside.

'Good morning, *Talatala*, good morning, *Marama*!' the girls chorused.

Elsie noticed the slightly startled look on the other girl's face. She was probably thinking. . . *Marama*?

'Welcome to our school,' she said. 'But you'll need to get used to being called "*Marama*". That is the term for all the white married ladies here. And "*Talatala*" for the ministers.'

The visitors did not stay for long. They were just on a tour of the mission station during a break from their language lessons and had called at the District Girls' School on their way, they explained.

5. *John and Jean Poole, 9 August 1940*

6. *Mavis Green, 1939*

7. *Elsie Wilson, 1939*

8. *Jean Poole, 1940*

The girls sang for them, they smiled graciously in the way of school visitors, had a cursory glance at the work on the desks and the maps on the wall and were gone.

Elsie went back to her class work. She was glad the visitors had not stayed longer. Even now, in her second year at the school, she preferred not to teach before an audience other than her students. It was a year since she had come to this large and challenging school, with its girls and married women in separate classes to be taught, accommodated, fed and chaperoned. In some ways she was still building her confidence to do the job well. It was very different from her first years of teaching in tiny bush schools in South Australia, with herself the only teacher. People sometimes commented on her youth, which did little to reassure her; surely twenty-two was adult enough to leave home for New Guinea!

Later that day, when the schoolgirls had gone off to do their afternoon gardening work in their food gardens, Jean Poole came back to visit Elsie. 'Do you mind if I come and have a proper look at your classroom?' Jean asked. 'I'd love to teach in a school like this.'

'But you can't — you're a married woman!'

'Only for the last three weeks and I'm still getting used to it.' Jean wandered around the room, obviously interested in the program for the girls, the academic subjects and the practical skills being offered to give young New Guinean women opportunities which had never been possible before.

Elsie watched her. You have to choose, you know, Elsie thought, but she didn't say it. Everyone knew that women could choose to be missionary teachers, or they could choose to marry. You couldn't have it both ways. That was the way things worked. There were one or two of the older single women missionaries who had been known to be quite cutting if a mission teacher or nurse decided to leave their work to marry — 'no commitment. . .', 'giving up their work. . .', 'denying their calling. . .' they'd say and be offended at the mention of the name.

Elsie did not feel like that. Yet she knew that she had to make a choice. For her, there was the pattern of the teacher who had preceded her at the school. Jessie March was attractive, intelligent, creative and single at forty. She could have married but chose to continue to teach, throwing her considerable gifts and energy into building up a fine school for girls. Elsie admired her very much.

The two young women walked from the school, following a path that ran through a parade of poinciana in flower. Beside a creek, schoolgirls spread damp washing on warm rocks to dry, their greetings and laughter following their teacher and her companion as they passed. The track narrowed through undergrowth then widened onto a beach of black volcanic sand and the glitter of the sea spreading out beyond the bay.

'Quite a few of the married women here used to be teachers in Australia,' Elsie explained. 'Mel Trevitt, Helen Pearson, Mrs McArthur, Mrs Linggood. Another teacher, Eileen, is soon to marry the mission accountant Wilf Pearce.'

They strolled back the way they had come. Elsie pulled a scented frangipani flower and tucked it into her dark hair. She did it without thinking. It was one of the bounties of the place, the wealth of blossoms waiting to be threaded into circlets for hair and neck, and the students often wore flowers in the springing masses of their hair. The young teacher was unconscious that she was beautiful.

'We won't all fit in the cabin.' The older man inspected his party of new recruits. Their bags and boxes were piled in the back of the small utility truck, along with bags of flour, drums of kerosene and their supply of groceries for the three months until a truck came with another load.

'John, you'll have to ride in the back with the boxes. Jump in, ladies.'

Jean Poole and Dora Wilson clambered into the cabin beside the driver. The engine sputtered and chugged into life and they were off, with the gardened beauties of Vunairima disappearing in their dust.

'Kalas won't be anything like Vunairima, you understand, Jean,' their driver Laurie Linggood chuckled. For years he had been patrolling through the Baining mountains and knew the area better than almost any other white man.

'It's one of the most interesting parts of the country, though. The people who live inland in the hills were the original people of this peninsula, but were forced back from the coast by later waves of aggressive migration. You'll find a wonderful mixture of culture and languages — and quite a bit of suspicion of you. You'll be the first whites to live in the area, and not just travelling through on patrol.'

Laurie Linggood did not take his eyes from the road, but Jean knew that he was studying her. The chairman, Laurie McArthur, had been the same. The chairman had set out the isolation, the newness of the situation and the complexities of language, warning her, watching her through his round spectacles for signs of anxiety. Now this other man, experienced in the country, fortyish, strong, seemed to be testing her, and Dora beside her.

'How do you think you two girls will find this life?'

Dora spoke. 'I've been getting ready for this for years, all through my nursing training. Ever since I was quite young, and the wife of our minister at church told stories of their missionary work in Fiji, I've been hoping to come to a place like this. She opened up a whole new world to me.'

'That's different from my experience,' Jean said. 'Six months ago, I had no idea that I'd be coming to New Guinea. But now that I'm here, I'm happy to have a go at anything.'

Behind her, on the tray of the utility, her husband bounced around among drums and suitcases. Ahead was their new home, recently built for them by Laurie Linggood. She couldn't wait to begin. It did not seem a good moment to mention to the practical man beside her that the science of domesticity was not yet among the sciences that excited her, and his kind wife Essie had needed to teach her, item by item, how to order her groceries.

They followed the road towards the hills. Plantations and villages flowed by. Staring children watched their passing and once a large pig bolted across the road in front of them and disappeared among bushes. Trees dripped with colour and every leaf, every vine seemed miraculously larger than life in the moist and heated atmosphere. It was very different from her beloved Australian bush.

The truck came in sight of a cluster of buildings and pulled up by a house. A darkhaired girl in white nurse's uniform hurried out to welcome them. 'Welcome to Malabonga Health Centre!'

Dora and Jean scrambled from the truck. 'Mavis!' The two nurses were delighted to see each other. While hospital orderlies carried Dora's bags into the house, Dora introduced Mavis Green.

'We trained together at Newcastle General Hospital in NSW, and knew each other well. Then Mavis went off to do midwifery in Sydney and came here last year. We never expected to share the nursing at a bush hospital in New Guinea!'

There was time for only a quick look around the buildings at Malabonga, a cup of tea and promises to walk back that way next Wednesday to have lunch together with the two nurses, and they were on their way again. Kalas was five miles further inland from Malabonga and the road was rough, bisected by little creeks.

At last, a clearing opened up before them, the end of the track. Tall bush timber pressed in about them, almost as if the little community in the hills was only there on sufferance, and through one break in the timber, blue-green ranges flowed away in the distance. A tall New Guinean man came to welcome them, the teacher of the new school, his hand extended in a strong grasp of welcome. 'This is Mikael To Bilak — and this is his wife Louisa,' said Laurie. Lines of barechested young schoolboys stood in rigid lines, bright eyes watching the arrival of the strangers. Beyond the lads, Jean could see a new timber house with an iron roof and their suitcases and boxes being carried inside.

Laurie Linggood stayed long enough to show them how to light their new primus stove. He pushed open the wooden shutter windows and propped them up to let in air and light. While the kettle boiled, Jean explored the rooms of their simple house. It smelled fragrant with the aroma of new timber. As she had not expected the luxuries of electricity or modern plumbing, she was not disturbed at the thought of living without them. She paused at an open window and gazed out across the clearing that was Kalas.

Kalas was indeed not another Vunairima. Instead of buildings on a grand scale, ringed by wide verandahs and set in magnificent gardens, the small school building of Kalas was of woven cane and thatch, as were the outbuildings and teacher's house, and the gardens were immature food gardens rather than spreading lawns and flowering shrubs. Instead of disciplined students in neat cotton laplaps and blouses, the pinnacle of the Methodist education system, the young Baining schoolboys roaming curiously around outside the house were the first of their people to be offered any formal education, and there was no sign of any schoolgirls at all.

'I'll be back in a couple of weeks to take John — and Dora, too — on your first patrol through the mountain villages.' Laurie Linggood was on his way again, home to his wife at their mission station on the coast.

'Me, too! I want to come on patrol with you, of course,' Jean responded.

'You don't have to come,' Laurie offered. 'Mission wives can choose to stay home. Unless you feel nervous about staying by yourself. . .'

Nervous? The thought had not occurred to her. Her mother used to say: 'Jean — five foot tall and scared of nothing and nobody.' If John and Dora were going with Laurie to visit the villagers in the mountains, then she would go with them. A whole new world of people and flora waited to be discovered.

Jean and John watched Laurie go. Inside the house were their suitcases, the boxes of wedding gifts and household things and the stack of bags, cartons and drums. Across the clearing was the thatched church-cum-school and smoke rose gently from a kitchen at the back of Mikael and Louisa's house. A few schoolboys were still watching them shyly from a discreet distance.

They looked at each other. They had come home.

Kalas, Jean discovered, was a delightful place to live. In the microcosm of their community in the clearing, she and John began to make friends. Mikael and Louisa were generous and friendly to the newcomers, and Jean loved their glossy brown-skinned fat babies. Louisa had been raised by missionary women, the child of a German planter and a New Guinean woman, and could speak to Jean in English.

Every day village women came to her door with fruit and vegetables to sell, and Jean shyly experimented with her small grasp of the language. She had always thought of herself as a perfectly ordinary person, but at Kalas she was an oddity. Old women came close to pluck gently at her white skin, to touch her soft brown curls. Mothers pointed her out to small children and then collapsed in peals of smothered giggles. There was time to be with John, sharing his learning about their new work; and there was time to stare at unfamiliar vegetation or visit the school or sketch.

Within a few weeks, Laurie Linggood returned, bringing Dora Wilson with him. He also brought one of the first two New Guinean men ordained to the Methodist ministry, a respected senior man called Akuila To Ngaru. They found Jean ready to go, boots on and hat in hand. Rucksacks and a patrol box with equipment for a week in the bush were loaded onto schoolboy carriers and Jean and Dora followed the men out of the Kalas clearing along the track into the Baining mountains.

As tropical rainforest wrapped them in green, Jean walked with delight. Filtered sunlight lit the track. Jewels of raindrops sparkled on leaves and flowers of vegetation she had never seen before. There was little time to stand and stare. The procession did not pause as they climbed and, if she hesitated to look closely at a spray of orchids hanging overhead or at nameless blossoms, she always had to run to catch up, slipping and slithering on the mud-greased track.

'I wish my botany teacher was here,' she said breathlessly to Dora. 'When I was a student at St George Girls' High, I had a wonderful botany teacher for my favourite subject, Miss Thistle Harris, who used to take me with her and her friends on plant-collecting walks in the bush. I'll have to write and tell her all about this.'

They travelled further and further into another world, a secret world of villagers who had rarely seen white women, a place with its own languages and knowledge, cut off from a world beyond the moist green of their mountains. Late in the afternoon they entered a village at the end of a day of walking, breathless, aching, covered in mud and damp with sweat. Jean joined Dora, John, Laurie Linggood and Akuila To Ngaru in accepting the offered ceremonial handshake of an entire village before they pulled off their muddy boots and prepared a meal.

Sitting in the thatched shelter that night, comparing aching muscles and tendencies to blisters, Jean caught John's eyes across the last glow of their small cooking fire. They had been warned that they ought to be very restrained in the way they behaved in the villages; village people would not understand the ways of a white honeymoon couple. But they were together, sharing the firelight, relishing the adventure, each feeling the excitement of seeing places rarely visited by other whites.

Linggood was telling the story of the time when he had been ready to sleep in one of these villages, clad only in his shirt, when a delegation of people came to solemnly shake his hand — 'We were very dignified about it and they were wearing even less than me!' Sharing the laughter, watching her husband, Jean knew that her life was very good.

They walked for days, deeper and deeper into the hills. One track, deep in shade and treacherous with mud, merged into another. Akuila To Ngaru offered his strong arm to the women in the steepest places and encouraged them when they tired. Some creeks were waded through and once the missionaries were carried across. Villagers stared at them and they gazed back. When at last they emerged on the north coast, a small coastal vessel was lying off the beach and Laurie Linggood decided to travel home with it, around the coast to Raluana.

'But you know the way now, so you'll be right to get back to Kalas. The schoolboys will make sure you don't get lost,' he said. And he was off, leaving the three newcomers with only a few mouthfuls of local language between them and days of hiking ahead of them in a land they had known for only three or four weeks.

'It's not that he's unfeeling,' John said, as they watched him disappear. 'He just thinks that we're here in a perfectly friendly place; he's shown us the way; what more help do we need?'

And they did get back to Kalas, as he'd known they would,

9. *Laurie McArthur,*
1937

10. *Laurie, Daisy and Malcolm McArthur, 1939*

without difficulty. Nonetheless, when Jean came to stick the photos of that September trip to Laup into her photo album, she had a naughty twinkle in her eye. Under one of a series of herself, Dora and Laurie Linggood being piggybacked one at a time across a river by their New Guinean companions, she printed neatly, under a photo of Linggood in mid-stream, 'Mr L just before he fell.'

The first three months of living in the mountains at Kalas passed very happily. Somewhere far away, the Germans, the British, the Australians and others were locked in a deadly battle, but the people of the mountains knew nothing of it, and Jean found herself more and more detached from news of it. Her world was focussed on her home, the school, Mikael and Louisa and their babies, learning the language, talking with village women. She and John were very contented, full of hopes and plans for years of work together in New Guinea.

Each Wednesday she and John walked the five miles to visit Dora and Mavis at Malabonga, or the two nurses came to see them at Kalas; they were becoming good friends. She was still sometimes astonished to find herself with John and in this strange and beautiful land, but had a strong sense of being in the place where she should be, the place where God invited her to be.

The three months were almost over. Soon Laurie McArthur would come driving up the track, as he had promised, and they would leave Kalas behind for a few weeks. It was the time of the annual church meetings when all the mission staff gathered from their places scattered across the islands. They would meet Rodger and Kath Brown again, and the people from Vunairima, and would have the fun of meeting all the other staff, many for the first time.

They were to meet at Raluana, where Laurie Linggood and his wife Essie worked, and Jean knew she would be expected to help Essie with the catering as she was not a member of the formal synod business meetings. Their bags were packed and it was going to be a delightful time, she was sure.

Later, when all that was left of those happy synod days was strips of tiny photographs in black and white, Jean remembered the colours, the perfumes, the laughter — and the food. Whenever the members of synod paused in their talking they were fed, and every time she saw John or the others they had a teacup in one hand and a buttery scone or a sandwich in the other. There were dinners and picnics, and afternoon teas under the mango tree looking across the bay and, as Essie Linggood's helpers, she and Kath seemed to be preparing food all day.

She knew that she would never forget the colours of Raluana where they met for the meetings. Their mountain place at Kalas had its own green and blue beauty, but Raluana was a jewel. The shading canopy of mango, breadfruit, poinciana and raintree framed the sun-glinted blues, jade and aquamarine of the waters of the bay as it washed across to the encircling rim of gently rounded volcanoes. Generations of mission staff had created gardens which flowed back from the palm-edged beach in floods of vivid colour. The perfume of frangipani mingled in the warm, moist air with inscrutable aromas of decaying vegetation, salty water's edge, a whiff of volcanic sulphur and the pervasive scent of copra — like a million coconut biscuits slowly baking.

Laughter and singing was part of it all, too. Australian, Chinese and New Guinean Christians reported on their work for the past year and planned for 1941, but whenever they relaxed together it was time for music, some impromptu games of cricket and for jokes. New Guinean leaders who often sat silently through official meetings in deference to their white colleagues would abandon their reserve when it was time for fun and would be at the centre of the wildest slapstick humour and the most riotous laughter.

At the family picnic for the mission staff, Jean met again women whom she had met in Rabaul and Vunairima during their first few weeks in the country and others who were strangers. Clustered together on mats of woven pandanus palm in the shade of the trees of the Rabaul Botanical Gardens, women and children had a rare chance to meet old friends. For the past year they had lived on isolated mission stations scattered around the islands of New Britain, New Ireland, New Hanover and the Duke of York group with little or no contact with their colleagues, and this was the time for being together, for shopping in a town and for the women-talk conversations for which they starved. Bunched together on their mats, they looked like the reunion of a large and lively family with their backs turned against the rest of the world.

On the far side of the harbour stood the grey-white scarring of Vulcan volcano, bare and forbidding, the hill that had risen out of the harbour on the day of Mel Trevitt's wedding, a silent reminder that the colour, peace and beauty of the area also had a dark side. Within a week or two, a party of some 500 people would be brought into Rabaul from an outlying island, plucked from the sea after surviving German attacks on vessels in the Pacific. Elsewhere in the world, armies were doing battle, and nations plotted to seize power and change the shape of things.

The newlyweds, Jean and John Poole, recording the events of the mission meetings with their camera, did not see these things. They saw their new friends, young men in tropical whites and women in florals, laughing under the mango tree. Life was good and the challenges of their new life and work spread before them without shadows.

When mail arrived long after, along with the prints of their photographs, they laid the small black-and-white prints on the table and stared at them. Images of the past months looked back at them, symbols of everything that had changed — newly discovered landscapes, new friends and an unfamiliar race of people.

'Look at you, all in rows at synod,' Jean laughed. 'If we'd given Mr Mac the cricket bat to hold on his lap, you'd all look just like the village cricket team!'

The photographs were good. They studied them with pleasure.

'They're good,' Jean conceded, 'but they are such little pictures. All the colours and the smells have been squeezed out of them, and you can't hear the laughing.'

She stared at the picture of the group of young men in their tropical whites, with John and Rodger sitting on the grass in the front row. The images stared back, a moment frozen in time.

It was New Britain, December 1940.

2

*Christmas 1940–
June 1941*

THE SOUND OF SINGING WOKE THEM. They had gone to bed on
Christmas Eve happily, even though everything seemed very
strange.

It was Jean Poole's first Christmas Eve without parents or
brother and sisters. There had been no crowded shops bright with
decorations, no visitors, no Christmas pageants or concerts. The
encrustations of the Christmas celebrations of the Australian suburbs had been stripped away. Yet the simplicity of the evening
had been beautiful. She and John had taken their lamp across to
the thatched building which served as both church and school
and, with Mikael and Louisa and some schoolboys, they had sung
carols together. There were small gifts to share from Australian
parcels and everyone went home into the quiet night with a gift.

Then, before dawn, they heard the singing. Pushing open their
bedroom shutter, John and Jean looked out. Clouds edged with
moonlight drifted above a dark curtain of trees. A hurricane
lantern, held high, illuminated the white of smiles against darkness. Harmonies were laid over the sound of wind in the trees,
the sound of Christmas carols from an almost invisible choir.

Jean did not recognise all the words of the songs, sung in
another tongue, but the tunes carried memories of other years,
other places, other people. Home. And this was home, too, this

mountain clearing in the bush with John — and with Mikael and Louisa and the others who were now their friends and neighbours, come to sing for them, a gift in the middle of the night. Tomorrow John would delight in leading his first Christmas service of worship among them, and later they would join Dora and Mavis at Malabonga for Christmas dinner.

Pulling a gown around her, Jean walked outside with her husband to greet the carol singers. They seemed like lantern-lit shepherds coming over darkened hills to Bethlehem as they sang, 'O come, let us adore him, Christ the Lord.'

On the night of the full moon a month later, the earth convulsed. Trees moved without a wind, grasses rippled, buildings creaked and shuddered. Water tanks stretched and flexed their corrugations, setting water sloshing against the metal.

Jean Poole was woken by a thunder of crashings and the strange feeling that her bed was in motion across the floor. She was staying with Dora Wilson and Mavis Green for several days at Malabonga Health Centre while John was away at Vunairima. Dora had offered to share her room with Jean.

'Dora? Dora — oh, this is a big quake!'

Both young women clung to their beds as they skidded to and fro. At last everything trembled into an insecure stillness. From the next room, they heard Mavis calling and the three searched in the dark for torches and hurricane lanterns. When a lantern shed its pool of soft light into the house, they were startled to see that their beds were in strange new positions and the floors strewn with fallen objects. Among the shifting shadows they saw strange intrusions thrusting through the floor. Their house had moved sideways and was now impaled on some of its own cement foundation stumps.

Outside, almost all the bush-materials housing for patients had collapsed, and the hospital stood precariously on shaken foundations, with smashed windows and broken medicine bottles. Corrugated iron water tanks had been jolted from their stands and water flowed across the ground. The three young Australian women joined the rest of the Malabonga community — medical orderlies, hospital patients and their attendant families — in sitting on the cement paths in the moonlight, talking and waiting for the small tremors till daybreak.

Some miles away on that night at Vunairima, Elsie Wilson woke suddenly, alone in the big Sisters' house. Somewhere in the house, nameless things were crashing to the floor. She wasn't usually nervous, but just then she wished that her friend Jessie or one of the other women teachers had been living with her still. It was no use wishing. The shrieks coming from the schoolgirls' dormitories were her responsibility. Sometimes she had the feeling that this sort of thing would be easier if she were at least ten years older and wiser. When at last the earthquake eased, Elsie went to see what had happened. None of the schoolgirls had been hurt but some of the timber, cane and thatch buildings had collapsed.

Through the trees in the Headmaster's house, Mel Trevitt reached for a torch. 'The baby!' she cried and tried to step out of bed to go to comfort him. The house lurched and shook, throwing her to her knees. It was impossible to get her balance and walk. 'Jack, help me!'

Crawling on hands and knees for minutes that felt like eternity, she clawed her way along the hall to her child's room until she held him safe in her arms. Through the screams of the baby they heard a crash and the sound of breaking glass further along the hall, mingled with a startled yelp and some muttering. In the beam of the torch, Mel and Jack watched their houseguest John Poole walk towards them along the hall, rumpled with sleep and trailing blood along the floor.

'That shake shook me right off the bed — and I've just sat on the lamp. It's smashed and I've cut myself!'

In the mission house at Vunairima, high on swaying piles, Helen and Howard Pearson struggled to their infant Donald, and found his cot crowded in among furniture which had danced across the floor into the centre of the room. Two of their heavy bookcases had been flung forward onto their faces.

When at last the sun lit the Bainings, Vunairima and Malabonga, it was possible to see the damage. On mission compounds and in villages, buildings made of bush timbers, cane and thatch had collapsed, tanks had ruptured, large permanent buildings had suffered some structural damage, equipment was broken, trees had fallen, and the earthquake, combined with months of dry weather, had damaged roads, bridges and garden areas. Akuila To Ngaru, their senior New Guinean minister, walked to Malabonga to make sure the Australian women and the hospital staff and patients were safe, and went on to comfort his people through the mountains. At Malabonga, the women spent the day clearing up the mess in the hospital and environs.

All day there had been minor tremors and, as dusk began its swift tropical descent, the three Australian girls decided that they didn't feel secure in the house. 'Let's sleep out on the grass,' one suggested, and they dragged mattresses outside and settled for the night under the stars.

Later, along the moonlit road they saw men coming, first Laurie Linggood and Laurie McArthur and finally, limping painfully along, John Poole. 'We had to leave the car some seven miles back — a bridge is out and there are landslips, too, blocking the road,' he said, 'but we had to get here, to make sure that you girls were all safe.'

John Poole had made an heroic effort to reach his wife, despite his discomfort from the unheroic wound. Jean was glad to see him. The group gathered in companionable fashion on the grass, prepared to talk their way through the unsteady night.

'We are not going to have a repeat of the big eruption we had four years ago — May 1937 — I hope.'

The women were curious. Each of them had heard bits of the story, but now, with a long shaky night to fill, they persuaded Laurie Linggood to tell what he had witnessed. As he began the story, Laurie McArthur set off to walk through the night to Kalas to check on the Pooles' house and Mikael and the others; he would return by dawn.

'That time, four years ago, began with a series of tremors, getting bigger all the time,' Linggood began. 'We wouldn't easily forget what happened, in any case, but the timing of it all, on Mel and Jack Trevitt's wedding day, meant that most of us were together that day. . .'

The story was told. Miss Melville Chaseling, as she was, arrived on the ship from Australia two days before her wedding to Jack, planned for 29 May 1937. The whole missionary community had been excitedly planning for the occasion and many guests had arrived from outlying mission stations and even from Australia. To the bride, newly arrived in a tropical community, the atmosphere seemed very oppressive and the frequent earth tremors startled her a little, but everyone assured her, 'Don't worry about it — we are always having these tremors.'

As the church in Rabaul was filled with flowers and a friend set out her best china and prepared a delicious garden wedding feast at the Kabakada mission house, people commented on the increasing severity of the earth tremors. Water tanks sprang leaks, things were shaken from shelves and the tide in the harbour moved in a most peculiar way; it seemed to add spice to the wedding day.

That afternoon, Mel and Jack stood before the chairman, the Rev. Frank Lewis, to make their vows, surrounded by their friends. 'Do you take this woman to be your wedded wife?'

'I do,' said Jack — and the earth shook. There was the sound of a violent, reverberating explosion and someone muttered, 'Electrical storm. . .' The bridal party watched, mesmerised, as great bowls of flowers on stands directly behind the minister began to rock, back and forth, threatening an avalanche of maidenhair fern, and then steadied slowly. Mel choked back giggles.

'I do,' said Mel, hardly daring to catch Jack's eye.

In the vestry after the wedding service, bride and groom were signing their names in the wedding register when another thunderous roar shook the building — 'a bad quake this time,' someone said. Mel came to the door of the church on Jack's arm with her bridal party around her and confetti floating around her head. Over the sound of laughter and greetings to bride and groom wailed a car horn held down. As they looked up, they heard shouting and saw the awesome sight of a gigantic column of dense smoke rising above the trees.

'The crater has broken! A volcano. . .'

Wedding guests ran to cars to drive to the waterfront for a

clear view. On the other side of the harbour, in a continuous roaring, an island which had not been there that morning rose up out of the water before their eyes, belching immense clouds of dense smoke, rocks and pumice.

Guests with cameras in hand for the wedding party focussed instead on the spectacle across the harbour, watching the unbelievable. The dark mass of cloud began to thin to a yellowed vapour high in the atmosphere and they could see flames and fiery rocks exploding from the rising land as the earth around them continued to vibrate. Then someone realised that the great dark erupting cloud was not drifting harmlessly up into the sky. The wind was beginning to carry hot dust towards the town.

'It will be better over the hill at Kabakada,' the mission party assured each other. Bride, groom, bridal party and guests joined the rest of the town — white, Chinese and New Guinean — in trying to escape on foot or in vehicles from the choking cloud.

The frightening cloud of hot ash was following them. Though they fled over the hill to the northern coast at Kabakada, it was not the haven they had hoped. Under the pall of hot ash and fearing a tidal wave, they hurried on. Women in wedding finery scrambled up the high sides of a copra truck to drive on to Vunairima. The bride was crowded in the cabin of a utility with her groom and several others. Villagers on foot pleaded for a ride in cars till every vehicle was overloaded.

As they drove, the swirling sulphur fumes poisoned the atmosphere, and volcanic dust fell as mud, intensifying into darkness, thick and palpable. Jack jumped down from time to time to scrape mud from the headlights to try to penetrate a little further along the lightless track, but driver and passengers were blinded by falling mud and deafened by continuing roaring explosions.

One car ran into a fallen palm in the darkness, and another slipped sideways into a roadside gutter. People walked on, calling to each other in the confusion. A wild electrical storm slashed through the stifling blanket of the atmosphere, sheets of lightning splitting the darkness briefly to illuminate the chaos around. In those brief flashes they saw coconut palms weighed down with mud, fallen timbers, blasted vegetation, people stumbling along together. Unrecognisable mud-coated apparitions said their names to colleagues. Those with towels, snatched up at Kabakada, tried to protect their faces so that they could breathe.

When, later, the dust cloud thinned and passed on and they gathered at the mission at Vunairima, they were a sorry lot. Hats were plastered to heads, and those who had been bareheaded had tight caps of mud. A wedding guest was mortified; her beautiful new morocaine dress had shrunk dramatically, leaving her barely decent. Women in saturated clothing tried to find something to borrow, with size and shape not a consideration.

A missionary wife, Jean Shelton, at Vunairima for her baby's birth two days earlier, could offer only maternity clothes. Instead of the beautiful wedding breakfast, over twenty mission staff shared soup served in whatever mugs and bowls could be found — with doses of quinine for dessert, urged on them by Dorothy Beale, Sister-in-charge of the mission hospital.

That night, in the safety and beauty of the Methodist mission compound at Vunairima, the party of over twenty wedding guests found places to sleep among the staff houses. Bride and groom said good night to each other; the bride slept with a group of women and Jack with the men. Under a covered table, the newborn Shelton baby was settled to sleep in a suitcase. No-one seemed quite sure whether to cry or laugh, though a shaky kind of laughter came easily.

'But I wasn't laughing,' Laurie Linggood concluded. 'I was sick with worry about Essie, pregnant and with our little boy at home at Raluana on the far side of the new volcano.'

He left Vunairima at first light, walking the miles towards his home through scenes of devastation. Plantations were reduced to burnt stumps, the town lay under a shroud of hot mud and pumice and the new volcano continued to pour hot ash and rocks high into the atmosphere. The harbour was carpeted with floating pumice. His horror grew as he discovered that several harbourside villages well-known to him and not far from Raluana, along with their people, had been buried under the storm of burning rocks and ash.

'And then it was like a miracle. Beyond all that death I came to a place where the eruption had not touched. Everything was still green, and whole, and alive. I found Essie and all our people coming out of church. . . Thousands of survivors, native, Chinese and white, waited on a northern beach till they were all taken off in an armada of shipping to safer areas.'

He looked at his audience, listening silently. 'This country is very beautiful but treacherous. You never can tell what surprises it may be waiting to spring on you.'

'Do you think we might be going to have another volcanic eruption?' one of them asked. 'Or could this big shake be an omen of something else?'

It was January, 1941.

The timber-cutters' boat chugged through the water. Kath Brown sat on the deck and watched the coastline pass slowly in a tangle of mangroves punctuated with crescent beaches. The further west they travelled, the further they felt from anything they had ever known before. They were on their way to Malalia in the Nakanai area on the northern coast of New Britain and already they had been on the way for three days.

The two Bell brothers who owned the boat, white timber-cutters, were in no hurry. They knew that anyone needing to travel to such a lonely place would have to wait until any boat was going that way, and would also have to tolerate the leisurely pace at which they travelled. At one beach or inlet after another the boat made anchor and the brothers went off to negotiate the sale of timber with the villagers.

Kath tried to be patient. The brothers had promised that they would reach Nakanai the next day and she was anxious to get there. For the past few months, they had been relieving for an absent minister, but now they were ready to begin what they saw as their real work in their own place. Rodger could barely wait. He was enjoying himself so much — making friends with New Guineans, rapidly learning the language. And now he was relishing a yarn with Lincoln Bell as they travelled, hearing stories of the islands from a man who had lived there for years.

Kath was happy to think of being able to set up her own home,

11. *Synod group, 1940*
Back row: *Gil Platten, Ben Chenoweth, Percy Clark, Jack Trevitt, Tom Simpson,*
Dan Oakes, Laurie Linggood
Centre: *Mary Jenkins, Essie Linggood, Laurie McArthur, Margaret Harris, Kath Brown*
Front: *Rodger Brown, Howard Pearson, John Poole*

12. *Jean Poole on patrol in the Baining mountains, 1941*

very much aware of their boxes stowed on board, bringing her wedding china, linen, household items and the silver teapot her mother had given them for their wedding.

Sitting under a shade cloth on the deck, she tried to picture what her mother would make of the scene. Her mother, a dignified widow with very high standards in housewifery, might have been able to accept the slow boat, the crude arrangements for ablutions, even the dark-skinned crew and the timber-cutters with their unpolished manners. But Kath wasn't so sure how her mother would feel about the large tin dish with many lives. She wasn't sure how she felt about it herself. It seemed a long way from embroidered table linen and silver teapots.

Kath eyed the wide tin dish. It was all good preparation for a missionary life, or so Rodger had whispered with a twinkle in his eye. Just the same, when she had her own house, she intended to insist on a bit more class at her own table. A woman's touch, perhaps. She decided that she would not mention the tin dish to Mother.

A New Guinean crew member came to collect the tin dish. Among its many uses it was a bowl for serving slices of freshly peeled pineapple, for washing-up, for personal washing and for dog food. She wasn't sure that she wanted to know what it would be used for this time. Faint echoes of lectures at missionary college stirred in her memory — missionaries should learn tolerance. . . accept the odd ways of others. . . sense of humour. . . She was beginning to learn.

Jean Poole clung to a protruding tree root and paused to stare up the mountain face. Her breath came in deep open-mouthed gasps and, though the mountain air was cool, sweat soaked her shirt. Jungle stretched high up into the sky overhead, leafy branches clawing their way up into the sunlight; begonia, balsam, ginger and orchid in the shade of the green canopy.

Somewhere up above her John climbed on with Laurie Mc-Arthur, striding at the front of the line of carriers. The mountain track strained up and up, each slippery clay step seeming to be on a level with her knees, and she regretted being short.

A New Guinean schoolboy, agile and muscular, waited for her

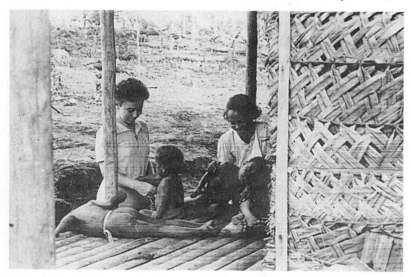

13. *Jean Poole with Louisa, wife of Mikael To Bilak, Kalas, 1941*

14. *Dancers in village in the Baining mountains, 1941*

on the steps above and others in the procession of carriers and schoolboys waited behind for her to move on.

'How far is it?' Jean was quickly learning all the many possible answers in the Kuanua language — very far, far, quite far, not so far, fairly near, very near and all the others.

Behind her a young man with a load on his back laughed and urged her on. 'Not far, only two more rivers and one mountain!'

Dragging herself up the next step with the help of a strong pointed stick, Jean knew that, despite being hot and tired, her boots covered in mud, her curls plastered to her head from sweat and with the muscles in her legs aching with strain, she would not have changed places with anyone.

Up ahead was John, a huge grin on his face, his eyes alight with the challenge of it all. Somewhere behind was Akuila To Ngaru, their friend and mentor, ready with his strong arm. And all around was a glorious rainbow world of birds and butterflies, of flowers and shrubs which she had never even seen pictured, of great strange trees and vines, of new fruits and nuts of which she had never heard. Best of all, in this land of far mountain vistas, they came to hidden villages of shy generous people waiting with food and shelter, whose languages were as mysterious as their customs, and as untouched by the rest of the world.

'What is that? Can you eat it? How do you use it?' Her questions bubbled out. Though her limited grasp of their language often knotted her tongue, she was sure that she would never exhaust the multitude of themes she was eager to ask the people about.

At the edge of yet another mountain stream they stopped, waiting for the group to catch up. Jean sat on a great rock at the water's edge, warm from the sun, and let her laboured breathing ease. Looking up, she saw John watching her. It seemed so natural to be together in that setting and she smiled at him.

The welcome of the villagers to the mountain village of Kulit was very friendly. There was food shared, the formal opening of a new village church and then men disappeared into a secret house to complete the preparation of masks for the dancing.

'May I come too, and watch them?' Jean pleaded, when the

visiting men were invited in.

'If you were one of our women, we would refuse,' she was told, 'because any woman who sees behind these secrets will become sterile — but come, you are not the same as our women. . .'

Through the afternoon she watched the bird dance. Into the darkness of evening, illuminated by a great bonfire, dancers circled in the secret snake dance, their vast fantasy masks and extravagant body decorations fit for giants. Bamboo spears were stitched to their bodies making them appear the height of three men; every part of their body decorated to exaggerate, to transform the dancers from mortal men to mythical creatures. By the light of the bonfire Jean sketched, her pencil striving to capture the detail of each kind of costume — the colours, the names of things; overwhelmed by the feeling of privilege at being present to witness the movements and mysteries of a hidden people.

Just before dawn, the dancers became very excited. The bonfire had died into glowing coals and dancers leapt through the coals, scattering them across the dancing ring. Only certain masks could be kept, though the identity of the wearers was still kept secret, and all the other fantasies of barkcloth, feathers, bamboo and blood were to be destroyed before the sun rose. With the growing light, giants and monsters were transmogrified into mere men.

Stretching cramped limbs and folding away her sheets of notes and sketches, Jean rose to her feet. It was going to be a long walk back to the ordinary world of the little mission station at Kalas.

On Anzac Day 1941, six Australian army nurses disembarked in Rabaul with men of the 2/22nd Infantry Battalion of the 23rd Brigade. Led by Captain Kay Parker, the six friends were disappointed to find themselves in a tropical town far from the war zones of the Middle East and Europe.

The nurses knew that their work would be limited to dealing with accident cases, tropical diseases, perhaps a few men with malaria. Not only did they feel that they were far from the scene of any real action, but the military medical officers did not seem particularly pleased to see them, as if they were intruding into a male domain.

'They only see us as potential social partners for the officers,' they complained, 'in a town with too few single women.'

The huge Chinese characters of bronze dazzled in the sun, dramatic against the high white facade and black granite pillars of the new school. In letters of red it announced in English, 'Overseas Chinese School'.

Daisy McArthur, with her new baby in her arms, was in the official party at the opening of the school in May. She was very pleased for the Chinese community in Rabaul. Some of the families had lived in New Britain for several generations and there were four streets of Chinese stores in the tree-lined town. The Methodists had provided a school and teachers for a number of years, but now it had grown to over 170 students and the Chinese families had been working for the past few years to build a fine new school. Daisy had seen the effort they had put into it, producing beautiful handwork, garments and paintings for sale, and entering their 'dragon' in the town procession.

The doors of the school were duly opened and Daisy followed Laurie, with hundreds of other guests, into the handsome building. They were ushered past new classrooms and the library into the main hall where a wonderful banquet was ready, a triumph of Asian delicacies, prepared by women who had been up since the first chickens were despatched in the early hours of the morning. Dainty Chinese girls, pretty as vivid butterflies in slim satin gowns, served their guests. Sitting at the table, Daisy was delighted to praise all those involved — the newly arrived minister, the Rev. Mo Pui Sam, the teachers, Thomas Mow and his wife Wai Yin Mow, and the Australian missionary Mary Jenkins — on their fine students and excellent new building. The whole Chinese community had a strong sense of pride in their people and their achievements.

'Next month,' Mary Jenkins explained, 'the children will be presenting their first concert on the new stage. You must be sure to come.'

Something was different. In the six months since they had last come to town, something had happened to Rabaul. Jean and John

Poole looked curiously around as the small truck bounced into town. New Guinean people were still carrying and selling their pawpaws and coconuts, taro and pineapples, in coconut frond baskets. White men in tropical whites and their women in summer florals still strolled down the street past Chinese girls under sunshades. The usual slow bustle of a hot and steamy harbour town went on.

But there were also the soldiers. Everywhere there seemed to be men in khaki, young Australians in the streets, in the stores, along the harbour front. When they attended the town Methodist church, where John had been invited to preach, a number of soldiers joined the missionaries and government officers who usually made up the congregation. A choir of soldiers sang for them in rich harmony; they were bandsmen who, in their peacetime life, had been members of several Victorian Salvation Army bands, all gifted musicians under the leadership of composer Arthur Gullidge. The congregation crowded into the home of one of the members for coffee and cake after church, and many of the young soldiers joined them.

John introduced Jean to one of them. 'This is Bill, Private Bill Harry,' he said. 'I've invited young Bill and some of the other boys to come out to Kalas if ever they get the chance. The lads don't often get out of town.'

They talked, each enjoying the company of other young Australians in a place far from home. From the quietness of the Pooles' home at Kalas, with no telephone and no teleradio, news of a distant war rarely reached them. Even here in Rabaul, suddenly coloured in khaki, soldiers were just new friends from home, people to share pikelets and cake with after church, and an excellent male choir of Salvos.

'They are saying that you should go.' Laurie McArthur spoke heavily.

Daisy looked up, puzzled. He looked out across the darkening garden to the harbour where the last of a sunset stained the tops of encircling volcanic hills. Lights were coming on around the ring of the waterfront and town. A clatter of crockery came from the kitchen where the house servant was washing the dishes. Their baby son was already asleep; soon she would go in to say goodnight to their seven-year-old boy, tucking him into the security of his mosquito-netted bed. Somewhere beyond the house, village choristers sang an evening antiphon with frogs.

'*Who* is saying? Go *where*?'

'Harold Page was talking to me today.' Page was Assistant Administrator of the Territory of Papua and New Guinea, with headquarters in Rabaul, and he and his wife were their friends. 'He says that the civil authorities have to decide what to do if — probably when — Japan chooses to enter the war. If they do, Rabaul may well be on their path. That's why the fellows of the 2/22nd are here. It's all just conjecture at the moment, but they have to plan. Page says that they have already chosen a narrow valley area on the edge of town where we can all retreat if necessary. Refuge Valley they are calling it.'

Behind his round spectacles, his eyes were very serious. Daisy had seen that look before, when the responsibilities of leadership had weighed heavily.

'And he says that you should go — you, and the children, all the Australian women and their children. They can't order you, but he strongly advises you to leave while there is time.'

There was a long silence. Daisy folded and refolded her table napkin, a meaningless busyness for her hands. Leave Laurie? Go back to Australia? But where could she go? She and Laurie were both the youngest in large families and older brothers and sisters would help, but how could she, with two small children, impose on them for more than a short holiday? Travel all that way without Laurie's help? Be without her beloved husband for weeks or even months?

He was her best friend, her soulmate, the one person with whom she fully shared her life. It had been that way since they met years ago in South Australia. They had come together to New Guinea, then when she became ill they had returned to Australia together, even though he must have been very disappointed to give up his work in education for several years until she was well enough to return. Laurie had always been there, supporting her and she supporting him. Now she was well, and they had a new baby, and Laurie was so much enjoying his work as chairman. Leave Laurie and go back by herself? How could she?

'Must I?'

'Perhaps as wife of the chairman, you ought to think of the example to the others — do the right thing. But you know how much I hate the thought of being without you and the boys.'

Daisy tried to think of all the families who would face the choice. Some had young babies like her own. Two of the mission wives were pregnant; others were settled happily in their places and would resent the disruption. It seemed impossible to picture their town and region the scene of invasion and battle. Even the presence of some 1 400 young Australian soldiers in town was not threatening; most of them seemed bored and frustrated by being cut off from the real war in this tropical backwater. If their community could live through the violence of earthquakes and volcanoes then they would not be scared by something that was only a rumour.

And yet, if Laurie thought it was wise for her to go and Harold Page recommended it, perhaps. . .

That night, before she slept, Daisy turned again to her Bible. Fourteen years earlier, before she and Laurie were married, he had given her that Bible for her birthday and written some verses in the front cover. Now she returned to the words of blessing he had copied for her then, from the ancient book of Numbers:

The Lord bless you and keep you;
the Lord make his face to shine upon you and be gracious
unto you:
the Lord lift up his countenance upon you and give you
peace.

Kath Brown walked slowly through the village. It was Friday, and on Fridays she followed the tradition for the missionary's wife to visit the village houses on an 'inspection'. The village was not far from their house and Kath walked carefully along the track, watching out for stray pigs and village dogs. Shy women waited for her, their houseyards neatly swept with twig brooms. Their homes were so simple, with so very little of material comforts in them, but Kath understood the pride some took in keeping their homes clean and providing their families with ample food gardens.

The weekly inspection was only a simple formality, but Kath enjoyed it. There were not many opportunities to get away from the narrow confines of her own house and the small community of church and hospital at Malalia now that she was pregnant. In front of her house lay the open sea and behind stood high, jungle-covered mountains.

She had once gone with Rodger in a very small craft on one of his visits to villages. Steep muddy tracks and high seas in darkness had been no fun and she was glad of the excuse to let Rodger enjoy his adventures without her. Apart from their colleague, senior mission nurse Maggie Harris, Kath had only seen two other white women, from plantations, in the many months they had lived at Malalia.

Now she walked among the houses of their neighbouring village, speaking with the women and avoiding the dogs. There was an invisible fence between her and the village women; two languages, two cultures. After the baby was born it might be easier, she thought. By then she'd have learned more of their language and the universal language of a woman with a child would also speak for her.

It was time to turn back for her own house. There was an evening meal to prepare and she was in the middle of sewing for her baby. After tea, she would write home to her mother and tell her more of her observations of village life, a life almost untouched by civilisation.

Perhaps, after the meal, Rodger might try to tune their teleradio to hear the national news, but then again, now that the batteries were getting a bit flat, he might prefer to save the radio till the regular radio contact with Rabaul in the morning. There would probably be nothing very interesting on the world news, anyway, she thought.

'But — aren't you coming, too? Back to Australia with your children?' Mrs Jean Shelton had just arrived at the chairman's house at Malaguna after making the crossing from Ulu Island in the Duke of York Islands group. She looked at Daisy McArthur with confusion and a hint of resentment. 'But I thought we all had to do what we were told, and the message came that we were supposed to go.'

Daisy McArthur did her best to explain. 'No, I'm not going on this ship,' she said, 'but it's only a few months before we'll be going on leave. Laurie has to be in Sydney for meetings in January. By then we'll all be glad to get away — the vulcanologist is warning that we could have more volcanic activity around the harbour and that has more people anxious than any imaginary threat from the Japanese.'

Jean Shelton had her two young children with her, ready to take the sea voyage. 'Winifred had her fourth birthday only a few days ago,' she commented, 'and she was born two days before the big eruption of Vulcan volcano. The poor little thing spent her first days sleeping in an open suitcase under a table, to try to keep volcanic ash off her! If it is happening again we should have stayed on peaceful Ulu.'

Ulu, lovely island: Jean Shelton couldn't help thinking of the comfortable home she had just left, with all her personal things and the glorious view across lawns, palms, garden beds and flame trees to islands scattered across aquamarine waters.

'It was so hard to say goodbye to the people,' she said wistfully. 'Crowds of them came to the wharf to see us off, and I kept saying, "You're not to cry, you're not to cry". . . But the women clung onto my hand and wept and wept, and the men, too. . . we've lived with them all for years and they are family to us. They think I won't come back. . .'

Jean Shelton with her children was on board the ship *Macdhui* with some seventy women when it sailed early in June. Whenever she saw her little girl's birthday doll, she could not help thinking of that last morning with Herbert, when she woke to feel the child and her doll snuggled in between her parents, ready for a morning kiss from her daddy. 'As soon as things calm down, I'll be back,' she promised her husband.

Within days of the sailing of the *Macdhui*, in June 1941, a volcano erupted on the northern shore of the harbour. Hot rocks, pumice dust and ash blew into the sky, the ash and dust floating down over the town of Rabaul and making life miserable for the residents. From as far away as Kalas, Jean Poole watched the plume of smoke and dust rising into the air beyond the hills.

In the town on Malaguna Road, Mary Jenkins with much regret took her classes out of their beautiful new Overseas Chinese School because it was impossible to work under such a pall of ash. She wrote a note to her teacher friend Elsie Wilson to tell her that their great concert, planned for that month, 'has been postponed indefinitely'.

Though the army was drawing up plans to build a sixty-bed military hospital in Rabaul, the civil administrators were deciding that earlier plans to transfer the entire Australian civil administration to Lae should be revived immediately. The plans had been designed after the catastrophe of the 1937 volcanic eruption, but public lethargy had seen them shelved. Several government departments were now under orders to begin packing to move as soon as possible. Women and children who had initially hesitated to travel south at rumours of a possible invasion decided that they would leave anyway.

It was most unpleasant to live in the vicinity of Rabaul while Tavurvur continued to fling dust and ash into the atmosphere. By the end of the month, some seventy women had already gone and another forty were waiting for the next boat.

Daisy McArthur did not go. She was aware that there was debate in the town as to whether women should leave or not. Several families from the mission had gone or planned to leave soon for their normal furlough.

'I know that the authorities want us out of the way,' she said to her husband, 'but I don't know whether I should go, as an example of obedience, or stay, because it might look to our people that I was running away. Anyway, I'm staying. After Christmas we'll all travel south together.'

3

June–December 1941

'WHAT DOES THE GENERAL SECRETARY SAY? Does Mr Burton think we mission women should leave our work?'

Daisy McArthur knew what her own opinion was. Laurie, who always liked to do the right thing, had written for advice and the reply from the mission's General Secretary had just come. She hoped that the letter would confirm her own feelings. People talked about war, but in the humid lethargy of tropical Rabaul there was little sense of urgency about it.

The town was full of young soldiers, but most of them seemed very bored, disappointed to find themselves in such a backwater. Preparations for battle seemed less than intense, with the lads of the anti-aircraft group practising their skills by pretending to shoot down the weekly mailplane, or lining up their sights on a toy plane carried around on a long pole.

People who had left town were beginning to come back again, and several of their own people who had been on leave were arriving back in town, including Sister Jean Christopher on her way back to Malabonga. The community, it was true, was being instructed in methods of preparing slit-trenches in their gardens. A leaflet had been distributed describing the arrangements for Refuge Valley on Namanula Ridge — the upper portion reserved for Europeans, the lower for Asiatics and a smaller area convenient to the Europeans for their native servants with 'car parking available'.

Ladies in the town were arranging for kits of pyjamas and for tea and scones to be available.

'A conflict of opinion regarding the seriousness of the situation. . .' Laurie McArthur read aloud. 'The mission board assures me that they have "full confidence in my judgment", but in the light of many opinions on the matter, they have decided to listen to the information coming from the national leaders in Canberra. We can send our families home if we like, but if we do we must pay the fares ourselves.'

Daisy took the letter. It was as she had thought. Only a few weeks earlier, Laurie had written to all his staff: 'Christian missions must go on, notwithstanding the war. . . By the faithful carrying on of our work, whatever the difficulties may be that confront us, we are making a contribution to the solution of the world's problems.' She agreed. The ponderous preparations for war in their area were merely role-playing.

'That's settled, then,' Daisy said. She looked again at the comforting words from the General Secretary.

He had written that there was 'no evidence of any specific danger in New Guinea and any general danger is not so serious as appears in the minds of some'.

Far from the sulphur-scented atmosphere of tropical Rabaul, secret letters and cables passed between decision-makers in Canberra, Washington and London as they studied what was for them a tiny mark on a map of Asia and the Pacific. If Japan entered the war, what would happen? Would they strike through the islands of the Pacific, and what would be their most likely route? Was Simpson Harbour in Rabaul significant or not? Ought they to set a minefield across the entrance to the harbour, or block it with a defensive net?

The discussions went on, heavily influenced by the United States military opinion. No decisions were made.

The young soldier at her table traced a map of their area with a fingertip on the tablecloth. Jean Poole watched as he outlined the east New Britain coast and doodled the position of the mountain ranges.

'We'd have to come through here,' Bill was saying. 'If the Japs come to Rabaul, we could hold them for a while — I think — but most of us reckon that we haven't the men or the defences to hold them out for long. We'd have to fall back, but none of us know our way around these mountains.'

Bill Harry was the country boy from Victoria whom they had met at church in Rabaul. Both Jean and John enjoyed his friendship. Now that he was working with a team on a comprehensive compass and chain survey of the eastern Gazelle Peninsula area, he was able to visit them. Sometimes he would stop for a cup of tea with Mavis and Dora at Malabonga Hospital and travel on to spend a night with the Pooles.

John had a suggestion. 'Do you want to come out on patrol with me? You'd get to know the area.'

Bill's face lit up. 'I'll wangle it, all right!'

It was clear as the two men talked that Jean was not included in their plans. This was to be a men-only patrol.

Several weeks later, she watched them set off. They disappeared into the dense green of the jungle and she found that she didn't mind. Two weeks of mountain climbing would be heavy going and, as rain began to fall, she was thankful that she would be sleeping in her own bed. She wouldn't be lonely.

Mikael and Lousia and their little ones lived nearby, and the schoolboys were always around. John had insisted that two young schoolboys should stay in the house overnight for company, but Jean was not nervous. She had never been afraid of the people of the area; she had no qualms about the fact that their house had no front door to shut and the only room that could be locked was the storeroom.

That evening, when the lamp was lit, she prepared to so some writing. While John was away, she had a long list of things she wanted to achieve, to show him when he returned. There were letters to write home, local language to learn and scientific sketches of local dances and botanical specimens. And there were the moths, common ones and sometimes rare and beautiful ones. In the evenings, moths fluttered into the orbit of lamplight and she had been collecting specimens, using a technique learned at home to transfer the gleaming wings, whole, onto the pages of a book. Now she bent over delicate moth wings, with two young boys watching, fascinated, while rain washed down on the iron roof overhead. Yes, she was content to be at home, this time. Next time she would travel with John.

When John and Bill returned two weeks later they were tired, dirty, and full of stories of their trip. Bill was enthusiastic. 'If I survive a Jap invasion, John, I'll head on out here to Kalas and join up with you. You and I could survive back there in the mountains for years — 7 000 feet above the sea, no roads, thick jungle, tracks that keep disappearing — we'd be right.'

Jean was silent. It was hard to imagine it. He was very young, of course. 'Plan to come back out to us for your twenty-first birthday, Bill,' she offered. 'I'll cook you a special birthday dinner.'

On the island of New Hanover, north of the long narrow island of New Ireland, a young woman opened her mail with delight. With her missionary husband Tom Simpson, Nellie had lived on their mission station since their marriage in 1937. Now the coastal schooner had brought an invitation to visit Kavieng for a weekend of social fun with the town community and the young soldiers of the Independent Company, recently stationed there.

Nellie loved her life with Tom on New Hanover. She enjoyed the students, the children, and occasional visits to the nuns who looked after the leprosy patients at the Catholic mission. A schooner with a friendly captain brought their supplies from time to time and she had the piquancy of having Errol Flynn's daughter helping her in the kitchen. She loved company of all kinds and relished any chance to visit the wider community.

'Mr Mac would be shocked!' Nellie had a wicked twinkle in her eye.

There were times when she rather enjoyed the thought of disturbing Laurie McArthur, who was so thorough, so particular and so conservative about everything. Nothing really dreadful, of course; just a few little things to satisfy her independent spirit. She

15. *Syd Beazley*

16. *Jack Trevitt*

17. *John Poole*

18. *Wilf Pearce*

remembered the questions that had been raised when Tom had arranged for her to be a member at the Kavieng Club, so that she could use the Club facilities on the rare occasions when she crossed the channel from New Hanover to the small town of Kavieng. It was thirty-five miles of ocean, often rough, and the Methodist mission station was miles away. But '. . .the club? Where all the men are there for the booze? Surely not a suitable place for a Methodist missionary lady!'

And now this. Nellie laughed and gave Tom a hug. 'Of course I want to go across for it. I haven't been to Kavieng since baby Margaret was born over there, and that's months. But just think of it. . . they've caught those brumbies and broken them in, and we'll have a race meeting, and then dancing at the Kavieng Club. Horse races and dancing — even if they don't spike your lemonade with something, like they did when Margaret was born. Just imagine poor Mr Mac's Methodist face!'

All those lads in Kavieng, she thought, just eighteen- or nineteen-year-old boys so she'd been told, despite their uniforms, stuck in an out-of-the-way place like Kavieng where surely nothing was going to happen. It was only a rumour that Japan might enter the war, wasn't it? War or no war, Nellie decided, it would be a lot of fun to go to Kavieng and, though her Thomas would be the best-looking and nicest man there, she'd enjoy dancing with as many of the young soldiers as invited her.

The cluster of dark-skinned girls in their loosely flowing cotton blouses giggled their way out onto the spreading lawns with arms full of wheels of dried pandanus leaves ready for weaving. Cleaning-day was over and they could relax. Freshly scrubbed bedboards had dried in the sun, floors were swept, bedding had been aired and cooking pots glittered with the high polish of hard rubbing.

All good training for their future lives, Elsie Wilson thought, as she watched them settle themselves under a poinciana tree and spread their work in front of them on the grass. Week by week the rhythm of the District Girls' School at Vunairima wove patterns of security and purpose around girls and staff. Community and work, order and discipline, self-reliance and learning of skills, a strict timetable to instil good habits; the eighty girls and young women were under Elsie's care while they were at the school.

She walked across to sit on the grass and watch them. Their fingers flickered in and out, weaving the supple, sweet-smelling pandanus leaves into the smoothness of sleeping mats. This was not a skill she could teach them. Older women taught the younger ones, as they also taught them the skills of making gardens to feed families. Her own role was in the classroom and as supervisor of their lives as boarders.

There were times when she felt ill-prepared as a single woman for the task of training a whole school full of teenage girls and women to be good wives and mothers. It was all a very long way from the little one-teacher school where she had been teaching in South Australia before she offered to work for the church. Those students had been young children; most of these students at Vunairima were either married already, promised in marriage or at least being groomed as potential brides for the young men being trained as pastor-teachers. These fine girls were chosen to come to the school from many scattered islands and villages, to be prepared to be literate, skilled homemakers, craftswomen, respected church leaders, offering leadership to other women.

Other women teachers had established the pattern, including her friend Jessie March. Now Elsie was happy to continue the work with the help of a number of New Guinean women teachers, even though it was a daunting task. She had the satisfaction of being part of creating a stable church leadership, where the wives of leaders could take their place as respected partners, and she was building up her own confidence in her work.

Watching the girls on the grass as they sang and wove their pandanus mats with skilful fingers, she had a strong sense that she was in the place where she was meant to be. This was her world, her place, her work. With little social contact beyond the grounds of Vunairima, and with no wireless to keep in touch with world news, Elsie saw no reason to think that her stable world might be shaken.

The drumbeats of war were almost unheard at Kalas during those happy months of 1941. Louder was the beat of the log drum calling villagers to prayer, or the rhythmic clash of bamboos stirring the feet of dancers.

Jean Poole relished her life with John: the patrols to remote villages where they were made welcome, the special occasions, the traditional dances. There was a trip to Malasaet high in the mountains, where Mavis Green had set up a clinic for the day. Laurie McArthur led the people in a special service; for the occasion the villagers had built not only a shelter for their guests but also homemade beds and chairs. On other trips, she collected botanical specimens and added to her notes on traditional customs. The people of Kalas became friends, not exotic scenery.

Her new house at Kalas was home now. Their weekly contact with the nurses at Malabonga was always cherished, though Dora's absence was a disappointment. Since the return of Sister Jean Christopher, Dora had gone to be the mission nurse at Vatnabara in the Duke of York Islands, some hours' boat trip away. Mavis and 'Chris' were welcome guests at her table on alternate Wednesdays, and Bill Harry called whenever he could and slept on their stretcher bed.

Kalas had been home for about a year when it became, briefly, a focal point for the whole area. For the first time, the annual thanksgiving, the giving of gifts in cash and kind for the work of the church, was held there. Two thousand villagers crowded into the clearing from all over the area on the edge of the mountains, bringing their gifts and their music and sharing in the feasting. Mission visitors, nine or ten Australians out for the day, filled their little home, more than Jean had ever entertained before.

All that day she hurried between the excitement of the annual gift-giving, with unaccustomed crowds filling the space where Mikael To Bilak ran his school, and her house full of guests. Every piece of wedding china was needed and they hadn't enough chairs, but Jean delighted in making them welcome. Laurie Linggood was there as the main preacher for the day with the nurses from Malabonga. Laurie McArthur had come out with his wife Daisy and their boys.

Daisy McArthur was planning to stay on for a week's holiday. ('The mission board says that we women don't have to leave because of the war,' Daisy told Jean. 'Leave?' Jean was puzzled. It was hard to remember at Kalas that a war was being fought on the far side of the globe.) Howard Pearson and Jack Trevitt had come out for the first time from Vunairima, and Bill Harry turned up in his army uniform.

Jean caught John's eye across the room. Their guests were deep in lively debate; linguistics and education, training of church workers and printing of literature — there was always something real to discuss. Their friends were enjoying themselves in the Poole home. The glance between Jean and John said: We must do this often, you and I.

Just before dusk, the last of their guests set off for home. The mission grounds had been trampled by thousands of feet and the aroma of chicken, pork grease and coconut cream lingered around the places where food had steamed for hours in trenches in the earth. It had been a good day.

Jean stood close to John as they waved goodbye. 'This time next year you must all come out again,' she called. 'Next year. . .'

Dora Wilson lifted the lid and peered once again at the steaming pot of chops. She had pushed it well to the back of the kitchen stove, but it had been cooking for so long that it was slowly disintegrating into a stew. The tables were set and the pots of taro, pumpkin and local greens were either overcooked or rapidly going cold. Her colleagues were late again, still talking, no doubt, over their mission business.

She went to the door. There was still no sign of them coming for dinner. The sun was setting across the water that divided her on the Duke of York Islands from New Britain, and the vivid flame tree in the gardens at Vatnabara was losing colour in the dusk. While the others were busy with the Methodist synod of November 1941, Dora's days were an endless cycle of meals. Jean Shelton had very helpfully sent some suggested menus and her husband Herbert had killed a beast to provide meat, but Dora had carried the responsibility for feeding them all. All the men were in, travelling to Vatnabara from New Hanover and New Ireland, distant Nakanai and the town of Rabaul just across the water: Australian ministers and laymen, New Guinean leaders like Akuila To Ngaru, the Chinese minister Mo Pui Sam. Sister Dorothy Beale and teacher Mary Jenkins were the only women staff members eligible and able to attend.

At last Dora heard the sound of laughter. They were coming. Herbert was as calm as ever as men trailed into the big mission house, still talking as they found their places at the table. After a year when many of them had been working alone in isolated places, or had been under pressure with their work, their annual meeting was a time of high spirits. Though they were all strong-minded people who did not always see eye-to-eye on issues, they were also mates and their general good-humour filled the room. Herbert, as their host and elder brother (at forty-four he was the oldest of them all), turned a blind eye to any youthful wildness that sometimes erupted when they were together. Dora hurried to complete her work and bring the plates to the tables.

It seemed that they were not even aware that they were late. The talk flowed on, and Dora caught up with fragments of news which had filled their day.

'Percy Clark is definitely leaving in the New Year and going back to church work at home. . .'

'We expect Syd and Beryl Beazley, and Mel Trevitt, back on the next ship. . .'

'Laurie and Daisy McArthur are booked to fly to Sydney straight after Christmas, in time for Laurie to attend the annual meeting of the board. . .'

Rodger Brown was anxious about his wife. Kath Brown had travelled to Rabaul in September to wait for the birth of their first child and was staying with the nurses at Malabonga while he was at synod. 'The baby isn't due yet, but I hope everything is all right with her.'

There was so much happening in the mission and the table talk was full of ideas and energy. There was the mission education program and the printing press with several recent publications of importance, including a new hymn book in Pidgin English and the major Kuanua-English Dictionary, the work of Trevitt and Linggood. Another topic discussed was the first six trained New Guinean ministers who would be in their new appointments before Christmas.

There was also the growing work among the Chinese community. Rev. Mo Pui Sam, recently arrived from China, had been recommended to become a full member of the NSW Methodist Conference, a rare thing for an Asian.

They were a very lively lot, Dora thought; noisy, cheerful, young and with some very able men among them, a good team. If anyone mentioned the war, it was of distant battles, of the Middle East, or of missionaries being evacuated from faraway China to their George Brown Missionary College in Sydney. The lads in khaki in Rabaul and Kavieng were not the war. They were frustrated young men left on the outskirts of what was happening elsewhere.

When the meal was over, the table was pushed back and the lamps hung from hooks in the ceiling. Beyond open windows, coconut palms creaked and rustled in silhouette against moonlit ocean. 'Time for charades!' someone said, and the peaceful night air was set quivering with roars of laughter, witticisms and sheer silliness.

When the evening tea cups had been washed and the kitchen tidied, Dora, Dorothy and Mary left the mission house with its overload of men and walked up to Dora's house to bed. In the light of their lanterns, they saw that their mosquito nets hung gracefully over the places where their beds should have been, but the mattresses had vanished.

'It's some of those crazy men! Like schoolboys mucking up when they get together. . .'

A search finally located the runaway bedding and it was returned to the Sister's house by unrepentant missionaries. Church meetings should not be too solemn and ponderous, they assured the women, and reminded them of picnics, boat trips and a cricket match planned before the end of synod; they should always be willing to take a joke.

While the synod met in solemn session the next day, skilled

needlewoman Dora sat in the mission house with her sewing. When she had completed her task, the sleeve ends and trouserlegs of all the pyjamas of all the mission men were securely stitched together and neatly replaced under their pillows.

Later, when she recalled the weeks around the birth of her first child, Kath Brown recalled one difficulty after another. The visit with Chris and Mavis to Malabonga had been a happy one and when Rodger came to take her back to Vunairima she had said goodbye to them with gratitude. There were only two more weeks to wait, she thought, and the weariness and unease of late pregnancy, overlaid with the constant weight of tropical heat, made her long for the time to come.

The truck jolted along the road, although Rodger drove with care. Several miles along the road, however, the engine spluttered and died. Despite all his efforts, the truck had broken down and Rodger could not revive it.

'You'll have to walk back to Malabonga.' Rodger was shocked. So was Kath, but there was no choice. On that back road they both knew that there was little chance that any other vehicle would pass their way.

So Kath had trudged back over the miles, back to the health centre at Malabonga, feeling hot, heavy and not at all well. Chris and Mavis were horrified to see her reappear, exhausted, at their door. Putting her to bed, Chris said sternly, 'Don't you dare go into labour here!' Kath woke at intervals that night to sense that Chris was there, by her bed, and was reassured and comforted.

It was just as well that Kath did not begin labour out in the bush at Malabonga. A repaired vehicle came to take her back and in due course she was taken to the Namanula hospital in labour. Kath herself had little awareness of what happened next, but for Rodger it was a nightmare.

Kath's labour was long and dangerous, with the baby presenting in the breech position. When at last she knew that she had borne a baby son on 10 November, it was through the vague mists of serious illness. Kath had come very close to death.

In the first week in December, many of the mission families began to look forward to holidays and Christmas. In Rabaul, the volcano on the outskirts of town continued to pollute the air with dust, making housecleaning a thankless task. Daisy McArthur began to plan for furlough while she cared for Kath Brown who was slowly regaining her strength after the birth of her baby Graham; the baby was very small and they would not be able to travel home to Nakanai on New Britain's central north coast for several weeks. Howard and Helen Pearson visited the Pooles at Kalas for a holiday after Howard's students left for their appointments and Elsie Wilson looked forward to the end of the school year.

At Kalas, Jean Poole looked forward with excitement to the visit of her sister, who planned to do the adventurous thing and fly from Sydney in time for Christmas. There was so much that Jean wanted to show her sister. She had seen none of her family since her wedding and daydreamed about the long conversations and the fun they would have when Joyce came. Jean had sent a gift and congratulations to Kath and Rodger on the birth of their son. It caused her a small pang to think of Kath with a new baby.

She was very content to be free to travel with John, to climb mountains, to collect specimens, and once she had small children she would have to put freedom and adventures behind her. But there had been no sign yet that she and John would be parents, and they had been married over a year. Still, she thought, there was plenty of time.

Across the Pacific, on 8 December 1941, in the place they called Pearl Harbour in the Hawaiian Islands, a storm of Japanese aircraft burst over the American fleet gathered there, leaving a chaos of death and destruction. The imagined and half-expected had happened. Japan had entered the war and the Pacific was no longer a place of peace but a path for ships of battle.

News of the bombing of Pearl Harbour and the implications of it spread rapidly through the township of Rabaul and, through the network of teleradio contact on remote mission stations and plantations, across the islands. Alone in his remote station halfway along the length of New Ireland, Methodist missionary

Dan Oakes wrote to his father-in-law. His wife Marion and the children had gone home to Australia already as they were due for leave, but Dan was delayed; the resignation of another minister in the area had meant that Dan was asked to stay on for a period. Dan missed Marion very much. They were a team and he valued her strong personality and capacity to do so many things well. She and the boys were at her parents' home in Sydney.

Now Dan Oakes wrote to her father of the news of Pearl Harbour. 'No doubt this will mean more difficulties in regard to shipping in these waters and also greater danger from raiders. Possibly there will be an attempt against this Territory and so Marion and the children are just as well out of it, aren't they?' He considered the possibility that the other mission women might also be evacuated and added, 'For myself I feel that it is more than ever my duty to stay here. I guess soon that other missionaries will be just as lonely as I am.'

Four days later a cable marked 'MOST SECRET AND IMPORTANT' was encoded and sent from the Australian Prime Minister's Department in Canberra to Washington, USA. Decisions needed to be made about the usefulness of Rabaul as a defended base. The cable suggested that Rabaul was 'too exposed for our slender forces' and there were questions about how much could be done unless there were help from the USA.

It was clear that Rabaul was not a key in the USA naval scheme; Suva, Noumea, Samoa, Port Moresby and Darwin were the names on their lips. The cable concluded: '[I]t is considered better to maintain Rabaul only as an advanced operational base, its present small garrison being regarded as hostages to fortune.'

4

18–22 December 1941

EVERYTHING SEEMED TO BE working against her, Kath decided. All she wanted was to get back home from Rabaul to Malalia. Since leaving home in September, she had been in hospital or other people's houses and longed to be back in her own home with Rodger, getting the baby settled into a routine. Baby Graham was still underweight, but well enough, and she was feeling much better. Rodger was free to go whenever a boat was travelling to the west, but it was well into December and, if no boat was available soon, they wouldn't even get home for Christmas.

Kath was visiting Essie Linggood at Raluana along the coast road when Essie's husband Laurie arrived to tell her that he'd heard that a coastal ship in the harbour was expecting to sail for the Nakanai coast and Malalia that evening.

'Kath, give me your grocery list for the next few months; I'll fix it up in town. Rodger and I both have to be at a meeting in Rabaul and as soon as Rodger gets back, you'll be collected to go to the wharf,' Laurie said.

Kath packed the things she had brought to Raluana, prepared the baby and settled to wait for Rodger's return. Across the open ocean beyond the house the rain was falling heavily and winds whipped up high seas. She watched apprehensively. Her longing to travel home was tempered by the sight of waves and the sound of wind beating through the palms. It was the change of season when hurricanes were common; the thought of being on a small ship in a storm, with a new baby and possibly a seasick husband, was daunting. She waited all day. Every three hours she fed her baby and waited, but there was no sign of Rodger.

At last Laurie returned. 'You've missed it — the boat left at half past five. Rodger hasn't turned up. You've got a big order of groceries and other supplies waiting to go back whenever you get another chance.'

Kath was very disappointed. Missing the boat seemed even more upsetting when an exhausted Rodger finally reached her with the tale of his day. It sounded like a bad dream where one calamity dissolves into another. After driving on one errand he was sent on yet another more distant one, then waited for passengers who delayed departure. In the storm, the car became bogged and he was forced to unload all the cargo in the rain.

After getting the car out of the bog he travelled on through mud and rain, breaking an axle just on dark. Leaving the car, he walked on, trying a shortcut in the dark across Vunakanau airstrip and was challenged by Australian soldiers on guard, then held and interrogated by the military until he was finally able to phone the chairman who went to his rescue. . . 'And now we've missed the boat!'

Kath could not deny her disappointment. Yet, watching the shadows of coconut palms and poinciana thrashing in the wind and rain outside, part of her was very thankful to be dry and safe in the Raluana mission house, with Rodger safe beside her.

Daisy was the first to know. Laurie McArthur came home that Monday morning in the week before Christmas with the news.

'This time they are insisting. All of our women and children are to be evacuated. I've been talking to Harold Page and he says that this time there will be no option for the women —

except a few who count as 'essential services' such as some nurses. The authorities feel that the war will be moving down into our area. There are rumours of Japanese fleets on the move travelling south and south-west from Japan. They attacked Malaya on the same day as they hit Pearl Harbour.

If they plan to include Australia in their Co-prosperity Sphere of Greater East Asia, they may well come down through these islands.'

Daisy was white-faced but calm. 'How long do we have? Can we have Christmas together?'

'No. Only days. Page says that they have called on the *Macdhui* and the *Neptuna* to come directly to Rabaul to take off as many as possible. I feel for Harold Page — half of the Administration departments have already left for Lae, the rest are in a muddle of packing to join them, and the Administrator, McNicholl, is very ill in Lae and is passing all responsibility to Harold. He plans to send patrol officers and police around to all the communities and plantations to let everyone know, but I want to send out my own messages to all our people. It's going to be a shock.'

Husband and wife stared at each other. Through all their own battles with illness and change of location they had always been able to stay together, each the one who made the other complete. She could see the pain on his face as he thought of his own family, and the families of all his dearest friends, being parted from each other at a time of national stress.

She laid a gentle hand on his. 'I'm very glad I didn't go six months ago,' she said.

Mr Mac's note arrived at Raluana and Essie and Kath studied the instruction. It was only days since Kath and Rodger had missed the boat home. 'If we'd caught that boat. . .'

'If you'd caught the boat, you would have made a round trip in a storm with the baby — the boat is picking up women off the plantations along the coast of West New Britain to be evacuated by the end of the week.'

Essie caught at a point in the letter. 'He says that essential services include nurses. I'm a nurse, so I can stay.'

There was no doubting the wisdom and practical skills of Essie Linggood, but her husband finally persuaded her that she should go. 'With our young Bill already with your people in Melbourne, at school, you must think of little Loloma — it wouldn't be fair to the child to keep her where there might be danger. I think you'd better start to pack.'

The District Girls' School stood empty of students on that hot, steamy afternoon. The last of the girls had left, carrying their rolled sleeping mats and few possessions, to travel home to their villages at the end of the school year. Elsie Wilson was glad of the quietness in the building as she worked. It had been a very busy year, with earthquakes, and exams, and the challenges of caring for so many young girls and women. Now the girls had gone and there was only the last of the end-of-year cleaning to finish before she would be free to begin her Christmas holiday. She would be glad to get home as she felt hot, sticky, untidy and very grimy.

A vehicle pulled up beside the school building and two young patrol officers stepped out. They began to speak to her and at first she was confused, not understanding. They spoke to her in Pidgin English, of which she knew little, and said something about telling the Australian teachers that they must leave.

'Excuse me, I don't understand — could you please give me your message in English?' she said politely, and saw a look of surprise on their faces.

'Sorry, we thought. . .' and she suddenly realised what the two men were seeing. She had inherited a pale-brown complexion from Channel Island and southern England ancestors. Now the two young Australians had mistaken her, young, grimy, hard at work and 'disgracefully brown' as she thought of herself, for one of her New Guinean students.

All Australian women were to be evacuated within days, they told her, and Mr Mac arrived at Vunairima not long after to confirm their message. The order affected not only Elsie, but also the nurses and the married women, Helen Pearson and Mel Trevitt, as well as Beryl Beazley who had only just arrived back in New Britain after two years away; Beryl had barely had time to unpack her things since she came with her husband Syd who was to establish a new technical training school, a continuation of his previous itinerant technical training in building skills. Mr Mac returned to Elsie after he had seen the married women.

'Elsie, it is possible that the single women like yourself may be able to stay on — certainly the nurses will have that option. Think about it and make your own decision about what you should do. There will be no pressure on you either way.'

That night she could not sleep. All night the questions circled around in her mind. Was it running away to leave? How much danger was there really? She knew about Pearl Harbour and Malaya, but Hawaii was a very long way from the peaceful gardens and black sand beach of Vunairima. Yet now that the schoolgirls had gone on holidays for weeks, what good would she do by staying?

Through the long hours of the night, she tried turning her pillow to the cooler side, tried lying on her left side and on her right, and scrambled out of bed to sit by the window to pray, trying to find some clear direction to guide her. When she spoke to the two nurses in the morning, Dorothy Beale who had a number of years of experience and Dorothy Holmes who had only been at Vunairima for a few months, both said that they planned to stay. Still Elsie was not clear.

Later in the morning, Laurie McArthur reappeared. 'Elsie,' he said, 'the latest word is that only the nurses have a choice about staying. You and Mary Jenkins from the Chinese school must go with the married women — pack your things and be ready to come into Rabaul tomorrow.'

The message came to Dora with the mail. When the canoe came ashore at Ulu Island, there was a very large parcel of gifts from groups of Methodist women and girls in NSW, as well as other mail. Dora tore open the parcel. As she had hoped, it was full of useful things for her medical work and she lifted out each item with appreciation. The civil administration did not pay for medical supplies for use in the mission hospitals, though they were generally the only source of health care for major population areas and, if it had not been for the help of such parcels, Dora and the other nurses would have been severely limited.

Putting aside the treasure trove of the gift parcel, Dora opened other mail and discovered the message from the chairman. She had a choice, to stay or to go with the other women being evacuated. If she chose to stay, it was probable that she, Mavis and the other new member of staff, Dorothy Holmes, might be transferred to the military hospital in the event of an attack, and the senior nurses, Dorothy Beale and Jean Christopher, would continue with the village work of general health care and maternal and infant welfare.

Dora, peace-loving and peacemaking, could not conceive of a situation where an enemy attack might happen. She had planned to come to work as a missionary nurse for years and she saw no reason to leave now.

The loud thumping on the front wall of their house dragged Jean and John Poole out of deep sleep. John groped for a torch.

'What's happening? It's the middle of the night. . .'

Jean waited, dazed and shaken by the sudden awakening. Voices spoke at the front door and she felt a rush of anxiety. Ordinary things did not happen at midnight in Kalas.

'We'd better light a lamp, Jean.' It was John standing in the doorway. 'There is a policeman here with a document from the government.'

In the circle of lamplight they read the message. All Australian women were to be in Rabaul in two days, ready to be evacuated by sea. They looked at each other in shock. They had had no idea that things could be so serious. At Kalas there was no telephone, no teleradio, no newspaper, rare contact with others who could tell them news. Through the nurses at Malabonga they had heard about the bombing of Pearl Harbour less than two weeks earlier, but they were often out-of-date with the events of the rest of the world.

Later, clinging to her husband in the dark, Jean remembered Bill Harry's comments — 'John and I could survive for months in the mountains. . .' Survive? Would the young Australian soldiers have to face a real battle with a real enemy? John was twenty-eight and much older than most of the infantry they had met, who were keen and courageous — and very young. Jean knew that she did not want to leave. She did not want to leave the people of the mountains whom she was growing to love, and she did not want to leave John. They had only had seventeen months together and their marriage was at its beginning.

Yet there was no choice. The next morning another message told them that a utility would meet her at Malabonga hospital the following day and she and John faced the task of packing. All day the choices went on, as they tried to decide what John needed and what she should take with her. Her collection of moth and butterfly wings, the photo album and camera with a half-finished roll of film taken during the synod meetings and picnics in the Duke of York Islands, her Kuanua Bible and new dictionary, most of their wedding gifts, and clothes went into her pile, while household equipment, crockery, bedclothes and blankets were for him. Each choice was a painful one. Their things belonged together, not in two separate piles.

All through the day of packing, people came to the door to weep and farewell her. The news had quickly spread that she was going and one person after another brought gifts of vegetables as an expression of their affection for her. Mikael and Louisa came to help. It was difficult to imagine what they must have been feeling to see the white women taken away, when Louisa herself had been Louisa Schultz with a heritage both New Guinean and German.

There was little time to talk with John, but in the middle of suitcases and bundles and piles of gift food they tried to talk about what each would do, to cherish the little time they had together, and to plan for the day when Jean would be able to come back and they would go on with their work together.

In the morning, with a party of schoolboys shouldering her suitcases and boxes, as well as the bundles of vegetables, Jean stood at the beginning of the road leading out to Malabonga and looked back at her home. The neat house stood in its clearing, wooden shutters open to let through the breezes, and the open entrance which had welcomed guests, brown and white. The little community of Kalas, the school building which doubled as a church, Mikael and Louisa's house, the bush materials wash house, the gardens; she had walked around them all so often, talking with the schoolboys, practising speaking the language with the women, playing with Louisa's babies. She didn't want to leave and she was sure that she would be back.

The walk from Kalas to Malabonga was sad and often silent. Jean and John walked with their thoughts, trying to imagine how the other would manage without them. They had often walked this eight kilometre stretch together, but John would have to do the return trip alone.

When they reached Malabonga, there were more farewells. Chris and Mavis were both planning to stay and continue their nursing as long as possible, and sent out letters with Jean. Malabonga people also came to the Sisters' house to weep over Jean, bringing more bundles of coconuts, pawpaws and sweet potato. 'I can't refuse to take any of this food,' whispered Jean, 'they'd be so hurt if we did — we'll try to share it out to people in Rabaul;' and so the small utility truck was piled high with suitcases, boxes and clusters of fruit and vegetables.

Driving up out of the mountain valley along the unsealed road, treacherous with rain and mud, the driver attached chains to the wheels, but even so the heavily loaded vehicle could not get enough traction on the steep and greasy clay track.

'Sorry, folks, you'll have to walk for a bit till we make it up this hill,' and Jean and John found themselves walking beside the vehicle as it spun its wheels and struggled to churn and slide its way to the top. At the crest, thick mist masked the mountain top, and when they climbed back into the cabin of the truck they crept forward slowly through a moving mystery of roadside jungle. Then the road carried them down towards the coast and, as they drove closer to the town of ·Rabaul, they saw the ominous backdrop of an erupting volcano, still spewing dust-laden steam and smoke into the air, spreading layers of pumice on rooftops and roadways like shifting, dun-coloured snow. Even the avenues of casuarina, raintree and mango seemed to droop under the weight of dust and grit.

Pulling up in the grounds of the Malaguna mission house, Jean leaned close to her husband. She was emotionally drained, tired and muddy, and there seemed to be no sign of relief from the sense that things were very wrong.

On the island of New Hanover, lying north of the furthest tip of New Ireland, Tom Simpson listened to his wireless set. Fragments of news had come crackling through the airwaves from time to time and he was aware of the growing danger from a possible invasion. One of the older men over at Kavieng, a sergeant with the Independent Company, kept saying to the civilian men, 'You blokes should be getting your wives out of here!'

Nellie said that she didn't have time for crouching over the radio. She had their eight-month-old baby daughter Margaret to care for. In any case, she often involved herself in tasks around the mission. ('We missionary wives do as much work as the men, don't we — we just don't get paid for it!' she often said.) Nellie did everything with verve and passion and that included her caring for her family and her mission work.

She saw Tom stoop over the radio, trying to capture every word through the distortion of sound. There was a sudden exclamation and he turned to her. 'This is it, Nell. I felt sure that it would come sooner or later. There will be evacuation ships sailing from Rabaul on Saturday and Captain Saunders is bringing his boat across here to New Hanover today to pick you up.'

Within hours, Nellie's world changed. After a frenzy of packing, with Nellie thinking chiefly of the needs of her child and filling a round hatbox with baby food, nappies and little clothes, while Tom tried to gather other things she would need for the journey, they saw Captain Saunders' boat coming towards their anchorage. There was no time to linger over farewells, but Nellie watched with tears in her eyes as people who had been part of her world on New Hanover waved goodbye.

Across the passage, Kavieng was thrown into confusion with women and their husbands arriving from plantations and missions for evacuation. The town was a small and close-knit community and even the recently arrived soldiers of the Independent Company had quickly become known through social and sporting events and the Kavieng Club. With so many people in town at once, the accommodation was stretched beyond its capacity. Nellie and Tom found themselves without a place to sleep for the night until the owner of the town garage offered them his workshop floor and a spare mattress.

'Not very romantic for our last night before I go!' Nellie said, spreading towels across the mattress and kneeling on the cement floor to change the baby's nappy. The room smelled of cars, petrol and oil, but Tom was there and baby Margaret, and Nellie wanted to hold them both in her arms and never let them go.

When they sailed, early the following afternoon, Nellie struggled with the idea that she was about to travel without Tom all the way to Adelaide. The little copra boat with about ten or twelve women on board set out under sail as the afternoon winds were rising. With his last embrace still warm around her, Nellie stood on the deck watching her tall Tom slowly diminishing in the distance as the waters of the passage separated them. Because she was the only one with a baby, the captain offered Nellie the single berth.

'This is the worst time to be sailing,' she said to the others. 'We know this passage between New Hanover and New Ireland — we've sailed it so often — and we are in for an awful trip. Just feel that wind!'

She was right. The copra boat wallowed from side to side through the passage, threading between little islands, threatening to be swamped. Women were miserably seasick. As they flew before the wind down the eastern coast, Nellie, anxious, pleaded for some sail to be lowered before they capsized.

At dusk their little boat found an anchorage and the women went ashore to do the best they could to light a fire for hot water, to wash themselves and find something to eat from the things they had brought with them. Nellie washed and fed her baby by firelight and wondered whether it would have been far simpler to stay at home with Tom on their lonely little island with a leprosy colony as neighbours, where surely no Japanese army would ever come.

In the morning they went on, passing beyond the southern end of New Ireland and beating their way slowly back north towards Rabaul.

It was a long slow journey, uncomfortable, crowded. Women began to be anxious that they would be too late to travel with the evacuation ships. The captain said reassuringly, 'Don't worry. They won't go without you.'

From all points the women came to Rabaul, bringing their babies, their suitcases, their camphorwood chests from the Chinese stores filled with family treasures. Some from the town like Helen Wayne had their households partly packed already, to transfer with their government department to Lae. Others like Nellie Simpson had not had time to pack much at all, snatching up essentials before the coastal boat sailed.

Kath Brown had come to Rabaul with a suitcase of maternity clothes and baby things months earlier; though she asked Rodger to ask Sister Harris on the teleradio to bring some of Kath's glorybox and wedding gifts on the boat into Rabaul, Rodger was ill with malaria at the time and didn't see embroidered traycloths and silver teapots as a top priority.

Exhausted women arriving with babies and bags of wet and soiled nappies after hours or days of travel found that the whole town was in the panic-driven confusion of an antbed that has been kicked. Needing consolation and cups of tea, the new arrivals found their hosts and hostesses distracted and preoccupied with their own urgent affairs.

Every household seemed to be striving to make their own emergency plans, to find space for husband and wife to discuss where she should go when she reached Australia, how she would be supported financially, bank accounts and wills, forwarding addresses; but such conversations were snatched haphazardly in the middle of turmoil, much as bags were being packed with strange assortments of objects that were nearest or dearest.

Women who had just come from idyllic islands or the clear air of the hills found that in town volcanic dust sifted over everything and the town water was unfit to drink. Even their freshly washed napkins, strung up to dry around the houses of their hosts, had taken on the depressing colour of pumice. Essie Linggood took care of Nellie Simpson, who knew very few people in Rabaul, producing a makeshift bed for her in a crowded household. Daisy McArthur had a constant stream of guests, mostly fellow-staff needing somewhere to stay in town; Daisy, who sang hymns softly in moments of stress, did quite a lot of singing.

Crowds of would-be travellers queued at the government offices to have official papers signed. 'They told us we have to go, but now they insist on having papers in triplicate giving us permission to leave!' they complained. Jean Poole dutifully filled in the papers and emerged with a document which announced that she, the person hereinunder described (Age: 27 Height: 5 feet) had permission to leave the Territory of New Guinea. Nonetheless, most were grateful that their passages to Australia were being paid by the government.

Husbands hurried from place to place around town trying to discover which ship their wife would be on, where their luggage should be taken, and how much money they could take from the bank. Jean felt that she scarcely saw John once they arrived in town; his list of tasks included distributing large quantities of coconuts and vegetables from Kalas.

Women visited Chinatown, Mel Trevitt among them, and discovered that no arrangements had been made by the Australian government for the evacuation of Asian or mixed-race people and the Chinese storekeepers were anxious and distressed. People were buying many bargains on impulse as the Chinese were lowering their prices. Elsie Wilson went to the house of her fellow-teacher Mary Jenkins and saw through her eyes the needs of the Chinese community: 'There is no love lost between Chinese and Japanese people — they've been at war with each other for years now — and if the Japanese were to attack Rabaul, all my Chinese friends would be in serious danger, I believe. Only the wealthy ones will be able to escape from here.'

Elsie was very touched by a conversation with Mr Mac. He told her that he had written a letter to the General Secretary of the mission, John Burton, requesting that Elsie be returned to New Britain to continue her work whenever that became possible: 'I just wanted to put it in writing that we wanted you back and were very happy with your work,' he explained.

By the end of the week, though the ships *Macdhui* and *Neptuna* waited at the wharves, torrential storms beat against the town, delaying loading. Acres of coconuts were blown down and roads were closed. Kath and Rodger, with the baby, drove into town to join the ships through a downpour; they came along a road skirting the water's edge which was known sometimes to fall away into the sea, and arrived saturated and miserable. There was still no sign of the coastal ship which had gone to collect the women from the West New Britain coast, as it had been delayed in the storm.

During the afternoon of 22 December 1941, at last women were allowed to go on board. Elsie and Mary joined other single women on the *Neptuna*, with other teachers, typists, shop assistants, and office workers, and the married women and children went on board the *Macdhui*. Laurie McArthur helped Daisy to find her cabin, with small seven-year-old Malcolm and the baby Glenn. Nellie Simpson and Helen Pearson with their little ones were sharing a cabin; it was very different from their first journey together to New Britain when they had been two young brides coming for their weddings.

Kath Brown was a little upset to discover that she was to share a cabin with a woman with a fourteen-year-old son. She whispered to Rodger, 'I'm not happy about having to feed the baby in front of that big boy.' Jean Poole surveyed her cabin with a sigh. 'If it is anything like our honeymoon trip up, I'll probably spend most of the time on board lying in here being very seasick!' Essie Linggood and Mel Trevitt were sharing, too, Essie with four-year-old Loloma and Mel with her little boy Bruce, eight months old.

Mission accountant Wilf Pearce settled his wife Eileen into her cabin very tenderly; they had only been married a little over a year and Eileen was due to have their first child within weeks. Wilf's sister Netta was sailing on the *Neptuna* and tearfully saying goodbye to her husband of little over a year, Ken Allsop, who was also closely involved with the mission community.

Beryl Beazley looked around the familiar spaces of the *Macdhui*; it was only weeks since she and Syd had made the journey north on the same ship and now she had to turn back once more — Perth seemed a very long way away. Old friends Ron Wayne and Bill Huntley were there to farewell their wives Helen and Hannah. Ron had been on the Methodist staff as a layman for fourteen years till 1939 when the downturn in the world copra market had seen both he and Bill Huntley leave their jobs as mission plantation managers to find other work in the area. Ron was now court interpreter and used his skills and experience working with Wilf Pearce in the church for the labourers of Rabaul, while Bill had become postmaster at Kokopo. Both families were still very much part of the mission family and the mission women welcomed Helen and Hannah as part of their group.

In each cabin, families tried to find the words to say good-bye. Fathers cuddled their babies. Husbands held their wives. People tried to be cheerful, but even jolly Ron Wayne with his endless good humour was struggling for a joke. 'We'll be back in six months — you'll see!' some assured their partners; it did not seem possible that any real danger could touch their tropical world.

In some cabins, couples sat wordlessly and in others prayers were whispered, pleas for strength in weakness and for protection in danger. Tears flowed as people embraced and placed each other into the hands of God. Some spoke the ancient blessing: 'The Lord bless you and keep you, the Lord make his face to shine upon you. . .'

During the afternoon the men were sent ashore. After the last clasped hand was released and the last man had reluctantly turned and walked away from his partner, more hours dragged by with the men standing on the wharf and the women lining the rail of the deck high above them. No-one dared to leave and the hours of painful waiting dragged on. It grew dark and still it was not time.

'Maybe they are waiting to see if the ship with the women from the west coast gets here in time,' someone suggested. Then there was a commotion on the wharf. Someone came running to say that a small vessel with a party of women to be evacuated had just come in from Bougainville. Women on the deck of the *Macdhui* and men below caught snatches of the argument — the two ships were already full, they were going to sail very soon, these people were too late, there would be other opportunities, other outstation women hadn't turned up yet, either. . .

Yet when they learned that the women had spent two days sailing through rough seas and heavy rain from Bougainville, some of them sleeping on the hatch as the limited shelter was taken by the women with the smallest children, all of them seasick, saturated and utterly spent, they were welcomed on board. It was true that the ship was full. The latecomers came aboard thankfully, even though the only place left for them was the floor of the music room and they were warned that there could be no baths till the morning.

Late that evening, under a heavy cover of cloud, the *Macdhui* and later the *Neptuna* began to move away from the pier. Through tears, Jean watched John following the slowly-moving ship, starting to run, hurrying to follow along a second and longer pier. They were all following — husbands and fathers, planters and missionaries, senior public servants and technicians, storemen and scientists, patrol officers and medical men, following their women with their eyes.

The mission women on the ship waved and waved, calling till their voices were lost in tears. The ship moved far beyond the longest pier and Laurie McArthur and Laurie Linggood, Jack, Howard, Syd and Wilf, Ron, Ken and Bill, Rodger and John blended into a white blur of men, with the crater of Tavurvur sending a glow of fire-lit smoke into the darkly clouded sky beyond.

5

Christmas Eve 1941– New Year's Day 1942

DAISY MCARTHUR STOOD AT THE DOOR of the ship's dining room, her baby on her hip and her little boy by her side. The sound of a room full of agitated women assaulted her ears. Last time our family sailed home it was not like this, she thought. That last time, when she and Laurie sailed from Rabaul on furlough, she had not been well, but her husband had been there to take care of everything. The voyage had been restful, a holiday. This was very different.

The dining room was crowded with women and young children waiting for their lunch. Each had been taken suddenly from her partner and forced into an independence which, for some, did not come naturally. The handful of men on board were either elderly or ill. Most of the women had been unprepared for such an abrupt departure and farewells had been hasty, confused and incomplete.

They didn't want to leave the islands and their lives on plantations, mission stations and in colonial townships. Most of them had come reluctantly and only because they had no option. Many were exhausted from the hazards they had encountered between their homes and the *Macdhui*. There were too many of them — some were sleeping on the floors of dining room or music room. The ship was festooned with babies' nappies fluttering everywhere one walked. And there was the unspoken knowledge that this ship might be attacked by an enemy.

Looking across the tables, Daisy saw a cluster of her friends from the mission staff who beckoned her to join them.

'Have you had a quiet morning?'

'Not really — the baby was very restless.'

'Last night I slept like a log. I was worn out and as soon as I dropped into my berth, after all the business of getting into Rabaul, and the storms, I put my head down, had a little cry and then fell asleep.'

'We won't see Jean Poole for lunch, I don't think — the poor girl is a very bad traveller and when I popped in to see how she was this morning she was seasick already. And Kath Brown was still busy feeding her baby — he's so tiny, the dear little thing.'

'Didn't the men all look so pathetic down there on the wharf last night! If some of the others are like my husband, they are in for a hard time — he has never had to cook a meal in his life — they probably think they'll soon starve to death unless their cookboys remember what we've taught them.'

'I kept hoping that I wouldn't have to leave after all,' Essie Linggood said, 'because they said that the nurses could stay and I'm a trained nurse. But they insisted. But by then it was too late to pack much. Still, Laurie will pack up anything he thinks might get broken while I'm away.'

'Christmas will be a bit funny for them all. . . and for us, too.'

'This doesn't seem real, at all, does it?' Women nodded agreement. 'For so long we've been told that Rabaul and New Britain and New Ireland were really well out of range of any war. No-one seems to have taken the Japanese very seriously — then suddenly they are bombing the Americans at Pearl Harbour and all the Allies are at war with them. Before we know what is happening, all of us women have been rushed off in a panic.'

'Surely this is just unnecessary caution,' one said. 'We all know that when Asiatics meet the might of the white world powers they can't win. Pearl Harbour must have been a fluke, and they had the advantage of surprise. The newspapers have been very clear — their air force is weak, compared to our side, and what they have is out-of-date and inferior.'

'Anything made in Japan falls apart — we all know that, too.'

'Just the other day I saw in a Sydney paper that so many of their youth have damaged their eyes from reading their sort of oriental characters that most Japanese have to wear spectacles and would never pass the medical tests we set for our military men.'

Another added, 'There was a big diagram in a newspaper showing a map of the Pacific and South-East Asia. They had drawn two great big circles on the map, showing where the danger areas are, one centred on Hawaii in the north Pacific and the other centred on Malaya in South-East Asia. And do you know, Rabaul and New Britain and our bit of the Pacific were outside both of the circles! We probably would have been safer to stay where we were.'

'It won't be for long, though, this business of going south. A month, maybe two, then we'll be coming back again.'

In the hot dusk of Rabaul, men wandered aimlessly or gathered in groups of friends in clubs or houses. Some began letters to the wives who had left them the previous evening. Ron Wayne, Methodist layman and court interpreter, wrote to his Helen, 'Rabaul was absolutely flat today. Nobody could work except by driving themselves to it. . .'

He wrote of meeting other men in the unexpected setting of the butchery, each wondering what to do with the pieces of meat they had just bought, of renewed earth tremors, of bits of gossip gathered from the network of the teleradio — 'No-one seems able to remember that this is Christmas Eve.'

Listing the group of friends who planned to gather at Raluana for Christmas dinner — McArthur, Linggood, Pearce, Allsop, Wayne, Huntley, Poole and Brown, with Shelton and Dora Wilson if the weather was suitable for sea travel — Ron Wayne added, 'If such a mob gathers around the festive board, then imagine it!

O, a-wailing we will be, a-wailing we will be,
What are our lives without our wives?
A-wailing we will be!'

With her baby in his woven cane basket beside her, Kath Brown sat through the ceremonies of Christmas Day on board the *Macdhui*. The sea was calm and the weather beautiful, but the spreading ocean beyond the *Macdhui* only reminded her of the ever-increasing gap between herself and Rodger. Only a few days ago she had still imagined that Christmas would be spent back in their own home at Malalia, with their baby safe in his bed and village choirs coming to sing outside their windows, and having the fun of cooking her own Christmas dinner. But not this.

Everyone had gone to such trouble to make it a special day for them all. Before the *Macdhui* sailed, the New Guinea Club and the staff of Burns Philp stores had brought aboard all the gifts, the tree and special foods prepared for the annual children's Christmas party which was usually given at the club. Two hundred Christmas stockings for the kiddies, they said, and sweets and chocolates.

Most of the mission children were only babies, six of them just a year old or younger, and so the excitement of a Christmas stocking presented by a Santa Claus with cottonwool whiskers was lost on them. But Daisy's Malcolm and Essie's Loloma were old enough to enjoy it. With over a hundred children on board, the noise of childish shouts and laughter punctuated by wails and the tears of over-excitement flowed over everyone, the intensity of their response tangling with the balloons and tinsel.

There was no sign of Jean Poole who was still sick, but others came to join Kath, most of them with babies on their laps, to watch the turmoil of children opening gifts. It was very confusing, a strange mix of festivity and anxiety, celebration and a sense of loss. Women called 'Happy Christmas!' to each other, but the words had a tinge of mockery. The aroma of roasting turkey floated on the air and they'd been told that they would all sit down to a sumptuous Christmas dinner of turkey and the trimmings with Christmas pudding, but celebration grated — none of them would be sharing the meal with their partner. Festoons of streamers competed with festoons of drying baby nappies.

There had been, earlier in the morning, a church service in the music room for those who wished to attend. For the mission women, it was a strong reminder of their husbands and those other years when Christmas had been celebrated with village friends. For some, there had been a sense that this year God would not be part of Christmas.

But then they heard again the story of the birth of the Son of God; the story of the young mother Mary, exhausted, far from home, searching for a place to lie down. They listened with a new understanding. Around them on the floor of the music room were the bundles of bedding and baggage of the women who had arrived so late from Bougainville, after a terrible journey through storms, and had almost been left behind by the *Macdhui*. The mother of the Son of God had been turned away as there was no room and was grateful for a poor substitute because she was carrying within her the urgency of a child about to be born. Even after the child was in her arms, she was forced to travel on, a refugee fleeing from danger — perhaps after all, the women thought, the Son of God would understand how they felt on this strange Christmas morning. . .

Yet another child, smeared with ice-cream and chocolate and sobbing over a burst balloon, was carried away to his cabin by a harassed mother. They watched him go, feet dragging, gifts trailing.

Someone said, 'Poor kid. I know how he feels. I'm not sure whether I am having fun or whether I feel like putting my head back and howling my eyes out.'

On the slower ship, the *Neptuna*, loaded with single women and those who had no children, Elsie Wilson and Mary Jenkins went to call at the cabins of friends. Eileen Pearce, looking uncomfortable in late pregnancy, sat by the bed of her sister-in-law Netta.

'Netta's feeling seasick.'

'Seasick! But you can't be — the sea is as flat as could be. Aren't you coming up for Christmas dinner?'

'No!' Netta Allsop looked pale, appalled at the thought of baked potatoes, gravy glossy with turkey fat, rich pudding.

Elsie remembered seeing Netta's face as the *Neptuna* had pulled away from the wharf. Her older brother and friend Wilf

Pearce, the mission accountant, had been down there, and her husband Ken Allsop with whom she had shared less than two years of marriage. Elsie knew that, much as she regretted leaving her students and her work, it was not the same as watching two of the most significant people in her life disappearing in the distance.

'Can I get you a cup of tea, then, and maybe a dry sao biscuit?'

'Thanks.' Netta's eyes were reddened and Elsie knew that she must have been weeping. 'I suppose I'm not really seasick, you know. It was much rougher yesterday and I was all right then. But it's Christmas Day and I'm just — sick. . .'

There were eleven of them sitting round the table for Christmas dinner at Raluana. John Poole had brought the two nurses, Mavis Green and Jean Christopher, from Malabonga for the day. They were disappointed that Dora Wilson had not arrived in from the Duke of York Islands with Herbert Shelton, but the weather had been wild and stormy and the mission boat had not been able to travel to pick them up. Bill Huntley had come in from Kokopo further along the coast, where he worked as postmaster, and Laurie McArthur had brought out Wilf Pearce, Ron Wayne, Ken Allsop and Rodger Brown from town.

Like a queen holding court, Miss Margaret Harris sat at the head of the table. Maggie Harris was by far the most senior among them, having first arrived in New Britain in 1918. Maggie had an endless fund of good stories about local personalities past and present, many of them hilarious yarns, and could keep a group of people, be they New Guinean pastors or Australian colleagues, laughing till they ached.

'The trip in along the north coast through the storm was a wretched one,' she said. 'Rodger, you should be very glad that you and Kath missed that boat. We picked up women and children along the way and most of them didn't want to come, of course — and then, when we finally arrived yesterday, the evacuation ships had sailed without us! Still, I'm told we'll be flying south in a modern passenger airliner! I must have sailed on all the ships on the islands line since 1918 — this time I'm flying.'

Over Christmas dinner they told stories about their work, about patrol journeys and plans for the future. Those who knew the community had stories of the latest gossip. Someone complained of a woman plantation owner, Mrs Bignell, who had somehow managed to evade the demands that all those Australian women who were not providing 'essential services' must leave.

'There have been a few hostile comments around town about that,' someone said, 'because if she could stay, why couldn't some of the other women?' The names of their wives and friends wove in and out the conversations; they were thankful that their families were on their way to safety, but they could not help missing them.

Men who had arrived looking dejected cheered up during the day as they ate an excellent dinner, talked and laughed, and then went walking to visit the relics of the old German colony. From the beauty of the Raluana gardens, they looked across the width of the entrance to Blanche Bay on the south to Praed Point on the north; if any of them thought of the battery of coastal defence guns established on Praed Point, no-one mentioned it.

As they gathered around their vehicles that evening, before setting off to drive home into the mountains to Malabonga, back to Kokopo, or around the beach road back to Malaguna, one of the men said: 'It's been a great day! This morning I was so miserable to wake to Christmas Day and know that my wife and baby were somewhere out at sea. There I was in my empty house, carefully washing the glass on the picture frames of my family photos. By the time I had finished, my spirits had ascended from the abyss to a morgue-like state of cheerfulness. . . But spending today with my mates has been good, after all.'

The rumours were the worst. Elsie Wilson tried to ignore them, but every time the women gathered for meals, or paced the deck in the sunshine, someone had something new to relate. For the women on the ships it was impossible to sift the truth from the vivid imagination of their fellow-travellers.

A few had radios which picked up fragments of world news and each snippet of news was drawn out, embroidered, enlarged. Women recalled seeing planes overhead, flying over plantations or small outpost communities: could they have been Japanese? Some had encountered Japanese visitors in town over past months, tourists with cameras: were they spies?

On Christmas Day, so the news went, British-held Hong Kong had been overtaken by a surprisingly efficient Japanese force and in the early hours of the following morning had finally surrendered. Fighting was continuing through Malaya and, though defeat there was unthinkable, the news reports suggested that it was no easy victory for the British, Indian and Australian troops there. Everyone had a story of something they had heard or read about Japanese atrocities in China: women being raped, looting, executions. They had seen Japanese people and shipping around Rabaul often over the years and knew that places like Truk in Micronesia to the north had been in Japanese hands since the Great War and Rabaul was much closer to them than Rabaul was to Townsville in north Queensland.

'The enemy listens,' they were told and Elsie took the warning to heart. Before they left Rabaul, the women were all instructed that they must not send cables home to warn their families that they were coming. 'If anyone does send such a message, it is sure to be picked up by the enemy and they will come after our evacuation ships. We can't risk that.'

Elsie was grateful for the companionship of Mary Jenkins on the journey home. The married women like Helen Pearson and Mel Trevitt who had been her neighbours at Vunairima were all on the other ship, the single nurses had all stayed behind and she knew few of the other women on board the *Neptuna* because she rarely visited Rabaul township. Her natural reserve combined with the dire warnings that 'the enemy listens' made it harder than ever for her to chat easily to acquaintances.

'I wish they had let us stay with the nurses,' she said to Mary.

Mary was serious. 'I can't help thinking of Rev. Mo Pui Sam and Mr and Mrs Mow. If it is not safe for me to stay in Rabaul, why should Mrs Wai Yin Mow be safe there?'

In the heat of a summer evening, the *Macdhui* ploughed on through the darkened sea. Groups of women strolled on the deck, grateful for the coolness of breezes off the water after the oppressive heat of the cabins in the heart of the ship. The ship rode on in darkness, with all external lights extinguished and interior lights hidden by blackout material. Daisy walked with Essie and Nellie, pacing quietly around the deck by the small light of stars and a slim moon.

'Look there! What is it?'

Moving towards the *Macdhui* through the gloom was another ship. It seemed to be coming in a direct line and it, too, was carrying no lights. The women stood very still. Daisy found her fingers gripping the rail till they hurt. No-one spoke. At last, as the ominous shape came nearer and nearer, Nellie whispered, 'Is it the Japs?'

The silence seemed to go on and on, but they suddenly realised that the two ships were passing each other, quietly, without any visible sign. Daisy felt her heartbeat steadying at last. She had felt frozen, unable to move, unable to rush to her children below, unsure what she could have done to protect them even if she had run.

'But who was that?' The question passed from mouth to mouth around the ship. 'Was it one of ours?' No official word was given and the rumours kept flying.

'If that had been the Japs, and they had attacked, who was going to help us?' women demanded. 'Apart from the crew, the only men on board are too old or sick to be any use — we'd have to save them as well as our children.' The thought was too awful to contemplate. One woman declared that as soon as they reached land, she wanted to get off the ship and travel the rest of the way by train.

Each woman carried her own private fears. Jean Poole was still too seasick to think about it very much, but she missed the presence of John coming in to comfort her as he had done during their honeymoon voyage. The presence of so many infants was very tiring — Kath had told her of an elderly man who had complained that 'every time I want to wash my hands there is a nappy in the sink!' Mel Trevitt spent most of her hours with her little boy who was ill for much of the journey.

On the *Neptuna*, Eileen Pearce watched anxiously for any signs of early labour; she longed to arrive so that her child could be born in the safety of an Australian hospital.

Kath Brown's fears were with her child. He was so little, so fragile, and every time she looked at him she felt afraid for little Graham. If only Rodger could have been beside her. The child began to cry and she moved to lift him into her arms from his basket. A woman nearby turned and spoke disapprovingly. 'Don't you believe in the Plunkett system of child care? You shouldn't go picking him up the moment he cries.'

Kath was close to tears herself. She was worried about Rodger, worried about the baby's health, worried about all the upsetting rumours that kept going around. 'I don't know anything about any Plunkett system,' she said, her voice wobbling dangerously. 'All I care about is getting back to Australia safely with this child!'

A single light in the ceiling of the church in Rabaul fell on the little group of men gathered for the English language evening worship. As the women had almost all gone and most of the young soldiers were on duty or out of town, there were only about fourteen people there, and they dragged the pews together into a circle under the light. One of the men played the organ and the singing was hearty; each one was grateful for the support of his friends and the quiet, homelike atmosphere. Laurie McArthur left the formality of the pulpit to come and stand with them by the communion rail as he preached.

It had been a most peculiar week. On the day after Christmas, people had been called in to work in their offices, even though most of them barely went through the motions. Men speaking of Christmas in the town said it had been very quiet and dull, with several town personalities ending the day 'as full as a goog', but there was little in the way of the usual giving and receiving of hospitality. No-one felt like it. Then there had been that plane overhead; it was clearly a Japanese plane and its presence had increased the sense of unease.

Two evacuation planes had flown out as expected. Many of the men from the mission had been out at the airstrip to farewell Maggie Harris and also Mrs Platten and her little girl who had been among other women coming in late from New Ireland. The loading of the departing women and children had been proceeding, every person and piece of cargo being weighed carefully, until there was a sudden warning — it was possible that Japanese aircraft were on their way. People and their bags were unceremoniously pushed on board and the planes were on their way after only three-quarters-of-an-hour on the ground in Rabaul. Yes, it had been an unusual week.

After the last prayers were said, the group went to share tea and cakes at a neighbouring house, sitting around the table munching scones, fruit cake and anzac biscuits produced by skilled cookboys.

'New Year's Day — we should go out to visit the Vunairima chaps,' Laurie McArthur suggested. 'Who wants to come?'

'Dear Mum,' Kath wrote, trying to phrase something to post home that would give a clue without alerting the watchful enemy, 'You'll have Graham mowing the lawn for you next month.'

She read aloud what she had just written and Jean Poole laughed. Graham lay in his cane basket, still very tiny, and flailed infant arms in the air. Now that they were coming into Cairns, Kath's earlier cabin companion was leaving the ship and Jean was joining Kath. Though both young wives had spent the past year in far distant settings, the friendship begun at the missionary college in Sydney continued. Ever since they had first met, there had been an understanding between the Pooles and the Browns; they enjoyed each other's company, were at ease together, had shared a similar vision for the work they hoped to do.

'How are you feeling today, Jean?'

'Still not well — but at least we are in Australian waters now.'

As they came into Cairns, the group of mission women who had supported each other through the strange voyage farewelled Essie Linggood. Essie had volunteered to leave the *Macdhui* at Cairns with a number of others who were being off-loaded there to relieve the overcrowding. Essie couldn't bear to see a young mother with tiny children facing the train trip without help and joined the train party.

The *Neptuna*, at last off the coast of north Queensland, crept delicately through the reef towards Townsville. Elsie and Mary stood on deck watching the land come nearer. Even now, within sight of their own country, they had been warned that there could be mines strewn along the entrance through the reef, and they remained tense till it was clear that they would be docking in safety.

'Don't forget,' they were warned, 'say nothing to anyone about where you have come from. The enemy could use any bit of information — there would be no point in the censor going to all the trouble of checking incoming mail for things that would help the enemy if you go chatting all about Rabaul, and the trip home, to everyone.'

At Townsville, some of the women disembarked from the *Neptuna* and were loaded onto a train. There was not enough emergency equipment on board for all of those on the crowded ship, they were told, so some had to be off-loaded. Elsie, Mary, Beryl and Netta were among them. They were grateful to be on Australian soil, but the journey in a very basic suburban train over many hundreds of kilometres from Townsville in north Queensland right down the east coast and across to Adelaide in South Australia seemed to stretch away into an infinity of railway lines. Beryl Beazley's journey all the way to Perth seemed endless.

At some point during the first night on the train, Elsie woke from uncomfortable sleep propped up in her seat to find that the train had stopped. A group of strange women and children were milling around with bags and bundles in the confused shadows of a half-lit railway platform and climbing into the railway carriages. They looked tired and bedraggled, too weary to question what was happening to them, just thankful to find some kind of seat on a train that would carry them further south. 'More evacuees,' someone whispered. 'This lot have come through overland from north Australia and further north in Queensland — they look a lot worse than us, poor things!'

The train full of women and children swayed and rattled on. From time to time it pulled in at country stations and local women were waiting with sandwiches and big pots of tea for the travellers. It was a trip of many stops and starts; sometimes the train would stand without explanation for periods and at other times they were side-tracked off the main line to let other trains rush by them. Two sleepless nights and a day passed before they reached Brisbane, where they were transferred to another more comfortable train for the journey to Sydney. Adelaide was still a very long way away for Elsie.

'Even when I get to Adelaide, I'll still have another long trip ahead of me. Dad was transferred recently into the country further west,' she told Mary.

The *Macdhui* sailed on to Sydney after leaving Essie Linggood at Cairns, calling at several Queensland ports then moving on to Sydney. The women on board had been told that those who lived in Sydney would be given transport to their homes and others would be cared for in hotels or with private billets till they could travel on to their own states.

When at last the ship docked in Sydney Harbour, the women came ashore carrying suitcases and small bundles, many with a small child or two clinging to their hand and an infant on their hip. Jean, grateful to be on solid land again, walked down the gangway with Kath. Jean had some boxes in the hold, but Kath had nothing but the baby basket and a suitcase of clothing.

As they passed through Customs, they had nothing to declare. Two Customs officers peered into the baby basket and smiled at the young mother.

'This one was born on the ship, wasn't he?'

'No, he's six weeks old,' she said, yet there was no denying her baby was very tiny. She longed to get him home to Adelaide and dreamed of her mother being there to help.

Outside the Customs hall, officials waited to offer assistance to the shipload of women. None of their families were expecting them so each one needed help. In that last muddled moment of being together as a group, the mission women said goodbye. Some had been close friends and neighbours, but now that they were back in Australia it was hard to know when they would meet again until the threat of war in New Britain was behind them and they could join their husbands once more. There were hugs and tears and then they were parted.

Daisy McArthur and her children planned to travel on as far as Melbourne to stay with relatives, after a night's sleep. Eileen Pearce was thankful to be in Sydney; the mission staff had arranged for her to stay at George Brown College and then to be admitted to the War Memorial Hospital, Waverley, for the birth of her child. Nellie Simpson, Helen Pearson and Kath Brown were booked on a sleeper to travel to Adelaide via Melbourne, leaving the next morning. Mel Trevitt would stay in Sydney; her own family lived in the country, but she hoped to be independent as soon as possible.

Jean Poole climbed into a taxi to take her to her parent's home in Rockdale. As they drove through the city, she was astonished to see great walls of sandbags against city buildings, blinds drawn over windows and signs of trench-digging in parks. The taxi driver said, 'They've turned off the lights on the Harbour Bridge as well as the street lights!' It hadn't occurred to her till then that she was returning from a potential war zone to a city which expected to be besieged.

The taxi dropped her at the front gate of the house which she had left as a new bride only seventeen months earlier. As far as her parents knew, their Jean and John were at Kalas, in the Baining mountains of New Britain. She walked in through the front door and called, 'I'm home!'

Essie Linggood arrived in Melbourne on New Year's Day. It was only six months earlier that she and Laurie had left Melbourne after their furlough, leaving their son Bill with his grandparents to attend school. Now on the platform at Spencer Street Station, Bill came running into her arms and, with Loloma and her parents holding her, she knew that her family was there to support her until Laurie came home again.

As for Kath, the long journey home finally came to an end and she found herself walking down the railway platform with her baby basket in one hand and her suitcase in the other. Somehow her mother had learned that the Adelaide women were coming home on that train and was there to meet her with Rodger's parents.

'But Kath, where is your baby?' her mother cried.

'Here, in his basket — he's still little enough to fit in the baby basket,' and she held up her first-born proudly to meet his grandparents.

Later, when the first excitement had died down, the family gathered in the familiar home. A grandmother cuddled the baby and her mother poured cups of tea.

'Kath, what I don't understand is where are all your things. You seem to have arrived with your baby, a suitcase and nothing else. Don't tell me that you've left that beautiful silver teapot behind, the one I gave you for your wedding!'

For a moment Kath was speechless. 'Yes, but I'm here.'

On New Year's Day, 1942, Laurie McArthur took his group of friends from Rabaul — Brown, Pearce, Wayne and Allsop — and drove out to visit the remaining staff on the north coast at Vunairima. They joined Jack Trevitt, Howard Pearson, Syd Beazley and two nurses, Dorothy Beale and Dorothy Holmes. A letter which had just arrived from their head office in Sydney caused some lively comment; the General Secretary wrote that the Department of External Territories in Canberra had informed him that missionary women and their children could stay in New Britain if they chose.

'Did the authorities here ever know that? We doubt it.'

'How some of the ladies will growl when they hear that! They will not be pleased.'

'Still,' said one, 'I'm quite glad that they got away when they did, even if they could have stayed,' and the others agreed.

It was a good day. There was chiacking about the plight of Howard, Jack and Syd sharing Howard's big house and none of them experienced at running a household. Vunairima was quiet with many of the students gone for the holidays and only the New Ireland families still in residence, so there was a sense of holiday among the party of staff.

Ron Wayne described the day in a letter to Helen: '. . .We had a ham Mac and Rodger cooked, and Christmas pudding Eileen left behind. It was food plus all day. An uproarious luncheon party of ten. A yarn, then down to the beach for a swim and afternoon tea. I forgot my bathers — the others hadn't even thought of theirs — Jack Trevitt wore shorts and gave his trunks to Rodger.

'I wore whose? I think a spare pair of Dorothy Beale's — tied the ties around my middle after rolling the superfluous top down like a tyre. Dorothy B pushed me into the briny most beautifully from a canoe, but fell in herself after me so we ended quits. Dorothy H twice foundered the canoe, by trying to crawl aboard over the bow — she little knows the ways and means of a canoe, but she'll learn. Hilarious high tea at Howard's place — coffee, chatter and off home no later than 8.30 pm. Beautiful moonlight night and we sang old songs (and some near-new ones) till we could sing no more. . .'

On New Year's Day 1942, the Area Commander, Colonel Scanlan, issued orders to the men of Lark Force, the 2/22nd; in the event of enemy attack on Rabaul, they were to fight to the last. The orders concluded, with the words underlined and in capitals: 'THERE SHALL BE NO WITHDRAWAL.'

6

2–16 January 1942

THE ORNATE METAL GRILLE DOORS of the lift-cage clanged shut and the lift began to rise sedately up through the heart of the Sydney city building.

Elsie Wilson watched the walls of the liftwell flow by beyond the filigree of metal. 'It seems a lifetime since I was here last,' she remarked to her companion Mary Jenkins, 'but it is only two-and-a-half years, I suppose.'

'Going to visit the General Secretary — I've always been rather nervous, even though the GS has always been very gracious and kind. Just the thought has been intimidating.'

The lift shuddered to a halt. The two women, as staff rather than the wives of staff, were expected to report to the Rev. Dr J.W. Burton, the General Secretary of their mission, before they travelled home. John Burton himself welcomed them with warmth. From his office in Castlereagh Street in the heart of Sydney, he had pastoral and administrative charge of missionaries scattered across the Pacific and through north Australia, each of them known and considered; as a church figure with a wide and inclusive view of world affairs, the implications of a world war weighed very heavily on him.

From the windows of his office they looked down on a busy city street, but within the room there were books, pictures and artefacts which stretched far beyond the limits of a city into the expanses of a wider world of thought and interconnectedness.

They talked. Burton was clearly well-informed and had visited New Britain on a number of occasions in the course of his leadership years. Each staff name and role was familiar to him and he asked for news on their colleagues whom they had left behind.

'What news of the nurses?'

There was little they could say. Elsie had left the two Dorothys at Vunairima several weeks earlier and had seen little of Mavis, Chris or Dora over past months as each woman had stayed in her own location working on her own task. Had there not been the inhibiting memory of the repeated instruction to avoid talking about where they had been, Elsie felt that she still would not have been able to satisfy Burton's need for news.

Her missionary life had been spent in a very contained area, all on a single mission compound with a well-defined group of women and girls; she had not even made many contacts with neighbouring plantation families in the way that some other staff had done. As a staff member still in her first term of service, she had not been a member of synod either, so had little in the way of current church news to offer.

'You could have stayed on, of course,' Burton said, 'if you had wished. We thought that message had reached you.'

Elsie was troubled. She had been bustled away from Vunairima so hurriedly, and Mr Mac had said that, after all, she had no choice. Had she run away from her work, after all? It was a very disturbing thought.

'You are both entitled to two months furlough,' Burton was saying, 'and then I suggest you find teaching posts, with a view to returning to your work in New Britain whenever the way is clear again.'

It was a long way to Adelaide. The train travelled on, steaming south through the night. Elsie Wilson sat staring into the darkness as the brief lights of farmhouses and villages twinkled and faded into deep shadows as they passed. She need not have come back.

This long weary journey could prove to be a foolish waste of time. If only she had known, she could have stayed at Vunairima and been preparing for the new school year.

She leaned back, trying to rest, but the train shook and roared and, even after she dozed off after midnight, the train halted at the state border at Albury and all the passengers staggered, bleary-eyed, onto the platform to change trains. There was a day to wait in Melbourne and then on again, west to Adelaide, through country that was parched and dusty with drought. It had been very hot all the way and dry heatwave winds blew through the train windows, not cooling but carrying dust and smoke and cinders from the dark clouds pouring from the steam engine. Even when she reached Adelaide, Elsie knew that she would have to travel on to join her parents who had moved to Minnipa on the west coast.

'The enemy listens. . .' People had drummed that thought into her mind. What did she know that could be of any use to an enemy, she wondered. Still, if the authorities told them to be silent then she was certainly not going to disobey them. The command was reinforced for her when she read in a newspaper a series of instructions for behaviour in the event of an attack: 'Sit tight. Do not spread rumours. Do not block roads. Keep a clear head and a shut mouth.'

She remembered the warning when at last she reached Adelaide and was able to visit her home church. It struck her, talking with old friends, that the people of Adelaide were not particularly curious about where she had been, or what she had been doing. Most of them were far more interested in talking about their own local affairs. It was not so very hard then, she discovered, to keep her own experiences and her long journey to herself. And yet, though she had been obedient, it was just a little disappointing that hardly anyone even wanted to know.

Elsie travelled on, by ship from Port Adelaide to Port Lincoln across Spencer Gulf, then by train again heading further west to join her parents at Minnipa. The hot dust whipped up across the open plains, carrying topsoil in whirling duststorm clouds. In her carriage travelled a group of soldiers, their khaki uniforms looking well-worn and their slouch hats battered as if they had travelled far and hard. They ignored her and the other travellers, absorbed in their own private world. She wondered whether perhaps they were men who had just returned from the Middle East; it was possible, but she knew she would not ask.

She felt very alone. The other women who had been with her on the wharf in Rabaul before Christmas were scattered across Australia now. Mary Jenkins and Jean Poole had gone to their family homes in Sydney to stay with their parents. Mel Trevitt, Helen Wayne, Netta Allsop and Hannah Huntley were also in NSW, Helen in the Blue Mountains and the others in Sydney. She had seen Jean Shelton in Sydney, too, with her two children, acting as housekeeper at George Brown Missionary College in Haberfield while she waited for her husband Herbert to come on furlough.

Eileen Pearce had gone into hospital and had given birth to a daughter, Rosemary, only a few days after they had arrived in Sydney. There was great excitement over the safe arrival of the child and messages had been sent off to Wilf Pearce in Rabaul — Elsie pictured him celebrating with his brother-in-law Ken and other Rabaul friends.

Marion Oakes from a mission station on New Ireland was also in Sydney with her two boys, they said, staying with her parents in the parsonage at Lindfield, though Elsie had barely met her and knew her only by reputation as a strong and capable lady. Burton had told her that Essie Linggood had gone to her parents in Melbourne, Beryl Beazley to Perth, and Helen Pearson, Nellie Simpson, Isobel Platten and Kath Brown to their families in Adelaide. Daisy McArthur was with an aunt in Melbourne; Mr Mac had his seat booked on a plane in mid-January to fly to Sydney for the mission's annual general meeting and they would be reunited then. All scattered. . .

Elsie sat in the train rocking with the motion of the carriage and stared out across a countryside that was not even the familiar landscape of her growing-up years. If her friends in Adelaide had felt distant after nearly three years away, how much more would the strangers of this country town where her parents were? If she were unable to share what had happened for her over the past years, then she knew she would feel very isolated.

It was not only the events of their sudden departure from Rabaul but all the learning, the disappointments, the mistakes, the fears, the delights and challenges of her teaching experiences with New Guinean girls and young women. She had never been one to force herself and her interests on other people and now she was afraid that much that was of deep significance to her would remain hidden.

It was then, as the train travelled on towards yet another little town strung out along that stretch of railway line that pointed on to the coastal port of Ceduna, that she noticed the soldier. He stared out of the train window, his hat tilted down over his eyes, watching the landscape of home spreading away to the horizon. Who knew what lay behind his eyes, what memories of other deserts, other battles? What were the things he would never tell his family? For now, before the moment of reunion, he let the silent tears run down his face, a wordless grief.

The dark-eyed girl looked away. She could not enter the stranger's pain, but neither, it seemed, would others be able to share in her own.

High, high overhead, almost transparent against a nearly cloudless blue sky on Sunday morning 4 January 1942, the first wave of bombers came over Rabaul. There had been rumours for weeks, all kinds of tales gleaned from all manner of sources including Radio Tokyo yet, despite the repeated myths, no-one had quite believed that it would happen.

The blasts of the alert siren startled Rabaul residents peaceably pottering around town, some looking for company at the New Guinea Club, others visiting friends or having a quiet sleep-in while their houseboys tidied up. Slit-trenches which had been seen as having little more than nuisance value in people's backyards suddenly went into use.

To those watching, it was clear that the object of the flight of some twenty Japanese planes was the upper aerodrome, Vunakanau, out of town. Australian Wirraway aircraft took to the air, but their speed and manoeuvrability were no match for the enemy. White puffs of smoke exploded at a great height from anti-aircraft fire, but fell far short of the high-flying bombers. New Guinean labourers in their labour compound near the aerodrome, free of work for the day, stood and stared up at the unfamiliar sight — and some fifteen men died violently and others were seriously injured as bombs fell out of the clear bright sky.

That evening, just after the brief tropical dusk, the sound of planes again pierced the quiet air. The sky was pearly-pale pricked with stars and the moon had not yet risen. Warned by the events of the morning, men who had been on their way to the Methodist service in English clambered down into slit-trenches and crouched there in stifling heat under roofing of iron covered with earth, waiting in the dark and slapping vainly at voracious hordes of mosquitoes.

Brief flashes of distant lightning split the sky, and there were rumbles that perhaps were thunder, they could not tell, but — 'I reckon the mozzies are doing more damage than the Japs,' someone said, 'and if this happens again, the first thing I'll grab to bring into the trench will be the bottle of citronella.'

In the warm evening on the island of Ulu, Dora Wilson stared across the water towards Rabaul. A tropical storm danced in the sky over the dark outline of distant New Britain lying across the horizon. It seemed, oddly, that perhaps some of the faint sounds could have been explosions rather than thunder. 'They must be practising over there,' she said, puzzled. Surely the soldiers took a day off on a Sunday, she thought.

'I think it's more than practising.' Herbert Shelton had been listening to his wireless and was more aware than the young nurse. She, like many, was shielded from fear by a sense that surely nothing so harsh as a world war could touch the beauty and quietness of a place like the Duke of York Islands. Wars happened in places like the Middle East, places where centuries of conflict were part of the very dust, not under fringing coconut palm or across rainbows of coral reef.

Inland at Malabonga, Mavis and Chris stood outside their door listening to the far-off hum of aircraft. From their community hidden in the hills at the edge of the Baining Mountains, it was hard to tell what might be happening miles away in Rabaul, yet it seemed that they could hear distinct explosions. Since New Year's Day, when John Poole and Laurie Linggood had come out to Malabonga to keep them company, they had heard no news, but John had just arrived from Kalas during the afternoon and planned to travel on down to Rabaul early in the morning for a meeting of the Methodist district committee.

'If anything interesting is happening, I'll let you know when I come back through in a day or two,' John assured them.

In a suburban home in Sydney, in the domestic orderliness of her mother gathering up the breakfast dishes and her headmaster father putting aside his newspaper to leave for school, Jean Poole was arrested by a minor headline in the discarded paper. The word 'Rabaul' leapt at her. Only yesterday it had happened. . .

'Long range bombers attack over RAAF aerodrome at Rabaul,' she read; '. . .slight damage. . . a few native casualties. . .'

The sound of a truck labouring along the road towards Malabonga brought Mavis to the door of the hospital. John Poole must be on his way back. Behind her, the hospital ward was crowded and she and the doctorboys had been busy all day. Chris had been out at a clinic in one of the villages and had just come in tired and looking for a cup of tea. With clinics for infants, daily outpatients, occasional maternity work and a hospital full of patients, both nurses were very busy.

Mavis found it all very satisfying. She loved nursing; with skills for managing things and people developed as an oldest child and inherited from a mother who carried authority as a natural gift, she was enjoying to the full being part of a staff who provided a health service to a people who would otherwise have had none. They formed quite a considerable community there in the hills and took pride in being the sole health care facility for the population of mountain people who still needed gentle persuasion to come to them with their diseases, accidents and maternity needs.

Behind the central timber hospital stood a row of simple buildings, one for each village in their area, where families of patients came to stay and to prepare food. At the time they had one hundred and fifty patients as well as all the family members.

John came into the Sisters' house, bringing mail and news.

'That wasn't just a storm on Sunday night, after all,' he said. 'It was an air raid over Rabaul. Then on Monday morning, when Mr Mac had all of us ministers in to work out plans just in case there is an invasion, there was another alert. We all headed up the hill from the church offices to Refuge Gully and got into trenches, but it turned out to be a false alarm. Laurie Mac wasn't going to be put off the job in hand, mind you — he's a very single-minded chap. There we were, all sitting round waiting for a raid that didn't happen, and he wasn't going to let us waste time. He made us all concentrate and work out a plan. He's a good leader, that man.'

'So what have you decided?'

'*If* there is an invasion — and we find it hard to take that idea very seriously — then we'll take you girls across to the Catholic Mission at Vunapope. With a number of German staff and a German bishop, you'd be safe enough there with the nuns. We plan to bring Dora across to join the two Dorothys. In the meantime, while things are a bit disorganised all round, we've decided that you nurses should do a series of clinic patrols by car — Howard Pearson will take the two Dorothys around the Kabakada circuit and Laurie Linggood will be the escort for you two, and probably Dora, around the Raluana area.'

'And what about the rest of you?'

'We will carry on in our circuits until something actually happens. Then, if the Japanese come, we've decided that we should wait to see what their attitude will be to missions. In the last war, the Australians let the German missionaries carry on their work here in New Britain for most of the time, though it was difficult for them, and a few were interned for a while in 1915 — we feel that we can't just leave our people because of enemy threat. In any case, where would we go? Percy Clark was retiring and leaves Kavieng within days, as planned, but we can't all go. Rodger Brown is hoping to get back to Nakanai as soon as possible and the rest of us will just keep doing our work as usual.'

He added: 'We're all glad that Howard Pearson's group of six New Guinean men have just gone out to their appointments. They are a fine lot of men and, if things do get more unstable, they will be a strong presence among their own people around the country.'

After John had gone, Mavis considered what was happening. Few of the young soldiers who had visited Malabonga had seemed to think that the Japanese would come to the area. That was why most of them were very frustrated to find themselves in New Britain, so far from any real action. They were eager for the enemy to come, talking with the enthusiasm of the young of the valiant deeds they would do, but didn't expect to. Even if the Nips did try it, they had told her, everyone knew that they had no decent equipment and a team of Aussies would clean them up in no time. . . 'One Aussie soldier is worth three or four Nips any day.' That's what they'd said.

But then there had been others who had been heard to complain that their own army was not getting the supplies they had ordered, reinforcements for their small force had been refused, and their armaments were dated, inadequate and almost certainly outclassed. She had heard occasional mutterings about the methods being adopted by the leadership and, though she knew that she had no knowledge of military principles, when people she respected seemed dubious about the wisdom of some decisions, she found herself wondering, too.

Surely, she thought, those bombings on Sunday were only an odd event, not to be repeated. She went on with her work.

When Laurie Linggood arrived on their beach to collect Dora, she was astonished. She saw the small craft approaching from the direction of Rabaul and even when she recognised Laurie she was not expecting to hear what he had come to say.

'We've decided that it would be better if you came across and joined Dorothy Beale at Vunairima while things are so unsettled. Just pack up enough stuff to bring for about two weeks — that should be enough.'

There was no time to consider what she should take. Laurie

was waiting for her. She could see him from the window talking seriously with Herbert Shelton as she went to find a suitcase. First she needed to make arrangements with her doctorboy to take care of their health centre in her absence, and to pass her keys over to Herbert. Then she gathered some clothes, a few personal things and her Bible, toiletries, sandals.

She looked in her cupboard at a few warm jumpers she had brought from winter in Sydney the previous year. There would be no need for anything warm in the steamy heat of Rabaul, she decided, and in any case she would only be away a few weeks. She closed her case, shut the door and went to join the men on the beach.

When their craft reached the wharf in Simpson Harbour and Dora disembarked, she found a very different town from the one she had last visited months before. Pausing briefly to collect some supplies for Vunairima at Burns Philp and the W.R. Carpenter stores, she observed that there were no white women to be seen. Laurie told her that the military and civilian nurses were still at work in their respective hospitals, but other than that almost no-one.

Men in military uniform outnumbered the white civilians by far and Linggood pointed out signs of army occupation through the town. In house yards, there were piles of heaped-up earth, or boards and sheets of iron, where people had dug slit-trenches for fear of air raids. On verandahs and under trees, men were building timber packing cases.

'In the past week,' Linggood explained, 'after dithering about it for years, ever since the 1937 eruption, the Administration has finally sent out an order that a number of government departments are to move to Lae — Supreme Court, Registrar General, Treasury, Crown Law and the Civil Administration — and to be there by 17 January. The others, like Agriculture and Public Works, will follow later on. Originally it was the volcanoes that had them worried, but this new order came through on the day we had our first bombing raid.' He chuckled.

'Our mate Ron Wayne, who works as interpreter for the courts, is in the throes of packing up his house things as well as the office for the judge — he reckons that most of the men are saying that, what with Tavurvur volcano blowing up gritty pumice dust, all the wives gone, bombing raids and trying to pack up everything to move to Lae, what more could you want? And one chap says you can't go insolvent because his files are packed — and another says that all births, deaths and marriages are off!'

They called on the chairman at the church offices in town. Dora had great respect for Laurie McArthur and was glad to have the chance to see him before she travelled out to Vunairima. She knew that he cared for the well-being of all the people under his care.

'Dora, are you quite sure that you are prepared to stay on?' he asked.

Dora was surprised. 'Of course. You gave me the chance to go before, but I said then that I was willing to stay.'

'Yes, but that was before the Japanese started to bomb the area. A ship has come in, the *Malaita*, and you could go if you wanted to. I need to tell you that our newest nurse, Dorothy Holmes, has been brave enough to come to me, since the bombing began, to say that she feels that she can't take it after all, that it has upset her so much that she is worried that she would break down and be no use to us as a nurse. She is being very sensible, I feel, and is going out on the *Malaita*.'

He pointed out that there were also other missionary staff travelling on that ship, too; John Rundle the chairman of the Methodist district in Papua and John Goldie from the Solomon Islands. 'They were a bit scathing when we said that we'd prefer to go into Rabaul to sleep, near some good slit-trenches just in case, instead of staying out at Malaguna near the wharves — thought we were being a bit weak, I think. Yet their ship came into the harbour during a raid — we watched it zigzagging across the water, so their captain must have been a bit apprehensive anyway.

'So far we can be thankful that the bombing has been very precisely aimed at military targets, mostly at Vunakanau aerodrome, and no bombs have come near the town at all. But you never know,' he said. 'Several of us are packing up boxes of things to send back to Australia to our wives — wedding gifts, some books, photo albums, that sort of thing — and we are sending them off on the *Malaita* tomorrow.'

Dora thanked him for his concern, but she had no sense that she ought to leave. It was always her way to put the most kind and optimistic construction on her circumstances and she thought that the present difficulties would be short-lived.

Out at Vunairima, she found Dorothy Beale at work in the Stewart Hospital, professional in uniform and crisp white Sister's veil, supervising her local staff in their medical duties.

'Now that we've just lost a staff member, you can take up her jobs,' Dorothy instructed. 'There is more than enough for us both to do, specially as they want us to take on some extra patrolling work in the villages.'

Dora unpacked her few things and explored the facilities of Stewart Hospital, which had been opened in 1930 to provide health care for the many students resident in the institutions at Vunairima as well as give training to local nurses and orderlies. It would be interesting, she thought, to have a few weeks working at this excellent hospital. Dorothy was the most experienced nurse among them and so she would probably learn quite a few useful things from working beside her.

It was pleasant living with another Australian woman again, Dora thought. For most of the months spent out on the island of Ulu, she had had the company of Duke of York Islands people and Herbert Shelton; Jean Shelton had taken the children and returned to Australia during that time. Now she had a congenial fellow nurse for company, a work colleague as well as a friend for after working hours. When she and Dorothy heard an air-raid warning, they each had the company of the other as they hurried across the darkened lawns to the slit-trench — and on shining their torches down into the trench they were of one mind.

'Let's risk the bombs — they never come out this far anyway,' they agreed. 'We're not going down there. That trench is full of huge toads!'

Across the city of Sydney, sweltering under a heat haze in that drought-dried January of 1942, women who had recently come from the dampness of tropical storms struggled to find their way. Where could they live, so suddenly torn from their island homes where some had lived for years? How could they support themselves, now that their husbands, the earners in their households, were so far away? Sooner or later arrangements would be made for some of their modest missionary income to be diverted from overseas to provide for the women and their children in Australia, but what could they do in the meantime?

Mel Trevitt had chosen to stay in hotel accommodation arranged by the government for the evacuees when she first arrived. She wanted to be independent, to continue to control her own life as competently as she had always done. Her teaching qualifications were good and she knew that she could go back to teaching geology, geography and other science subjects when the school year began at the end of January. In the meantime she needed to support herself and little Bruce. Mel went in to the city to the Department of External Territories to ask for an advance until such time as more funds came through from Jack. It was not a great success.

'How much money have you?'

'Only two pounds.'

'Come back to us when you have run out altogether.'

Where to teach, then, and where to live? Though she went to Jack's people for a period, she went reluctantly, not wanting to impose on them. For a short time, she and Helen Wayne considered finding a place to share, each woman with teaching qualifications and with small children to support and care for, but in the end they found teaching appointments far apart. Mel discovered that she would be accepted, even with a young child, at the Methodist Ladies' College in Launceston, Tasmania, and that there was accommodation and child-minding available close to the school. She went to see Burton. 'When Jack comes, send him down to Tasmania.'

Burton was amused. He knew this gifted couple. 'Love will find a way!' he assured her. Once Mel had left Sydney later in January, she would be out of contact with the other evacuated women and separated from her earlier networks of friends in Sydney as well.

For Marion Oakes, the separation from Dan, which they had imagined would be only for a few months until he came on furlough, was stretching on and on. She had been angered by the news that Dan would be staying on because another minister was leaving earlier than expected. It was not fair, she thought. Just because Dan wanted to do what he saw as the right thing — his 'duty' — and not leave a circuit without leadership, their whole family would be disadvantaged.

Also she would have to continue to bear living with her parents. It had never been easy, the relationship between strong-willed daughter and authoritarian father; her growing-up years had seen many conflicts and the frustration of being forbidden to train as a nurse because Father did not approve. Since marriage to Dan, she had been free to learn and grow, discovering many ways of exercising her quick mind and vigorous personality as part of the team with Dan. In the isolation of Pinikidu on New Ireland, she had discovered in herself skills in communication and teaching, and between them they had initiated basic health care for their villagers. But now, back in Father's house as a mature married woman in her early thirties, the old battles were being fought again.

Despite her father's grumblings, she had found work at a nursing home and planned to begin nursing training at Royal North Shore Hospital, while her younger sister cared for her boys. Dan would be back in time, she was sure, and they had agreed that when he came they would return to an ordinary circuit in New South Wales after nearly ten years of missionary service. When Dan came home. . .

Her parents' home was a haven for Jean Poole and she saw herself as being very fortunate, compared to other women who searched in vain for a place for themselves and their little children. She and her sisters and brother had always been close friends, with interest in each other's scientific discipline. Yet she knew that she could not sit around the Colditz house indefinitely. She needed a job.

Nor was life easy for anyone at that moment. The group of women who had just arrived in Australia from Rabaul were not alone in their feeling of disruption. Other parties of women and children had been arriving in Sydney over recent weeks and months from China, from Malaya, from Singapore, from Papua and other parts of the Pacific, and though people like the Red Cross organisation were very helpful to people in transit, once the women arrived at their destination they had to fend for themselves to a great degree. The whole community was suffering too much stress to spend much time on evacuees.

The feelings of estrangement from her home city which had struck on the day she had first arrived back continued over the next weeks. Though the Japanese forces were fighting in distant Malaya and a fleet was still somewhere far north of New Britain, the people of Sydney seemed to expect to see Japanese soldiers marching through their streets any day. Everywhere there was an undercurrent of fear.

Casual conversations mentioned people who had left the city, selling up quickly after Pearl Harbour the previous month and moving out to country centres like Bathurst or Bowral. People spoke of putting their children's names down for evacuation to the country and hoped that the National Emergency Services people knew what they were doing with their plans to 'evacuate 100 000 children from vulnerable areas'. Newspapers complained bitterly of the way the 'empire had been lulled into a false sense of security' and laid blame at the feet of Sir Earle Page and General Sir Thomas Blamey for their 'glowing statements about Singapore's impregnability' when everyone knew that battles were being waged in Malaya and Allied troops were being forced further and further back towards Singapore each day.

'If Singapore were to fall, we'd be next,' they said.

On her first day home, Jean had seen the city streets darkened, the unlit harbour bridge, walls of sandbags against city buildings and blackout materials on windows throughout the suburbs. Earthworks in public parks and school grounds turned out to be slit-trenches and air-raid shelters. When she commented on the piles of sand dumped on street corners she was told, 'We have to go with a wheelbarrow to collect our share and get it home to our place. The sand is for putting out fires from incendiary bombs.' From time to time, the chilling wail of an air-raid siren galvanised the whole community and people hurried to shelters, half-knowing it was only a practice but never quite certain; they listened for the sound of approaching aircraft and remembered that wardens would blow whistles to indicate incendiaries and ring handbells if gas were present.

On the daily news were announcements that the Red Cross was appealing for a thousand volunteers and that Sydney hospitals had just evacuated 2 500 patients to country districts to provide beds 'for casualties in the event of an air raid'. And despite the extreme summer heat, even the idea of a trip to one of Sydney's beautiful beaches lost some of its charm when Jean heard that great spirals of barbed wire had been laid along the sand of a number of beaches to repel invaders.

Even the weather added to the sense of impending doom. After a long drought, the city's inadequate water supply was dwindling so critically that severe water restrictions were imposed on New Year's Day, allowing only four hours of domestic use of water in the mornings and four hours in the evenings, with no more than a gallon of water per person to be stored through the day. Hot water systems were forbidden, no plants could be watered and there was a limit of four inches of water in the bottom of bath tubs. The drought conditions were affecting milk production, too, and there were threats of milk rationing.

Bushfires raged in bushland around the city, sending walls of red terror towards outlying suburbs till wind changes saved them. Hot high winds carried dust, darkening the land. News came of severe dust storms blanketing Melbourne and Adelaide in choking clouds.

And for Jean, doing her best to fit in with her family and to find a teaching position, there was always the thought near the front of her mind of John, somewhere in the Rabaul area. Was he at Kalas and had Mikael and Louisa stayed on there? Were all the school children still away? Did he still try to visit Chris and Mavis on Wednesdays, and were the girls really safe there at Malabonga?

She had received some letters, telling about Christmas and New Year festivities. Her own Christmas on board the *Macdhui* didn't count and their first Christmas together, last year, seemed to belong to another world.

That morning, in the newspaper of 8 January, was the message: 'Rabaul Again Bombed. No casualties. Two attacks. Damage to planes on ground.'

On 16 January 1942, the Chairman of the New Guinea District of the Methodist Mission began to write a long and difficult letter. Laurie McArthur weighed his words carefully. It had not been an easy morning. There was so much uncertainty in the air. If the military knew what they were doing, they were not sharing it with the civilian population. Rumour and speculation filled every conversation as men who had lived and worked in the area for years — friends, adversaries, acquaintances — put in their two bob's worth of comment. Since that first day of bombing there had been two more raids, with little damage. But the story was around that an Australian pilot had flown north from Kavieng and brought back news of a large Japanese fleet lying off the Pacific island of Truk some 700 miles away. Rabaul, they decided, would be an ideal base for the enemy to use for an attack on Australia, unless the Americans smartened up and came in first.

That was another of the stories; the US navy would come in and use the harbour as a defensive base for the region. 'When the Yanks get here. . .' people said hopefully, complaining bitterly about the lack of military support they had from Australia. 'The navy has sent nothing — not so much as a dugout canoe! The air force chaps are great, but what can they do with only ten Wirraways, four Hudsons and an occasional visit from a Catalina?'

Men experienced in the area questioned the placement of coastal defences facing north: 'Don't they realise that with the nor'wester season on us, no-one in their right mind would try to land anything along the north coast? If the Japs come, they will come right round and enter Blanche Bay and Simpson Harbour — and everyone knows that the men manning the battery at Praed Point at the harbour entry are working with obsolete guns.'

Others muttered about the way there seemed to be little preparation for a withdrawal from the beaches, no sign of supply dumps back in the hills, little training in bushcraft and too much free time for the troops which some filled with hard drinking.

Laurie McArthur sighed. He thought again about his conversation the evening before with his friend the Acting Administrator Harold Page. Page had been at the church quarterly meeting Laurie had called and been part of their discussions over how to manage the town church work in such a time of difficulty. With Mo Pui Sam they had decided to continue to treat the Chinese and the Malay congregations as separate groups, and to carry on with services in English on Sunday evenings.

It was not easy for the communities remaining in town. After the meeting was over, Harold Page stayed to talk for a while. He looked tired, burdened with the weight of responsibility and decision-making on behalf of the civilian population. The Administrator, McNicoll, was very ill and Page had been instructed to take charge.

'All the signs point to an invasion by the Japanese,' he had said. 'It probably won't be long now — only days, perhaps. There is no sense in keeping the Australian civilians here — half the departments are moving out in a couple of days in any case, and if we just kept on enough essential men to keep basic services running, we could leave the place to the military. In the morning I'm sending a cable to External Territories in Canberra, asking permission to send out most of the civilians on the Norwegian ship that came into harbour today. I've given this a lot of thought and I'm sure it's the right thing, but I have to go through the proper channels. Let's hope they realise that this is urgent.'

Now Laurie McArthur looked out across the harbour. The freighter *Herstein* was at the wharf at Toboi, loading copra. It had come in with a load of Bren gun carriers (but no Bren guns), anti-tank guns (but no ammunition), large quantities of beer for the troops and some two thousand bombs for the RAAF. Truckloads of bombs were being unloaded into a dump about 100 metres from the Headquarters New Guinea Area within the town, until they could be taken to their final destination.

19. Mo Pui Sam

20. Jean Poole in the garden at Kiama

21. Ship in Simpson Harbour, Rabaul, 1941

After several years of depression in the copra market, the Japanese invasion of other coconut-producing areas had brought a sudden demand for New Britain copra, and some 6 000 tonnes were being loaded into the *Herstein*. He stared across towards the freighter. Ought at least some of his men, and the nurses, be sent out on the *Herstein*, instead of copra?

Even as he began his letter, the desk where he sat trembled from a minor earth tremor, one of many over recent weeks. The volcano seemed to be working up to something, in keeping with the instability everywhere else. He hesitated, fingering his pen. Would the mission board and Burton see him as being cowardly? He had thought and prayed long and hard about this and it was for his people and their families that he wrote.

He asked of the board: '. . .what provision it is proposed to make for these dependents in the event of things turning out badly here. . . if the enemy invades this Territory. . . the best that we can hope is that we will be interned. . . Will the board continue to support our dependents throughout such a period of internment? Or if one should be more unfortunate and lose his life as a result of enemy action, what provision will the board be able to make for his dependents?

'. . .I dislike writing a letter like this lest it should be interpreted as an indication that we as a staff are showing undue concern about our personal welfare. On the contrary, the men are quite steady and cheerful, and are doing their very best to reassure the native people. We all realise that the men in the services are facing far greater personal dangers than we are.'

He went on. 'If the authorities, with the knowledge they have of enemy movements and our ability to withstand them, should at any time decide that civilians should leave the Territory, are we to assume that our period of usefulness as missionaries has come to an end for the time being, and withdraw? Or are we to carry on until we are prevented from doing so by internment or some other means?'

He concluded the letter with a request that the board commit themselves to supporting the missionary wives and children, whatever happened, and asked for advice on how to proceed.

After Laurie McArthur sealed the letter and put it aside, he pulled the writing pad towards him again. If the letter to the Board had been difficult, this letter to Daisy was going to be far worse. He couldn't bear to think of the look in her eyes when she read it; the disappointment, the loneliness. They had been apart for over three weeks now; he and Daisy were only whole when they were together.

How was he going to tell her that he was cancelling his plane ticket to Sydney? Was there a soft way to say, 'I'm not coming home next week as planned. Things are too uncertain to feel justified in leaving at this time'? He knew that he could never get on that plane to go to Australia and to his family, even though the plan to travel to the annual meeting had been in place for months, and leave the other men and women behind in New Britain. His seat on the plane could be used by one of their friends from church, a mixed race woman who was going to friends in Australia. Laurie dipped his pen in the ink and began to write.

(At the hour that McArthur was writing, the Methodist Overseas Mission Board continued a meeting in Sydney. They approved plans for furlough during 1942 of a number of staff. The names were read: Laurie McArthur, Herbert Shelton, Dan Oakes, Mavis Green, Elsie Wilson. . .)

Shortly after noon, the air-raid siren blasted. A flight of twenty-six bombers bearing the red circle of Japan flew over Rabaul and unloaded their cargo of destruction on to the aerodrome at Vunakanau.

Harold Page called in briefly on his way home, his face angry.

'I've had my answer back from Canberra, Mac,' he said. 'I'm not sure who is behind it, External Territories or Treasury. They didn't waste words — it just said, "CONTINUE LOADING COPRA."'

7

20–22 January 1942

THE TRUCK GRUMBLED TO A HALT outside the hospital at Malabonga and the soldiers jumped down.

'We've got to unload,' they told Mavis Green. 'It's mainly food for the troops, in case we need to withdraw into the bush.'

As she pointed out a suitable building where the stores could be kept, they added, 'There will be one or two more truck loads coming out, we're told. We're not sure whether this means that the officers have decided to change the plan or not — till now they've been saying things like "no withdrawal" and "we'll fight them on the beaches" like Churchill, but at least one officer is sending some stores out here to Malabonga. Don't know whether they are planning any other dumps of stores behind the lines — haven't heard of any.'

The soldiers came in to lunch with Mavis and Chris. Though at twenty-six Mavis was the youngest of the remaining missionary staff, the soldiers seemed very young to her, mere boys in their late teens and early twenties. They relayed the latest rumours and told about blocks on all the roads into town.

The military seemed to have taken over most of the town, there were communication wires running from tree to tree beside most roads and the new Chinese school was packed to the doors with foodstuffs and ammunition. The military hospital had moved into what had been the Governor's residence on Namanula Hill.

They spoke of their training in the use of weapons. 'What I can't understand,' Mavis said, 'is how the cut of a bayonet could kill anyone.' As a nurse she had a practical knowledge of wounds, but couldn't imagine how a bayonet wound would inflict such injury. Her life in quiet rural areas and her time of study in the Women's Hospital, Paddington, in Sydney had not prepared her for their answer.

'You push it in hard, then twist it around and pull it out again,' they said off-handedly, as if it were just a mechanical exercise.

Mavis was silenced. Suddenly she pictured an enemy armed with a bayonet coming towards her. Every coloured drawing in her physiology books, every abdominal surgery she had ever witnessed hung before her eyes in every detail, ready to be gouged by the bitter blade of a bayonet. It was the stuff of nightmares.

It had seemed easy enough at first to say confidently that she was willing to stay on after the other women left. That was before the bombings began and before trucks brought stores out to Malabonga to supply troops in the event of a withdrawal from an invasion. Though she didn't like to say so to Chris, perhaps it was not going to be so simple after all.

The morning of the next big raid, on 20 January 1942, Mavis and Chris had spent a busy morning in their hospital. Children with pneumonia, men with yaws, women with new babies, people with malaria and tropical ulcers passed through their hands all morning. The medical orderlies worked beside them, using the many practical skills they had learned through the teaching of the Stewart Hospital training program. When they heard the drone of many engines, it was early afternoon and they watched with awe as flights of planes converged on Rabaul from several points of distant space. In the past, they had watched ten planes, even thirty planes, fly over in formation, but this was on a scale they had never seen before.

'How many do you think? I keep losing count.'

'Too many! Over a hundred, maybe. . .'

It was later that day when another army truck pulled up near the hospital that the story was told. When Mavis went to greet the drivers, the men looked horrified.

'Don't tell us you two girls are still out here in the bush! It's time you were somewhere safer than this. Things aren't too good at the moment in Rabaul and it looks like they'll get worse.'

They described the raid the girls had seen from a distance. There had been some 120 Japanese aircraft, Zeros, float planes, dive bombers, heavy bombers and fighter bombers — 'the fighters are the ones we nicknamed "Mavis"!' — against a total of eight Australian training Wirraways. From the beginning it was impossible, a massacre. The young Australian crews must have known it as they grasped their courage and took off into the teeth of a foe whose numbers and weapons and aircraft were so far superior to their own. In seven minutes it was over for them. Three had been shot down, two had crash-landed, one had crashed while trying to take off into a rain of falling bombs, one had landed with damage and only one aircraft remained whole. Crews were killed and wounded in those seven minutes of bravery and carnage.

'After that, you would have thought it was an air pageant with the heavy bombers and the seaplanes going round in formation, a few aircraft having the hide to do a few aerobatics while the Zeros ripped the guts out of whichever target they chose. The wharfs, shipping, the two airfields. They had been talking about sending more civilians out on that freighter, the *Herstein* — probably you girls would have gone on it — but you can forget that idea. It's on fire and adrift in the harbour: it took some direct hits.'

'What made us mad, though, was that we had almost nothing to answer them with. No air force left. No naval backup. Equipment that doesn't work. Guns without ammunition. And all along they've been feeding us this story that the Japs only have rubbish for aircraft. . .'

'Anyway, you girls shouldn't be out here in the bush by yourselves,' they said as they prepared to go. 'We can't kid ourselves any more. The enemy must be heading this way and we'll see them in Rabaul sooner or later — probably sooner.'

It was no surprise to Mavis and Chris, then, when they saw the mission utility heading along their road next day and Laurie McArthur telling them to pack immediately.

'Things are getting more difficult each day,' he said, 'and now the *Herstein* is gone. We'd hoped. . . You two, with Dorothy and Dora, will go to stay with Laurie Linggood out at Raluana — that's probably far enough out of town to be safe. Laurie has gone out to Vunairima to collect them.'

It was not an easy day. At least eight years of mission involvement had brought the Malabonga hospital to the point where village people were coming for health care. There were about 150 patients there, and it hurt to leave them. Moving through each section of the hospital, the two women handed over the care of patients and supplies to trusted national orderlies. 'You are in charge here till we get back,' they explained, handing over keys. Their friend and New Guinean mentor Akuila To Ngaru was there, talking earnestly with Laurie McArthur about what might come to his people. Each man had a deep concern and love for the people of the district and each tried to comfort the other as they faced the unknown.

Dusk was falling swiftly when they were ready to leave. The truck was surrounded by patients and orderlies, and by small children standing subdued beside their parents, not understanding why the Sisters were both going away. Mavis found it hard to say goodbye to the children; they had become friends — she had often found them squatting outside her house, waiting to skip beside her to the hospital, clinging to her hand. Men and women who had been helped in the hospital extended their hands for a dignified handshake of farewell. 'We'll be back as soon as we can,' the Sisters said.

'Don't be afraid,' said the big man who had become their spiritual father there in the hills. Akuila's broad brown hand enveloped their own. 'God will care for us all.'

And then they were on their way, their suitcases bouncing in the back and the two nurses silent as they drove away from their work and their friends, travelling through the last gleams of sunset. Mavis, who was never carsick, was disturbed by unexpected nausea and forced to stop the car more than once as they drove towards the coast.

A lantern swung in the dark in front of the road block and a soldier halted them. 'You were heading for Raluana, sir? I wouldn't do that, sir. Colonel Scanlan has issued orders for a company of men to go to Raluana Point near the mission. Raluana mission won't be a safe place for the ladies if there is fighting there.'

'In that case, we'll go direct to the Catholic mission at Vunapope.'

'That's a wise move, sir. There have been a lot of troop movements today; the companies on the north-west coast have been withdrawn and moved to points around the harbour, and men have been sent out of the military camp on Malaguna Road near the waterfront on exercises.'

(Colonel Scanlan was in a position of inevitable defeat and he knew it. His garrison was undermanned, undersupplied, a mere token on the map of world conflict. The Americans' talk of using Rabaul as a base had as yet come to nothing. The purpose of the presence of the 2/22nd and the other troops in Rabaul had been stated as being solely to protect the RAAF stationed there; most of the aircraft of the air force were now lying wrecked, the crews dead or wounded, and the survivors were flying out today with their wounded. Yet when he contacted headquarters to ask what was the role of the force now, and was Rabaul to be held, the only answer had been to keep communication open and wait for further news.

That morning the colonel had told his senior officers of the approach of an enemy fleet and ordered his men out of their camp 'on exercises'. To his officers he said, with grim memories of the War of 1914–1918: 'I do not intend to allow the troops to be massacred by naval gunfire.')

They drove on. Across the dark harbour, the glow of flames still rose from the *Herstein* as its cargo of copra burned. McArthur glanced towards it and looked away. It was too late now. His friend Harold Page had told him how he had tried repeatedly to stir the authorities in Canberra to give permission for him to send out the civilians on the *Herstein*; there had been no reply. Now the *Herstein* was drifting across the harbour, broken and burning.

Beside him in the cabin of the truck sat the two nurses. Page had spoken of the nurses: 'Your mission girls, the military nurses and our staff at Namanula Hospital — I know they all volunteered to stay on, even though I urged them to reconsider, but there is no good reason to keep them; there are other medical staff who can do their work in an emergency. I hate the thought of the nurses still being at risk.'

(McArthur was not to know that at that moment a message from the Prime Minister's Department in Canberra lay partly decoded on a desk in the new Administration headquarters in Lae. Decoding had been interrupted by a bombing raid over that town. When the decoding was completed the next morning, the message would ask for figures of 'non-essential civilian population in order that consideration be given to evacuation of these people'.)

The reflection of flames on dark harbour waters mocked McArthur. It was too late now.

There had been other news that morning, too, before he left town. Kavieng on New Ireland had been bombed early on 21 January and the news was that the Kavieng mission house had been bombed and his colleague Dan Oakes had received a minor head wound trying to rescue papers from the burning house. On his way through Rabaul, one of the ministers who was retiring, Percy Clark, had told about a happy Christmas spent in Kavieng with Dan Oakes and Tom Simpson, with vigorous games of tennis with Dan, Tom and some of the soldiers.

It was hard to imagine Dan, a man so full of good humour and energy, being wounded by any sort of enemy. Nothing was stable any more. Nothing was as it used to be. In another, more predictable world, he had imagined that this week he would be on a plane flying south over jade, turquoise and amethyst reefs, flying home to Daisy and his boys.

In his mind, he cried out as he drove on through the night to the Catholic mission, 'Lord, have mercy. . .'

It was very late, well after ten o'clock at night, when they drove into the grounds of the Sacred Heart Mission at Vunapope along the southern coast towards Kokopo. Mavis had never been there before. For generations of missionary endeavour, the Catholics and the Methodists had not been at ease with each other. Mutual suspicion, intolerance and distrust had seemed normal, an inevitable part of the fabric of life. But now, as they drove towards the black bulk of buildings set among trees, the light in the open door of the convent signalled welcome and safety.

Nuns of the convent of Our Lady of the Sacred Heart — Australian, Dutch, Irish and German women — came forward to draw them inside. At any other time, Mavis might have found the statue of Mary the mother of our Lord, the crucifix and the religious pictures an assault on her Methodist upbringing, but now, clutching a suitcase of hastily gathered belongings, tired, thirsty, confused, distressed and with a sour taste in her mouth, there was great comfort in the welcome of the nuns. She was surrounded by kindness in nun's habits and some of them even spoke with the accents of Australia.

She discovered that they were expected, as Laurie McArthur and Laurie Linggood had already asked permission to bring the women to the convent, and beds were ready and the kettle simmering. At midnight, more headlights came up the driveway and Dora and Dorothy came in, delivered by Laurie Linggood.

'You'll be safe here,' Laurie McArthur said as the men prepared to leave them. 'As there are quite a lot of German mission staff here, and Bishop Leo Scharmach is Polish-German, if the Japanese come at all then they will surely leave their Axis partners alone. In any case, you women would probably be sent home if the Japanese arrive. Laurie, Howard Pearson and I will join John Poole at Kalas and perhaps some of the others might come out, too — Kalas is far enough out in the bush for us to be out of the way till we see what their attitude will be to missions. We plan to take the patrol box full of church records out with us and we'll hide it.'

The four mission women watched them go. Narrow bars of light from headlights swung up and down beyond the trees along the driveway and briefly lit strips of dark ocean before they turned out on to the road back towards town. Then they were gone. Behind the women was the safety and unfamiliarity of a Catholic convent and in front were nothing but shadows.

When they woke on the morning of 22 January 1942, it was to the sound of rain on the roof. It was going to be another warm, wet day. Dora stared curiously from the convent window out on the grounds of Vunapope. Buildings which had been nothing but black shapes at midnight when she arrived now resolved themselves into three convents and hospital, boarding schools, cathedral, bishop's residence, priests' presbytery, seminary for New Guinean students for the priesthood and other staff houses. It was a very large and impressive complex set on a hillside in gardens of great beauty, with the mission wharf in front and coconut plantations and bush climbing the hills behind.

Even though Vunapope was new to her, in some ways it felt familiar. The fine tropical buildings and gardens were very like the Methodist complex at Vunairima. Across the ocean, Dora could see through the misting rain the islands of the Duke of York group; only a few weeks ago she had been over there peacefully getting on with her village clinics, weighing babies and giving injections for yaws.

The sweet familiar perfume of freshly cut grass was in the air as muscular brown-skinned schoolboys swept scythes of sharpened hoop iron across the wide lawns as the rain stopped, just as they did on the Methodist mission stations. Harmony of *a cappella* voices drifted across from the cathedral, and the laughter of children from school dormitories. There was order and work to be done, faith and worship of God, a sense of community, friendship between brown and white.

And yet there was a dissonance. Even her own presence, and that of Mavis, Chris and Dorothy in the convent was a sign of something odd. What were four Methodist mission nurses doing at the Catholic mission when they had their own work to do? They all knew the answer. A clashing discord greater than anything the nurses or the nuns could imagine was about to burst upon them. There was nothing they could do but wait.

The normal peace and simplicity of the convent breakfast was not long over when they first heard the planes. The droning of aircraft swelled in volume, louder and louder. In flight across the bay went some forty-five heavy bombers and dive bombers heading for the aerodrome at Vunakanau on the plateau above the harbour. Crowded side by side in the mission slit-trenches with nuns from Europe, Australia and New Guinea, the nurses listened to the wild percussion of falling bombs, machine-gun fire and explosions.

As they stared out across the water, looking through the broad entrance into Blanche Bay and on into the inner Simpson Harbour, the phalanx of bombers swept out across the harbour to drop death on the battery at Praed Point. Somewhere on that point on the far shore of the harbour entrance were young soldiers, the company responsible for the two coastal defence guns and the searchlights, but all the watching women could see was the swooping of planes, bursts of smoke and earth exploding upward and flashes of fire until the point was hidden in a dark pall of dust-laden smoke and the sound of engines faded away into the distance.

The women stared at each other in horror.

'If the battery with the big guns is gone. . .'

'What will be next? The town? The military camp? Us?'

'Surely it won't get to that point.' Someone spoke with the confidence of one whose history was filled with stories of rescue at the last possible moment. Always there was the triumphant shout of the beleaguered people, with the enemy pounding on their doors, as they saw their rescuers riding at speed to save them. 'The Australian Air Force will come.'

'More likely the Americans. The Americans have said they'd be taking over Rabaul; they won't let this place go into the hands of the Japanese; they'll be here any minute.'

'Even if they don't bring their whole navy here, at least they'll come and take us off. They always do — think about Gallipoli, and Dunkirk.'

They waited, talking, doing their best to encourage each other. When at last the all clear sounded over the mission grounds, the women moved back to their work. Dora, Mavis, Dorothy and Chris were invited to join the nursing nuns in the mission hospital not far from the beach and they were there when the first twelve wounded men were brought in.

If they could help nurse the wounded, there was some point to it all, Mavis thought, and took up the tasks in the hospital ward with energy.

As they worked, one of the nuns murmured: 'Our mission doctor, Dr Joseph Schuy, is having a very busy day — as well as caring for our own native hospital and these extra men, his wife is in labour with their fourth child.'

It was a very strange day. In the gardens at Vunapope mission, in the brilliance and colour of magenta bouganvillea, bronze and gold hibiscus and pink-tipped frangipani, brown and white nuns moved about their work in the grace of long habits and veils. From their distance of some thirty-five kilometres away, the town was a distant blur across the water, yet they were filled with a great unease when they thought about it. There seemed to be signs of fires burning near the wharves or the military camp and, though there was no sign of Japanese aircraft at the time, they heard the reverberations of a great explosion somewhere in the town.

At a quiet moment in the day when she had been given no further tasks, Dora walked along the length of the hospital verandah. A sudden brief tropical sunshower was pouring its force over the gardens and she was glad to be under shelter. At intervals along the long low building, doors opened from wards onto the verandah, and a separate cookhouse and storeroom stood nearby.

Centred in the middle of the building she found the surgery and a chapel. Slipping quietly into the chapel, she sat in silence. Beyond the walls were the people of the place, a large international community, all tense with the insecurity of those who do not know what is happening around them and are afraid. Some talked too much, others were irritable, some wore miserable faces and a few upset everyone else by panic-stricken dithering. It was good to be by herself for a few minutes.

Looking up, her eyes turned to a crucifix hanging on the wall. It was not part of her own tradition, and yet she recognised the Christ figure, twisted against the bar of the cross, exhausted from carrying undeserved pain, accepting the misery of the world into his own person. There always had been pain and grief and fear; it was part of being human in a failed world. She closed her eyes, shutting out the crucified figure of plaster and paint. Yet even in her darkness, the wounded person of Christ remained, feeling her fear, understanding, knowing, loving. . .

Across the quietness cut the sound of vehicles driving in convoy up the driveway, and shouting voices, commanding, calling for action. Ambulances were pulling up by the verandah, Australian army nurses were jumping from private cars behind them and more cars could be seen coming in the distance. The 2/10th Field Ambulance detachment and over eighty patients had arrived.

Within the space of a few hours, the order of the Vunapope Native Hospital and some of the school buildings had been arranged into a military hospital. In the middle of the confusion of patients, the very ill and the wounded, Mavis and Dora saw six Australian army nurses at work, staff with the 2/10th Field Ambulance. Doctors, known and unknown, hurried past; civilian and military men worked together to make the sudden transfer of patients to what they hoped would be a safer place. Private cars and army trucks continued to arrive with more patients and staff as the afternoon went on. Many of the patients were soaked from the heavy rain and in pain from injuries and illness.

'It's been a rough day,' someone said.

In snatches of conversation as they worked together and when groups of them sat down to a meal prepared by the nuns, some of the story was told. The severe bombing of Praed Point had left men dead and injured and the coastal defence guns were silenced. Some of the soldiers had been buried under deep earth when a dugout where they were sheltering was hit; though some were dug out by their mates, it was too late for others.

Though some parts of the town were affected by the bombing, the hospital was untouched and was stretched to the limit with the wounded being brought in. The wards were still full of Norwegian seamen from the *Herstein* with burns and men who had lost limbs in bomb blasts in the attack two days earlier. The staff estimated that perhaps thirty or forty men had died. For hours they had all worked without pausing, bloodied swabs being tossed to one side as they attended to the next victim with the urgency of knowing that still more wounded men were waiting.

'And then there was the most terrific explosion. The whole place shook. We were all sure that it was a naval bombardment from the enemy who must have got into the harbour while we were hard at work. I was able-bodied and the nearest to the door, but most of my patients jumped into the slit-trench before me! If it hadn't been so frightening it would have been funny. . .'

At that point the hospital staff had no idea what had happened, but within twenty minutes a truck arrived at the hospital door with orders for them all to evacuate immediately. With no time even to dress their patients, staff grabbed whatever they could, sent any walking patients back to their units and joined the hasty convoy of trucks and any cars which could be commandeered to drive through town out to Vunapope mission near Kokopo. No-one knew the whole story, but fragments and rumours passed along the convoy.

'Have the Japs arrived?'

'Not yet — that explosion was our own blokes at work.'

'But what is going on?' Nobody knew.

(It was not until later that some of many confusions of that day were known. Only days earlier, the *Herstein* had come into harbour with a cargo of bombs for the use of the RAAF. Because of the size of the cargo, 2 000 bombs including 500 pounders and 250 pounders, they had been stacked temporarily in the town waiting for transport to the airfields. No-one had seemed troubled that the dump was only about a hundred metres from the New Guinea Area Headquarters.

With the Japanese fleet within hours of Rabaul and the RAAF planes reduced to wreckage, the order was given for the bomb dump to be detonated. When the immense blast had finally shuddered into stillness, men were seriously injured, buildings in the path of the blast had been demolished or had their frontages wrecked, telephones had been blown from walls. The major radio transmitter with one hundred lines of communication was put out of action, cutting off Rabaul from the rest of the world.

Colonel Scanlan was trying to send out messages to say that a large enemy fleet had been sighted approaching from the north-west, and the authorities in Lae were trying to pass on the message from Canberra asking for details of civilians to be considered in a possible evacuation, but the radio link had been silenced.

On Malaguna Road where it intersected with Mango Avenue, bronze Chinese characters lay haphazardly across the rubble of the pillars of the facade of the new Overseas Chinese School; under threat of volcanic eruption and enemy invasion, the handsome facade had been damaged by the hand of friends before the Chinese children had presented their first concert there.)

'Everyone is on the move, getting out of town as fast as they can. The place will be empty soon.'

They had been caught up in a movement which touched everyone in the community. Companies of soldiers were being deployed to new positions, with the survivors of Praed Point joining others near Vulcan crater, while an improvised company composed of batmen, cooks, clerks and others from the abandoned military camp found themselves guarding Raluana Point not far from the Methodist mission.

As there were no prime movers available to move the anti-aircraft guns from their isolated position on the peninsula, that company was under orders to destroy their guns and withdraw because they were in danger of being cut off from the other Australians. Headquarters staff moved for some hours to the Methodist rest-house at Tomavatur on the plateau overlooking the harbour.

The confusion in the town was heightened by air-raid sirens which sounded very similar to the all-clear siren so that people were not certain whether they ought to be coming or going. Some Chinese families from Chinatown in Rabaul — including Rev. Mo Pui Sam, Mr and Mrs Mow from the school and many Chinese merchants and community leaders — gathered what they could and drove over the hill to seek refuge at Vunakambi, the Methodist plantation near Vunairima, while other Chinese and Malay people went to their section of Refuge Valley. There was a bitterness among many that their women and children had been left behind in the evacuation of white families.

A very irritable party of white civilians gathered at Refuge Valley, angry that there seemed to be no clear direction, no serious moves to evacuate civilians who were not in essential services, and all the key administration figures appeared to have departed elsewhere, leaving them to their own devices: 'They're useless — can't make their minds what they are up to,' some complained, 'sending out messages saying "invasion is imminent", but in the next breath saying "carry on normal duties"!' New Guineans who were able to leave set off for their villages, but labourers who had been brought to Rabaul from other parts of the country had nowhere to go.

Clouds of dark smoke rose over the town from burning fuel and bomb dumps. The smouldering wreck of the *Herstein* had floated across the harbour and some of the wharves were burning as well, the result of other demolition work across the town. Staff of banks and other businesses burned records or locked and hid them before boarding the *Matafele* at dusk, an inter-island BP ship which had come into harbour. Some one hundred men from the RAAF followed a pre-arranged plan and were lifted out from Wide Bay by plane.

A party of civilians set off for Kokopo by schooner and others were finding their way from the town, some climbing the hill to the huts of Refuge Valley, others by truck, by car, perched on the running boards of passing cars, on foot, by bicycle, heads bowed against teeming rain, sliding and slipping on mud-slicked ribbons of road. Darkness began to fall without its usual blaze of molten sunset as cloud and rain and smoke shadowed the sky and the harbourside volcano Tavurvur sent sulphurous dust boiling into the air.

At the convent of Our Lady of the Sacred Heart at Vunapope, the nuns tried to find beds for everyone. The place was crowded with extra patients, military personnel and the nurses. Dora, Mavis, Dorothy and Chris introduced themselves to the other women. Kay Parker, the leader of the military nurses, was a tall and impressive woman. They all looked very weary.

It was late when the new women were free to take off their

Sisters' starched veils and aprons.

'What are we going to change into in the morning?' one of them asked, looking at her soiled uniform, stained from a long day of caring for the ill and wounded. 'They rushed us off into the cars at such a rate that we had no chance to go back to our house to pack anything. If we are not wearing it, we haven't got it!'

'In the morning someone will go back into town and collect our things. Some of the fellows have gone back already to collect more medical supplies and equipment to add to all the things we grabbed on the way out this afternoon.'

In the morning. . .

That night, mission nurses shared their sleeping quarters with the army nurses. Mission men settled to an uneasy sleep at Vunairima, Refuge Valley and out in the bush at Kalas. In Australia their wives re-read recent letters that had come from their husbands, brooded over reports of the bombing of Rabaul on 20 January and prayed for their men. At Vunapope, Mrs Schuy the doctor's wife gave birth to a baby. In dugouts at points around the darkened harbour, soldiers waited and watched, talking in subdued voices of home and family.

Before midnight there was the sound of a plane overhead. Parachute flares were dropped over Vulcan crater and Raluana, lighting up the whole harbour. Violet and white searchlights stabbed at the Rabaul foreshore and the harbour edge. A solitary aircraft traced a line with a searchlight along the harbour shoreline from Rabaul town round to Raluana Point. Very soon soldiers would see landing craft and moving figures silhouetted against the fiery glow of the burning dumps of Rabaul.

8

23–25 January 1942

IN THE DARKNESS BEFORE DAWN of Friday 23 January 1942, the peal of a mission bell rang out, calling the faithful to early morning prayer. Women in the convent lay awake already. It had been a night of little sleep. There had been strange lights in the sky, then some time after midnight they were sure they heard distant gunfire.

Dora stared into the gloom, listening to the night-breathings of unfamiliar companions. A few of the army nurses had been called out during the night, but she was not sure what the whisperings had meant. Any strange sound might mean that the enemy was at their doors.

When the mission bell rang out, Dora sat up. A few of the women were already on their feet. There was a gasp and she saw the outline of heads crowded at a window.

'Look at that! What's happening?'

She scrambled to her feet and stared out. The dark sea which flowed out from the beach in front of the mission at Vunapope was spangled with light signals flashing on and off, giving tantalising glimpses of an armada of shipping.

'Thank God!' cried the old Australian nun, Sister Borgia. 'The Americans have come in time.'

'Sister, we don't think it is the Americans. . .'

As dawn slowly washed the dark from the windows, they looked out on a sea full of shipping. A wall of thirty-one large vessels lay across the harbour entrance with minesweepers, tankers, transports and two aircrarft carriers. A string of destroyers steamed up the harbour, while others waited outside beyond Kokopo and off the coast towards the Duke of York Islands. Landing craft were scattered along the harbour foreshore. During the hours of darkness, a large navy and thousands of men had come to Rabaul and, as they had known they would be, they were Japanese.

A few of the army nurses appeared in the doorway.

'They've landed,' they said. 'Some of our own men have come in with gunshot wounds. They were at Raluana Point when they heard landing barges scraping up on the sand and suddenly marines dressed in black were among them. It sounds very confused. . .'

The sun began to rise beyond the distant bulk of New Ireland, illuminating a sea filled with ships. Fragments of the story, roughly stitched together with bits of rumour, odds and ends of distressed imagination and with gaping holes of lack of information, formed a ragged blanket of anxiety which spread over everyone.

No-one was clear what was happening, but whatever it was it did not seem to be going well with the Australians. It seemed that landing barges loaded with Japanese soldiers had been landing at points all around Simpson Harbour. At some points there was strong opposition, but even where the Australian troops were well established and despite their courage, they were all aware that they had only enough ammunition for a very limited defence, in one case only enough for one minute of rapid fire.

At other points, companies of men had only moved into that position within the past twelve hours or less and had had no time to dig trenches, spread barbed wire or make any other preparations for defence. Men who had been working in clearly understood groupings with tasks they knew well found themselves adrift, withdrawn from their earlier position, with mates dead or wounded, their weapons destroyed and no clear direction.

The worst of the confrontations were in the dark of night, with darkness adding to the confusion and men relying on sounds and shadows. Once it was daylight, Zero fighter planes swooped towards any group of men who remained visible, spitting machine-gun fire. Drivers with truckloads of retreating men were forced off roads, sometimes plunging into the signal wires suspended between roadside trees.

Communication between companies and headquarters became more and more difficult as signal wires were severed; the key radio network had been destroyed in the explosion a day earlier. The headquarters moved on from one point to another and were out of contact for extended periods; and the heavy teleradio units, which often gave trouble due to corrosion from volcanic fallout at the best of times, refused to function and in some cases were abandoned. Different directions came from different officers, each trying to discover the mind of others, but left with the insecurity of messages passed by troops on the move.

One order came: 'Hold out as long as possible. . . thereafter all personnel to go bush and continue guerilla fighting.' The other phrase, 'Every man for himself', was passed from man to man, yet no-one seemed to be sure whether that was the order from headquarters, countermanding the earlier order 'No withdrawal', or whether it was simply a practical response to the inevitable.

With companies dispersed, leadership unable to communicate, no naval or air support and overwhelming numbers of opposing forces flooding onto the beaches and up the hillsides against them, resistance became impossible, and group after group of Australians were forced to move back.

On foot or in any vehicle they could find regardless of who owned it, men moved back, following roads and tracks up onto the plateau above the harbour or along the southern coast. There was the possibility that they could continue to harry the invaders from behind the lines, becoming guerilla warriors, or at least survive to fight another day on another front. Stories came through the hospital wards as retreating soldiers called at the mission, told of the confusion they had witnessed and set off in assorted parties to find tracks to the north or south.

In the green folds of tree-clad Refuge Valley, clusters of men discussed their position. The neat bamboo-and-thatch huts of Refuge Valley with the names given so flippantly only a year ago — Hampton Court, Regent's Park Hotel — and plans made there for the local ladies to serve hot tea and hand out packs of pyjamas and toiletries to any who sought refuge there, now seemed a mockery. Each section contained men who had spent the night there in the thin security of the European, Asian and New Guinean areas. It was clear to them all, after a sleepless night, that an invasion had taken place, their own military was in disarray, the town lay empty, most of the civilian leaders had departed to wait at Kokopo or beyond, and that their party and some villagers were cut off from their fellows on the wrong side of Blanche Bay with nowhere to go.

Most of the men were very angry indeed. No official opportunity had been offered for civilian men to be evacuated and no ordered plan for withdrawal to safety had been made. Even in their most disillusioned moments, some of them had clung to the hope that, in a blaze of drama at the very last moment, Australians from Port Moresby or Americans from anywhere in the Pacific would suddenly appear to rescue them, that the delay had been an elaborate plot to trick the enemy into a false sense of security, to lure them into a trap. Now it seemed that Rabaul was to be abandoned as a minor casualty of war and its people with it.

Three men who had made New Britain their home for many years made up a white flag party, walking with deep apprehension down from the hill along Namanula Road until it intersected with Casuarina Avenue. The busy tropical town they knew so well was empty of its familiar residents in their white tropical clothing or the military in their khaki. The Chinese and Malays were nowhere to be seen and villagers were staying away in their own places to try to escape from the madness of war. As they walked into the eerie uninhabited street, unsure of their own fate, a party of Japanese soldiers met them. With armed soldiers and interpreters beside them, including men they had known in the past as interpreters on visiting ships to Rabaul, they climbed the hill again to collect the others still waiting in the refuge.

When next they walked down the hill into the deserted town, it was filling with new inhabitants, small men who were systematically emptying each building of its contents before taking over as the new masters. As for the bitter and disconsolate Australian civilians, they were prisoners.

Before the sun was well up, more news came to the convent from the mission hospital at Vunapope. An army nurse who passed it on looked stunned.

'They're leaving.'

'Who are?'

'Our two army doctors and most of the twenty orderlies. They say that there is our mission doctor and some of the civilian doctors to look after the patients. And us nurses, of course. They should be with the retreating troops, they say — the retreating soldiers won't have any medical help if they don't go with them.'

Someone muttered a comment about 'every man for himself'. Two medical orderlies had volunteered to stay behind with the nurses and some eighty or ninety patients, but the rest of the Field Ambulance, with two ambulances and most of the medical supplies, were preparing to move off as quickly as possible. The Anglican chaplain, Padre John May, prayed with them and sent them on their way with blessings into the unknown roads and bush tracks of jungle and mountain they had never before seen, under the continuing fire of many Japanese aircraft.

The nurses watched the ambulances and an assortment of trucks and cars disappear down the drive. The harbour was filling with a Japanese navy before their eyes. The hospital behind them was full of sick and wounded men, the men who were not fit enough to attempt an escape. There was nowhere to go.

'We wouldn't have left the patients, anyway,' said one nurse.

'We weren't offered a choice,' said another. 'No-one suggested that we fly out yesterday with the RAAF wounded.'

'They probably took "every *man* for himself" at face value,' a woman said acidly.

However they looked at it, it was too late. The ambulances had gone and most of their medical supplies with them.

'We'll be battling to look after our patients, anyway, whatever happens.'

None of them wanted to look too closely at the immediate future. Whatever was going to happen next would be happening very soon, and they knew it. Practical women, the nurses and nuns began to prepare as best they could for the arrival of alien guests. Sister Columba gathered other Irish nuns and a mission truck and drove to nearby Kokopo to collect as many truckloads of food supplies as they could get from the Burns Philp store; the store manager willingly opened the doors to them and they were able to bring in stocks of food for the many residents of the large mission compound as well as the hospital so recently taken over for the army.

Nurses decided to attempt to make it plain that they were staff and patients of a hospital and therefore non-combatants; bed-covers marked with a red cross were displayed prominently outside the hospital. Women wore their distinctive nurses' uniforms with Red Cross armbands and nuns' habits, hoping that perhaps the garments would form a protective shield. Chaplain John May, the only officer left, gathered any military firearms brought in by wounded troops and locked them in a cupboard and the other nurses persuaded Captain Kay Parker to surrender the tiny pearl-handled pistol she kept in her handbag.

Dorothy Beale convinced Mavis that she should pass on the church synod minutes from the recent meetings at Vatnabara to one of the Catholic nuns for safekeeping; 'with so many German and Italian missionaries here, our church papers will be safer with them than with us Australians,' she urged. Nothing felt very safe, even so.

At nine o'clock that morning, Rodger Brown switched on his teleradio to make his daily contact with Rabaul. It had been difficult to remember that the island might be in danger of invasion once he was back at work at Malalia. He missed Kath very much and tried to picture his tiny son, now a month older than the last time he had seen him. Kath's mother would be delighted to have her daughter home with her again, he was sure, and his beloved family would be cared for very lovingly in the safety of Adelaide.

Yet, though he missed them greatly and found his home very empty indeed, there was always work to be done in his circuit and no reason at all to avoid doing it. He thoroughly enjoyed his growing friendship with the local pastors and leaders, and revelled in the patrol work through the mountainous coastal district of Nakanai.

On the previous morning their radio schedule time had been interrupted. 'We're having a raid — stand by till the all clear and I'll come back to you!' He had gone outside and listened. Even at a distance of 200 kilometres he could just hear the reverberations of explosions and he knew that bombs were dropping on Rabaul.

This morning he spoke his call-sign and waited for the familiar reply to come crackling through the static. There was nothing. Again and again he tried. Were his batteries getting flat? he wondered. The radio operator in Rabaul wouldn't have forgotten.

Standing outside his mission house, he tried to hear anything that would tell him what was going on in Rabaul. He thought that the faint echo of explosions came through the quiet air but he could not be sure. For the time being he had to rely on his imagination and the rumours he had heard that invasion was imminent. There was nothing he could do about it. Rodger went on with his work. The pastors and leaders were coming in for a quarterly meeting and he needed to complete his preparations for it.

Under an Australian sky clear blue with summer drought, a train slowly steamed through cuttings gouged out of the rock of an ancient mountain range. Jean Poole leaned back in her seat and watched the grey-greens and olive greens of eucalyptus, banksia and melaleuca flowing out over long vistas of the Blue Mountains.

She loved the Australian bush, yet her mind was on another mountain. Somewhere far to the north, John was at work at Kalas, there in that area where the mountains were so young that they still shook with volcanic action.

Jean tried to imagine him on this Friday morning. School holidays were coming to an end and so perhaps he was working with Mikael To Bilak to finish preparation of buildings for the new school year. Maybe he was taking the chance to go on another patrol or preparing his sermon for Sunday, working on the translation into the Kuanua language and revising lists of new words to be learned. She pictured their house with the windows propped open to let in the morning freshness and one of the young lads washing John's breakfast dishes and singing.

Jean gazed wistfully from the train window as they descended from the mountains out onto the drought-brown plains. She wasn't at Kalas. She was on her way to Bathurst. It hadn't been easy to find a teaching position. Married women usually lost their jobs from the time of their marriage and even in these troubled times, with men enlisting, the Department looked critically at an application from a woman who had a husband to support her. Certainly she could not be on a permanent staff. Still, she had found a place at a church-run girls' school in the provincial town of Bathurst, and had written to tell John that she had found work and not to worry about her financial position while they were apart.

In his next letter she would hear his comments, she supposed.

In a city office in Sydney, General Secretary John Burton framed a letter in reply to one he had just received from the chairman of one of the Methodist districts. Laurie McArthur from New Britain was asking for advice on whether the mission staff were free to accept evacuation if that were possible.

As to whether the missionaries should leave the Territory of Papua and New Guinea, Burton wrote: '. . .I cannot offer an opinion. I think that every man will have to decide these things for himself. I rather imagine that there will be no choice and that in all probability you will be interned, though I understand that in similar circumstances missionaries have been given their parole and allowed to go on with their work.'

McArthur had asked for promises of financial help for the wives if the men were killed. Burton thought of his staff scattered across the Pacific and in north Australia, and of all the ministers and their families across Australia. Outside his window, lined with heavy blackout material, Castlereagh Street was walled with sandbags. Shop-fronts were being boarded up. Piles of sand waited on street corners to extinguish incendiary bombs and children in the schools were being issued with gasmasks. Everyone said it was only a matter of time.

He continued the letter, but he felt that he should be cautious about financial help. The whole thing was so complex and uncertain and the board was responsible for so many people in such farflung places that promises seemed impossible. He wrote: 'It may be that sooner or later we all here in Australia will have the same risk of death by bombing. . .'

With Laurie's letter open in front of her, Daisy McArthur tried to hide her disappointment. He wasn't coming at the time they had planned. His letter had tried to say it gently, but there was no kind way to say it. She did her best to understand.

Of course, he couldn't just catch a plane and leave his people when things were getting difficult. Of course, it was the time when, as chairman, the New Guinean people needed to have him with them, encouraging them, offering hope, going from village to village, from district to district, bringing the comfort of stability and familiarity. Of course, he couldn't wave goodbye to the mission nurses and the other men staff and just fly out of Rabaul as if their welfare didn't matter. Certainly, he couldn't appear to be facing the future with less courage than their own.

She knew all that. He had to stay. But as she folded his letter away carefully, Daisy found herself scooping up her baby from the rug where he was crawling among his soft toys and holding him tightly, composing her face carefully so that when her seven-year-old boy came in from play he would not see any sign of tears.

It was a very strange morning for the nurses at the hospital at Vunapope. Patients still needed to be bathed and given their medication. People still needed to be fed. The morning was passing and though everyone was waiting tensely for their first sight of Japanese soldiers, the community would soon be looking for their lunch.

Mavis and Chris were busy helping the staff in the hospital; Mavis discovered a familiar face among the wounded lads. A young soldier said, 'I know you, Sister — I came out to visit Malabonga one weekend with some other chaps and we picked fruit for you' — and she remembered that the boy had admitted to being only seventeen.

Mavis was in the hospital and Dora was helping in the kitchen when they came. Mavis heard someone say, 'They're here.' She went to a window and stared out at a sight that was unbelievable.

Men were running up the grass from the waterfront, shouting as they came. The uniform was recognisable before any faces were clearly visible, the uniform she had seen in propaganda drawings of fanged and evil men with round spectacles on their noses. They were shouting with a violence that chilled her, their words a jumble of meaningless gibberish to her ears, moving swiftly towards the hospital. She saw machine-guns, bayonets, swords. . .

John May stepped from the verandah and moved quietly towards them. Mavis watched him with a mixture of fear and deep admiration. He had chosen to stay with them. The unarmed chaplain was making signs to the invaders, pointing out the spread bedcovers with the Red Cross symbol, walking with their officers to show the patients in their beds, the nurses in uniform by their side. He offered an open hand with a key and showed them the cupboard where the rifles had been locked away.

Orders were being given, and Mavis realised that some of the officers and men spoke English. Everyone was ordered onto the verandah that ran along the front of the low building. Nurses and patients, even the cot-cases, as well as men who had come to the mission hospital for refuge, were hurried out to stand in rows before their captors. Dora heard the shouting and came with others from the kitchen.

Eye-to-eye they stood there. An order was translated into English: 'Hands up!' Mavis held her hands high in surrender. She was outraged, but there was no choice. Japanese soldiers were ranged in front of them all, aiming weapons at their bodies. From the corner of her eye she saw other soldiers move around behind them with fixed bayonets. Ten Australian nurses and about seventy-five sick men, some nuns, Chaplain May, some missionaries from the Seventh Day Adventist Mission, the manager of the Burns Philp store at Kokopo, the two medical orderlies and a few others stood waiting. Beyond their party gathered on the hospital verandah they could see other groups of soldiers moving rapidly up through the grounds of the mission, on their way to take control of the bishop and his priests and nuns, the seminarians, the staff and the families who lived at Vunapope.

Their freedom was over.

Dora found herself too numb to be afraid. It was as if she were watching a melodramatic movie, something removed from herself. They were such funny little men, she thought, so small and slight compared to her own tall stature. She found herself staring at their shoes, such strange shoes like mittens, with a division for the big toe; she had never seen anything like them and in the strangeness of the moment she wondered whether they were comfortable to wear. Officers marched up and down before them, shouting questions, interrogating one and then another, the rapid flow of incomprehensible commands being interpreted into English.

Many of the soldiers looked very hot, and dirty, and she guessed that they had been shut up in a ship's hold for weeks, waiting to go into battle. Some of them looked so very young, and valiant, charged with the great task of taking all before them for the emperor. Their great moment had come and weapons in hand, intoxicated with patriotism, fear and tension, fingers on the triggers, they were facing their enemy. Their enemy. . . We are their enemy, she thought, nurses and sick men, nuns and mission staff. It was ludicrous — and terrifying.

One of the nuns spoke to an officer. 'Would you like drinks of cold water?' The officer stared, astonished at the incongruity of the question; the courteous offer of a cup of cool water to a traveller on a hot day had seemed natural to the nun, but she was quickly brushed aside.

Along the row they went. One man after another was questioned. Slow or unsatisfactory answers were rewarded with a slap, or with a blow from a sword-scabbard on bandaged ulcers. An officer demanded food for his men and the watching Australians wondered when the troops had last been fed; perhaps, they thought, they were kept a bit hungry to make them crankier.

They discovered quickly that it was important to bow, and to bow deeply, in reponse to the demands of the officers. One of the army nurses, Tootie Keast, was begrudging in her bow, unwilling to bend before the enemy. She was struck and knocked to the ground, and when she scrambled back to her feet, she and the other women were ready to bow, deeply even if reluctantly.

'Where are your doctors? You have no doctors so you women are not nurses. Don't try to deceive us. You are really Comfort Women for the use of the troops!'

Standing near one end of the line of prisoners, Mavis was beyond fear. The wicked gleam of a bayonet blade shone somewhere behind her. Ever since that idle conversation about bayonets with Bill Harry, in the lost peace of the house at Malabonga, her mind had tortured her with images. Over and over she had seen the blade, felt the thrusting and twisting, the ripping, the agony. Now she struggled to make her mind a blank, to erase the horror. Now all the symbols of war which had been feeding her imagination were before her eyes, near enough to touch.

Little men in the uniforms of the enemy stood before their prisoners with the evil eye of their machine-guns trained on her. A soldier was threatening to shoot them all and she only heard him faintly through the pounding of her heart, as she tried to focus on the strain of upraised arms and the ache in her shoulders.

She found herself looking along the line of fellow-prisoners and at the man from Burns Philp who stood beside her at the end of the line and thinking, 'At least I'll be second to go — thank God, I won't have to watch all the others being. . .' She couldn't even think the words. 'I won't have to see the others go before me. . .'

If there were prayers, they were not the careful words of church services, or the peaceful conversations with God of private prayer. There were only the wordless cries, the cry, 'My God, where are you?' Dry-mouthed and rigid, Mavis closed her eyes and waited.

And then a voice announced, 'You will not be shot today.'

Confused and trembling, they heard orders to continue their work. A table for a guard was set in the middle of the hospital verandah and they were told to bow deeply when they passed it. It was impressed upon them that they had the good fortune to be under Japanese military discipline during the continuing international conflict. It was hard to believe that they were all still alive and unharmed.

The chaplain John May and another man were loaded into a car, thrust in among a tangle of swords, bayonets and rifles. They were driven away and the women wondered whether they would see them again. Nurses and nuns huddled in little groups, grateful for the company of others, talking in subdued voices as they helped their patients back into bed. It was hard to believe. They were prisoners, under the guard of an enemy they had always supposed to be their inferior, an enemy armed and edgy with the tension of battle.

A few hours later, the women were relieved to see the chaplain and his companion walking back towards the hospital, escorted by a Japanese soldier wheeling a bicycle. The two men were puzzled by what had seemed a meaningless exercise. They had been taken, they said, to sit by the roadside near a refrigerator shed, seated at a table.

'We were given lunch,' John May said. 'A bottle of lukewarm beer, a tin of IXL jam — and a pair of chopsticks! After a while, a Chinese lad came by and offered us a packet of Kraft cheese. Then they gave us a bundle of mosquito nets and sent us back here.'

The women were very grateful to see him. As the only officer among them, he carried the authority of someone who might be able to take charge in a situation so fraught with confusion.

John May added: 'Can I ask you women not to think of trying to escape? It seems to me that you will be far safer if you stay here, part of a large community than if you attempt to get away into the bush. I've given the officers an assurance that you will stay here, accepting internment without making trouble — and if any of you attempts to escape, I will answer for it with my life.'

The motley procession of people walking down the hill from Refuge Valley to the baseball ground was unlike any seen in Rabaul before. The white 'masters' were no longer in control. They were herded along the road at gunpoint, mingled among the Asian and New Guinean residents. No-one carried their luggage for them. No-one deferred to them.

When they arrived at the baseball ground and the white civilians moved to take their places in the shade of the grandstand, as befitted their place in society, they were shocked to be ordered down into the sun while Asians and New Guineans took the preferred places. The world had truly been turned upside down.

Shaken and disturbed, a cross-section of the civilian population of Rabaul listened to an address by the Japanese. Among the group, uneasy in such an unnaturally mixed multitude, were highly-placed government officials, traders, plantation owners, Chinese storekeepers, business executives, artisans, Malay tally clerks, court judges, domestic servants, the Methodist accountant Wilf Pearce; every part of Rabaul life was represented. They listened with disbelief as the official message was read aloud to the New Guineans and Asians.

'The soldiers of Japan have arrived here in order to improve your condition. We have seen how the English and American people have exploited you in every way. . . They are anxious that the people of Asia and the many people near Asia do not progress . . . The Japanese army is only fighting the English and the Americans. We are your friends and protectors. You must not be afraid of the Japanese. . . This island no longer belongs to the King of England. Your people here must rise to a new prosperity. . .'

When they were taken later to spend the night at the Kuo Min Tang hall, the races soon sorted themselves into familiar groups. There was no food that night and men who were accustomed to the colonial comforts of the New Guinea Club were grateful to find tin cans or bottles in the gutter to catch water from a pump to drink.

Wealthy men searched the Chinese hall for anything they could scrounge to use as a pillow and lay down on tables or the floor for a restless sleep, images of armed guards, ignominy, threats and the overturning of everything they knew passing through their dreams.

When, the next day, the men of the South Seas Force of the Japanese navy arrived in large numbers at the Catholic mission at Vunapope to take up residence there, the nurses were still feeling stunned. The bishop was evicted from his house to make way for the conquerors and moved in with Dr Schuy and his family. Mission buildings were taken over by soldiers.

The native people who lived at Vunapope were sent away, including some thirty-four New Guinean nuns and seminarists; the Japanese made it clear that their quarrel was not with the native people of New Britain but with the white races. Captured Australians were seen arriving to be quartered on the mission grounds. It seemed that not all those who had tried to get away had been successful.

Dora heard young Australian soldiers, ill in the hospital, talking together in complete disbelief as they gazed out to the distant harbour crowded with modern Japanese shipping. They were shaking their heads.

'We were told they were half-blind, ignorant, didn't know how to build any sort of plane or ship or armament — we were told that the Japs had to get the Germans to fly their planes for them.'

'Just take a look at that out there now. I didn't know the Japs had the brains.'

That night, trying to settle in the downstairs room they had been given by the nuns, the mission and army nurses talked among themselves. Although the two groups of women had no previous links, it was quickly becoming clear that they were being viewed as one group of nurses and their future would be bound together whether they chose it or not.

With Captain Kay Parker, the army nurses formed a closeknit team which she had chosen before they sailed for New Britain, women with whom she had nursed in the past and who were selected for their good sense and skills: Tootie Keast, Mavis Cullen, Lorna Whyte, Eileen Callaghan and Jean Anderson. The Methodist girls had much in common with the others in training, nursing experience and age group (single women between twenty-five and thirty-five years were the rule for army nurses) and they had yet to discover what else they might share.

That first evening in captivity, knowing that Japanese soldiers were in control of the whole mission compound, the women had good reason to be anxious. The army nurses whispered that they had collected phials of morphine and put them in their pockets.

'We'll keep them on us day and night, just in case things get too bad. Then we'll have a choice between suicide and being raped,' they said.

It was a shock to hear the thing being named like that. It was one thing to imagine horrors that were without name, unspeakable. To have one's fears spoken aloud by another brought them very close. It was no longer possible to say sternly to oneself, 'Don't be ridiculous — you're imagining things!'

'Not me, I won't be using the morphia,' murmured one of them, the one they called Cal. 'I'm a practising Catholic and I know I couldn't choose suicide. It's not because I'm not allowed, but because it would go against everything I believe. . .'

The listening Methodist mission women were glad to know that they would discover fellow-believers among the group.

In the middle of the night, when the women had settled to an uneasy rest, they heard voices outside their door, voices speaking in a language they did not understand. The door was bolted but they waited, hardly daring to speak in a whisper, feeling the strengthening presence of each other. The banging began, fists thumping on the door of the room, demanding that the door be opened. Laughter, coarse and demeaning, pierced through the thickness of the door.

'They think we're prostitutes. . .' Dora and Dorothy, Mavis and Chris huddled together with the others. This was even worse than the sight of bayonets. The hammering of their hearts seemed almost loud enough to drown the sound of the knocking. They tried to pray and the whispered words were cries from the heart, a desperate plea for protection, a terrified reaching out for God in the darkness.

The invasive drumming on the door continued at intervals

through the night. To the sleepless women, it seemed to come at longer and longer intervals until at last the silence stretched out into hours.

When dawn lightened the shadows in the room, it was very quiet. Dora stirred and turned over. She could just distinguish the outlines of her companions. Her heartbeat had steadied, but there was still a tight knot of anxiety in her stomach. A strange thought had occurred to her, and she lay there thinking of her family. They would be thinking of her today, of all days, and her mother would be sure to speak of her.

The sun had risen when at last the women cautiously opened the door and stepped outside. Around the doorway and out across the lawns lay sleeping Japanese soldiers. Dora stepped carefully over some Japanese boys who blocked the doorway. She looked down into their faces, young and vulnerable in sleep. They seemed so very young and she felt a sudden unexpected compassion.

'It's my birthday, girls,' Dora said, as they threaded their way past enemy soldiers on their way to breakfast. 'Today is 25 January and I'm twenty-nine today!'

9

25 January–19 February 1942

DORA'S BIRTHDAY. . . With their stable world so suddenly tipped upside down, flinging everything into disarray, it was one tiny, ordinary thing to clutch.

'Happy birthday!' they said, even though it could not be that.

That day the mission nurses were forbidden to work in the hospital with the army girls. When they offered to help the nuns, Dora and Dorothy were asked to carry the bread from the convent to the hospital. They walked through the vivid gardens, along paths bordered with croton and hibiscus, under cascades of magenta, purple and apricot bouganvillea, with the aroma of fresh bread drifting up from the basket. A very big basket was balanced between the two tall women, loaded with loaves, high and glossy, crispy-crusted, the ordinary stuff of life with a clean white cloth flicked over them to protect them from dust.

They walked down a track through a mission plantation. Dora listened to the quietness, hot wind ruffling palm fringes, the occasional thud of a falling coconut, aware of birdsong and the distant voices of children at play. Below on the open sea they could see the movement of the ships of an enemy and the faraway flight of aircraft over Rabaul, but the women watched them from a distance, as one might watch the action of a play from the most remote seats of a theatre.

New sounds reached them, magnifying quickly. A dive bomber roared over the hill, swooping over the wide grounds of Vunapope. It seemed to Dora that it was plunging straight at them, the circle of red suns on wings, machine-guns focussed on them, roaring, diving. . .

It is a bad dream, it must be, Dora thought. Her limbs seemed to be turned to stone, the only movement the drumming of her heartbeat. Fingers tightening around the cane handles of the bread basket, commonsense shouted in her head: Run! You're supposed to run. . . into the shelter of the trees. . . throw yourself down! And she could not.

With the pilot, it seemed, almost staring into their eyes as he dashed his tool of death towards them, the nightmare paralysis suddenly left her. She snatched the sheet from the basket.

'Bread! It's only bread. . .' Her voice was lost in the thunder of engine as the plane pulled back hard and rose up over the mission, banking away to seek a different target for its hail of bombs and bullets.

Dorothy stared at Dora, trembling. 'Why didn't you run? We should have run. I was never more scared in my life.'

Dora was white. The unthinkable was happening. There was nothing to prepare her, nothing to compare to this. Even after the fears of the night before, she still found it hard to think that someone would seriously want to be her enemy, to wish her ill. Surely there must be another explanation for the plunging aircraft.

'I thought maybe they just wanted to see what we were carrying in the basket, under the sheet. . .'

Later, when the army nurses returned to the convent, several of them spoke with great agitation about the behaviour of some of the Japanese soldiers. 'They were really horrible — so suggestive and disgusting — they were wanting to get us upset and they were succeeding, too.'

'And did you hear what happened to Eileen Callaghan? She was really tired after a sleepless night and went to lie down for a while, and woke up to feel something cold on her cheek — a Jap bayonet! She yelled, poor thing, and the man ran off, but it was nasty.'

The curious thing was that despite all that was offensive and frightening there was a small ray of hope. The interpreter, a young man named Sugai, introduced himself to the mission nurses. He had learned English as a student in a Christian school in Japan and understood some of the ways of Europeans, he said, from his contact with the missionaries.

'It is not your custom to bow in the Japanese manner. However, I advise you to show proper courtesy and good manners,' he urged, 'and bow as we do. And, please, lock your doors!'

When they found the HQ staff car, abandoned on the track beyond Malabonga on the way to Kalas, the three soldiers of the 2/22nd were very disturbed. The young private, Bill Harry, had led the officers Captain McLeod and Lieutenant Figgis in pursuit of the headquarters staff. They believed the senior officers were travelling in front of them with the vital teleradio they carried.

In the middle of the night after the day of invasion, the three had walked through pouring rain and darkness with a party of seventeen men out towards Malabonga. Malabonga, so recently a busy hospital and place of welcome, was deserted except for two soldiers, one injured, who urged them to keep going as they expected the Japanese to arrive at any minute. They had set out again and, after a few hours of uneasy rest in a native hut by the track, had gone on at first light.

Though there were no signs of the local population, there were many signs of their own people; abandoned military and private vehicles, motorbikes and push-bikes, as well as cases of tinned food and grenades. The walls of jungle rose around them and men began muttering bitterly about the uselessness of canned peaches to men who had at least fifty miles of steep mountain country ahead of them. Because of his knowledge of the area, Bill Harry had taken McLeod and Figgis on the Kalas side-track while the others went on towards Rabata village.

Yet the abandoned car was an ominous sign. Searching in the undergrowth, they found to their dismay the remains of the teleradio, deliberately wrecked. With its bulk and heavy batteries, the radio would have been impossible to transport through the mountains without a large team of carriers, but the sight of the ruins of their only hope of communication was shocking.

For three more hours they walked on. This was well-known territory to Bill Harry; in these hills he had explored with John Poole, eaten at Jean Poole's table, watched the Bainings dancers with Mavis Green, become friends with Akuila To Ngaru and Mikael To Bilak.

When they came out into the clearing at Kalas, the mission house stood as Bill remembered it from earlier visits, among the scattering of buildings — thatched church, dormitories and cookhouses — but the usual clusters of smiling schoolboys were gone. The small party of Australian soldiers approached the mission house with caution. Bill was relieved to see the familiar face of John Poole.

'Come on in, Bill. You know all these chaps, don't you?'

The three soldiers greeted the mission party; Laurie McArthur was there, with Laurie Linggood, Howard Pearson, Ken Allsop and their host John Poole. Food was put on the table and the mission men spoke of the headquarters staff who were the only Australians who had travelled through Kalas during the past twenty-four hours.

'They didn't look very happy,' someone remarked, 'what with broken-down vehicles and having to walk from the end of the road and wade rivers. All the rain has turned the tracks into bogs — it's fiendishly hot — they'd had no decent food for a couple of days. All that, with blisters on their feet and Jap planes strafing them every time they poke their heads out of the jungle — we wonder how they'll go over the mountains.'

'Bill, you've walked these tracks. Even with the help of the local villagers, the best time you could hope would be a six-day trek out to the coast and then find a canoe to travel further west. It could take weeks.'

One of the soldiers pulled a leaflet from his pocket and passed it around. 'And this,' he said. 'This was one of a lot of leaflets air-dropped over us this morning.'

They read the words: 'Surrender at once! And we will guarantee your life, treating you as war prisoners. Those who resist us will BE KILLED ONE AND ALL.'

They were silent for a while, then Bill asked: 'Are you coming with us, John? Mr Mac?'

'We don't feel that we should.' Laurie McArthur was grave. 'As a team we decided that we should find out first whether the Japanese will allow us to keep on working, even in a limited way. If there is a chance that they will, we don't feel justified in trying to escape and leaving all our New Guinean friends behind. It's different for you — you are the soldiers they are fighting. We are unarmed missionaries. And there is something else.

'We took the four nurses — Dorothy, Dora, Chris and Mavis — to the Catholic mission, thinking they'd be safe there. But the whole mission may be under Japanese control by now. So no, we're not coming. We'll stay here at Kalas as long as we can, but when they come to round us up we'll accept internment if that is what happens. We can't leave those four girls behind.'

'Who'd like another cup of tea?' John Poole offered the teapot and Bill Harry pushed his cup forward. He was not to know that it would be his last cup of tea for several months. Soon he would shoulder his arms, farewell his good friends and disappear with the officers into the mountains of the Bainings.

The board room, shrouded in blackout curtains, wore the patina of decades of solemn meetings. In the heart of the city of Sydney, only half of the members of the board gathered for the annual meeting of the Methodist Overseas Mission.

It was not an ordinary annual meeting. They all knew that. The interstate delegates had been warned against travelling at this time of uncertainty and potential danger. Instead of the usual four days of meetings they did their task in four hours, making no attempt to make decisions on finances, appointments or policy. They didn't even have the annual social afternoon tea.

The names of missionary women who had been evacuated from New Britain, the Milne Bay area, north Australia and the Solomon Islands were read. So many families and individuals were being affected. The main task before the board was to draw up a plan in the event of things worsening and more missionaries being obliged to return to Australia. It was decided that if that happened and men came back to Australia from Fiji, Samoa, India, and all the other places where the Methodist church had missionaries, then a few key men, preferably chairmen of districts like McArthur or Len Kentish from north Australia, would be retained on the mission staff for deputation work and a quick return to their fields after hostilities were over. The others would be helped to find work in the home congregations across Australia.

The matter of the earlier letter from the Rev. Laurie McArthur was raised in which he asked for advice on possible evacuation and care of the wives, and the General Secretary's reply was duly endorsed. It was urged upon the members that this was to be treated in the strictest of confidence.

The General Secretary commented that he was glad that most of their overseas churches were already mature. 'The native churches themselves would be able to carry on, even though the European missionaries were evacuated for a year or two. There would be no collapse of the church. . .'

The nuns at Vunapope were troubled. The women at the mission, particularly the white nurses, were very vulnerable. As the sun set on the evening of Dora's birthday, some of them came to the nurses.

'The Japs are leaving us nuns alone, but we don't want you girls to have another night like last night. Tonight, we'll drag some mattresses upstairs for you and put you out of harm's way, in the sacristy.'

That night, ten women crowded into the sacristy among the liturgical vestments and locked the door. There was only space on the floor for a few mattresses and they lay down wherever they could fit. Dora and Mavis tried to sleep side by side on top of a wide cupboard filled with linens and sacred vessels for the Eucharist. It was very cramped, very uncomfortable, but somehow felt a little safer.

A shout woke them, then another. The thud of feet reverberated through the convent, running up the stairs, along corridors, and voices yelling and commanding. Had the men come for them again? Was this the moment that they most dreaded? Fists pounded on doors and they heard the nun's answering words.

An urgent tap on their door brought the nurses to their feet, and then they heard the nuns. 'Girls! You'd better show yourselves. The officers couldn't find you and they thought you'd all escaped. All this rumpus is the search party out to catch you.'

Reluctantly they opened the door. An angry officer ordered them out into the corridor and insisted that they line up to be counted. The interpreter turned the shrieked commands into words they could understand and the women stood there, dishevelled, confused with sleep and tense while the counting was done, over and over until the men were satisfied that ten women were still under their control.

At last they were permitted to creep back to their crowded mattresses in the sacristy. 'My phial of morphia is still in my pocket,' one said. 'I thought I might have to use it tonight.'

Over the next days, the tension did not ease. There was always a current of anxiety flowing under everything that the women did, even when the surface of things seemed calm. It was impossible to know what their fate would be and whether to believe the courtesy of the interpreter or the crudities and threatened violence of some of the soldiers. Sometimes a few of the army nurses chose to sleep in relative shelter under the beds of Australian wounded in the hospital.

One night, a courageous Australian civilian, Pastor Malcolm Abbott, leader of the Seventh Day Adventist Mission in New Britain who had arrived at Vunapope with several other SDA staff, stationed himself outside their locked door, planning to sleep there. Though he was a stranger to almost all of the women, he offered to shield the women with his own body. During that night, the women heard scufflings beyond the door; Malcolm Abbott had been removed.

The discarded pile of folded newspapers was ready to be used to light fires when Jean Poole picked them up. She had arrived at a private school on the outskirts of Bathurst in NSW, ready to begin teaching, and was settling into the staff quarters.

The word 'Rabaul' leapt out from the pages as she read. 'Widespread Raids', it said, with stories of a cloud of a hundred and more aircraft attacking the town; 'Enemy Fleet Off Rabaul'; and on 23 January the headline read 'Rabaul Silent Since 4 pm Yesterday'. Jean read each article intently. The Prime Minister, Mr Curtin, had said: 'Anybody who fails to perceive the immediate menace which this attack constitutes for Australia must be lost to all reality.'

The war cabinet, among other things, urged Australians to make Australia Day, 26 January, a day of record production instead of a public holiday. Government Ministers for the Army and the Navy explained that 'the object of the Japanese would be to secure bases from which to attack the Australian mainland'. A journalist, writing from Port Moresby, would announce on 27 January that the AIF and the militia in Rabaul 'were now in action against the Japanese invaders who landed in Rabaul on Friday' and were 'fighting magnificently'.

But Jean, searching for any crumb of news, saw the repeated phrases of uncertainty. 'It is not known at present whether any Japanese force has attempted to make a landing. . . The fate of the garrison stationed in the town is not yet known. . . It is believed that. . . The fate of Rabaul, in New Britain, is still not known.'

Australia Day, 26 January 1942, was a Monday. Many Australian schools were ready to begin their first term the next day, after the public holiday.

In Bathurst, NSW, Jean Poole went for a walk through the town, looking around at the silent streets, with shops closed for the day. In the morning she was to begin her new work, teaching at the Marsden Church of England College. She had always worked for the NSW Education Department before, and this new school would be very different. It was hard to concentrate her thoughts on the present.

All around the handsome provincial town, the countryside spread out in undulations the colour of lightly browned toast. Drought had shrunk dams into cracked mosaics of dried mud.

People were saying that drought and war would bring ruin to many. In the churches people were saying prayers for rain. As Jean walked she was not seeing the browns of drought-dried Australia but the moist greens of Kalas. What was really happening in Rabaul? Was John still safe at Kalas with Mikael and Louisa? What did those newspaper articles really mean when they wrote 'not known'? Did John know that she was coming to Bathurst?

In Tasmania, far to the south, Mel Trevitt prepared to begin teaching the next day. She was grateful to have found accommodation and work at the Methodist Ladies College in Launceston, and someone who lived over the road from the school to care for small Bruce while she was teaching. She had not taught since her illness before her marriage in 1937 and, though she had confidence in her own competence in her field of earth sciences, it was still enough to make her feel a little apprehensive.

Tasmania was so far away from the familiar landscapes and friendship networks of NSW and further still from New Britain. Mel wished she could discuss it all with Jack. Though she had read newspaper accounts of the silence from Rabaul, she pictured Jack safely in Vunairima, planning his timetable for the new term.

(In the crowded confusion of the Kuo Min Tang hall in Rabaul, one of the prisoners produced paper and pen and began his evening record of 26 January. He was a journalist, editor of the *Rabaul Times*, Gordon Thomas, and he was determined to keep daily notes of what was happening around him.

He glanced back over the entries for Saturday 24 January: '. . .no food yet, this is my third day w/o food except occasional scraps. . . Everyone lolling around and very fed up. Nobby asking for whites to be put in New Guinea Club. . . mooning about all the a.m. and then at 1 pm we had our first meal rice and ham — very welcome — same food as Asiatics and only a few spoons provided. Back to the natural.'

He named men who had been brought in from the north coast and described how on Sunday 25 January they had worked at the wharf 'unloading 554 transport, not hard work — fairly good *kai* [food] and treatment — we working on wharf and trucks, Chinese on ships'. He also wrote of Saturday night: 'Last night heavy bombing and anti-aircraft fire. Two missionaries, Trevitt and Beazley joined us. . .')

On Australia Day 1942 other women, scattered across the face of Australia, thought of New Britain. Kath Brown, at home with her mother in a hot Adelaide summer, wished Rodger could see their growing baby; she had heard of the bombing of Rabaul but Rodger was a very long way from Rabaul. In the security of their family homes in Sydney, Adelaide and Melbourne, women cared for their children and listened anxiously for news of Rabaul. Women like Helen Pearson, Nellie Simpson, Beryl Beazley, Eileen Pearce and Essie Linggood were grateful for family support.

In Sydney, Marion Oakes was working in a nursing home and wished Dan was home, though at least he was a long way from Rabaul. Helen Wayne found a teaching position in the Blue Mountains, NSW, and arranged for a place for herself and her two young children until they were free to rejoin Ron. Netta Allsop found a small bedsitter in the middle of the city and began work with the City of Sydney National Emergency Service; her mother and sister lived too far out of town for her to be able to travel from there each day.

Jean Shelton had come to Sydney from Brisbane, expecting her Herbert to be joining her soon; the mission board had invited her to act as housekeeper at the George Brown College at Haberfield, and she was grateful for the accommodation.

Passing with her children from household to household, Daisy McArthur longed for a place of her own. Her own family and Laurie's were kind, and she knew that they were always welcome at Laurie's brother's farm, but what she needed was a settled place where young Malcolm could start school without disruption while they waited for Laurie to come on leave.

For years, she and Laurie had shared the decision-making and it was not since her years as a high school teacher, before her marriage, that she had ordered her life alone. The strange silence of the newspapers over what was happening in Rabaul was unnerving, too, and — though some suggested that the silence from Rabaul was simply a strategic radio silence — she felt sure that they were only guessing. By now, Laurie must be in a place of conflict.

Elsie Wilson, newly arrived in a small rural community in the east of South Australia, thought of the handful of children who would come to the one-teacher school near the railway station where she would begin teaching the next day. This was not at all as she had imagined the beginning of the school year for 1942 would be. When she had arrived first at her parents' home from Rabaul, she had been almost penniless and her clothing consisted of the faded summer dresses of nearly three years of tropical wear. Elsie was grateful to her parents for a loan of five pounds to help her till her teaching salary began to come. She was also grateful to the family who were offering her board for the year; they were descendants of German settlers, farming people, and seemed very kind.

Yet even though the Education Department had appointed her to this country school, she could not get the faces of the New Guinean girls and young women out of her mind. Tomorrow she should have been opening the doors of the District Girls' School at Vunairima. The dark-skinned girls, many with peroxide-blonded frizzy hair and colourful loose blouses, should have been arriving from their villages to begin first term, woven pandanus sleeping mat bundles poised on their heads. It might be months, she thought, before she could go back and get on with her work.

'I should have insisted on staying,' she thought with regret. 'Even if the Japanese did come to the area, they would not be likely to want to interrupt the work of a girls' school. If the nurses were staying, I should have stayed, too.'

Before January 1942 came to an end, the first of the men who were trying to escape from New Britain came straggling into Port Moresby. They were the men who had managed to get out before the final fall of Rabaul and had only fragmentary reports to offer. Before the end of January, across the Pacific the Japanese forces were attacking Ambon and the Allies had been forced back from Malaya onto the fortress of Singapore Island. Kavieng on New Ireland had been bombed and taken by the Japanese forces and Lae and Salamaua on New Guinea had been bombed as well.

Writing in his notebook, handwriting reckless with frustration, journalist Gordon Thomas noted by the end of the month:

'General opinion is our general military organisation is up to putty — Jap most thorough — some vituperation over our leaders . . .'; 'Jap AA fire very effective. What the Japs have done in a week for the defence of the town compared with AIF eighteen months' work — all in favour of Jap efficiency. There is no doubt they get things done. . .'; '. . .still revilings on heads of heads. . .'

On a moonlit night at the end of January, the people of Rabaul watched an air raid pass overhead. No longer were they subjected to raids from the Japanese; now they submitted to over two hours of bombing by the Australians from Port Moresby, planes slipping in and out of the lines of searchlights while the Japanese troops fought back with pompoms, anti-aircraft fire, machine-guns, tracer bullets — everything, Thomas wrote, 'except bows and arrows and shanghais'.

Within days, the first bombs fell on Port Moresby and troops saw that the Japanese advance was relentless and rapid. A day later, though the world did not know it, a terrible calamity befell a large party of Australian troops making their way along the southern coast of New Britain as they passed through Tol Plantation; bloodied bayonets left pierced corpses among the palms.

In NSW, Jean Poole and the others combed any news reports for the smallest clue about what was happening to their husbands and friends in New Britain. One church paper writing of the fall of Malaya and the uncertainties about Rabaul wrote: 'The enemy comes closer to Australia and the nation, from all the signs, is about to face the supreme trial of her history. What our defences in men and material are, we cannot know. . . We are realists enough to see that a mighty foe will be likely to hammer at our gates, but men of faith and courage enough to see the foe defeated.'

Another church paper wrote, under the headline 'The Bombing of Rabaul': 'We are anxiously waiting for detailed news, but meanwhile our hearts go out to our brethren and our four sisters remaining there. What the future holds, none may know, but the prospects seem dark and we deeply sympathise with our native friends. . . At present, our missionaries have given up normal work and are exercising a steadying influence by patrolling the villages.'

It was not so much what had happened to them that made the nurses tense in those first weeks of captivity. It was the thought of what might happen to them at any time. The threat of assault, rape or violent death hung over them like a miasma.

There were sixteen of them now and the nuns had moved them into the convent vacated by the New Guinean nuns who had been sent off the mission compound. The newcomers were the nurses from Namanula Hospital, the Rabaul hospital for Europeans. The civilian nurses from Namanula were under the leadership of recently-arrived Matron Joyce Oldroyd-Harris and had had little time to adjust to the new regime. With her were Alice Bowman, Joyce McGahan, Jean McLelland, Grace Kruger and Mary Goss. A Chinese nurse, Angela Choi, had been sent home to her family, and no-one knew what was happening to the Chinese community.

In that disrupted world, strange things took on the glow of good news. There was the day two weeks after the invasion when one of the nurses came into the convent with a shout of delight. 'Guess who has just arrived! A shipload of Japanese prostitutes. There is a rumour that there are two hundred of them housed in the Cosmopolitan Hotel in town and more here at Vunapope — in the bishop's house, no less!'

'Thank God for that, then. They'll probably leave us alone now.'

(The Australian women, grateful for their own reprieve, were not to know that many of the women brought to Rabaul for the satisfaction of the invasion forces were Korean girls who had been snatched from school grounds and other public places, the stolen women of a subject people, wrenched from home and family to disappear without trace for the duration of the war. They would be known as Comfort Women.)

Another glimmer of hope was a proclamation over the title of the Japanese Commander-in-Chief, delivered on 11 February. It appeared to have been printed locally in English and the women studied it carefully. There were some lively comments over the statement: 'Japan's mission is to first accomplish the establishment of a great mutually prosperous Asia and then to contribute greatly to the peace and happiness of all mankind. It is your misfortune that you were forced to surrender. . .'

In among paragraphs with threats against all who resisted, they discovered a statement which gave them new hope. It read: 'It is hoped that arrangements can be made for the early release of civilian prisoners and that, after the termination of the war in the near future, all prisoners will be permitted to be returned safely to their own country.' Early release of civilians, they said to each other. Twenty days of captivity was quite long enough.

As February went on, more and more people came into Vunapope; young soldiers captured while trying to escape, civilians found on outlying plantations, mixed race women and children from across the community, missionaries from bush mission stations. Though most of the national families and seminarists were sent away from the mission, back to their villages or the villages of their friends, the population of the Catholic mission grew to well over three hundred people.

Then one day one of the nuns brought news. 'Some of your Methodist missionaries have just been brought in. They are being held on the other side of the mission compound.'

With some difficulty, Dora and Dorothy were able to get permission to visit the men. It was a month since McArthur and Linggood had left them at Vunapope and it was a great relief to see them again.

Laurie Linggood's greeting was happily ordinary. 'Do you girls have any soap?' he asked. 'We've run out!'

They were only permitted a brief time together and there was much to tell. Laurie McArthur told them of the long wait at Kalas and of the help given to them by their New Guinean friends. Men like Mikael To Bilak, the student Saimon Gaius and the Rev. Akuila To Ngaru had been with them, supporting, encouraging, bringing food, and praying with them. If Christian faith was to survive among the people, the responsibility for carrying the words of hope would lie with the people of the place, not with missionaries. The Australian men were distressed at the way they were being torn from their work, leaving their New Guinean friends to carry on in a time of such danger and disruption.

'We stayed at Kalas together for about two weeks,' McArthur said, 'expecting the Japanese to arrive for us at any moment. From 23 January on, groups of Australian troops came through, and a number of officers. We fed them and welcomed them, but I must admit that we were always glad when they moved on. It made us all nervous to have groups of armed men with us — we felt that we had a better chance as unarmed civilians, prepared to surrender. We heard from New Guinean people that the Japanese had already taken over Malabonga. One day a Jap float plane came overhead and circled around the mission house. . .'

'And we didn't hang about — we headed for the bush!' Linggood added. 'We watched it circle and then saw two bombs fall, one on each side of the house. They knew we were out there, you see, and from then it was just a matter of waiting till they came.'

'In the end, we came to the point where we felt we should go and give ourselves up. It was almost a relief,' McArthur said. 'It seemed better to go and meet the Japanese openly, rather than wait on and on in suspense. So we left our friends at Kalas in the first week in February and started walking. We ran into the Japanese at Taulil. I tried to ask whether we would be allowed to keep working, but they didn't listen.'

He went on, telling the story of the amputation of the white missionaries from the body of Christian believers in New Britain. It would not be right to frighten the women, he decided, by telling every detail. He knew that some New Guineans had witnessed the beating they had received and that the news of it would pass among the people. Nor did he mention that they had been taken back to Malabonga to see the destruction of the Sisters' house there. The nurses had enough to worry about without him adding to it, he was sure.

'They've taken us here and there, and now they've brought us here to Vunapope. We don't know how long they'll leave us here.'

Laurie Linggood added: 'We'll probably see our New Guinean friends again — they've promised to try to bring us food. Those good brothers of ours won't forget us.'

'But couldn't you have got away?' One of the nurses asked it. 'If you'd gone straight away, couldn't you have escaped?' Surely McArthur, Linggood and Poole, perhaps the best-known white men to walk the tracks of the Baining mountains in recent years, and Pearson, teacher and friend of a number of the New Guinean pastor-teachers stationed in the area, could have simply walked on into the bush. They could have followed the paths they knew, receiving help along the way from known friends among the villagers, and gone on to join Rodger Brown well along the north coast at Malalia.

'We couldn't go and leave you girls here. We thought that, maybe, if we accepted internment at least we'd all be together.'

Nellie Simpson hadn't written about the new baby until she was sure. It wouldn't be kind to get Tom excited for nothing, she decided. In her previous letters to Tom, Nellie had told him about how she had arrived home in Adelaide to find her parents away on their summer holiday, and how she had appeared on a kind neighbour's doorstep with her suitcase and baby Margaret. She told him all the details of settling in again with her parents, and how delighted they were with their lovely grandchild.

It was hard to write. She didn't know what was happening for Tom. She had written to the mission Board people in Sydney asking for any news, but Mr Burton had written back to say that they had no news at all about Tom. They said that Kavieng had been bombed, but Tom would probably be safe over on New Hanover. Maybe Dan Oakes had gone over to join him, out of the way of danger. Even if the Japanese had landed at Rabaul and Kavieng, why would they want to be bothered with a small island as remote as New Hanover? Yet it was a month since she had last received a letter from Tom and there was no way of knowing what was really going on.

'This news will cheer him up, anyway,' Nellie thought, 'and

give him something good to look forward to.'

'Guess what!' she wrote. 'We are going to have another baby some time in August. Maybe a son for you.' She laughed, a mischevious gleam in her eyes. 'Do you remember that last night in Kavieng, when we had to stay in the garage? It must have been that cement floor!'

It was a strange week, that one. From 15 February, each day brought news of events that were cataclysmic, convulsive, extraordinary. For the ordinary people of Australia, including women like Jean Poole, Daisy McArthur and Kath Brown, each passing day tightened the tension, turning the screw until they felt they could not bear more news. Each day the Japanese forces came nearer and nearer and daily the stories told of failure, imprisonment and flight. Daily, people asked: why? The mystery of the tangled and knotted skein was impossible to unravel.

On 15 February, Singapore Island, that fortress which was said to be impregnable, was surrendered by the Allies to the Japanese and thousands of Australian fighting men found themselves suddenly and unexpectedly prisoners. Among the many in flight from fallen Singapore was a large party of Australian nurses travelling with patients on the *Vyner Brooke* which had sailed a few days earlier. On 14 February, their ship was bombed and sunk. Those who survived bombs, drowning or being swept away on a raft, struggled at last, after twenty-four hours adrift, onto a beach on Banka Island in Indonesia. There twenty-two nurses were mown down by machine-gun fire as they stood knee-deep in the surf; one wounded woman survived, a captive, to tell the story. Her story was to remain hidden from the Australian public till the war was over, years later.

On the same day as the Banka Island massacre, articles appeared in the Australian papers about the amazing escape of a group from the British Solomon Islands. A telegram had arrived at the Methodist Overseas Missions office announcing the arrival of a party of New Zealand Methodist missionaries, who had just arrived in Mackay in North Queensland on 12 February. The telegram read: 'Leadley myself four sisters landed yesterday proceeding Sydney weekend book first available passages plane or steamer New Zealand. Signed: Rutter.' Missionary women reading the story in the papers read every word, wondering if their own people could be attempting similar feats.

With six others, Dr Rutter, mission education officer E.J. Leadley and mission Sisters Jones, McDonald, Harkness and Cannon had survived an eighteen-day adventure in a seventeen metre launch covering 1 760 kilometres of open ocean. When the news reached them that the Japanese were bombing a nearby settlement, within two hours they made the decision to leave in the mission launch. The launch had food and water on board, but even the person chosen as skipper had no experience of sailing. One man said that he could steer, or at least point them in a westerly direction so that eventually they should bump into Australia.

They left Tanaka in the British Solomons under the protection of a rain squall, clouds obscuring the view of the Japanese planes overhead. Through storm they travelled, at last reaching the coral wall of the Great Barrier Reef where they were stuck on the reef several times, bumping backwards and forwards over several days and only by a miracle avoiding being holed and foundering. But they had arrived in Mackay, north Queensland exhausted, penniless, without luggage — but alive.

On 16 February 1942 General Sturdee, Chief of General Staff wrote a significant policy paper. With the weight of great responsibility on his shoulders, Sturdee wrote: 'We have violated the principle of concentration of forces in our efforts to hold numerous small localities with totally inadequate forces which are progressively overwhelmed by superior numbers. . . the present policy of trying to hold isolated islands with inadequate resources needs review.'

The Methodist women that day were not interested in military strategy. The news began to pass among them that one of their mission men was home. Gil Platten had just arrived in Sydney from New Ireland.

Gil Platten was their husbands' colleague. He had first gone to the islands as a missionary in 1927 with his wife Isabel and was working at Namatanai on the east coast of New Ireland. He and his wife had only just returned from furlough before Isabel was evacuated with their children on the last plane out of Rabaul. Now he was in Sydney but, to the disappointment of the women, he had no accurate news of the other men.

He told his story, of the 'sinister sight of a skyful of bombers' and then hearing the thunder of the bombing of Rabaul across the seventy-seven kilometres of St George's Channel followed by the silence of broken radio contact. New Guinean villagers coming across the narrow neck of land from the west coast told him of watching Japanese transports under naval escort sailing down past New Ireland on their way to land in Rabaul in New Britain. He had moved around the villages of his area, explaining to the villagers that what they called the 'great confusion' had come. Some villagers were building huts hidden in the jungle to hide their women and children.

Platten then encountered a party of Australian men, mostly from the New Ireland plantations, led by the district officer. After days of hiding in the bush, he joined the group to attempt the journey by launch to Tulagi in the British Solomon Islands. As they travelled they saw enemy cruisers landing along their coast, attacking native villages and the Chinese plantation. They heard the drone of aircraft engines overhead, but were thankful that an attack was foiled by heavy obscuring tropical rain as at last they set off. They set out to try to sail to Tulagi equipped only with a map of the world in a school atlas to steer them through countless tropical reefs.

On the journey, they sailed through torrential rainstorms, were dogged by a seaplane dropping bombs which somehow missed their target, and were lost and found among small islands. When they eventually reached Tulagi, which was to fall to the Japanese on 2 May, they were able to travel on to Australia across open ocean in an inter-island ship.

The women, hearing the story, asked: 'Could John. . . could Laurie. . . could Rodger be attempting a voyage like that, right now?' There had been no news, no letters since those posted a month earlier, and anything might be happening.

When Platten arrived home in South Australia, Kath Brown

was one of those who visited him. 'Do you know anything about Rodger?' But Platten, from another island and hundreds of miles distant from Rodger, knew nothing.

On the north coast of New Britain that week, Rodger Brown had a visit from the Australian Assistant District Officer for the area, Keith McCarthy, and heard that a plan of escape was being organised. McCarthy and other Australians working along that coast, in the absence of any coordinated evacuation plan being offered by the military, or any rescue attempt by the Australian government, were seeking out soldiers and civilians escaping through the Baining mountains and doing their best to provide an escape route back to Australia. It was a work of desperation, attempting to gather up hunted men who had been walking through the bush.

Even though McCarthy was doggedly determined to keep men alive and moving away from the concentration of Japanese around Rabaul, he was forced to admit that he had no idea what he would do with his men if he were able to shepherd them all the way from east to west across New Britain. 'Something will come up,' he said; 'we've got to get them there first.' He sounded very unimpressed by the lack of clear action and direction from the authorities in Port Moresby and was grateful for the initiative and independent action of local men such as plantation managers, timber-getters and miners who were offering their small schooners to help collect the men. McCarthy was relieved to find that Rodger had a functional teleradio and took it over to re-establish communication.

'I plan to stay on,' Rodger said. He looked at the rough map McCarthy had sketched out, with a collection point for the escaping men at Pondo plantation in the east and a destination at Talasea in the west on the far side of a wide crescent of open sea. 'Don't worry about coming to pick me up — your boats won't be coming anywhere near here at Malalia in any case.'

Rodger had his own plan. From late in January he had begun to make arrangements in the light of the decisions made with his fellow-missionaries early in January. He prepared a hidden cache of food, medicine and clothing in the bush and, in the event of

Japanese troops coming to the area, he planned to retreat into the mountains. He talked with the New Guinean pastor-teachers and also the minister-on-probation Ilias To Vutnalom about the difficulties ahead of them all.

To Vutnalom asked, 'What will the Japanese do about our religion?' Rodger did not know the answer. 'I don't think they will do anything about it at all — we don't know. But' — and on this he was sure — 'whatever happens, nothing on this earth can separate us from God.'

If there were moments in the early weeks of February when he wondered whether he had chosen the right path, he did his best to silence such thoughts. In many ways his work went on as always. The school children chanted their lessons with their teacher and people came in for basic medical help from the medical orderlies. The small trade store did its usual trade and he met with villagers and church workers. Most days there was the interruption of a flight of Japanese planes passing far overhead.

Rodger had warned the teacher and children to run from their school when the planes went over, just in case, but after weeks of running to hide in the bush there had never been a threatened attack and most days the planes had been only a distant sparkle in the sky. Once, on the day that Rabaul was taken, a solitary pilot had swooped to inspect the small and isolated mission at Malalia, but he had flown on and not returned.

Now Rodger had chosen his course. He would not leave and join the escape party.

That week in February wasn't over yet. On 19 February, Darwin in north Australia was bombed for the first time. An ill-prepared and vulnerable town with over forty ships in the harbour was fiercely attacked in waves of terrifyingly effective Japanese bombing. Elsie Wilson, teaching in a school so far from the conflict, heard the news with shock.

The ship *Neptuna*, which had brought her and the other single and childless women in safety from Rabaul to Townsville, had been at the wharf in Darwin, loaded with explosives. Now the *Neptuna* was ablaze, with dead men engulfed in an inferno in the place where she had shared Christmas dinner with the other women less than two months earlier.

The following day the Japanese forces landed on Timor. Soon more Australian families would learn that their sons, brothers, husbands, sweethearts and friends were captured and imprisoned till some day in the future when the war would end.

10

20 February–15 March 1942

THE AIR-RAID WARDEN'S UNIFORM hung in the garage at her parents' house when Jean Poole came back to visit the family home in Rockdale. Her father's car was there, too, tyres fixed in place with chocks, immobilised for the duration because of petrol shortage.

Among the garden rakes and tins of paint, the warden's uniform seemed a little sinister. It was so odd to imagine her headmaster father patrolling the quiet suburban streets to make sure that neighbours were blacking out their houses. She had seen pictures of the London blitz. Those air-raid wardens had been clambering over the debris of bombed buildings, silhouetted against billowing black smoke; perhaps soon her father would have to help his neighbours from the smouldering wreckage of Rockdale.

Jean had leave from her school for a few days in order to attend the NSW Methodist church's annual conference in Sydney at the end of February. She was to bring a greeting at an afternoon missionary rally, mainly for women. The program was being advertised in bold letters as a chance to meet 'Our Missionary Sisters. . . Nothing more tragic has happened in missionary work in this generation than the disruption of our work in Papua and New Guinea' and she knew that many would want to know what was happening there. She wished that she knew herself.

Sitting on the official platform in the new Lyceum building in Pitt Street, Jean had very mixed feelings as she looked out across the crowded hall. Under that sea of ladies' hats were women with so many heavy things on their minds. The conference had begun with the announcement of the bombing of Darwin, only days earlier, and friends had commented that the conference delegates listened to matters of conference debate with one ear and to the latest news with the other.

Some of the women had sons and husbands in the armed forces, fighting in Europe and the Middle East, or in training camps across Australia, preparing to go to theatres of war. Many had men who were important to them caught up in the disasters of the past month — Rabaul, Ambon, Malaya, Singapore, Timor and Java — and were waiting for news, any news, of what had befallen them. With her on the platform were other women who had been through the distress of evacuation: Jean Shelton from New Britain and others from north Australia, China, Papua and the Philippines.

In the past, when she had attended such events, there had been elaborate programs of music and presentations of various kinds, but this time everything was very simple, very real, very honest. Each speaker had her own story of sudden disruption, separation, anxiety; a woman from Papua described her escape 'in a boat built to accommodate twelve, but packed with 132 passengers, including Chinese'. News was passed on of damage to mission properties, as observed by Allied bombers flying over. Jean Poole and Jean Shelton exchanged shocked glances when it was announced that Vunairima on New Britain had been bombed and that the once-proud George Brown College and Stewart Hospital were now charred ruins.

It was not a time for superficial things. Jean watched the faces of the women in the congregation as they listened. No family was untouched by the pain that was attacking their land. Each person in her own way was looking for strength to go on, despite the ominous rumours of invasion, despite the astonishing news of battles lost, despite worrying over whether or not to evacuate their children to the country, despite the silence that had fallen over their men who were perhaps captives, fugitives or dead.

The sea of hats rippled as they bowed their heads in prayer. Each woman had her own plea to God. Jean listened and joined her own heart's cry with theirs. Someone was saying a prayer on behalf of them all, naming their missionaries — Dorothy Beale, Jean Christopher, Dora Wilson and Mavis Green, Laurie McArthur, Laurie Linggood, Wilf, Dan, Tom, Howard, Syd, Rodger, Herbert, Jack. . . and John. John and his friends — 'somewhere in New Britain'.

Flanked by guards, a bedraggled white woman was marched towards the convent. The nurses saw her arrive with some astonishment.

'It's Mrs Bignell! Didn't she go with the other women when they left?'

'Obviously not. Mrs Bignell always has had a mind of her own. She is the one who wouldn't leave after the 1937 eruption, either.'

The woman who walked towards them looked weary, soiled with hard travelling and angry. She had lived in the tropics since her marriage in 1914, on plantations in the Solomon Islands and on New Britain, and for a period had taken a lease on the Rabaul Hotel where she had insisted on staying when Rabaul was devastated by the volcanic eruption in 1937. Though some had disapproved of this sole woman catering for the many men left to restore Rabaul's services, to others she was a heroine and she was awarded the British Empire Medal. No-one, including her husband and family, had ever succeeded in making Kathleen Bignell do what she did not choose to do.

Now she had chosen to stay on her plantation out of town, then to join a party of men attempting to escape across the jungle-clad hills to the north coast, only to return after a month of adventures when she learned that her soldier son Ted was still in the Rabaul area and searching for her. Returning to her plantation in the hope of locating Ted, she had been captured and brought to Vunapope.

Life at Vunapope had begun to take on a rhythm of its own. Mavis, Dora and the others spent much of their time with the Australian and Dutch nuns, helping where that was possible. The pattern of their day was punctuated by the shrilling of whistles. Each morning the whistle called them just before 7.00 am and in five minutes they were due at roll call. From then on the whistle divided their day, cutting it into neat slices as prescribed by the printed daily schedule. For everything there was a time; work, meals, Japanese language lessons, and retiring to bed at 8.30 pm. Even the bits of the day marked 'Free' were controlled: 'anybody who wished to be out to the ground must get permission,' read the notice. A verse of Kathleen Bignell's was passed around with appreciation. She called it 'The Whistle':

They blew it for cooking, for drinking and eating,
They blew it for dressing, for bathing and sleeping. . .
They blew it to stop us from playing or walking,
But no whistle invented could stop us from talking.

Official notices were displayed and the women studied them with curiosity and sometimes disdain. There was mockery at the sometimes erratic English grammar of the notices and annoyance at the demands that they should all 'learn the Japanese language in the earliest possible time now that all the Territory belongs to the Empire of Japan'. There were prohibitions on listening to the radio, intercepting messages, publishing printed matter, writing to each other, meeting, photographing, going out at night and communication with any other territory.

They began to realise that they were living in isolation and that, little by little, they would lose contact with the rest of the world. For the mission, nurses the order which caused some heartache was one which announced: 'Propagation of a religion and meeting by European missionary are prohibited.'

'That answers Mr Mac's question about whether we'll be allowed to keep on working,' they said ruefully.

Afterwards, Daisy McArthur was not sure which gave her the greater surprise, the sight of her own handwriting on a letter in her own letterbox or the red official stamp across it. At first she was puzzled. Then she read the message stamped red across the letter she had posted to Laurie: 'NOT TRANSMISSIBLE, SERVICE SUSPENDED.'

Slowly she carried the letter up the path into the house. She had held this letter before. This same letter had been written one evening some weeks earlier, after her little ones were settled for the night. She could see herself sitting at the kitchen table by the kerosene lamp, pen in hand, trying to find the right words to tell Laurie about her loneliness without upsetting him, to tell him the pleasures of a day with her baby and her little schoolboy, wanting the words to carry the weight of her love for him.

But here it was, back again. Laurie had not received it. Perhaps, she thought, the post office had made a mistake. She would write again, and be very careful about the address. Again she turned the scarred envelope and stared at the re-addressed message and the smudged red words that shouted at her, 'Service Suspended'. Was the continuing silence from Rabaul to be deepened with the loss of all communication, even the lesser link of letters?

There was little to distract the nurses at Vunapope from the rumours that circled around the mission compound — no current newspapers, no radio, no travel, not even satisfying work. Even within the limits of the convent, enough news came through to tickle the ears of everyone.

Most of the women had friends, acquaintances or family members among the men who were coming into the mission grounds, and every crumb of information was eagerly gathered up and shared. Kathleen Bignell had been able to have a brief conversation with her son Ted and learned that her son-in-law Dudley was also a captive. Jean Christopher had seen her cousin Howard Pearson. Mrs Goss, one of the Administration nurses, asked everyone whether they had seen her husband Tom, but it was thought that Tom Goss was still somewhere at large.

They heard that Dr Robertson, who had gone with the other 2/10th Ambulance team to follow the fleeing troops, had been captured and returned to Vunapope, but the army nurses did not wish to see him; though other troops assured them that the doctors and medical orderlies had done fine work for the Australians in flight, the women had not forgotten that they had been left behind. Nurses from Namanula Hospital, who had lived for several years in Rabaul and knew all the white civilians, started making lists of men they had seen in the grounds at Vunapope and, when a party of Australian men was sent from Vunapope to Rabaul in late February by the coastal ship the *Duranbah*, they were able to record their names.

Some of the stories were told in whispers. Women had seen and heard things they would rather forget. There was the ill and injured young soldier who turned his face to the wall, gave up hope and died. 'We're not going to let that happen to us; we'll keep on going as long as we can!' the women assured each other.

They were told that some of those recently brought to Vunapope had seen a group of natives lashed together around a coconut palm in one of the streets of Rabaul and beaten. There was a vast pile of burning papers in Rabaul town, it was said, much higher than a man and heaped with the records of Customs, the Crown Law office, Treasury and the banks, the written story of people and transactions becoming curled and blackened fragments of ashen history.

The Rabaul Chinese community seemed to be particularly vulnerable. Stories of indignities and cruelty reached them — rapes, beatings and the execution of three senior Chinese community leaders in the Botanical Gardens. The whole Chinese community had been forced to acknowledge in writing their allegiance to the Wang Ching Wei regime in China. Japanese soldiers had demanded that a group of Chinese girls be delivered to them. Some of the girls tried to disguise themselves, hiding in the anonymity of the enveloping black clothes of old women.

A group of terrified Christian girls joined their fathers, brothers and sweethearts in praying for protection. Then one of them was stricken with an attack of dysentery and a friendly doctor let it be known that all the girls were highly infectious. The ploy shielded them until the arrival of the so-called Comfort Women. The mission women thought of Mr and Mrs Mow, all the bright-eyed children of their school, the Rev. Mo Pui Sam and the many pretty girls of their church — and remembered that the Japanese and the Chinese had been enemies much longer than the present conflict.

Very early in their time at Vunapope a story filtered back to the nurses through the nuns who heard it from the religious brothers and the New Guinean seminarists. One of the Brothers who was the mission baker told of the presence of some Australian soldiers in the bush not far from Vunapope in the first days after the Japanese landing and that he had been able to send them bread. But then one of them was captured, tortured and killed.

'Some of the young men from our seminary were there — they saw everything except the final execution,' whispered one of the Sisters, white-faced. 'But they say that there is a new grave just on the edge of the seminary food gardens, in the direction they saw the Australian officer being taken at the end.'

The story haunted Mavis and Dora and the others. The images of cruelty and sadism burned in their minds. There was the story of the captain bound to a coconut palm for many hours, facing the sun with his hat thrown away so he had no shelter; the taunting and impossible questions which did not quell his courage; the beatings; the demand that the New Guinean on-lookers who were digging trenches under supervision should climb the palm and drop weighty coconuts on him. 'They refused, made up some sort of excuse about the palm, but they wouldn't do it.'

There were the ants, the big green ones, deliberately shaken onto him, and the hours of thirst. 'Our students said that he shouted for water and one of them moved to help him, but the interpreter, Sugai, warned them to stand back and not interfere. "You'll be shot if you go near him," he told them. "There is nothing you can do". . .' They said that there were two officers who were the cruel, brutal ones; the others obeyed orders.

Sugai the interpreter. The women found it hard to put the two pictures together in their mind: Sugai the spokesman and witness to an atrocity, and Sugai the courteous and helpful man. It made no sense. But then, very little made sense for them at that time.

Yet, despite all the things which frightened them, there were still those things which, in their very normality, gave some comfort. For Dora and Mavis, the continuing kindness of the nuns reminded them that goodness, peace and faith in a God who did not forget his people still remained. The gardens still flowered around them — cassia, croton, bougainvillea and the rest — even though in the kitchens the food supplies were beginning to dwindle.

Though the mission girls had been refused permission to continue working in the hospital, they took on the ordinary tasks of cooking the meals for the others, and experimented with bread-making. Sometimes they were allowed to go walking around the grounds and strolled through the quietness of the mission cemetery, reading the inscriptions on the headstones of long-gone priests and nuns whose enemy had been tropical disease.

Though some of the Japanese military were rough, cruel and on occasions sadistic, others were not like that at all. Some of the soldiers were perhaps as young as fourteen years old, very confused and very frightened.

'It's not right!' raged one of the army nurses. 'Some of these lads thought that they were going on a cruise, not setting out for a battle in the South Pacific' — and announced that she was going to take some of the young boys in hand and teach them how to knit in their free time. Their courteous Japanese friend, Sugai, continued to speak with words of good sense and understanding.

Out walking in the grounds one day, Mavis and Chris heard a loud cough from the far side of the fence and found New Guinean minister Akuila To Ngaru waiting among the bushes. The gentle Akuila carried a package woven from a coconut frond and, when he unwrapped it, they saw that he had brought eggs, beans, tomatoes, sweet potato, a chicken.

'I brought some food for the guards, too,' he explained, 'so that they would let me walk around here.'

Akuila had also gone to their house at Malabonga before the Japanese arrived there and rescued some more of their clothing, a packet of synod minutes and a copy of the Kuanua-English dictionary. Passing these things over the fence, he spoke quickly of the troubles that had befallen his own people. New Guinean families were moving back to hide in the bush. Men were sending their women back, well out of sight, for fear of assault and rape. Food gardens and plantings of coconut, pawpaw and other fruit trees were often used by the conquerors, leaving the rightful owners short. New Guinean men were often being used as carriers and labourers, with heavy demands made on them. No-one was unaffected by the impact of invasion.

The visit of Akuila lifted the spirits of the mission nurses. Though the news he brought was not encouraging, at least it was some sort of news. The food and the clothing were greatly appreciated and the sight of his face on the other side of the fence was a comfort. He had been like a father to them all, helping them with their language skills, hurrying to check on their well-being when the area had been struck by earthquake in early 1941, ushering them through riverbeds and dragging them up hillsides on patrol. His concern for them had not been discouraged by the sudden loss of prestige of the white population with the coming of the Japanese conquerors. He was still prepared to run risks to bring them food.

'Next week one of us will come again,' he assured them. 'We have made a plan. Each Saturday a different village group will come with food.'

Then he was gone, disappearing among the trees and hurrying away to the comparative safety of his people in the mountains. The value of his visit far outweighed the nourishment brought by his parcel of food and the women were thankful.

The day of the picnic at the beach was hot and sunny, a true Adelaide summer's day. Kath Brown drove with her mother and baby Graham to Glenelg and, among the beach umbrellas, clusters of sunbakers and swimmers she found the others. Daisy McArthur was there with her boys, Helen Pearson with Donald, Nellie Simpson with Margaret and others of the Rabaul community who had been evacuated with them. They had not been together since they had arrived home in Adelaide early in the new year.

With the bigger children heaping up sandcastles and the babies dozing under umbrellas, the women talked.

'What do you think is happening to them?' Kath asked. 'If the Japs are in Rabaul, and none of us are getting letters, they must be prisoners.'

'If only we knew what was going on it wouldn't be quite so hard,' Daisy said. 'We are all only guessing.'

'They'll be all right,' Helen said with confidence. 'God won't let anything happen to them.'

'Rodger must be down at Nakanai by himself. I've had a couple of letters written since Christmas that have come through and in one he said that he was planning to leave Rabaul for Nakanai the next day. So he must be there. The Japs wouldn't go to Nakanai, would they?' Kath looked for reassurance. She remembered her own journeys to and from their remote station and was comforted to think how far away it was from Rabaul.

'Maybe our husbands from around Rabaul have travelled down to Nakanai to join him, but they can't get mail out — mail from Nakanai is slow at the best of times.'

It was a relief to each of them to talk freely about their men. Since they had arrived back in Adelaide they had all felt as if there were a gulf between themselves and the people of their communities who had never been in the islands. Several of the women commented that there had been little in the way of comfort offered by their ministers. 'You'd think they could call in and ask how we were getting on,' Kath said. It seemed that the whole community was busy with its own affairs and had no time for a few women who had not heard from their husbands for two months, even though they might be prisoners of the enemy.

Daisy McArthur was leaving Adelaide soon. Laurie's older sister, postmistress in a little South Australian town on the long road leading north, had offered two rooms to Daisy and the children in her home behind the post office.

'Do you know anybody out there?' the others asked.

'No. Only Laurie's sister. But it will be somewhere to stay till he comes home. We've lived in parsonages since our marriage — it is strange to have nowhere of our own to go.'

They were gathering up sandy towels, picnic baskets and cranky children to travel to their homes when Nellie spoke. 'Tom doesn't even know,' she said. 'I've written to tell him but the letter came back. I'm going to have another baby in August — and Tom doesn't know. . .'

At dusk on 12 March, as the sun was dropping beyond the distant Willaumez Peninsula, Rodger Brown watched an unfamiliar schooner coming in towards the beach at Malalia.

'The Japs have come to get me,' he thought. As the weeks had passed, he had been waiting for the axe to fall. He was in touch, through village contacts, with Keith McCarthy, and knew that McCarthy was experiencing many difficulties and frustrations in his task of collecting Australian soldiers and civilians. He had heard that the vessels which McCarthy had hoped to use to take the men off from Pondo plantation were all unavailable for one reason or another — damaged by enemy fire, taken for another purpose — and so he was forced to bring the men by short and painful stages on foot around the coast with the help of only one small schooner.

It was not easy to push a canoe out into the water that nightfall and go to meet the shadowy vessel, a silhouette against the last gleams of sunset. It could be, he knew, his last few moments of freedom. Then he saw the hat, a distinctive Australian slouch hat waving in greeting, and he found he could breathe freely again. A red-headed young man leaned out over the railing and shouted a friendly remark and an older man called down, 'This is the *Gnair*, from Salamaua, part of the Harris Navy!'

The Harris Navy. . . It was not long before Rodger discovered what that meant. The redheaded young man was known as Blue Harris, a patrol officer who had been in Lae just before that town fell to the Japanese, and had responded to Keith McCarthy's call for help for his refugee men.

With the cooperation of a team of volunteers, he had raised a flotilla of schooners from the places between Madang and Salamaua on the eastern coast of the mainland of New Guinea: *Totol* from Madang, *Bavaria* from Finschhafen, *Umboi* from Siasi.

They had sailed across the Vitiaz Strait to the northern coast of New Britain.

'The British did it for Dunkirk,' Harris said. 'We can do it, too — ordinary blokes in their own small craft going to rescue their own people from an enemy.'

Blue Harris and his goldminer mate, Bill Money, were looking for Keith McCarthy and for any of the fugitive Australians. 'But we've been going along the coast all day and haven't spotted one of them,' they said, puzzled.

'If they are like me, they all thought you were a Jap boat and went bush,' Rodger said. 'I'll give you a message addressed to any of our New Guinean church workers to let them know who you are, and they'll be sure to pass the message on to any soldiers hiding in the bush near them.'

That night, as his guests ate at his table, Rodger learned about the people who had volunteered for the 'Harris Navy'. Lincoln Bell, the timber-cutter who had brought him and Kath to Malalia in 1941, was ferrying men in the *Aussi* and there were a couple of goldminers and government officers, but most of the volunteers were Lutheran missionaries. Australian and American Lutherans from the many Lutheran missions spread along the east coast of the mainland had been willing to risk their mission boats and their own safety to attempt to save their friends.

'It's a funny world,' Bill Money commented. 'We've been hearing so much about the horrible Hun and the rotten Nazis. But these blokes who've come to help — do you know what their names are? Freund, Obst, Radke, Rohrlach, Neumann. . .'

At dawn the next day, the *Gnair* left to search again for the men who were struggling along the coast. When it returned, there were some forty men on board. Others began to walk into Malalia or come in by canoe, until about eighty men had passed through the mission. Rodger was disturbed to see their condition.

It was now nearly two months since Rabaul had fallen to the Japanese and the men who came stumbling into the mission were half-starved, wearing the last shreds of their uniforms. The sun had burned their unprotected bodies, blistering skin and lips and mosquitoes had raised itchy welts. Some had wrapped hessian and cloth around their feet when their boots had fallen apart and others could barely walk with the pain of tropical ulcers and the misery of malaria. Yet those who came along the many miles of black sand beach, mangroves and jagged coral rock were the fit ones. Over seventy wounded and sick men were being ferried on to Talasea to the west of Nakanai.

As each group of men came along the track, Rodger and Corporal Mac Hamilton worked to provide rest and food and instructions for the next stage of the long, long journey west. Always, as another group of men came in sight, Rodger wondered whether this time his friends might be among them — Laurie McArthur, Laurie Linggood, John, Howard and the others. But as one group after another was given help and sent on their way, his friends were never among them. No-one had any news of their whereabouts.

Over and over again, however, exhausted men told of the way they had been cared for by Methodist church workers along the way. The litany of names of New Guinean men he knew and trusted was a great comfort to Rodger: Misiel Tiriman, Saimon Gaius, Epineri Kopman, Darius To Kalia, Mikael To Bilak and others.

'Wonderful blokes,' men said. 'Looked after us with such care and great hospitality, even though we all knew what would have happened if the Japanese had come along and caught them helping us. One of them, Iolam To Vaira, fed us chicken and then offered finger bowls for our greasy fingers!'

'You'll have to come with us, Padre,' men said. 'We've seen what was happening in Rabaul. Sooner or later, it's going to come out here. As far as we can see, the Japs don't have a fight with the natives, but they are out to get us whites.'

It was a very painful time. To leave or to stay? Rodger did not know what had happened to any of his colleagues because the silence from Rabaul had been complete. On the night of 13 March he did not sleep. A number of fugitives were staying at the mission, trying to gather their strength to go on in the morning and Rodger spent the night walking quietly around the mission grounds, thinking and praying.

How could he leave his friends, his fellow-Christians of the Nakanai area? How could he leave the work he had begun with such delight only eighteen months earlier? How could he go back on his sense of call which he felt had come from God? Was it cowardice to join the troops and the other civilians, running away from danger which perhaps would not even come?

But. . . on the other hand, if he were to stay on at Malalia, would that place his New Guinean friends at greater risk for having a white man among them? There was already one coastwatcher in the mountains behind the Nakanai coast, so was there any sense in having another one? If, as seemed likely, his colleagues were already prisoners, as the only Methodist mission staff member free to escape, ought he not to attempt to do so? Men coming through had already told him that the Japanese were sending out notices banning Christian mission work. The thoughts went round and round in his head, confusing, opaque.

'What am I to do? Show me, Lord!' he pleaded. As the dawn lightened the ocean, it seemed that he had no real choice but to stay.

But that was before more men came in during that day. At last there was some news. The newest arrivals had been behind some of the others and had more information. Rodger grasped every word. The nurses, one said, had been taken to Vunapope Mission and were nursing Japanese and Allied patients — or so some Catholic natives had told them. Another said that a party had been captured at Vunairima, and that Jack Trevitt had been among them. The speaker did not know Syd Beazley, but Rodger presumed that they would be together.

Others told him that the Japanese had taken over Malabonga and gone on to Kalas. Then a few men spoke of coming through Kalas days after the fall of Rabaul and described the missionaries there: McArthur, Linggood, Pearson and Poole.

'They were there for at least ten days after Rabaul fell but, with the Japs taking Kalas, they almost certainly won't be there now.'

No-one could tell him anything about the whereabouts of Shelton, Oakes, Simpson or Platten, but because each of those men was stationed well out of Rabaul he hoped that they were safe enough.

Late that morning there was a ripple of excitement. Another party had just arrived. When Rodger encountered the newest group he discovered that they had come, with great difficulty, from the south coast, led by Frank Holland, an employee of W.R. Carpenter company, and a team of trusted New Guinean men who had gone to try to find any other men who could join the escape plan. Among them were a number of men of rank, Lieutenant Colonel Howard Carr, commanding officer of the 2/22nd, four captains, a lieutenant and the Commissioner of Police, Mr W.B. Ball with three other police officers.

'Does anyone know what happened to Colonel Scanlan?'

'He decided that, for the troops' sake, he should go and surrender. A tough decision. He got a message that didn't leave him much choice. They wrote direct to Scanlan: ". . .you have no means of escape. If your religion does not allow you to commit suicide, it is up to you to surrender yourself and beg mercy for your troops. You will be responsible for the death of your men."'

'We don't give him much chance, though.' The men who spoke were sombre. 'There are a couple of chaps coming in on Lincoln Bell's "sick ship" with the sick and wounded who are lucky to be alive. Frank Holland brought them back — somehow they survived a wholesale massacre on Tol plantation, but one hundred and fifty others, our blokes, have been killed. . . a horrible business.'

The police officers had a message for Rodger. His friends at Kalas had been seen on the road, going to give themselves up in line with their earlier decision.

It was a subdued and weary group who sat around Rodger's table that evening. The officers were persisting in their quest to get as many of their men out to safety as possible; other officers and men had made other choices because of the hazards of the long trek across country and the uncertainty as to whether they would be rescued or die of hunger, disease and exhaustion after months of walking. But the dreadful news of the slaughter at Tol shocked and oppressed them.

'Padre, you'll have to come with us. Your friends are already in captivity. There's no point in waiting here to be cut down when the Japs arrive. They are not going to take a single prisoner out here — too much nuisance. McCarthy will drag you out, whether you want to come or not. And once we move on, you won't get another chance. McCarthy has hung on an extra week hoping that Holland would make it back from the south coast to join us but, now that he's come and we've heard about what happened at Tol, we'll be on our way at first light tomorrow.'

It was one of the most difficult things Rodger had ever done. He gathered his New Guinean teachers around him and told them he was going. There were many tears as they farewelled each other. He walked through his house, taking apart the fabric of his home where he and Kath had lived for most of a year, packing books and household effects into a big box to be left with one of the teachers. As he wrapped Kath's cherished wedding presents — the silver teapot, the crystal jug, the linen Kath had stitched with such skill — he remembered with a pang that Kath had not even been able to bring their baby son back to their home. As he nailed the box shut, he wondered whether he, Kath, the baby and these objects which had such family associations would ever be together again.

At dawn on Sunday morning 15 March 1942, they sailed from Malalia in the *Gnair* and the *Aussi*, carrying soldiers and civilians, the sick and the weary, as well as some mission goats and the bulk of his food store for the journey. As they passed along the coast, collecting McCarthy and others at Valoka on the way and going on to Walindi plantation, someone saw what they thought was a flight of Japanese planes coming towards them; there was great relief when the 'planes' proved to be frigate birds.

That night at the plantation, another small vessel of the Harris Navy arrived, the *Umboi*, one of the Australian Lutheran mission boats. A man from the *Umboi* introduced himself to Rodger as the Rev. Harold Freund and said, 'I believe that you are a missionary. Yes? So am I.'

'Where are you from?'

'South Australia — Waikerie.'

'I'm a South Australian, too. From Mt Mary, forty miles from Waikerie!'

Kept awake through much of the night by mosquitoes, the two men talked, discovering many common things, things of faith, things of home. Lying nearby were the officers and key civilians. This was the first time many of them had been together since the catastrophe of Rabaul nearly two months earlier and their voices continued on through the night, disillusionment and rage colouring their tones.

'A shambles. . . a disgrace. . .'

'We've been betrayed by our own government, dumped in a place which they knew we had no hope of holding and left to rot.'

'No communication. If they'd even let us know what was going on we'd have had some hope of being able to handle things, but men sent to battle stations thinking it was only an exercise, without quinine or rations — and no training in bushcraft and survival skills for anyone, even though it was obvious we'd need to retreat into the jungle. . .'

'What were any of us to do with Lewis guns left over from 1916?'

'And it looks as if the Australian government has decided to abandon its men who are trapped here — none of us have seen a single friendly aircraft looking for us in seven weeks, and there is no sign that Canberra is sending any rescue ships to get us out. If it wasn't for men like Keith McCarthy, Blue Harris and Frank Holland — the ordinary civilians who have lived in New Guinea for a few years and know the ropes — we'd have no chance!'

That night Harold Freund wrote a letter to his wife in South Australia. Neither he nor Rodger Brown had any idea whether they would survive the next weeks or years. Even McCarthy did not know at that point how he was going to move two hundred or more men from a series of isolated plantations along the north coast of west New Britain to a place of safety and, though he assured the men 'Something will turn up', there were moments when the words sounded very hollow in his own ears. Freund sealed his letter and handed it to Rodger Brown.

'If you make it home to Australia, I'd be glad if you'd post this to my wife.'

11

Easter 1942

'ONLY ONE PAGE! How can I fit two months of news into one page?' Dora looked around at the other nurses, each busy with pen and paper. 'Still, I guess we can be thankful they are letting us write anything at all. Mum must be sick with worry, not knowing where I am.'

After two months in captivity, with no opportunity to make contact with families, those interned at Vunapope as well as the men in Rabaul were given the chance to write home, one page each. The letters were to follow a set formula, beginning 'I am writing to you by kind permission of the Japanese Imperial Army . . .', but Mavis was not the only one who was scornful about such a heading. 'Not much of a kind favour, when they have us here as prisoners and haven't let us get in touch with our families or the mission or anyone!'

It was better than nothing, they all decided, and they did their best to choose their words with great care. Some included the names of close friends known to their families who were with them, in case one letter got through and another did not. Someone wrote, 'We are getting used to the diet of rice, fish and milk.' In the former army camp at Malaguna, a man wrote, 'Matupi volcano is going it hot and strong and we are living in a permanent rain of pumice.' Another wrote, 'We are fortunate in having a padre with us' and yet another, 'Have said more prayers than ever before in my life.' It was hard to find the words to make a strong connection between the captive writers and those whom they loved at home.

There were things which they knew they could not write. Even if it had not been for the knowledge of the censor who would read the letters, there were things for which they had no words. How could they write to their parents of the Seventh Day Adventist missionary who had arrived at Vunapope very ill and had died of his illness while a prisoner? How could they speak of stories they had heard of villagers being herded down into the sea and then machine-gunned? Or of the day when they saw two village men marched past them at gunpoint, going towards the cemetery, and then they heard the shots. . .

'But how are they going to get these letters to Australia?' One of the nurses sounded puzzled and spoke for the rest.

'The post office isn't going to send a man round on a bike to collect this mail.'

With a sigh, the General Secretary laid the black telephone handpiece back in its cradle. The unanswerable questions and the complaints kept coming from all directions. Whatever course he followed, there were people who would be hurt and angry. From his office in the brick and sandstone labyrinth of central Sydney, lines of communication and responsibility ran out to his people working in the Pacific and north Australia.

In theory, John Burton was in a position of power, but he had rarely felt as powerless. Mission staff were on the move, following a mix of orders from a range of sources. He could neither stem the flood of contradictory advice nor reach many of his people with advice of his own.

The women from New Britain and New Ireland had been evacuated safely, and arrived in Australia just before New Year. But their men and four nurses were missing and his office had been receiving those 'Not Transmissible' red-stamped envelopes. Experienced missionary staff, ready to return to New Britain after their furlough, had resigned because it seemed that return was impossible. Both men and women in the Solomon Islands and from the Papuan islands in the Milne Bay area had followed government instructions to leave and had also all arrived, after many adventures.

Since the bombing of Darwin, there had been a new urgency about evacuating the married women staff from north Australia, and both Australian and Fijian women and children were somewhere on their way, travelling overland through the heart of Australia, but their men were staying on. There was the question of the staff, mostly women, still with the newly established settlement for part-Aboriginal children on Croker Island off the coast of Arnhem Land; with four mission nurses already missing in New Britain, their position worried him.

And the children who were their responsibility, what of them? Should they be treated as black or white, be evacuated or not? If he made the decision to bring them, how could they bring ninety-five children from Croker Island to Sydney? Ought he to recall the mission staff from Fiji and Samoa, too? Was the great exodus a sign of foolish panic, running away from serious work, or was it the only wise path to follow? It was impossible to know.

Burton thought of his friend J.R. Halligan, government Minister for Territories, who carried responsibility for the evacuation of Australian civilians. The public expected men in their position to know what to do. But how could they be wise in these circumstances, with such limited information and no clear guidance on what the future held for their nation? Halligan shared with him what little he knew, but it was so insubstantial.

He began to draft a letter to send to the state conferences of the Methodist church around Australia. He wrote of those who 'grow impatient from lack of news and suggest sometimes that we are doing less than we might to obtain information and guard their loved ones, and those ardent souls who think that in no circumstances should a missionary leave his work and upbraid us for not insisting that each should stay at his post. I can only plead for a calm spirit and that no judgments be made until all the facts are known.'

It was hard to admit it, but he felt he should add something.

His earlier opinion had been that women and children living on remote mission stations would be safer than in southern Australia but now, in the uncertainty of the hour, he conceded that this idea was 'probably quite erroneous'.

A few days after leaving his mission station at Malalia, Rodger Brown found himself among over two hundred men at the plantation at Iboki, west of the Talasea Peninsula on the north coast of central New Britain. On foot and ferried by the craft of Blue Harris' navy, men had gathered. Rodger was among the very few who were fit; most had been travelling for many weeks and were exhausted, malnourished and ill. McCarthy made use of the mission teleradio and a second teleradio which had been brought around by boat and Rodger worked into the night helping to transmit messages.

That night, as Rodger worked to decode a radio message from Port Moresby, the tension among the men could be felt. For days there had been no sign of enemy aircraft but. . .

'They must know where we are. They've waited till we had a big mob in one place — they'll probably turn up tonight,' they said.

McCarthy's strength, which had supported and pushed so many who might otherwise have given up, was strained to the limits. He waited impatiently as the message was being decoded, but before it was completed he had lost his temper. The instruction was to sail to the mainland of New Guinea, land south of Madang, then walk his men inland over the mountains to Chimbu. Cursing the brainless fools who had sent the message, he demanded that a reply be sent. The officers and men around him were ill with malaria, half-crippled with the pain of tropical ulcers, undernourished, exhausted. With comprehensive epithets he railed against the authorities.

'Have any of them attempted that walk? It must be seventy-five miles over the ranges into the Highlands — those ranges go up to six or seven thousand feet and more, very hard walking — a month on the track, maybe — and what do we do when we finally make it to Chimbu country?'

He was only a little mollified when a further message read, 'Use your own discretion.'

That night, despite their fears, there was still no sign of the enemy, but a decision had been made. Blue Harris and his flotilla would carry all those who were at Iboki across to the Witu island group almost one hundred kilometres to the north. There, Mc-Carthy had commandeered the *Lakatoi*, a Burns Philp ship carrying copra from island plantations. They would dispose of the cargo of copra, despite its high value, because of the danger of fire, add sand ballast, and attempt to sail with the whole party to the Australian coast. Though they knew that there were other men still on New Britain, the time had come to try to get out with those who had gathered, and Harris, Lincoln Bell, Freund and other missionaries with small ships would do their best to locate and help the others.

There was no way of knowing whether they would pass safely through the straits between Japanese-held locations. Civilians, soldiers, a woman and a girl finally went on board the over-crowded inter-island motor vessel ready to make the attempt.

'You're a missionary,' they said to Rodger. 'You can pray us out of this. God is on your side — is he on ours?'

In a few more days it would be Palm Sunday 1942. In the churches, men and women would think of Christ as he entered Jerusalem, surrounded by crowds shouting welcome; soon the applause would turn into betrayal, judgment and death.

On dusty roads through central Australia and on railway tracks carrying people south from north Australia, a party of thirty-five missionary women with their children travelled on. Two of the Fijian women went through childbirth on the way, one at a settlement well north of Alice Springs and another on the train as they passed through Victoria.

Along the road, the wife of the chairman of the north Australian district of the Methodist Overseas Mission, Mrs Violet Kentish, passed through the tiny town of Marrabel without know-ing that the wife of the chairman of the New Guinea district was sheltering there. (Behind the Marrabel Post Office, Daisy Mc-

Arthur tried to keep herself and her sons occupied in their two rooms. It seemed to her that Sydney's Overseas Mission Board had already forgotten her.)

As the women from north Australia paused on their way through Adelaide, Kath Brown was among the church women who came to offer food and cups of tea. She saw their weariness as they continued their flight from an enemy who threatened their northern mission settlements. Could any of their own men in New Guinea be escaping, too? There was no news and none of them could do more than guess.

Somewhere on the Coral Sea, an inter-island motor vessel, the *Lakatoi*, dangerously loaded with passengers and well out of sight of its familiar islands, ploughed on through the sea hoping to make landfall at Cairns.

In the Baining mountains, pastor-teacher Mikael To Bilak calculated the cycle of the moon and remembered what Rodger Brown had once told him about the method of identifying the correct time for Easter. 'Next Sunday,' he told his people, 'we will celebrate Palm Sunday.'

At Bathurst NSW, Jean Poole looked forward to going home soon for the Easter holiday. She was not very happy at her school. The weeks of waiting to hear from John stretched on and on and she needed to be with her own people.

Rodger Brown couldn't believe it. He and the others had been sure that the Australian public must be waiting with keen interest to discover what was behind the long silence from Rabaul. There was little sign of it, however, when the *Lakatoi* moved at last into place beside the wharf in Cairns on the north Queensland coast on Saturday afternoon, 28 March 1942. Bearded, bootless, bone-weary and bedraggled men disembarked, thankful to be back in Australia, but were greeted by officers from the local garrison as if they had no business to turn up in Cairns in such a state.

The local Methodist church, thought Rodger, would be different; they would surely be wanting to hear news of their missing missionary staff. He was soon disappointed. When he located the local church, he discovered a student minister who had little idea of current war news in the Pacific and even less of Methodist missions or missionaries, missing or otherwise. Nor did he seem particularly interested in the stories Rodger was bursting to share. He was busy, finishing his sermon for the next day and choosing hymns; Rodger, who had just lived through several weeks he would never forget, found no common ground.

'I might as well have stayed with you fellows,' he said to the others when he rejoined them later at the hotel where they were accommodated. 'That visit was a dead loss.'

'You missed out here, too,' they assured him. 'They took us all down to the local stores while you were out and fitted us out with new clothes! And most of the blokes have spent the rest of the day getting very drunk and two are in jail for getting into fights — you missed that, too. Anyway, they're putting us on a train south early tomorrow.'

As the party of civilians and soldiers steamed down the east coast it was Palm Sunday. At intervals the train paused at country stations and women from the communities served them tea, sandwiches and cigarettes. The men were quick to correct anyone who called them 'refugees'. 'Not refugees — escapees!' they said proudly. Interest was beginning to grow as people began to see something of the magnitude of the disaster that had befallen Rabaul. Men found themselves telling and re-telling their stories, and some of the stories began to gather embellishments and embroideries along the way.

It didn't feel much like Palm Sunday to Rodger. Certainly there was no chance to join in a church service. The previous Sunday when they had anchored and gone ashore for a brief while at Lutherhafen on an island off the western end of New Britain, McCarthy had recalled them all to the ship urgently because a cloud cover offered some protection as they threaded their way past Japanese bases.

Rodger's plans for a church service while they were ashore had been lost. On the voyage, there had been a number of men who took the chance to talk about God to an impromptu chaplain as they sailed on, crowded, vulnerable, insecure; then, they wanted to ask about prayer and urged him to pray for them.

But now, rattling down the line towards Brisbane, relieved to be nearing home, Christian faith, perhaps useful in an emergency, seemed no longer to apply to them. They were back to the safety of being males in control of their lives. 'See, Padre? We didn't need your prayers after all!'

White sheets and nappies flapped in the Adelaide sunshine as Kath Brown carried another clothes basket full of damp washing out to the line in the back garden. It was Monday, washing day, and Kath and her mother had been up since early, lighting the fire under the copper and starting a full morning of laundry work. Her mother had just boiled the kettle to make the starch for the table linen and offered to make them a cup of tea as soon as the starching was done.

Kath thought she heard the postman's whistle in the street and, as she pegged the last of the garments on the clothes line, she knew that she must face again the possibility of finding the letter box empty. Day after day she had gone to the box, hoping to find a letter from Rodger, even a few words saying where he was, but for over two months there had been nothing.

From the back garden she walked around the house, holding onto hope until she lifted the lid on the letter box. Nothing again. She turned back and chose to walk back into the house through the front door.

It was then that she saw it. Tucked behind the locked flyscreen door was an envelope, a telegram, delivered by a telegraph boy who had not been able to get the attention of the women working in the back of the house. She snatched it up. Afterwards she wondered why it had not occurred to her that it might hold bad news. Tearing it open, she read the message: 'ARRIVED IN AUSTRALIA. BROWN.'

That was all, but it was enough. Clutching the telegram in one hand and trying to open the locked front door with the other, she found herself circling, overcome with delight, too excited to think, whirling round in front of the shut door and then running off the verandah, down the path, round the house, calling, laughing. . .

'He's safe, he's safe — he's in Australia!'

The unfinished washing lay in cooling soapsuds. The kettle went off the boil and the teacups waited empty on the table. An elderly neighbour hurried over to see whether Kath's news was good; her excitement had been observed from across the street. With the baby hastily snatched from his crib, Kath's mother backed out the car and they set off to tell Rodger's parents, with Kath running through her father-in-law's orange orchard, shouting his name and calling the news until she found him.

The bald telegram told them little, but it was enough to give them great joy. Questions remained. Where was he? How long would it take before he was home in Adelaide? Was he unharmed? How had he travelled?

'We'll find out in time,' they said to each other.

'I must let the other women know,' Kath said eagerly. 'If Rodger is back in Australia, the other men may be with him —or at least he'll have news. I must contact Mrs McArthur, and Helen and Nellie and the others. Thank God, he's safe!'

Outside the Methodist church offices in Castlereagh Street, Sydney, Rodger hesitated momentarily. Around him city workers hurried by, well-dressed women out for a day of shopping, servicemen in uniform.

As he had walked through the city from Central railway station, he had been aware of the incongruity of his travel-worn, dirty khaki trousers, unwashed shirt and the tropical solar topee on his head. He felt very disreputable to be presenting himself to the General Secretary of the mission, weary after three days and nights sitting up in trains bringing him and the others 3 000 kilometres from Cairns and heading for a hot bath and a bed. Apart from one night in Cairns, it was more than two weeks since he had slept in a bed or had a washing-day for his clothes. His pockets were empty and he had arrived in a city that was not his home. The only place to go was to report to his mission, to ask to see General Secretary Burton.

At the top of the stairs any anxiety melted. The secretary at her desk caught sight of him and gaped, astonished, as if he were a ghost.

'Rodger Brown!' With incoherent words of welcome, she hurried to tap on the door of the General Secretary. 'A visitor to see you, sir.'

Rodger stood in the open door and saw the face of John Burton as he looked up from his desk. Rarely had he seen such welcome, relief and thankfulness. The senior man stood and held out his hand. 'Thank God!' he said.

There was no doubt about the welcome he received. Rodger was taken from office to office through the Methodist building, exhibited as a trophy, one rescued from disaster by the grace of God. Burton insisted that a photograph be taken of him in his crumpled and grimy clothes, to be published later in the mission magazine over the caption: 'Rev. Rodger S. Brown as he arrived from New Guinea.' He sent a telegram to Kath telling her to expect Rodger to arrive on Saturday and arranged for him to stay at George Brown Missionary College in Haberfield in the meantime.

The question had to be asked, of course, and Burton was quick to ask it. 'What about the other men? What about the four nurses? Have you any news?'

There was so little to offer. Only rumours, sightings by men in flight who often did not know the missionaries well. The four women, he'd been told, were at Vunapope and nursing Japanese and Australian wounded. Of the men on the outlying islands, Simpson, Platten, Oakes and Shelton, he had heard nothing. Trevitt had been taken, with other civilians, from Vunairima, but his informants didn't know Beazley. McArthur, Linggood, Pearson and Poole had been seen at Kalas.

'I tried to send a message to them,' Rodger said, 'but I don't think they can have got it. If they'd chosen to, they could have come through to join me at Nakanai — six days walking through the mountains, where they'd have had a lot of help from our New Guinean pastors, and then about two weeks canoeing along the coast. But after two months they still hadn't come. It was their intention to wait and see, to stay at some place nearby till things settled down. Then they hoped the Japanese might have allowed their mission work to go on.'

Burton noted every detail about his staff with great care. The many demands from family members for news of their people had been a dreadful burden to him, but at least Rodger Brown had some fragments of news to offer them. 'Write everything about this down for me,' he said. 'We'll bring it to the Board of Mission and then publish it in *Missionary Review*. Everyone is desperate for news, however slight.'

When there was nothing left to tell, Rodger caught a suburban bus to take him to the missionary college. He was very tired, indeed. Burton had told him that Jean Shelton, his colleague's wife, was housekeeper at the college while she waited for her husband and was expecting him.

No sooner had he rung the doorbell than Jean Shelton swung the door open. To Rodger, it seemed that she barely saw him but was looking beyond him, seeking another face. 'Where is Herbert?' Her voice was sharp, anxious.

As he stammered that he had no idea, no news of any kind of her husband, she was taken aback.

'Their fleet came past the Duke of Yorks on their way into Rabaul, I was told, so he probably met the Japanese early,' he said.

'How can you say that? You can't possibly know what happened at Ulu when you were hundreds of miles away. . .'

It was true. He didn't really know. How could he, a young and inexperienced missionary, be safely in Sydney and her beloved husband be missing somewhere in New Guinea? Was she angry with him for being there instead of Herbert? He felt somehow guilty that he had come back without Herbert. How was she going to bear to have Rodger around for the few days while he wrote up his report and attended a board meeting?

And yet, the next day, he discovered the kindness of Jean Shelton which went beyond her pain. As Rodger walked through the hall of the college from the bathroom, he collapsed, spilling toothbrush and soap, shaving gear and towel in all directions as he fell. Jean Shelton was quickly beside him. 'Malaria — and exhaustion,' she said.

Though Rodger had little memory of the next days of illness, he was aware that the woman who cared for him did it with great tenderness, perhaps seeing him as a representative of the men who were the friends and colleagues of Herbert, even though her heart must have been crying out for her husband.

Good Friday that year fell on 3 April.

When she left Bathurst for the Easter holiday, Jean Poole felt the first cool edge of coming autumn sharpening the last warm days of summer. Soon winter would come. In the simplicity of Rockdale Methodist Church, sitting with her parents among the subdued worshippers who had come — far more than in normal years — to find some kind of contact with God, she joined in singing the sombre hymns of Good Friday. Many of their neighbours had feared that before Easter their city would have been attacked by the enemy; and now they came to pray, uncertain and anxious for the future.

At the front of the church was the place where she had stood less than two years earlier, bridal in the luxury of lace and tulle and breathing the perfume of her wedding bouquet. There was the place on the carpet runner where John had stood beside her. Where was John now? Their good friend Rodger Brown was in Sydney, she'd heard, though he was sick with malaria, but when John Burton contacted her he'd said that there was no clear news of John.

Jean tried to fix her mind on the words of scripture being read, to focus on the dying Christ, but her eyes kept returning to that space on the carpet runner, the place where John had been. But some words of scripture penetrated to her heart: 'Surely he has borne our griefs and carried our sorrows. . .'

Elsie Wilson, that Easter weekend, waited on the little country railway platform for the train. Across the tracks she could see the cluster of village houses and the little school where she taught. A dark plume of smoke heralded the coming of the train and she happily climbed on board as it paused with a great snort of steam. The train was a lifeline for her, carrying her off for the weekend to a town some twelve kilometres further along the line where the Methodists had made her welcome among them and a local family had opened their home to her whenever she could come. The family where she boarded were very good to her, and often did their best to squeeze her into their already overcrowded car to take her with them to their Lutheran church — but it was always good to get right away for a weekend.

As she travelled, Elsie thought of her mentor and friend Jessie March. The news had passed around the church grapevine that, although the evacuating missionary wives and children from the mission settlements in north Australia had passed through Adelaide a week or so before Easter, Jessie March and two other single women staff, Olive Peake and Margaret Somerville, had stayed with the children on Croker Island. Though Elsie had confidence in Jessie March's strength and good sense, she tried to picture her friend on an island north of Australia, probably on the path of enemy planes flying to bomb Darwin. It was known that Darwin had been bombed a number of times and that much of the population of Darwin had fled south, but Croker Island was small and isolated. The Methodist community had only begun its work with children there four months earlier.

In her prayers that weekend, as she often did, Elsie remembered Jessie March, her fellow-workers and the children in the north, and her friends Dorothy Beale, Jean Christopher, Dora Wilson and Mavis Green in New Britain. It was sometimes hard to live with herself, she was finding, when she thought of other single missionary women who had stayed at their posts. She had been given no choice, but nonetheless she found it hard not to feel guilty that she had come home.

(Though Elsie would not learn this till later, Easter was a significant time for Jessie March and the others on Croker Island. On Good Friday, just after their morning service, a baby was born to the one remaining missionary wife, Mrs Adams. They knew that the mission boat the *Larrpan* would be coming any day to take them to the mainland to begin the adventure of attempting to cross Australia with ninety-five children, and worked hard to prepare food and luggage for such a journey.

On Easter Day at dawn, they gathered in the early grey light around a cross of white-painted stones laid on the ground to show aircraft that they were a mission station. As the children's voices sang 'Christ the Lord is risen today, Hallelujah!' a red sun rose out of the waters of the bay, turning the sea to gold.

That afternoon the mission boat arrived with their chairman Len Kentish and Church Missionary Society missionary Jim Harris, and at twilight they gathered on the beach to sing and pray with the children. Jessie ended her Easter Day with a simple Holy Communion service by lanternlight with the adults of the party. By Tuesday she and the others would have left Croker Island on a trek which would take seven weeks and carry them across the continent.)

It was like no other Easter they had ever known. Though the nuns had been given permission to attend Mass every day, this did not apply to the army and civilian nurses, and a number of them missed the comfort and strength of worshipping God together. To a degree they were confined to the convent and had little contact with the hospital, except through the army nurses, and no contact with the Australian men who were also interned at Vunapope except through messages carried by the New Guinean people.

On Good Friday morning Dora watched as priests, nuns and New Guinean Catholics processed into their cathedral. It was hard not to think wistfully of her parents and friends setting off for church at home in New Lambton and to wonder whether her mother had made hot cross buns this year. There would be no hot cross buns at Vunapope; the mission bakery supplied their bread, but with dwindling stocks of flour every slice of bread was precious and, if it had not been for the New Guineans' kindness in bringing food from time to time, they would have been very short.

Later that morning, accompanied by the other women, Dora walked quietly into the convent chapel. They had been invited to join the nuns for the Stations of the Cross. On one level she was very aware that this was very un-Methodist, alien to her upbringing, the aroma of incense and the succession of painted images of the road to the Cross unfamiliar. Yet in a deeper part of her this was known, rich with memory, part of her spirit.

The women moved thoughtfully and with prayers from one Station to the next, remembering the Christ who was betrayed, unjustly accused, threatened, beaten, mocked, made to carry a heavy cross till he stumbled and fell, crucified. . . Outside the chapel, enemy guards waited. In the mission grounds hastily dug graves hid the corpses of victims of violence. Once again, women waited at the foot of the cross, weeping for the pain of the world and for their own grief, waiting with the One who felt and carried the bitterness of a world in chaos.

An unexpected gift lightened Easter Day. 'Chaplain John May has permission to come up to the convent on Sunday morning to celebrate Holy Communion with us! The priests have offered to loan him a mass-kit, with vestments, communion vessels, wafers and wine and everything,' the army nurses told them.

Early that morning the little chapel was dressed with fresh scented flowers from the gardens and the women waited for the young Anglican chaplain to come. They watched him walking through the garden to them, surprisingly without a guard, and heard young New Guinean children calling greetings, 'Happy Easter, *Masta*, Happy Easter!'

They were all there, Kay Parker and her army nurses, Joyce Oldroyd-Harris and the nurses from Namanula Hospital, Dorothy Maye in from Kavieng, Mrs Bignell, Dorothy, Chris, Dora and Mavis. The chaplain and his prayerbook were Anglican; the chapel and the wafer on their tongues were Roman Catholic; the women receiving the eucharist were Methodist, from other Christian churches or from no church. But for these believers, there was a strong sense that Christ was alive among them, that dawn would follow darkness, that hope could defeat despair.

After the eucharist, the women said: 'Come to breakfast with us, Padre, you are allowed. We haven't any chocolate Easter eggs, but we have a real egg for you!'

The women moved into another room in the convent where a simple breakfast was waiting. Mavis produced the egg, a gift from Akuila To Ngaru, and set about cooking it. When John May realised that in fact there was only one egg, and the seventeen women were breakfasting on tea and bread, he was embarrassed.

'I can't eat this. Surely someone else needs this more than me — can't we share it?' he begged.

Around the table the women laughed at him. 'It's all yours,' they assured him. 'Have you ever tried sharing one egg into eighteen bits? No, this is our Easter morning feast and we are just glad you can be here with us.'

Of the other men in the camp, they knew little. The mission women spoke among themselves of Mr Mac and the others. Had the men been able to celebrate Easter together? Had others joined them? There was no way of knowing.

12

April 1942

'I'M SORRY. I DON'T KNOW where John is. I only wish I did.'

Jean Poole looked at Rodger Brown, sitting there so unhappily in her mother's house. The poor man looks as if he has to apologise for being alive and here, she thought. It was hard for him to come to visit her, without her husband and his friend.

The newspaper for Monday 3 April lay open between them, its headlines shouting in indignation at them. There were articles on the arrival that day of the 41st US Division in Australia, under General Macarthur, the thirteenth bombing raid over Darwin by the Japanese and attacks by the Australians on Japanese-held Lae in New Guinea, but that was not what held their attention.

'Terrific Odds Faced at Rabaul: 1 399 Against Over 17 000', it said, and 'Sheer Cold-blooded Heroism' of the RAAF pilots of the doomed Wirraways and 'Stood Firm in Hour of Terror'. The first reports from eyewitnesses to the fall of Rabaul were at last in print.

Jean had been poring over it when Rodger arrived to see her. Among passages of purple prose, designed to build Australian confidence in their own heroes and to depict the enemy as not only evil but stupid, she found nothing to disguise the fact that the Australians had indeed been defeated in Rabaul. Phrases like 'bloody struggles' and 'incredible privations' did nothing to encourage her, nor did the statement that though numbers of

Australian soldiers were reaching safety in Australia: 'it is possible that full Rabaul casualties, including prisoners, number about 700.'

'Do you think John might still be coming? Could he be with another group like yours?'

'It is possible, but I don't really think so.'

They sat in silence for a while. The small comforts of the teapot and homemade biscuits were reduced to tepid tea leaves and crumbs.

'I can't get the others out of my mind: John, Howard, Mr Mac and the rest — and the New Guinean people. And the nurses, too, Dora and the others. The only good thing about being back,' he said, 'will be getting back to Kath and my baby son. The sooner I can get back to work, the happier I'll be.'

Jean did her best to sound cheerful. It wasn't Rodger's fault that she had not heard from John.

'Kath will be so thankful to have you home,' she said.

The whole world that April seemed to be in transit, no-one in their usual place. In city streets, American servicemen now seemed to outnumber the Australians. In factories and businesses, more and more women were taking the places of men workers. Missionaries like Elsie Wilson who felt they ought to have been at their work in the country of their appointment were reluctantly in their home states.

Rodger Brown was attending a meeting of the Methodist Board of Mission in Sydney instead of being at work in Nakanai. In every neighbourhood, families waited anxiously for news of husbands, fathers, sons and friends who had vanished since the fall of Rabaul, the fall of Singapore, the fall of Timor, Java and Ambon.

Mary Jenkins, fluent speaker of Cantonese and friend of the Chinese community in Rabaul, spent time with one hundred and twenty Chinese women and children suddenly torn from their homes in New Guinea and brought to Sydney. Families from the warmth, simplicity and bustle of tropical Chinatowns were finding a large, shared suburban building with unaccustomed facilities a very cold and strange substitute for home.

Each one asked, 'Where are the rest of our families?'

Daisy McArthur, from a verandah on the edge of the long road leading north, watched military trucks rumble through, carrying ever more men from the security of their farms, businesses and professions on to unknown northern destinations.

In the far north of Australia, another pilgrimage threaded its way from Croker Island. With responsibility for ninety-five children, Jessie March and the other staff travelled by coastal lugger, slept on a northern beach, walked endlessly through grasses higher than their heads and bounced on the back of mission trucks through trackless bush.

As they travelled south, in Sydney John Burton was doing battle with the Ladies' Committee for the children's home where he had expected that the children would be accommodated. The ladies had decided that it was neither appropriate nor convenient for a group of such children to stay within the institution they governed. Burton's outrage and the flurry of letters on the subject in the church press did not persuade them. As the children were being transferred from mission utility trucks onto the back of open army trucks for the long drive through the centre to the railhead at Alice Springs, Burton was grateful to be offered the use of a church youth camp site at Otford, just south of Sydney.

During those April days while the children and women from Croker Island drove south through clouds of choking dust, more Australian men waited in hope on a beach on the south coast of New Britain. Among them was Bill Harry, the young soldier who was a friend of John and Jean Poole.

For over two-and-a-half months they had struggled through unforgiving country, small groups of men searching for food, constantly wet, sick with malaria and dysentery, narrowly avoiding Japanese patrols, encountering antagonistic villagers. Some of their number had turned back to walk along the coast to give themselves up to the Japanese at Kokopo or Rabaul. Others had been able to take advantage of the chance to trek across the island to the north coast to travel out with the *Lakatoi*, but many others were still waiting.

They were bitter over the way the Australian government had

abandoned them, with no attempt at a rescue. Men among them were dying. But now help had come, not from the Australian government, but from officers of the Papuan administration. At last the yacht *Laurabada* came in under cover of darkness, waited in hiding during the day and took off the 128 survivors to carry them to Port Moresby. They were on their way home.

For Dora Wilson and Mavis Green, nothing and nobody was in their proper place. Instead of being at work among New Guinean villagers on a Methodist mission, they were under the guard of Japanese soldiers on a Roman Catholic mission. Instead of being free to improve their fluency in the language of the local people, they were having classes in German, taught by some nuns. Instead of having the leadership and counsel of their chairman, Laurie McArthur, Mr Mac had even less freedom than they did: they had only seen him once since he arrived at Vunapope. From the position of comparative power they had once enjoyed as respected white women in a colonial society, their status as whites had been greatly diminished and they were under the control of an Asian power.

Almost daily, planes flew over Rabaul and dropped lethal bombs on the town and wharf area; the planes were Australian. In the overturning of everything they had once understood, the people offering them care and comfort now were the Catholic nuns, a few humane Japanese guards and New Guinean leaders like Akuila To Ngaru. It truly was as the village people described it: the 'great confusion'.

'He wouldn't come,' Bill Harry said.

Jean Poole knew that he had seen the look of hope on her face when he had arrived on her doorstep, a look that had flared and died too quickly. For that brief moment she had thought, if another group of men has come through from Rabaul, if Bill is here, maybe John. . . Jean watched Bill's face, their young friend whom they had entertained at Kalas on his twenty-first birthday, and saw how hard it was for him to tell her the story.

'I went through Kalas and saw John there late in January. I asked him to join us, like we'd said in those days when the two of us went out into the bush on those long patrols. But he said he couldn't.'

The story was told of Bill's escape. Since the *Laurabada* had come safely to Port Moresby, they had sailed on the *Macdhui* to Australia — 'I came on the *Macdhui*, too,' Jean said. He and a few others who were still fit had asked permission to return to New Britain with radio equipment to do intelligence work, but they were refused. There were still other men on New Britain, hiding, waiting, but those who would still escape would be helped by local men, the timber-getters, patrol officers and missionaries of Lutheran, Anglican and Catholic churches who risked their lives. Some would not return.

The parts of the story he could tell were of the difficulties, the dangers, the physical feats of strength and endurance Bill and others had attempted through those weeks. There were the tragic moments: a close mate for whom he had been best man had been carried to safety aboard the *Laurabada* desperately ill, but had died that night. There were the ridiculous stories: 'I'd been carrying some tinned food for those months — emergency rations. One had no label and, when I opened it in the end to see what I'd been carting around, it turned out to be tropical fruit salad!'

'But what else about John?' Jean asked.

'I think they were expecting the Japs to turn up at any moment and it was almost an anticlimax when it was us. They had all dressed in their whites, as if they were ready for a formal church occasion: John, of course, with Laurie McArthur, Laurie Linggood, Howard Pearson and two Methodist laymen who used to be on the staff, Ron Wayne and Ken Allsop. They gave us our last cup of tea for months. Kalas was empty except for the missionaries — they had sent all the children and teachers home to their own places.'

Jean could see it all in her mind; the little room in her Kalas house with its simple furniture and the pattern of the cups for that farewell cup of tea. She could see John in the white shirt and trousers she had often laundered, and his missionary friends. She could almost hear their voices as they made their decision together.

'John said he couldn't come. He could easily have made it

through the bush with us — we both knew that. But they had decided that they couldn't escape and leave the mission nurses behind in Japanese control. He told me that they all felt they should accept the same fate and do their best to see that the Japanese treated the women with respect. John saw us off Kalas and that was the last time I saw Kalas — or John.'

Jean was silent. Duty — doing the right thing — taking hard decisions because it was a correct choice, not because it was pleasant; it was part of their lives. She had been holding onto the hope that John would one day come home with one of the parties of men escaping from New Britain, perhaps thin and weary, but home. Now that hope died. If John and the others had decided that it was their duty to stay with the nurses, that is what they would do. She would have to wait until the day when the Allies freed Rabaul.

Surely, she thought, that would not be long.

Volcanic dust hung over Rabaul, obscuring the sky. The sound of aircraft throbbed in the air and the women at Vunapope knew that yet another raid would soon strike the wharves and the harbour with its Japanese fleet. The nurses were not sure whether to feel secure from bombs or not. Did the Allied pilots know that many Australians, Dutch and Irish were below them at the mission or in the former army camp at Malaguna not far from the wharves? What of the people of the Chinese community, or the villagers who had a war thrust upon them?

A fearsome explosion reverberated, its waves carrying the sound across Blanche Bay. Black smoke rose in a column above leaping flames as a transport ship loaded with ammunition blew itself to pieces. Later in the day another wave of bombing left fires ablaze along the waterfront, igniting oil tanks and ammunition dumps, shattering buildings, shredding everything in its path. Bombs fell on the military camps and blood stained the orderly army quarters.

That night a Japanese soldier wrote in his diary of the terrifying scenes of the day. Of the prisoners he wrote: 'They must all be very happy after seeing today's bombings. Among them probably are some who clapped their hands. All the members of my unit who heard this talked mutually that it was better to kill them off one after another. . . If we changed places and were in their position, we might also be happy as they. I guess it is natural to be happy. And yet, knowing that the prisoners clap their hands, I presume it is natural to say "Finish them off!"'

He wrote of the sea of flames and the great amounts of blood and noted: 'Everyone's face had forgotten to smile. . . we seemed to have forgotten to work and, without a word, just looked at the scene. It is probably quite regretful to die now without killing one enemy. . .'

The letter was very fragile. The careful hand of a censor had snipped holes along lines of writing leaving a sheet like a lace paper doiley. Daisy lifted it from the envelope with great care. Her hands were shaking so much that she was afraid she would tear it before she had even read it. Laurie's handwriting — she could see the familar and beloved signs of her husband — word from Laurie, at last.

Spreading the cobweb of paper before her, Daisy saw the opening words: 'By kind permission of the Japanese Imperial Army. . .' Laurie was a prisoner. With trembling fingers, she touched the words that her husband had written. Already those words had been read by the censor, his hateful scissors stabbing and slicing into the things that Laurie had wanted to say to her, leaving her with little more than a message of love on a fragment of paper lace.

Yet his name was there, his handwriting. At some time, not very long ago perhaps, he had been alive and sitting with pen in hand. He had touched this paper as he put his thoughts on it, making contact with his wife and little boys. Fragile though it was, this letter was a direct link with the man she loved and she was thankful.

The letter was even more precious in the light of the news of the previous week. For the past two weeks, the Allies had been attacking Rabaul almost daily and descriptions of fires along the harbour front and running figures seen trying to escape from a hail of machine-gun bullets filled her with horror. Her island home was on that stretch of waterfront. The daily papers carried stories of how, despite the government 'doing all possible', there was still no news of troops and civilians missing in Malaya, New Britain and elsewhere.

There had been a hopeful headline, 'Japan Names Prisoners', but when she read the story it proved to be a list of British prisoners after all. In case the public had been tempted to complacency by recent Australian efforts, a message from the authorities in Canberra reminded them that 'Japan is still on Australia's doorstep. . . still regarded a Japanese invasion of this country a real danger.'

Though the letter from Laurie arrived in an army envelope, at first Daisy did not think to question how it had reached her. Later, when she contacted some of the other families — the Pearsons, the Christophers, Nellie Simpson and Essie Linggood — she learned that others had also received a letter from their men or the nurses and she heard the story.

Late in April several mysterious objects fell from Japanese planes over Port Moresby, trailing long white streamers. At first, they were thought to be bombs and, even when soldiers had inspected them more closely, there was a fear that they were booby traps and should be detonated by a disposals squad. Fortunately, someone had the courage to open one and bags of mail addressed to families in Australia were discovered.

To the amazement of the Australian military who had assumed their enemy to be remorselessly evil, the Japanese authorities in Rabaul had allowed and delivered letters from their Australian prisoners. Only then did the men in Port Moresby realise that what they had thought were bombs falling harmlessly into the ocean had in fact been other bags of mail, now lost forever. Some women, including Jean Shelton and Netta Allsop, had to face the fact that there was no letter for them.

When the mission women saw their chairman Laurie McArthur coming to the convent with Laurie Linggood, their first thought was that perhaps the guards were relaxing regulations.

'No,' McArthur said. 'They've let us come over to say good-bye to you. We are being sent in to Rabaul, to the camp there. They are looking for more labourers, so the rumours have it, to work on the wharves loading and unloading ships.'

Rumours percolated through the mission compound almost daily. The latest was that all the Australian men were to leave Vunapope, as groups had already done over the months. The army nurses had come back to the convent with the story that the hospital was to be closed to Australian patients and that Chaplain John May would be leaving with the final party of men.

'Something big is happening, but we don't know what,' the men said. 'There seem to be a lot of ships in the harbour and rumours of a lot of activity. Are they off to Port Moresby — or even Australia?'

Though they had seen so little of their mission leaders during the three months they had been at Vunapope, it was hard to see them go. There had been a sense of security in knowing that Mr Mac and Laurie Linggood were somewhere in the same grounds as they were, and Jean Christopher was glad of rare glimpses of her cousin Howard Pearson.

'Akuila To Ngaru has promised to keep in touch and look after you as well as he can,' Laurie McArthur said. 'We can all be profoundly grateful to have men like him.' He looked anxious. 'I'm not happy to be leaving you young women here, but we have no choice.'

Their visit was short. 'After the war. . .' they said — and then they were gone.

The ceremony, beside the timber memorial cross set in reef-stones and circled by flowers, was solemn. The nurses with the nuns and priests, the New Guinean seminarists and the Catholic bishop had been instructed to come.

'It is to honour your brave Australian dead who died when we invaded Rabaul,' they were told by interpreter Sugai. On the other side of the memorial a Japanese colonel and the other officers in full dress uniform stood with a detachment of soldiers. There were deep bows and speeches in Japanese, Latin prayers and a hymn for the departed by the Catholics, all offered with respect and dignity.

The women watched in silence. It was hard to forget the men who had been lost. Some had been good friends, known through the hospitals or socially. The Methodist women thought of young Australian men who had visited Malabonga or Vunairima. The story of the tortured captain whose grave was somewhere not far away on the border of the mission grounds tugged at their minds. Already weeds and grasses would be disguising that place, but they had not forgotten him.

Some time earlier, the mission cathedral had been used by the Japanese for a private ceremony at which a solemn procession of military had accompanied some twenty small boxes containing the ashes of their own men killed in the invasion: the ashes, much revered, were to be returned to Japan. Young men dead — and who knew how many more were to be destroyed by the conflict of nations?

To the nurses, the ceremony at the memorial cross was a mockery. As they were escorted away from the place, the women shared their feelings of confusion. It was not only the barrier of language which obscured what had happened. 'What was that all about?' they asked each other. 'If they could kill men — sometimes torturing them horribly — why are they honouring them now they're dead?'

'Is it something like placating the dead? Are they afraid of their spirits?'

'Is it political, some sort of showcase to the world to show how well they treat their prisoners?'

'Who knows? You can't understand these people at all.'

Something important was happening. United States pilots, waiting in frustrating inaction in Australia for a threatened attack which failed to materialise grumbled: 'If Nippon is going to strike, she had better hurry up — we plan to be home by Christmas and don't want to leave the work undone.'

Yet Dora and Mavis and the other nurses saw signs of unexplained action from many directions. Early in May, they could see a great many more military and naval vessels passing the mission on their way into Rabaul harbour: warships, cruisers, destroyers and transports. Flights of aircraft left Rabaul every morning and they could only guess where they might be going. Some nuns brought the story that the Japanese colonel who had taken over the bishop's house had ordered it to be cleaned before he vacated it — the bishop was told that they were 'moving out for an unknown destination'. The priests and brothers began to hope that they would be permitted to go back to their own houses.

When Methodist villagers came with their leaf baskets of vegetables and chickens for their mission nurses, they told stories of young village men being recruited to go on the Japanese ships as carriers and labourers. Watching from a distance, the villagers had seen their young men scaling rope netting slung over ships' sides 'like ants crawling up a coconut palm'. Following so soon after the departure of the last Australian men from Vunapope to Rabaul, it seemed that the invaders were preparing for action.

On the waterfront and wharf area in Rabaul, Australian, Chinese, Malay and New Guinean men continued to labour on loading and unloading the ships as they came and went. It was clear to them that there would soon be troop movements out of Rabaul and it was hard to imagine what that might mean for themselves.

Working in the heat of the day to carry cargo, three Methodist ministers were briefly reunited as they passed each other among the processions of labourers. Laurie McArthur and John Poole saw a familiar face among the Chinese men bent under their loads. Rev. Mo Pui Sam called their names and they were able to pass fragments of information. The Chinese community was being kept separate from the rest. A large group of Chinese had moved out to Vunakambi plantation near Vunairima and Mr and Mrs Thomas Mow, the teachers, were part of the leadership there. McArthur and Poole named some of the Methodists known to Mo Pui Sam who were with them at the camp — Linggood, Pearson, Shelton, Beazley, Trevitt, Pearce, Oakes and others.

On 3 May, ships began to move out of the harbour. Where were they going? Port Moresby? The Australian coast, perhaps to Cairns or Townsville — or even Brisbane or Sydney? Till this time, every forward thrust of the Japanese forces had pushed the Allied troops backward, in flight or surrender. They could only hope that this time it would be different.

In the hold of one of the Japanese ships, a Japanese soldier added to the notes in his diary. Only days earlier he had written of the restrained celebrations in Rabaul for the emperor's birthday, men finding it hard to be festive knowing that they were to go into battle any day. He had written: 'It is a great strain to all to think that, among those present, there will probably be some whom we will never meet again.' There had been a ceremony to honour troops who had already died and he had written what he knew could be his last letter home to his family.

Now, below deck somewhere in unknown southern waters of the Coral Sea, he was aware of the whine of attacking aircraft, the reverberations and shudder of distant explosions and knew only complete helplessness. There was no shelter, no escape from whatever fate had for him. He wrote now, knowing that he and his diary could soon be lost forever: 'We, the machine-gun unit, what are we for? We are in the hold just praying that our side won't sustain any damages. . . Our lives are so uncertain that we don't know when we'll die.'

For days over his head the battle waged. American, Australian and Japanese ships, though out of sight of each other, manoeuvering to avoid air attacks while sending out their own aircraft to seek out and destroy their enemy. Walls of water were thrown up by barrages of projectiles and torpedoes tracked through clear blue water towards targets of metal ships. Pilots sent their aircraft to lunge low over vessels, raining machine-gun bullets as they passed. Blots of dark smoke, falling bombs and flashes of flame pocked the bright sky as man strove with man, weapon against weapon. Ships staggered from their wounds and some sank, ablaze and mortally stricken, into the blue-green depths.

When, after some days, the Japanese fleet limped back into Rabaul, the women saw them coming past the mission, ships marked with battle scars and carrying back their wounded and their dead. Though the returning troops told the nuns that they had returned in victory, having sunk many American ships and shot down their planes, only returning because they had run out of water supplies, other stories were told. It seemed that both sides had suffered severe losses, though both claimed the victory and, if nothing else, the Japanese fleet had been deflected from its goal of taking Port Moresby. The mission hospital and some other buildings were filled with wounded men, and Japanese nurses, efficient and hard-working in immaculate white, arrived to care for them.

Within days the Australian newspapers carried stories of the Coral Sea battle and more suggestions that an invasion of Australia was threatened. The people of Port Moresby gave a sigh of relief at their reprieve. Meanwhile, the Japanese diarist, who had escaped death during the battle, was grateful when his ship took him to the quiet and peacefulness of Kavieng. There he recorded the pleasures of life away from conflict — letters home, putting on a picture show and a sports day complete with tug-of-war with the natives, going fishing and getting drunk.

There had been a time, in what now seemed the very distant past, when there had been contact between the mission wives. Then, even if the women were living on isolated mission settlements scattered through the islands, there had been friendships: the normal exchange of recipes, the passing on of baby clothes from one family to another, messages brought by husbands when they came home from synod or district committee meetings, the fun of being together from time to time for celebrations and special occasions. Women living on the same mission station had known each other well.

It was different now. Most of the mission wives were scattered, not among island mission stations but across the states of Australia. The remaining links were tenuous. It was hard to write. Stories sometimes passed among the waiting women of this one or that who had heard something — never anything substantial, nothing to go on, just enough to build precarious houses of straw, to be blown away in the next wind of rumour. Each woman was faced with making her own way, finding her own place in a world where nothing stayed as it had once been. Each one found herself in a society where no-one gave any special sympathy to a woman whose husband was a prisoner of war in a war zone. Twenty thousand Australian families had sons and husbands who were prisoners of the Japanese, quite apart from those who were missing — wounded or killed in action — while serving with one of the forces.

'We're all in the same boat,' women said to each other.

In Western Australia, Beryl Beazley focussed on her pregnancy, the new life growing. Did Syd know that he was going to be a father, she wondered.

Nellie Simpson in Adelaide also waited. This baby must be a boy, she decided — a son for Tom, even if he didn't know about him yet. Nellie had received one of the letters like a child's cutout and there was nothing in it to suggest that he had heard her news of the coming baby. Nellie kept in touch with Helen Pearson and knew that Helen had no news either.

In Sydney, Marion Oakes fought against the expectations of her father. It had never been an easy relationship and now, as an independent married woman, she longed for the freedoms of her own home with Dan instead of the bonds of being a dutiful daughter in her parents' house.

Netta Allsop would have been glad to live with her family. After her daily work with the National Emergency Service, she returned to the empty loneliness of her bed-sitter in the centre of the city, clinging to the thought that on Fridays she could travel out to the warmth of homelife on the fringe of town.

Helen Wayne with two young children had found a place to board in the Blue Mountains and a teaching position nearby and Jean Shelton continued to live and work at George Brown Missionary College.

As autumn chilled towards winter, Mel Trevitt in Tasmania felt ill. She recognised the symptoms of fever, familiar from her years in New Britain. It seemed incongruous to be struck with malaria while the autumn rain streamed down outside and the evenings grew cold. In their New Britain days, she and Jack, careful in their tropical setting, had taken their regular dose of quinine there at

Vunairima and had tucked in their mosquito net around the bed. Even so, they had both suffered from attacks of malaria from time to time, as everyone did. Here in Tasmania, she would probably have to give her own diagnosis to the doctor who might never have encountered it. Though things were working out reasonably well for the daily care of her small son and she was growing in confidence in teaching science subjects at the girls' school, it was obvious to her that she still carried a lot of the islands in her blood.

In her small school in a rural community in South Australia, Elsie Wilson felt very far from news of Rabaul. The people of the community had their own understanding of the pain of war, but they had no links with the world she had known in the islands. There was no-one to whom she could say: What is happening to the schoolgirls and are they safe? Have their villages been attacked or bombed? Where are my colleagues, Mr Mac and Jack and Howard from Vunairima? Or how is Jessie March managing, travelling on that long, long journey across Australia with all those children from the north?

No-one in that district knew Mr Mac, or Jack, or Jessie. No-one could picture the island schoolgirls. For the Lutheran family where she boarded, war brought its own griefs, painful memories of persecution of their German-Australian family during the Great War and costly loyalty in the present conflict. Elsie knew that she could not expect them to enter into her very different experience. Yet she continued to feel somehow apart with other knowledge, other memories, bearing the loss of a calling and the loss of a place.

From the familiar security of a home in Melbourne with her parents and sister, Essie Linggood waited for further news of Laurie. There had been that one letter, tantalising in what it could not say, and the knowledge that he was a prisoner in Rabaul. Yet Essie was grateful for several things. She and the children felt very welcome with her family and her home church had received her back with great love. As well, Essie had joined the newly formed New Guinea Women's Association. Women who had lived in New Britain before the war or whose men had been with the 2/22nd in Rabaul, who shared a common need to discover what was happening to their husbands, had banded together in mutual support. It was important to Essie to meet with other women who understood in a way that the wider community could not.

Of all the mission women, only Kath Brown and Isabel Platten knew where their men were. Rodger had come home safely to Kath and she was profoundly grateful. The church leadership had asked him to work as a travelling deputationist to home churches, telling the story of their mission work, after several weeks' holiday. They hoped that this would leave him free to go back to New Britain as soon as it was possible. Kath's own days were happily filled with child care, household work, church activities, tennis and her many handcrafts, but Rodger without a full workload was an unsettled and unsatisfied man. Knowing that almost all his colleagues were prisoners made him even less able to rest and 'waste time'. She knew that she'd be glad to see him back at work again.

As for Jean Poole, she had come to a decision. From early in the school year she had been unhappy at the girls' school in Bathurst. The patterns and attitudes of a private school for the daughters of privilege were in such contrast to the little thatched bush school for the sons of mountain villagers at Kalas that it made her very unhappy. At a time when she was most in need of spiritual comfort, the school demanded that she be present at Evensong as a duty, but refused her the eucharist because she was not an Anglican. Lonely for John, disturbed by the students whose interests and priorities had no connection with her own and, excluded from holy communion, she knew that she did not belong. As a married woman, she had forfeited her right to teach at a school of the NSW Education Department — or so she had thought till a few weeks ago.

Then she saw that in April, due to the great reduction in numbers of male teachers available because of their war service, the Education Department was re-employing retired teachers — and married women! Only as temporary staff, mind you, but still.

John was a prisoner of the Japanese, as Bill Harry and Rodger Brown had expected. She had his first letter from capitivity. She might have to support herself for quite some time, till John was free. Jean knew that she was not free to move into any other kind of work — teaching was 'a restricted occupation' — though the army was calling for 1 000 women recruits and all kinds of war work were opening doors to women through the manpower program. Still, she knew that she was a good teacher. Without regret, she applied for a position with the Education Department and waited for news.

A bright moon lit the camp. Against the starred curtain of night sky the silhouettes of volcanoes — the Mother, the North and South Daughters and Tavurvur — stood as a strong backdrop with a column of volcanic dust rising high into the puffs of cloud. In the tents and huts of the internment camp, over a thousand Australian men slept. Some of them had been in custody there since the first days of the invasion while others had recently come in from Vunapope. A number of men were underweight and ill; they had been among those who had attempted to escape through the mountains but had been captured or had been forced to give themselves up, coming into the camp after weeks or months on the run.

One of the Methodist mission men propped himself up on one elbow and listened. Through the night noises of the snores and breathings of many sleeping men he thought he could hear the sound of a distant aircraft. He hoped he was wrong. Too often there had been the sudden wail of an air-raid siren and the scattering of men, grumbling on their way to slit-trenches. Now he was tired and his shoulders and back were aching from the unaccustomed loads he had been carrying on the wharves, weighty boxes and bags of cargo for the Japanese; in the New Britain he had known, white men never carried heavy cargo.

A shaft of moonlight fell across sleeping faces. Nearby were his close friends and colleagues, the men with whom he had worked for years as fellow-missionaries. Other men had become close friends over recent months, men like the Anglican chaplain, Padre John May, the Salvation Army bandsmen with their leader Arthur Gullidge, as well as Australian missionaries with the Roman Catholic and Seventh Day Adventist missions.

In these strange circumstances they were finding common

ground in their Christian faith. Somewhere in the shadows were some of the most senior of the captured military officers in Rabaul, as well as youths who had come to Rabaul with the militia. These boys had been too young to be sent beyond the bounds of Australia with the regular army, but had been sent to the supposed safety of an Australian territory. Men who had been among the most influential of government officers in the country before the war tried to sleep. Plantation managers, shop assistants and mechanics from large and small communities in the islands had uneasy dreams. Many were strangers, while others had become good friends through the Methodist church services and after-church suppers in the homes of members.

The sound of aircraft deepened and the missionary sat up. 'Sounds like a raid coming,' he murmured as he nudged his companions. 'Are you coming out to the slit-trenches?'

A few muttered that they were half asleep and they'd risk it. As air raids became commonplace, some had become casual about them. Others stumbled to their feet and began to stream out towards the greater safety of the slit-trenches.

'It's a real bomber's moon tonight,' they said as they squatted together, slapping mosquitoes and watching the high dark objects that moved against the clouds overhead.

'Our Aussie blokes up there always go for the wharves, not our camp,' someone said. 'They know better than that.'

As the whine of falling bombs masked their voices, men hoped that the Allied aircrew were having an accurate night of work. From the area of the wharves and from close at hand they could hear detonations and explosions, and see bursts of earth flinging up into the air. Flames and the wheeling of searchlights il-luminated the sky. At last the planes were gone and men clambered back out of the trenches to inspect the damage.

There was a shout of rage. No-one had been injured, but stray shards of shrapnel had left damage behind in the internment camp.

'Look at this! The handle has been knocked off this stew pot with tomorrow's breakfast in it. That's a bit close for comfort!'

13

May 1942

THE CIRCLE OF THE DECK tennis quoit whirled through the air towards her, and Mavis caught it and tossed it back. Beyond the high net, two nuns stretched to try to reach it, but it fell safely to the grass. There was a burst of applause from the cluster of on-lookers. 'You've won! Good game, Mavis. Well done, Mrs Bignell.'

With her partner, Mrs Bignell, who had played for many years in colonial tennis matches on her family plantation in the Solomon Islands, Mavis walked from the court. Most of the nuns and the nurses were fit, younger women who enjoyed their sport.

'There is a little prize for the winners of the tournament,' Sister Columba said and handed Mavis a dainty handkerchief, edged with fine tatting. 'I did the tatted border in my free time.'

Free time. . . That was one of the very strange things about life at Vunapope. If it had not been for the enemy guards, Mavis decided, a visitor might think they were all on holiday. For women who had spent years in the discipline and hard work of nursing training in major hospitals, then come to the islands as medical staff for New Guinean and white communities, it was very unusual to have no work to do. There were no clinics, no patrol work, no daily admissions of patients or ward rounds, no injections for cases of yaws, no medications to prepare, no babies to deliver.

Long days were filled with household tasks for the women,

conversation, some sewing. Dora Wilson had been working on her skills with the Kuanua language, studying her Kuanua Bible and hymn book, and Mavis Green had been collecting recipes from the nuns. A few nuns had been keeping diaries of the events of the past few months. The bishop had encouraged his large community of priests, brothers and nuns to keep themselves well occupied; priests studied theology, languages and philosophy together, Brothers worked on building maintenance and some nuns from the convent of the community from Europe were teaching French and German to the other women.

Yet behind the groups of women busy with their fancywork or lists of French verbs were enemy guards. Any suggestion of holiday freedom was only a facade. One day the nurses and nuns were instructed to sit among the flowers and play a game of cards, while a Japanese photographer moved among them with his camera.

'Propaganda, of course,' the women muttered to each other. 'We'll probably feature in a Jap newspaper somewhere as an example of the very civilised way we internees are being treated.' It was the lesser evil of house arrest rather than the brutality of barbed wire, but even so they were forbidden to leave, forbidden to work in the normal way and cut off from their families.

Dorothy Beale, the senior Methodist nurse, talked with her colleagues, Chris, Dora and Mavis, at a time when there was no risk of being overheard. 'Akuila To Ngaru sent a message the last time he brought some vegetables and a chicken.' The village Christians had continued to provide extra food from their gardens every week, brought in secret and passed over the back fence. 'He says that they will help us escape and hide us in the bush.'

For a hairsbreadth of time, Mavis considered this route to freedom.

'Of course, I said no.'

Of course. There were too many reasons why it could never be. They all knew that. Chaplain May had asked them not to try it, or he could forfeit his life. The risks of attempting an escape were too great and they were probably far safer in the uneasy security of the mission. The dangers to their New Guinean friends if they were captured were too great to be borne. And there were already rumours that at least one Catholic priest at an outpost had met his end for helping Australian escapees.

'We couldn't try it — for everyone's sake,' Dorothy said. 'But how brave of Akuila to even offer it.'

Mavis put the thought of escape away. They would just have to wait. But wait for what? The frustrations of inaction and constant enemy supervision were gnawing away at her. As she folded away the handkerchief with its delicate tatted edge, she felt sure that things could not go on like this forever. But what would change?

The sound of the bus stopping just beyond the hedge at George Brown College in Sydney brought Jean Shelton to the front door.

'They're here,' she called to the other staff, and went out to meet the load of children who had at last arrived from Croker Island. They had been on the track from the far north for seven weeks and the bus ride from Central railway station had been the final stage of a journey which had traversed the nation by mission lugger and utility truck, on foot, in open army trucks, in railway cattle trucks and finally in passenger trains from Adelaide and on through Melbourne to Sydney.

About twenty-five of the older children stumbled down the steps of the bus onto the footpath, clutching little bundles of belongings and looking confused and weary. It was eight years since she had met an Aboriginal person, but Jean Shelton had a strong sense of recognition. Ten years ago she and Herbert had begun their missionary lives in Darwin among people like these. Now she led them through the gate and up the curving gravelled path to the wide front door of the College. Exhausted, touslehaired, grimy with travel, displaced, the children stepped into the unfamiliarity of the high-ceilinged Federation house.

It was an odd feeling, Jean Shelton decided, to be running hot baths and handing towels for these so-familiar children in enormous bathrooms designed for an earlier generation of the rich. Very different parts of her life were unexpectedly mingling. It was as if actors from one well-known play had accidently strayed on stage in a different play.

The college building was familiar; she and Herbert had studied here as new missionaries ten years earlier and it had been shelter for her and her children for several months now. Aboriginal children like these had made friends with her in the years when she and Herbert had lived in their corrugated iron house in Darwin, when she and Herbert were newly married. Seventy-five other children had gone on to their future home at Otford, south of the city, and they said that Jessie March was with them. Jessie had been there with her and Herbert in New Britain that day when her daughter was born, just before the volcano erupted. In every memory — Sydney, north Australia, New Britain — Herbert was always there.

Where was Herbert? Other men had come back, even though it had been hard and dangerous. Even these children had come, though several former colleagues from the north were still somewhere in Arnhem Land and perhaps at risk. Some other mission wives and wives of civilians from Rabaul had received scraps of censored letters saying their husbands were in the hands of the Japanese, but she had received nothing.

Jean Shelton moved around the dining tables, helping the exhausted and disorientated children with their meal. She was glad they had arrived safely. But. . . her own Herbert had not come. Later, her little girl found her huddled in the window seat of their room, staring blindly out at the garden through silent tears.

That morning in late May, Laurie McArthur woke to the sticky heat of another day of captivity in Rabaul. It was hard to sleep. It wasn't only the heat, the restless tossing with sweat-dampened skin or the insistence of hungry mosquitoes. He had been used to that for years. Nor was it the early hour when the camp came to life. Early mornings had always been the best time to work, before the full glare of the sun gathered strength.

If only, he thought, he could be waking to this same tropical heat, in this same town, with Daisy beside him and his little sons in the next room. If only he could be starting a day of his own work, visiting, planning, writing, discussing — and coming home for lunch with Daisy.

It was impossible. His New Guinean friends were out of reach beyond the high fence of the internment camp. Most of the other Methodist male staff, as well as two Australian Catholic missionaries and some Seventh Day Adventist pastors, were with him in captivity and none of them was free to do the work he believed God had called him to do. Perhaps today he might be chosen to work on the wharves, but more likely another day would drag by with meaningless, trivial tasks and time-filling occupations. Months had gone by and there was no word from Daisy and the children. Were they safe and well? Where were they living? How was she managing financially? The silence hurt.

As he lined up for a plate of breakfast, some of the men spoke of the letter which they had been permitted to write recently. 'The Japs probably won't send the letters off, anyway,' they said. 'And if they do, our families should be able to see through them. It won't take them long to see that we were writing what we were told — not our usual style at all.'

Laurie McArthur recalled the stilted phrases, the limited expression allowed, the dictated wording: 'By Japan winning the war, I hope extraordinarily that the war will come to an end and that peace will come again to us all.' There were other things that he longed to write to Daisy, other questions that he needed to ask, but no real communication was possible.

The attention of the line of men was taken by a commotion at the entry gate to the camp. Heralded by the shouts of sentries, a truck entered and four Australian men who had not been seen for three months climbed down. The four men had been taken to work for the Japanese to maintain the town's commercial freezer and had been kept in semi-isolation in the township area. The news passed quickly around the camp that something was happening; the newcomers said that they'd been told that the Japanese army was handing over responsibility for the prisoners to the navy and that the army would soon be moving out somewhere.

'They want to see how many of us they've got — a general muster, we think,' they suggested.

For a short time, the visitors moved among their civilian mates, glad for the chance to meet again with the men who had made up much of the European network of government officials, plantation managers, health and education workers, business men, technicians and mission workers. They seemed surprised to see how many civilians were still in Rabaul, about two hundred of them, and there was a lot of discussion about what might have happened to the men who had tried to escape overland. Had they made it safely? No-one knew.

Once again the sorry story of the last days of Rabaul before the invasion was told, with recriminations against the Australian government, the military leadership ('With no organised line of retreat, the troops were running around like hairy goats!' accused one) and the Administration in Rabaul who had not insisted on sending out the remaining civilians before it was too late, whether or not Canberra gave them permission. Many of the prisoners felt deeply betrayed, abandoned to their fate by their government who left over a thousand young soldiers and their officers to survive if they could and completely ignored an entire community of Australian civilian men. (The difficulties of the Chinese and Malay communities, whose women and children had been offered no way out, or the native New Guineans or people of mixed race, did not loom so large in their thinking; whites had always taken a superior role in Rabaul society and they found it hard to see the lordly white men so demeaned.)

'You wouldn't recognise the place,' the visitors said. None of the Australians had seen more than, at most, the road from the camp to the wharves over the past months. 'Sentry boxes on every corner, a few bomb craters and smashed houses from raids, every vacant bit of land filled with vehicles and temporary houses — and you should see your own houses! Places where two or three people used to live seem to have up to thirty or forty soldiers camped in them.'

'And have you seen the harbour? There is everything from landing barges to transports crowded out there, anchored from close in shore to beyond Vulcan volcano. Where are our air force boys? What a target!'

'They've asked us quite a few times if we'd like to go to Japan — have they asked you, too?'

As the heat of the sun increased, the men of the camp were ordered to fall in for a general muster. For hours, Laurie McArthur stood with a group of fellow missionaries as a party of Japanese officers moved through the ranks. Line after line of men waited their turn, hundreds of Australians resentful at their captivity, the sun beating on their heads and sweat trickling under shirts. Servicemen and their officers stood in their units — AIF, militia, New Guinea Volunteer Rifles and other units. Civilians waited restlessly, offended at the impotence of their own situation.

When at last the recording officers arrived among the lines of civilians, they began with the most senior of the men, Harold Page the Deputy Administrator, and the group of heads of departments, with judges, lawyers and doctors, most of them men in their forties and fifties with years of experience of the Territory. McArthur watched the slow progress as the list-making proceeded, man by man, checking existing lists and adding details of the cross-section of the colonial community. Men murmured complaints as they waited. A sick man, brought from the hospital tent wrapped in a blanket, swayed uncertainly then collapsed. The count went on.

'How long is this going to take?' someone muttered. 'We'll all be keeling over soon in this heat.'

The recording team stood at last before their group. It was not a simple task. The details of each man — name, age, nationality, occupation and place of work — were being recorded and each item had to pass through the interpreter to the Japanese scribe who marked it in Katakana characters.

A group of missionaries was recorded together, Methodists, Catholics and Seventh Day Adventists clustered as Australian internees in a way which blurred the old rivalries of denominational difference.

'Number 140, Pearce, Ernest Wilfred, age 41. . . Beazley, Sydney Unwin, age 32 . . . Trevitt, Jack William, age 28. . .' then Father McCullagh and Brother Brennan, with Pastor Abbott and T.V. Collett of the Adventist church. 'Number 146, Pearson, Howard James, age 28. . . '

There was hesitation over the next name and the interpreter

tried several times to pronounce it for the scribe. Friends glanced at Laurie Linggood. Would 'number 147, age 40' be recorded as Langwood or Limgood or something else again, and what had they made of the placename 'Raluana'?

Laurie McArthur stood tall as the smaller men of the Japanese army paused before him. How would he be identified? By a number and the simplistic summary of age and occupation. He knew that he was more than that. He was Daisy's husband, Malcolm and Glenn's father, graduate, educationalist, minister of the church, chairman of the district, friend of the New Guinean, Chinese and Malay communities. Today, none of that would be counted beside his name.

'Number 148, McArthur, Laurence Archie, age 37. Australian. Missionary Rabaul Methodist Church.'

Beside him, John Poole ('Age 28. Australian') prepared to answer to his name. The next group stirred and grumbled, thirty Scandinavian seamen who had survived the bombing of the copra ship *Herstein* in the harbour, the ill-fated ship which might have taken all these civilians away to safety. It was too late now. Too late for the seamen who were outraged to find themselves in captivity (the Japanese scribe added an annotation beside their names: 'These persons adopted hostile attitude at Rabaul') and too late for the civilians.

In other rows of men, the name of Herbert Shelton was recorded next to his friend, Guy Allen the planter from Ulu, and Dan Oakes' and Tom Simpson's names were with the other men from Kavieng and New Hanover. His good friends, the Methodist laymen Ken Allsop and Ron Wayne, had been recorded with others in their line of work. Though there had been groups of men coming into the camp as recently as the Kavieng lot on 11 May, there was no sign of the other ministers, Rodger Brown or Gil Platten. Perhaps, he hoped, they had escaped.

Nor did anyone know what had happened to the former mission plantation manager, Bill Huntley. His Chinese colleagues Mr and Mrs Mow and the Rev. Mo Pui Sam were, he supposed, with the Chinese community; from time to time some of the younger Chinese came to the fence of the camp and tossed their Australian friends some useful small items salvaged from family stores.

When, finally, the last man had been named and checked against the roll, the order was given to dismiss. Hot, weary and frustrated, men moved off into the shade. Mission staff congregated to compare notes. 'So what happens now?' they asked.

Just over a week later, on 31 May 1942, Marion Oakes left her parents' house in Lindfield NSW to go to her work at a nursing home. It was Sunday afternoon and she was due to begin night duty. Back at the house, her young sons George and Parker were trying to restrict themselves to the quiet things approved by their grandfather as fitting for the peace of a Sunday in the parsonage. Her sister Joy would keep an eye on them and make sure they did not get into trouble.

That afternoon the sun sank towards the purple-blue rim of the Blue Mountains on the west of the wide spread of the city of Sydney. Endless red-roofed houses lay in a mosaic along the lines of highways and suburban streets, the glow of sunset warming russet tiles. Late autumn was blending into the coolness of winter and on the waterways and harbour of Sydney there were few pleasure craft.

The Manly ferry sliced through pearl-grey watered silk as it carried families home after a Sunday outing and seagulls swooped over fishermen on peaceful harbour jetties. The last reaching rays of sunshine set the sheltered waters of the harbour glittering where it encircled incongruous signs of war — four military cruisers, a pair of armed merchant cruisers, destroyers, minesweepers and corvettes. Long shadows dragged from the tall city buildings shaded streets full of men in uniform, Australians and Americans, and darkening shadows made boarded-up shop windows and walls of sandbags seem more sinister.

And yet, for the servicemen and their girlfriends looking for an evening meal in the city or for Marion Oakes on her way to work, it was hard to take any of it seriously.

'The war isn't here,' Marion thought bitterly. 'The war is real in New Britain and New Ireland — the enemy is real to my Dan, wherever he is, and Dan ought to be here!'

That night the sound of a great explosion on the harbour shook houses around the foreshore. Sirens wailed and long stabbing fingers of searchlights pointed into the night sky, groping for a malign unknown. Marion heard the rumours. Someone at the nursing home had been listening to the wireless — a Japanese attack; no, just a military exercise; Sydney was being bombed; no, that was ridiculous. . . Something was happening, though no-one seemed to know what it was, and she worried for her sons.

In the morning, when at last she was free to come off duty and return home, the boys were full of their story.

'Auntie Joy put a table in the hall in the middle of the house, and made us get under, in our pyjamas, with blankets over us!' they told her. 'We were supposed to be asleep in bed but we heard air-raid sirens. It was really dark with black paper on all the windows, so we couldn't even see any moonlight — we sneaked out to the lounge room and Grandfather and Grandma and Auntie were listening to the wireless and talking about an enemy attack. That's when Auntie made us get under the table.'

Within a few days, the people of Sydney learned what had happened that night of the full moon. Three Japanese midget submarines had left their mothership submarine some forty miles offshore from Sydney harbour and had negotiated an entry into the harbour without being detected. Their intention was to destroy as much Allied shipping in the crowded harbour as they could. One had become trapped in a harbour boom net and the two-man crew finally chose to self-destruct. One sent torpedoes towards the cruiser USS *Chicago*, but instead struck and sank a ferry HMAS *Kuttabul*, being used as a dormitory ship; nineteen men died in their bunks. The crews of the tiny submarines died that night, somewhere among the storm of machine-guns, pompom shells, tracer bullets and depth charges.

The complacency of a Sydney which had begun to think of itself as far from the realities of war, merely play-acting through the motions of warfare, was much shaken. Marion Oakes and the children in the suburbs of Sydney, and Dan Oakes in a prison camp in Rabaul, were each caught up in the web of conflict.

Escape from entanglement would not be easy.

14

1 June–1 July 1942

CRAWLING ACROSS THE CHILL of the bedroom floor with her big scissors, Jean Poole thought regretfully of the wardrobe of winter clothes she had so blithely given away. It was not even two years since she and John had been married. She had thought at the time that it would be at least three years before she needed a warm coat again. A mistake, she now realised.

'If I'd known. . .'

But there was no way in which she could have foreseen that war in the Pacific would have engulfed her new home, her marriage to John and her new life in the tropics. The bride Jean, happily distributing woolly jumpers and her warm dressing gown, had not pictured herself shivering in a Bathurst winter, alone. She smoothed out the blanket on the floor. The blanket would have to be sacrificed. The cold weather had begun to bite at the same time as the government announcement that clothing, shoes, hats and gloves, linen, dress materials and blankets were soon to be rationed, and supplies would be immediately reduced.

When she went shopping, the shops were crowded with anxious people trying to buy up as much of the limited stock as possible and she had not been able to buy all the warm clothes she needed. Prime Minister Curtin had said, 'The darning needle is a weapon of war,' but that assumed one had a garment to be darned.

The scissors sliced through the warm wool of the blanket, steering a path through the maze of paper pattern pieces and the barbed wire fence of pins. Fragments of wool fell away as Jean lifted the pieces to pin them into position.

As she worked, she thought of John. It was two months since the censored letter had come, as slashed about as the ravaged remains of the blanket. Since then, nothing. He must be somewhere in Rabaul, she thought. At least he wouldn't be cold. But she wanted to be with him, to ask what he thought of her latest plan. Would he think it was a good idea to apply for a teaching position with the Education Department? Perhaps he would not have heard that there had just been a call for another 318 000 extra manpower workers, married and single women, retired men, anyone who was able to shoulder a job. She had written to tell him that she had just been appointed to Kiama on the south coast of NSW, to move there very soon. Had he received her letter? She had no choice but to act independently, as she had done in the days before she had become John Poole's wife.

There was a knock on the door and a member of the school staff appeared.

'Do you want a hot cup of tea to warm you up? There is tea and hot toast on in the dining room. By the way, what was the name of that ship you said you came back on, from New Guinea? *Macdhui*? They just said on the news that the *Macdhui* was bombed by the Japs, in Port Moresby. . .'

The pieces of blanket material bunched in tightened fingers. She could picture it. The *Macdhui*, so familiar to people travelling to the islands. She could see the cabin where she had lain, miserably seasick, the dining room where Kath Brown and the others had eaten Christmas dinner, the decks where women and children had walked on their way home to Australia, the strings of baby nappies slung wherever the overcrowded women could hang them. She could hear the voices talking: 'What if we are attacked on the way south? What if the ship sinks?' She could still feel the grip of the railing where she had stood as the *Macdhui* moved slowly away from the wharf that night when she waved goodbye to John.

With the ears of imagination, she heard the whine of a bomb plunging downward. Against the backdrop of Port Moresby hillsides, she saw the *Macdhui*, now a troopship at anchor, and shuddered as a bomb tore into its heart. Flames were leaping, devouring, a funeral pyre for soldiers on board, and slowly the ship slipped sideways, its back broken, to settle at last on the shallow floor of the bay.

When, some time later, she saw a newsreel of the bombing of the *Macdhui*, she could not help the rapid pounding of her heart as she watched. She had known just how it would be.

The women in captivity at Vunapope heard no news of the *Macdhui*. Any news at all was mostly rumour. But, as it happened, within two days of the sinking of the troopship the Methodist women had a visitor. They had seen none of their colleagues since the last of the Australian men were taken from Vunapope to the internment camp at Malaguna near Rabaul at the end of April and now it was 20 June. Ron Wayne, former Methodist missionary and more recently court interpreter, had been brought from the internment camp with a party of Japanese, to act as interpreter in a vegetable-buying expedition.

'The last time we saw you was on Christmas Day, with Mr Mac and the others at Raluana!' That was Mavis and Dora. Dorothy and Chris spoke of the New Year's Day picnic and high jinks in a canoe at Vunairima.

None of them knew this man very well, as he and his family lived in town and they had all lived on outlying mission stations, but even so Ron Wayne was part of the mission family.

'What's happening? Are all our people safe? Who has come into the camp at Malaguna?' There were so many things they wanted to know.

'All our men are in,' he told them, 'except Mr Platten and Rodger Brown. They've been bringing in groups of men collected from all the plantations; patrol officers, timber-getters and the rest. Some soldiers had tried to escape, but ended up being caught and brought in.'

There was little time to talk before he was taken to help

interpret between Japanese and villagers. Before he left, Dora and Mavis quickly gathered a few useful things and made up parcels. 'Please take these back to Mr Mac and anyone else — there are needles and thread, soap, a few first aid things. You'll have to sew on your own buttons!'

As they watched him go, they could not help wondering when they would have another chance to send a gift or a message to the men who were like their brothers.

It was still dark the next morning when Dora woke to the sound of tramping feet. Men were marching heavily around the verandah downstairs. Women sat up, whispering and staring into the shadows, until shouted orders demanded that all the women come down immediately.

Half-asleep, Dora pulled some clothes around her and stumbled down the stairs. Nuns and nurses mingled in confusion. Men were shouting, 'Hurry! Faster!' and they heard the sound of bayonets being clicked into position. As they came out onto the lawns, distant sounds suggested that others were also being called out at that early hour. Dora was lined up with the other nurses. Dutch and Australian nuns formed a squad nearby.

Moving shadows began to become clearer. Dora realised that they were surrounded by an armed guard with a group of Japanese officers in front of them. With the officers were other men carrying something which was indistinct at first. A lantern was moved into position and Dora felt the pulse of fear quicken into a rapid drumbeat in her ears. The dark shapes were ropes and spades. . .

A search was to take place immediately, they were told. Someone, perhaps several people, were suspected of hiding a radio transmitter and making contact with the Allied enemies. A spy must be in the camp, communicating by forbidden letters, or signals, to warn and advise the enemy. When any incriminating material was discovered, there would be punishment.

'The bishop is suspected of sending out messages and has been taken away for interrogation by the *Kempei-tai*.'

There was a gasp of horror from the nuns and murmurs of outrage.

'Silence! While we search the houses, you will not move or speak. After the search, you will be interrogated one by one. Disobedience will be severely punished.'

Leaving the women behind their barricade of armed men, officers and soldiers disappeared into the convent.

Little by little the darkness lifted. The ropes and spades were still there. Standing still, trying not to fidget, Dora stared at the spades, then tried to tear her gaze away. It was not so long ago that they had watched as New Guinean men were marched past them, led by soldiers with bayonets and men carrying spades and ropes; later some of the villagers had told them, whispering through the fence, 'They were taken to the mission cemetery, made to dig their own graves, and bound. . .'

She had heard the final shots. Perhaps, she thought, if they find anything, this will be the end for us.

If they find anything. What might they find? She did not know of any radio transmitters, but maybe one was hidden somewhere on the property, among the seventy or more buildings of the Catholic mission. They might find some incriminating diaries; she knew that a couple of nuns had been recording what they had observed of Japanese ships leaving Rabaul and returning, battered, or not returning at all. And some funny cartoons. Would they be offended by the drawing of the diminutive interpreter Sugai giving orders to the tall nurses, like herself and Captain Kay Parker, who towered over him? Might they think that her notes in Kuanua language were some mischievous coded message?

The sun climbed up in the sky, lighting the anxious faces of the women and reflecting off the faces of spades. It became hotter and hotter, but still they waited. Their guards took turns to leave them to have breakfast, but Dora could only dream of a glass of water or a slice of pawpaw to moisten her dry mouth. She was weary of standing so still in the sun, very stiff, very sunburned, very thirsty. The hours went by.

A sudden order came to the Mother Superior to go to help the search. Dora saw the wisdom of the older woman as she made the suggestion that it would speed the search if each woman collected her own papers and spread them out for inspection on the grass. Released from the prison of enforced stillness, each woman took the opportunity to ease tense muscles — and to attempt to deal with incriminating material.

Lined up once more, the women waited with their books, letters and papers spread. Mother Superior was instructed to examine the person of each woman, which she did with dexterity and discretion. Dora noticed one nun kneeling in an attitude of submission and piety, her veiled head bowed and voluminous habit draped around her. Others waited nervously as the drawing of Sugai was frowned upon and other papers were also taken away to be examined. At last, at about ten o'clock in the morning, it seemed that the ordeal was over. No radios had been found. The women, though still under guard, were free to go.

'I was sure that they were going to make us dig our own graves,' Mavis said later.

'So was I.'

An Australian nun whispered: 'Me, too. Mother has made me burn it in the kitchen fire now, but out there I wasn't just on my knees praying — I was kneeling on my diary!'

It was very early on Sunday morning, 22 June 1942, one day after the unsuccessful search for radios at Vunapope. In the internment camp at Malaguna, shouted orders broke through sleep.

Laurie McArthur groaned. 'What's the matter this time?'

'I think they said we're moving out.'

'Who? Where?'

'Civilians and Other Ranks. They didn't say where. They've been telling us about the beauties of Japan, but who knows?'

'Why at this hour on a Sunday morning, then? They could have waited till sunrise.'

By the time the sun had exploded up from beyond the distant rim of New Ireland mountains, a brilliant fanfare of colours trumpeting a rose, amethyst and violet glory across sky and harbour, the men had put together their things ready to travel. The rumour had it that they were to go on board a ship which was lying at the wharf, but the wharf was not visible from the camp and they could only guess.

It seemed a very strange Sunday morning. On other Sundays in the camp, there had always been a church service. With eight Methodist ministers and other lay preachers, the young Anglican chaplain John May, the Adventist pastor and the gifts and music of almost the entire band of Salvation Army musicians from the 2/22nd (one of them had escaped), there was always a service of worship for Protestants. Many of the young soldiers had been drawn to the Methodist church and the hospitality of mission homes in the months before the invasion. Others, who would not have called themselves religious, had found comfort and hope in the times of prayer since their capture, and Chaplain May was a young man whose personality and faith drew other young men to think about God.

Father McCullagh had brought a Mass-kit from Vunapope when he was interned, and the bishop had been permitted to send him altar-wine and hosts; Catholic soldiers and civilians valued the chance to receive Mass. Today, however, there would be no Mass celebrated, no morning prayer, no Methodist hymns or Salvation Army choir.

'What about the officers? What's happening to them? Won't they be with us?' No-one knew.

As the lines of over eight hundred soldiers and two hundred civilians passed slowly by the hut where sixty officers were quartered, McArthur and his group heard calls. Among officers' heads crowded at windows was the face of Chaplain John May.

'They've locked us in. Whatever is going on, they must have other plans for us.'

'We're off for a holiday — they say that a sea voyage is good for the health!'

Some of the missionary men began to joke among themselves, quick wits sparring with words, pressing back the encroaching edges of fear with humour and laughter.

The chaplain signalled urgently for some men to come as close as they dared. 'Tell the others — in the Prayer Book the scripture marked for the 22nd Day is part of Psalm 107. I'll read it to you, if there is time before they move you on, but pass it on — I think it will help.'

His clear voice began to read, 'Let the redeemed of the Lord say so, whom he hath redeemed from the hand of the enemy. . .' and boys from the anti-aircraft unit remembered standing with him on the high windy hillside above Rabaul some months earlier. Then he had been praying the Lord's Prayer when they heard the sound of aircraft coming from behind them. 'Lead us not into temptation — it's all right, boys, they're our own Wirraways — but deliver us from evil. . .'

Now the same calm voice spoke, reading the ancient words to mariners, and men who were lined up near to the officers' hut listened, and officers listened, pressed around windows and watching their men through cracks in the walls:

> They that go down to the sea in ships, that do business in great waters,
> These see the works of the Lord and his wonders in the deep.
> For he commanded and raiseth the stormy wind, which lifted up the waves thereof.
> They mount up to the heaven, they go down again to the depths; their soul is melted because of trouble.
> They reel to and fro and stagger like a drunken man, and are at their wit's end.
> Then they cry unto the Lord in their trouble and he bringeth them out of their distresses. . .

The lines of men began to move, passing beyond the sound of the chaplain's voice. Along with his friends, McArthur hoisted his bags onto his shoulder.

Following the long lines of Australian prisoners, they moved out through the camp gates. On previous occasions, they had walked down this road to the wharf for a day of work unloading cargo. Today, they carried their belongings. At intervals along the road, sentries with machine-guns guarded against attempts at escape. McArthur saw Chinese men along the roadside who were known to him through the Chinese church and could see the surprise on their faces; they had probably never seen a white man carrying his own baggage before.

The road led to the wharf. A large passenger ship of just over

10 000 tonnes lay at anchor, waiting for them. The name on the side read 'Montevideo Maru'.

'We must be going to travel in style,' someone said. 'I've heard of this ship. It's one of the Rio de Janeiro Maru class and has been a first-class passenger ship on the run between China and Korea — very posh — beautiful music room panelled in mother-of-pearl. Though the service may have deteriorated lately. . .'

Among the last group of Chinese on the wharf, just before they climbed the gangway, Laurie McArthur saw a familiar face. He nudged John Poole.

'Look across there. Our friend Mo Pui Sam.'

The Chinese minister was watching them from his place among the labourers, a great sadness on his face as his eyes greeted McArthur, Poole, Pearson, Trevitt, Beazley and the others.

Later, when he had been led down into one of the holds of the great ship, one among many waiting to sail into the unknown, Laurie McArthur pulled his Bible from his bag and read the end of the passage from Psalm 107. John May's message had been passed up and down the ranks. The words read:

He maketh the storm a calm, so that the waves therof are still. Then are they glad because they be quiet; so he bringeth them unto their desired haven.

With her coat hugged tightly around her, Jean Poole walked along the wintry beach. Waves ran up and back leaving a glassy surface on the sand. Cold wind sculpted the dunes. Beyond the headland lay the coastal town of Kiama with the school where she had just begun teaching, and the house near the beach where she had just unpacked her belongings. Already she felt that Kiama would be a good place to wait for John to come home.

She stood still, her feet sinking into the cool damp sand, and looked out across the ocean. Somewhere to the north, where these grey waves washed into the blues and aquamarine of warmer tropical waters, John was a prisoner on New Britain. Between them lay this endless restlessness of waters.

At dusk the surface of the ocean divided as a submarine rose into sight. The USS *Sturgeon* had been on patrol in the waters west of the islands of the Philippines since leaving the Western Australian port of Fremantle on 14 June 1942 where Two Squadron, Submarines, South West Pacific was base-ported. The American crew was looking for action.

For more than two weeks they had followed the same pattern, as recorded daily in their war patrol report: 'Patrolling off Luzon; dived at dawn, surfaced at dusk. No contacts.' Only once had they encountered the enemy during that time. The rest of the long hours were spent submerged during daylight and surface-running after dark, often after the moon had set and the glassy sea was barely visible. Once or twice they had seen smoke on the horizon and had given chase, and once had strayed too near to fishing grounds off Bojeador Lighthouse and been temporarily hemmed in by fishing nets. Otherwise, nothing.

Tonight was 30 June 1942 and they were travelling on the surface to the north-west of Bojeador. An edgy crew half-hoped for action and half-expected another quiet night. Then, not long after 2200 hours, the lookout spotted a darkened ship to the south, travelling at high speed.

Lt Commander W.R. Wright wrote the following patrol report later. He reported:

He [the ship] quite evidently had stood out of Babuyan Channel, headed for Hainan. Put on all engines and worked up to full power, proceeding to westward in attempting to get ahead of him. For an hour-and-a-half we couldn't make a nickel. This fellow was really going, making at least seventeen knots and probably a bit more, as he appeared to be zig-zagging. At this time it looked a bit hopeless, but determined to hang on in the hope he would slow or change course towards us. His range at this time was estimated at around 18 000 yards. Sure enough, about midnight he slowed to about twelve knots. After that, it was easy.

In the submarine's control room, Wright talked with his men as they pursued their prey. An officer checked the distant outline against his standard selection of silhouettes of shipping types to attempt an identification.

'It's the enemy, for sure. Bigger than I thought at first — looks like one of the Rio de Janeiro class, or maybe even bigger. When you write up the report, put the target down as probably a combination freighter-passenger ship of about 10 000 tons — very high, flat superstructure with only one stack. There is no sign of an escort.'

'Any identification?'

'No, sir. Nothing we can see.'

The patrol report went on:

1 July 1942. Proceeding to intercept target as before. Altered course to gain position ahead of him, and dived at 0146. When he got in periscope range, it could be seen that he was larger than first believed, also that his course was a little to the left of west, leaving us some 5 000 yards off the track. Was able to close some 1 000 yards of this and then turned to fire stern tubes. . . At 0225 fired four-torpedo spread, range 4 000 yards, from after tubes. . .

Piercing the dark water, four torpedoes with high explosive warheads fanned towards the ship, rushing towards its cargo of sleeping men. The submarine commander immediately put on full rudder bringing the bow tubes to bear in case of a miss.

The Torpedo Data Calculator Lt C.W. Nimitz Jr said: 'We won't have to use any more. One of those will get him.'

Silent death stalked through the moonlit waves. The submarine crew waited, tense, expectant, until they felt the vibrations of a violent explosion.

'Two hits, starboard quarter. . .!'

Lights showed briefly on the ship's deck, then died as power was lost. Flames leaped up from the heart of the vessel as it began to list to starboard. Four, five, six minutes ticked by and in the capsule of the submarine the crew felt the jarring and heard the sound of two more explosions. Two torpedoes which had missed the ship had exploded deep under water. The officer reported, 'His bow is well up in the air already.'

Three lifeboats were being lowered as the order was given to abandon ship. All capsized and one was too damaged to be used. Crew who had been on deck only minutes before struggled to right the lifeboats and pull some survivors on board. The terror in the sinking ship and in the churning waters around it was too distant for the crew of the submarine to see, but they knew that they had completed a successful strike against the enemy.

The commander completed his war patrol report. He wrote:

Location of attack: Lat. 18 degrees 37 N, Long. 119 degrees 29 E; Type of target: 10 000 ton passenger ship (unescorted); No. of torpedoes: 4 (stern tubes); Firing intervals: 8 sec.; Firing range: 4 200 yards; Results: 1 hit. Target sank in 11 minutes. . . At 0229 heard and observed explosion about 75-100 feet abaft stack. At 0240 observed ship sink stern first. 0250 surfaced, proceeded to eastward. . . Dived at dawn. No further contacts. . .

It was not the moonlight that woke her. It was the noise. The young woman who had been sleeping quietly in her room at the boarding school in Tasmania was jolted into wakefulness. Mel Trevitt lay stiffly, clutching her blankets over her, hearing over and over wild reverberations in her ears. Through the window, the sky was full of stars. Bare branches were sketched against the frosted garden. Her two-year-old son lay asleep and everything around was very still. Yet the terror of sound in her mind went on.

'I'm having a nightmare — it's only a nightmare. I must be remembering our wedding day when Jack and I said "I do" while the volcano was erupting,' Mel thought, willing herself to be calm and reasonable. Jack was always in her thoughts, an invisible part of her world.

The violent sound went on, explosive, a tumult of detonations. And then there was a great and overwhelming quietness. In the deep silence, Mel Trevitt knew, without knowing how she knew, that Jack was not coming home.

15

3 July–28 August 1942

THE HIGH, SWEET VOICES OF CHILDREN floated across the audience at the bishop's birthday concert and, under cover of the sound, messages passed along the rows of people. News from the outside world came slowly to the internment camp at Vunapope, and when it came it was often confused and unreliable. It was always hard to know what to believe.

'The news is that most of the men in the camp near Rabaul town have gone somewhere — nearly all of them, I understand,' the message was whispered. 'Chinese labourers saw them last, on the wharf boarding a ship, and they told New Guineans — and now the news has come through to us.'

'Do you think our missionary men would have gone?' Mavis, Dora and the others were anxious to know.

'Probably. We hear that the officers are still there, but the others sailed some time in the past two weeks.'

Mavis was disturbed. It was very hard to imagine that the group of men on whom she and the other mission nurses had come to rely — the chairman Mr Mac, Laurie Linggood, John Poole, Jack Trevitt, Howard Pearson and the others — might have already left the island. Wherever the Japanese had taken them, and she supposed it was to another prison camp somewhere, she and the others had been left behind. She felt bereft, abandoned.

The children's song came to an end and the boys and girls from the boarding school for mixed race children filed back to their places among the priests and brothers, seminarians, teacher-trainees and nuns from the three convents. A priest with a guitar took their place, and the concert for the bishop went on.

('It's not the bishop's birth date, you understand,' the nuns had explained earlier. 'It's the Feast Day of his patron saint, Saint Leo, on July 3, and that is when we always have a celebration. Bishop Scharmach said that even though we are all under house arrest, we can still have our concert — he tends to get his way with the Japanese officers when he insists.')

'Where do you think they might have gone?' They knew they were only guessing. 'And why have they moved them all away from here, anyway?'

A band of young New Guinean men moved forward with drum, cymbals and brass instruments and burst into a lively rendition of a tune for brass. In the front row, lines of Japanese officers applauded with enthusiasm. The concert concluded with a choral work arranged by a priest who was a gifted musician and sung by a choir of Germans and Australians, Italians and New Guineans, Dutch, Polish, Irish, French and Czech.

It had been a very good concert. Mavis joined in the applause, but the news of the departure of the men weighed heavily. 'Do you think we might be sent away, too?'

They did not have long to wait. On the day after the bishop's concert, a group of Japanese naval officers arrived to inspect the nurses' quarters and their clothing and to ask after their health. (Not everyone had experienced good health; there was the constant need to find quinine to combat malaria and a diabetic nun was running out of supplies of insulin.) The officers promised to return in a month.

The next morning, 5 July 1942, the women heard the sound of a truck pulling up in front of the convent. Mavis and Dora took no notice until one of the nuns suddenly appeared in the doorway. She was breathless and shocked.

'The nurses!' she gasped. 'The navy has come for the nurses

and they say that they are to come as soon as they've packed — the truck is waiting out the front — with guards.'

Young women froze into a tableau, a room full of immobilised figures, card-players poised with cards in hand, darning needle suspended over work, pen stilled in mid-sentence, book open but unread. Then the frozen figures melted into a turmoil of action, questions, confusion. A guard appeared behind the nun and urged them to move quickly.

Mavis and Dora hurried to the room where they had been sleeping. There was not much to pack. Dora had brought very little from Vatnabara in the first place, expecting only to be away for a few weeks at most. Mavis, Chris and Dorothy had a suitcase each and gathered up everything they had. The army girls had come to Vunapope direct from the hospital on the day of the invasion, and had only what New Guinean house servants had been able to collect and bring to them weeks later. Nuns had given them some sheets from which they had stitched dresses for them-selves. Dorothy urged Mavis to give her Kuanua-English dictionary to Sister Felistica — 'She might be able to use it more than us, if they are taking us away from here' — but no-one was brave enough to say aloud the thoughts that preyed on their minds.

Were the women being taken to another camp? Or was there an even more sinister plan?

As the mission, army and government nurses, and the sole civilian woman Mrs Bignell, were gathering their things together, the nuns stayed with them.

'Don't rush,' they whispered, 'let them wait. They've given you no warning.'

Australian and Dutch nuns who had given hospitality to the eighteen women for nearly six months did not want them to leave empty-handed. One after another came to the nurses, thrusting into their hands blankets, sheets, quantities of cotton wool and a few medical items. They had very little to spare, but they couldn't bear to see the other women going into the unknown without whatever gifts they could provide.

Mavis found a little package of coloured embroidery threads

being slipped into her hands by a nun who knew that she loved handcrafts.

Outside the convent the truck was waiting with impatient guards, but permission was given for a farewell. Bishop Scharmach and the Irishman Father Barrow were called. Someone suggested a song, and women's voices joined in the familiar airs of 'Home Sweet Home' and 'Auld Lang Syne'. Mavis thought of home, of her beloved parents, her younger sister and brother, of the hills around Maitland. No-one had words for farewell, but nuns embraced nurses and each one tried to say with her eyes the comforting things, the hopeful things, that they scarcely dared to think.

'Go with God. . . The Lord be with you. . . God bless you. . .' they whispered, but they all knew that they were at least a little afraid.

Bishop Scharmach asked, 'Where are these women going?'

'To paradise,' was the answer, 'where there is no malaria.'

And then Mavis found herself being hauled up onto the back of the high truck with the others, squashed in with their baggage, and the truck's tailgate clanged shut behind them. She clung on with both hands as the truck jolted into life and moved off, leaving behind the group of waving nuns with their bishop. Through the dust rising behind the truck, she saw for the last time the gardens of Vunapope, the twin-towered cathedral, the schools and hospitals, the beautiful mixed race children staring open-mouthed as they passed and the convent that had sheltered them. Then the truck swung out onto the coast road and the headquarters of the Sacred Heart Mission at Vunapope disappeared behind a wall of coconut palms.

Bouncing along the road, Mavis found it was all she could do to hang on and watch the road and the harbour. Villagers watched them pass and Mavis waved. Surely some of them would tell Akuila To Ngaru, she thought, that they had seen a truckload of white women, not nuns, on the road to Rabaul. Akuila, tall, black and gracious, was the last of the ministers from the Methodist church that they had seen and now they were being taken away from Akuila, too.

The truck rattled to a halt at the wharf. Mavis scrambled down with the other women, clutching bags and bundles. Guards clustered around them, urging them along the wharf, away from the waterfront sheds and warehouses. It seemed a very long walk, every step taking Mavis and her friends further away from the security of land and the people and places of New Guinea. Waiting at the far end of the wharf, she looked down into the water slapping below it. Pale pumice floated in ripples, washing to and fro in the tide. On one side of the harbour the grey-white cone of Vulcan volcano rose up from the water, still bare of vegetation, and opposite it a column of volcanic ash continued to pour from Tavurvur volcano, still climbing up into the hot sky and sifting ash across the town.

Looking back along the waterfront, there were the marks of Allied bombing, damaged buildings and smashed trees. Across the waters of the harbour more than one sunken vessel protruded a section of hulk above the water. On the unshaded wharf, perspiration began to trickle damply. A soldier handed the women hard biscuits as they waited — 'What's this? A dog biscuit?' muttered someone — but they dared not reject them as there was no knowing when next they would be offered food.

A barge came alongside the wharf. Guards signalled to the women that they were to climb down into the barge. One after the other, the nurses stepped down, their precious bags and bundles still clutched to them. Mavis looked questioningly at Dorothy and the others. She knew it was no use asking them what was happening to them. They knew no more than she did. Yet she was bursting to demand an explanation, to complain to the authorities. None of this was right; nothing was fair!

The barge moved off across the harbour towards a ship at anchor. As they approached, the name on its side became clearly visible. *Naruto Maru*, it read. A rope ladder dangled over the side and, as they tossed up and down beside the high-towering side of the ship, the guards made signs that the women were to climb the ladder. There was no choice.

Clinging to the rope with clammy hands, Mavis pulled herself up till she was dragged over the final space onto the deck by sailors, following Dora, Dorothy, Chris and the others, a procession of eighteen confused and anxious women. There was a last look at the bright sunshine on the harbour and the tree-rimmed town before she found herself groping her way backwards down another ladder into the hold.

John would be pleased to hear about Kiama, Jean Poole decided. She pulled the writing pad towards her and dipped the pen into the ink bottle.

'My dearest John,' she began, and paused. Through the window the sun was shining from a sky of clear winter blue. The breeze was cool, but inside the house the sunshine was warming the room through the glass, and she would not need to light the fire till evening. It was much milder than the chill of Bathurst, with its coal fires, hard frosts and sometimes even snow.

How should she describe Kiama? She wanted to paint a word picture for him so that he could imagine her in a place they had never been together. She wanted him to know about the cottage so near to the beach that the sound of waves lulled her to sleep every night and sand had a habit of walking its way onto her clean floors. She wanted to tell him about the pleasant woman friend, another teacher, who was sharing the house with her, and how she liked it so much better than living in staff quarters.

The school had welcomed her, too, as she began to teach boys and girls of a small seaside community and a few from dairy farms nearby. Even though she was a married woman, she was able to teach again, and she had always loved to teach.

Already she had begun to make some friends in the town; one of her students was the child of the local Anglican minister and his wife and the Mainstone family had begun to welcome her to the rectory with special warmth as they learned that her husband was a prisoner. So, even though it was awful to be so far apart and to have had no news for months, she was trying to see the bright side of things.

She wouldn't tell John about the times when she walked along the beach, angry, questioning, worried, alone. She wouldn't disturb him with tales of sleepless nights, or frightening dreams.

There was no point in upsetting him. If he was a prisoner, he'd have enough worries of his own and her letters should be as cheerful as she could make them. Perhaps only some of her letters were reaching him. Women whose husbands were prisoners had been advised to write care of the Japanese Red Cross, but it was hard to know how much mail would get through. All the more reason to write letters to make him feel that she was safe, and reasonably content.

The pen nib had dried out while she had been thinking. Now she dipped it again in the ink and began her letter.

The hot, empty space of the ship's hold received them. Dora and the others looked around with dismay. Bare floor boards, high walls, some shelving — and nothing else. No beds, no chairs. Wherever they were being taken, this would not be a luxury cruise. At least the hatches were open, letting in some light and air, and there was ample space for the eighteen.

Hours later figures appeared above, and men began to climb down into the hold. There was a stir of anxiety among the women until they recognised the khaki trousers on the descending legs.

'It's the Major! Colonel Scanlan. . . Chaplain May. . . It's our own officers!'

As men climbed down, one by one, the women recognised many of them. The army girls knew them all well from their work, and the government nurses had met many of them socially at functions in Rabaul. Dora and the other mission nurses knew very few of them, but the sight of Chaplain John May was a great comfort. Perhaps he would have news of their own mission colleagues. By the time the last of the men had joined them in the hold, they numbered sixty officers and eighteen women.

Soon after noon on 6 July, the ship began to move and they knew that they were leaving the harbour at Rabaul. The motion of the ship increased as the hours went by and Dora was glad that she was a good sailor. A rope was strung by the guards between men and women, giving the women a corner for themselves, but they were all close enough to talk together.

'What about all the other men?' the women demanded. 'The

doctors? All the government officials and all the chaps of the 2/22nd and the 1st Independent Company? Is it true that they sailed a few weeks ago?'

Mrs Bignell pleaded for news of her son Ted and son-in-law Dudley, and Mrs Mary Goss, the oldest of the government nurses, asked anxiously whether anyone had seen her husband Tom — 'He would be with the Volunteer Rifles,' she said.

'We saw them all marched out of the camp at Malaguna early on the twenty-second of June, with their baggage. They didn't come back into camp. We were told that they had sailed and a guard told us that they were being taken to the island of Hainan off the coast of China.'

Chaplain May moved to a position where he could talk with the mission nurses. 'I saw the mission men — we often talked and spent time together. The last I saw of them was on the Sunday when they were marched away. I was with the other officers, locked in the hut, but they were near enough for me to pray with some of them. They went off in good spirits, laughing. . . They have probably arrived by now at their new camp.'

It was a comfort to have the officers with them, but Dora found that it was in some ways a mixed blessing. The space in the hold was stiflingly hot and airless as the hatches had been closed. When it was time to sleep, there was not space for everyone to lie down on the floor at the same time. 'Let the women lie down,' a senior officer ordered. 'The rest of us will take it in shifts to stretch out.'

Lying in the dark in the suffocating hold, Dora tried to be grateful that she was able to lie down. The floor was unrelentingly hard. At intervals a guard paced along the narrow passage marked by the dividing rope and his steps made the floor boards under her body shift uncomfortably. I'll end up with a big bruise on my hip, she thought. The heat was intense, the metal sides of the ship absorbing the tropical heat of the equatorial seas through which they sailed, and she felt the sweat soaking through her clothing. It was getting hard to breathe and the odours of sweating bodies filled her nostrils.

There was another physical problem, too. She thought wistfully of those days when it had been a private and discreet matter to use a toilet. The women had been embarrassed to find that the toilets were light timber cubicles overhanging the side of the ship's deck. They giggled about it: 'I don't know which is worse — the humiliation of almost being a public spectacle or being scared that I'll fall overboard to the sharks while I'm in there!'

Days passed slowly. There were clear advantages in being with a party of Australian officers. Between them they carried enough authority, ingenuity and powers of persuasion to make the journey less difficult than it might have been. In the first few days, the men were able to persuade the Japanese guards to permit them to have an hour on deck and then a little longer, until they were allowed to spend most of the days on deck, sheltering from the hot sun under an awning. The weather was fair and the sea calm and there were days when Dora found that it was almost possible to shut her eyes and to imagine that she was travelling on a cruise ship.

Not for long, of course. As soon as she opened her eyes, she could see the Japanese guards and sometimes, in the distance, a destroyer which was travelling with them in convoy. Sometimes, the *Naruto Maru* changed course unexpectedly, zigzagging across the South China Sea, and there were whispers that there might be submarines in the area. Any brief delusions about a holiday cruise quickly disappeared when they were ordered below for their meals, bowls of rice eaten while they squatted on the floor of the hold. The officers had somehow managed to bring on board fruit and other army rations from Rabaul which they were able to cook for the group and they were all thankful for that.

The slow hot days dragged by. Dora and the other women dreamed of private bathrooms with deep baths, foaming with soap-suds, clean, wet hair, mirrors, a shining wash-basin, thick towels. Her skin was itchy and rough with the saltiness of sweat.

After dark, when she did not feel so exposed among the men and other women, she tried to cool down and wash with her ration of washing water, held in a small tin which had once held butter. Dipping a cloth in the water, she pressed the coolness against her hot face and trickled droplets of water over her body with a coconut shell, but it was only slight relief.

Somewhere in the north-west Pacific Ocean, the most senior of the mission nurses, Dorothy Beale, became very ill. Jean Christopher recognised the signs of cerebral malaria. It was hard to persuade their guards that they needed medical help. There was little they could do for their friend, in the hold of a ship and without medication, but between them they did their best to support Dorothy. The one thing that they could do was to pray and they prayed with great urgency. As the days passed, Dorothy's condition improved and she was left exhausted and shaken, but alive and recovering.

Sitting under the awning on deck, the Australians thought of home and tried to imagine their future. Men spoke of wives and children at home, showing photographs of girlfriends and wives, or family groups, kept safely among their most treasured papers.

'They'll be wondering where we are,' they said. 'We had only two chances to write since we were captured, and we are not sure whether either lot of letters was sent. If only we could put our families' minds at rest and let them know something.'

'But we don't even know where we are ourselves, or where we are going.'

'We can't be sure what the Japanese Imperial Army is up to, but our guess is that we prisoners are a nuisance to them, a large group of men to be guarded when they have other plans for their troops — maybe they wanted us out of the way while they got on with the business of attacking other targets.'

'As for you women,' the officers assured them, 'you are just an embarrassment to them. There aren't very many of you and they can't put you in with a big camp of men. We think they'll use you as a bargaining chip — exchange you for other Japanese civilians who are interned somewhere. In a month or so, you'll probably all be home.'

As the *Naruto Maru* sailed north, a disturbing rumour began to circulate among the communities of Rabaul. It was first whispered among the handful of Australian men who had been kept in Rabaul to maintain the commercial freezer. On 11 July, one of them waited until no Japanese were in earshot, then passed on the story he had just heard from a Japanese officer.

'The ship that took all our mates is supposed to have been torpedoed and lost with all hands.'

The others found the story unbelievable. 'Baloney! The worst sort of propaganda. They are just trying to keep us unsettled.'

At the Catholic mission at Vunapope, Japanese officers called on the bishop. They were men he had not previously met and, when they offered a tale of the sinking of the prison ship by the Americans with total loss of life, he found their story very unconvincing. Japanese authorities had never before divulged any news about losses to the empire, though he was convinced that such losses must have taken place. Why should they do so now? When other officers told him the same story on other occasions, he became more and more suspicious of their motives and feared that the story was a cover-up for a massacre of fearful proportions.

Though they did not want to believe it, the four Australians at the freezer were appalled at the possibility that the story just might be true. If it were true, then they had just lost almost every man who had been their close friend — or well-known adversary — in the close network of pre-war Rabaul, lost in one fearful blow.

'It can't be true,' they said, 'but just in case. . .' and they began to compile a list of names of every man they had seen that day when the nominal roll had been completed at the camp at Malaguna, or every man seen under guard around the town, who had not been seen since 22 June 1942.

There was a great deal of activity around the harbour during the next weeks of July, with convoys of Japanese troops coming and going in what they later learned were attacks on the northern coast of New Guinea, and Australians were aware of great tension among their captors. Yet during those days they all searched their minds until they had made up a list of 168 names and an additional unnamed group of Scandinavian sailors from the *Herstein*. For the time being there was no contact at all with their own people, no way to check the dreadful rumour, but their list was ready for some time in the future when people might come to ask questions.

Ten days after they sailed from Rabaul, the women and men in the hold were aware that their ship had arrived in a harbour.

'Where are we?'

'You have arrived in Japan,' their guards told them proudly. 'We have come to the great harbour of Yokohama.'

The first hours on land were tiring and confusing, with encounters with a variety of police, medical officers and even searches by Customs and immigration officers. 'Customs inspections, for goodness sake — whatever do they think we might have to declare!' It reinforced their impression that their captors were not sure how to treat them, whether as inconvenient foreign visitors, hostages or prisoners of war.

Then the women were separated from the men and loaded into a truck. Rushing through city traffic in the back of a three-tonne truck, being flung from side to side as the truck forced its way through crowded streets of unfamiliar architecture with every sign in Japanese script, Mavis and Dora felt overwhelmed by the strangeness of it all. Mavis had not been in any kind of city for almost three years, and this city was unlike anything she had ever seen.

The truck pulled up outside a two-storey building not far from the harbour front. As the women scrambled down from the truck, they saw a covered porch with a large sign over the front door which read 'Bund Hotel'. Mavis nudged Dora in disbelief. The open front door was flanked with garden beds and potted plants and there were lace curtains at the windows. As the guards led them through the entry foyer, they were startled to realise that they had been brought to a tourist hotel which had previously been designed to provide hospitality to Western guests.

Some of the women were on the verge of giggles. 'The men told us that they didn't know what to do with us!'

Carrying their bags and bundles with as much dignity as they could muster, and very aware of the incongruity of unwashed and bedraggled prisoners being ushered through the well-appointed rooms of a good hotel, the women followed their guards. Doors were opened from a hallway and Mavis and Dora found themselves allotted a double bedroom. 'A real bedroom. Look at this — proper beds and everything,' they sighed.

It was hard to believe. The bathroom they had dreamed of was there, too, and they each soaked in a luxurious hot bath, trying to cleanse away ten days of discomfort in the ship's hold. There was a good meal in the dining room and they were introduced to the hotel manager, Mrs Saito. Later, clean, well-fed and comfortable, Mavis and Dora were allowed to go for a walk with the others.

There was something very bizarre about it. They walked out from the dining room and the lounge room with solid furniture and potted ferns, out through the hotel gardens and on into a park on the waterfront. Across the water they could see shipping of all kinds and the silhouette of the city of Yokohama ringing the harbour, larger commercial buildings mingling with traditional timber and paper private houses. Over their meal they had been told that Yokohama, and particularly the area where they now were, was where foreigners had lived and worked since Japan had first opened its doors to the West some eighty years earlier and that the harbour of Yokohama, within the safety of breakwaters, was one of the world's finest.

Strolling along the harbourside paths on that long summer's evening, watching Japanese families passing by, it was hard to reconcile the conflicting images. The Japanese were 'the enemy', evil men in an alien uniform who made them afraid and controlled their lives, wrenching them away from their work and their home. Yet the Japanese on the paths of the waterside park were family people, women dressed in exotic traditional garments or in Western dress, small children running and playing, who stared curiously at the group of foreign women.

Most of the nurses came originally from country districts in New South Wales and Queensland with little opportunity for travel, even in their own country. The onslaught of impressions in a country so very unlike rural Australia was overwhelming.

They spoke of the hotel. 'I don't think much of the food,' said one. 'I'd been hoping for something substantial like proper lamb chops and potatoes and not all that strange Jap food.'

'Oh, I quite like it. Did you notice the beautiful cutlery — and the woman in charge, Mrs Saito, seems quite nice. She can speak reasonable English — from being hostess to lots of Western visitors, I suppose — and she said that they used to put on big banquets in the hotel gardens, with lots of courses before the war.'

'The place has gone downhill recently, then,' another remarked. 'I'm sure there are rats in the bedroom where I am.'

'And dogs have been tied up in the yard just outside our room — there's an awful smell.' Dora wrinkled her nose. 'Mavis and I might pull our mattresses out into the hall to get away from it.'

'Anyway, it shouldn't be for long. If our officers were right, they'll just keep us at the hotel until they can exchange us. Then we'll be on our way back home, out of here!'

But then they returned to the Bund Hotel and encountered someone whose presence shook their confidence. An older woman waited for them among the potted palms. She rose to greet them with tears of relief. 'I'm so thankful to see you girls,' she said. 'You can't guess how glad I am. I've been here by myself for a month and I thought I might go crazy. I'm Mrs Etta Jones.'

Mrs Jones, a short and stout American woman of sixty years, told them her story. With her husband she had lived in the far north of the Pacific, in the Aleutian Islands which formed a bridge between Alaska and the Soviet Union. Her husband had been responsible for the radio station. He had received word from the American authorities that he should dismantle the radio transmitter because the Japanese were expected to attempt to capture the Aleutians as the northern-most strategic point in their grand plan of controlling a great ring of the countries of the Pacific rim. After the radio was destroyed, early in June, they saw a ship coming into harbour.

'We thought it was the Americans coming to take us home. But it was the Japs. They ordered my husband to put the radio back in working order, but he said he didn't know how. So they killed him. . .'

Mrs Jones had been taken prisoner and put on board the Japanese ship. In her fear and grief, she had attempted to slash her wrists, but had been stopped. She had been brought eventually to the Bund Hotel, shattered and desperate.

'The first time I caught sight of myself in one of the hotel full-length mirrors I barely recognised myself. It was horrible — but I knew that I had to survive. And now you dear girls are here and, if I can stay with you, it won't be so bad.'

A Japanese naval officer sat to compose a letter to a company of shipping owners. It was a little awkward, but that was among the fortunes of war. The navy had been using a passenger ship commandeered from the ship owners for their own purposes and now he had to report its loss.

Reluctantly, he looked for the words to explain to the ship owners that their ship the *Montevideo Maru* had been torpedoed and sunk by the Americans off Luzon Island in the Philippines. Very unfortunate, as only seventeen members of the crew and three of the naval guard who had been on deck at the time had escaped, out of all the 1 053 prisoners, 71 crew and 62 naval guards on board. He dated his letter 20 July 1942.

For two weeks, the women stayed at the Bund Hotel. They watched the harbour eagerly for any sign of a ship which might have come to take them home. One day, they saw a party of Americans having lunch in the hotel and, though they were forbidden to speak to them, a few of the women were able to snatch a few words in the corridor.

'They are missionary families, brought in from China as internees, like us,' they reported.

Briefly they hoped for their company, but the next day the Americans were gone and did not return. 'Perhaps they were exchanged,' women said, 'but what about us?'

The woman who managed the hotel, Mrs Saito, arranged for them to send shopping orders with her and, though they had little money, they were able to replace small things like toothbrushes and soap. Several women asked her to buy notebooks and pencils for them. Dora chose to buy coloured pencils for drawing and Mavis bought several small notebooks with strong black covers.

'I want to start a diary of everything,' Mavis explained, 'to take home to show my family. I'll start with the things that happened in Rabaul.' With promptings from Dorothy, Chris and Dora, she began to write up dates and notes of the events beginning with New Year's Day 1942 and the note 'John Poole and Linggie out to Malabonga'.

It seemed a lifetime ago since she and Chris had shared their New Year lunch with the two men, and they had talked together about whether Jean Poole and Essie Linggood and her children had arrived safely in Australia with the evacuation ship. Now Mavis tried to capture the key events of the past months, those moments which she was sure she could never forget.

They wouldn't be in Japan for long, they assured each other, and so tried to observe what they could of the strange land where they found themselves. They were offered English editions of Japanese newspapers which they read with interest and a degree of scepticism. Mavis noted peculiarities in her notebook: 'Their kinds of shoes, cars, buses, baths, little lorries, bicycles, dresses. . .' Even the simple act of watering the hotel potplants was not done in a familiar way; the cleaning woman sprayed the ferns with a fine spray of water squirted through her teeth. Nothing was what Mavis had always thought of as normal.

There was the day when a funeral procession passed along the street in front of the Bund Hotel. With other nurses, Mavis and Dora leaned out of an upstairs bedroom window to watch the crowds lining the street below, the houses draped with flags. Bands were playing as men in vivid traditional dress and high black headdresses carried the ashes of the dead in solemn procession.

'The ashes of a fallen soldier have great power, so I'm told,' said one. 'It makes them almost like gods, able to do amazing feats for the emperor. They say that it would be almost unthinkable for a soldier to surrender — a terrible, shameful act, anyway — because he is supposed to be so loyal and committed to serve the emperor that he is always willing to die rather than give in.'

'They'd rather come home as honoured ashes than come back alive but defeated.'

They watched until the last of the procession vanished from view and the people lining the street went on their way.

'Well, I'd rather see our men get home alive, win or lose,' said a nurse. 'And I'd just as soon go home that way, myself, not in a little box of ash. I don't understand these people.'

On the last day of July, the Catholic mission doctor, Dr Schuy, was on the verandah of the hospital at Vunapope when he heard the sound of a truck. It came along the road, rattling and bumping, trailing a cloud of dust. He watched as it passed. It was only as it went by, on the road towards town, that he recognised some of the men riding in the back. They were Australians.

One he knew well. Bill Huntley was postmaster at nearby Kokopo where he used to collect his mail; Huntley had previously worked for the Methodist mission as a plantation manager. Another was Tom Goss, a well-known Rabaul identity. Mrs Goss had been among the nurses who had been taken away at the beginning of July. There were others, five of them and Dr Schuy tried to be sure who he had seen. These men must have been in hiding in the bush all these months and only now had been captured.

The truck disappeared from view. He would not forget his last glimpse of the Australians, the doctor thought. If he survived himself, the day might come when it would be important to know whom he had seen and when.

With very little warning, on 3 August, the women at the Bund Hotel were ordered to collect their things and prepare to move. There was an upsurge of hope. Perhaps this was the day when they would be taken to a ship and exchanged. The nineteen women, the nurses with Mrs Bignell and Mrs Jones, boarded a bus with their bags and drove a short distance across the city to another waterfront site. Their guards herded them off the bus towards a gate leading through high walls.

'Where are they putting us now?' one of the girls demanded. 'What's this place?'

They stared at the handsome building before them and then several of them started to laugh. The sign over the door read 'Yokohama Amateur Rowing Club'.

'It's a private club for Westerners, for goodness sake! Just look at this. . .'

There was very little time to examine their surroundings as they were led through the downstairs rooms and up the stairs, but as soon as they were alone again they compared notes. It was clear that they were being accommodated in what had been a beautifully appointed recreational club for foreigners. Women mentioned that they had seen a tennis court, table tennis tables — even a swimming pool in the grounds. Not only that; as they entered they had seen a number of the Australian officers who had travelled with them on the *Naruto Maru*, evidently accommodated on the ground floor.

Because of the nature of the building, it had no private bedrooms, but the women were issued with straw-filled Japanese mattresses which they spread out in the large upstairs hall which previously had been used for social functions and dances. The bathrooms were very clean, they were provided with toiletries, and Mrs Saito from the Bund Hotel sent gifts of extra food and useful items.

'This just goes to prove the point,' they said. 'The plan must be to treat us decently until they can exchange us, maybe even in the next few weeks. This place isn't bad at all.'

If they had known when the gates shut behind them what they would learn in time, they might not have been so cheerful.

In Adelaide, South Australia, on 15 August 1942, Kath Brown watched her oldest friend Grace walking up the aisle to meet her groom Gordon Young. Kath and Grace had been friends since their first day in kindergarten, then through all their growing-up years, living only a few streets apart, in and out of each other's homes. Kath had introduced Grace to Gordon and watched their friendship grow.

On that day in January when she had arrived home in Adelaide, exhausted and relieved, with baby Graham in his basket, she had insisted on calling in on Grace on the way from the railway station.

Now Grace and Gordon were being married. The wedding was like many other wartime weddings, with the limitations of rationing and absence of many men who might have been guests in other times. Though Grace came from a wealthy family, she had needed to scrape up enough coupons to buy a wedding gown and had borrowed a veil. In the safe familiarity of Spicer Memorial Methodist Church where the girls had grown up, the undercurrent of war could not be easily forgotten. The groom and other men were in military uniform and most guests had someone in their family who was away in one of the services.

Later, when friends gathered for the wedding breakfast, women shared their news. 'Have you had any word from your husband?' 'Any news of your son?'

Some were able to report happily of a brief letter from somewhere in the Middle East, or a censored but reassuring card from Port Moresby. Girls in uniform, friends of Grace from the Australian Women's Army Service, laughed about girlfriends who had been posted to the Northern Territory with the Signals Operation sections and were having more trouble with mosquitoes and sandflies than the enemy, or described their work on anti-aircraft gun sites. Others whispered quietly that a friend had just received word that her husband or brother was missing in action, or had been killed.

Someone asked Kath Brown, 'How is Rodger?'

'He's well. Away again, as usual,' Kath said.

At least, she thought, she knew where he was. Rodger had wanted to enlist, to play his part, but the church would not release him. He had thrown himself into his work with all his energy, travelling constantly around South Australia and interstate to visit churches with map and slide show to tell his missionary story. His hard work was his way of somehow sharing the burden with his friends who had not escaped. Consequently, Kath and their baby rarely saw him at home. She was grateful to be in the security of her mother's house. So many other women were in a situation much worse than her own and she was in no position to complain.

'Did you know that Nellie Simpson had her baby yesterday? And Beryl Beazley from New Britain is due in the next week or two, over in Perth,' someone said.

'Nellie's had a little boy and I hear she is going to call him John. Tom Simpson will be tickled pink when he hears that he has a son. He'll be wanting to teach him to play cricket!'

Within a few days at the Yokohama Rowing Club, the women settled into a new routine. With the help of partitions, they marked out spaces to spread their mattresses on the floor, giving a little privacy to each group.

'It won't be for long — it will be a bit like a Girl Guide camp,' they assured each other.

Already, over the months they had been in each other's company, clear groups had emerged among them, with mutual interests and similar background. The army girls, led by Captain Kay Parker, set themselves up at one end of the large room, with the civilian girls as a group in the middle beyond a partition. Dorothy Beale, Jean Christopher, Dora Wilson and Mavis Green were together at the other end and Mrs Bignell chose privacy in her own corner. A Japanese woman was put in charge of them and made her bed in the same room. They called her Mama-san.

Although they were not supposed to have any contact with the Australian men downstairs, the girls discovered ways of communicating. It wasn't hard to throw notes down over the balcony, or toss little gifts of soap or other things they had acquired, or sing carefully worded songs. Some of the officers had been sent already to other camps, and the mission women saw no sign of Chaplain May.

It was not easy to see across the harbour, because a high fence blocked their view, but between the cracks in the fence they watched one ship very closely. The officers had told them,

'That's the exchange ship — it's across the harbour, there, and you are sure to go out on it.' The Japanese cook at the club said the same thing, in his careful English. Through the cracks in the fence they watched it, a ship with large white crosses marked on its sides.

On 24 August, they realised that the Australian men downstairs were being moved out. 'We'll be next,' they said hopefully.

But after a few days one of the women peered through the cracks in the fence and came to the others in distress.

'The ship with the white crosses has gone! And we are still here.'

16

September 1942–
April 1943

THE SILK-CORDED THREAD SLID RAPIDLY through Mavis' fingers as she knitted. She had always been a good knitter, ever since the days when she was a young girl and her mother taught her. Mother was a craftswoman who created exquisite white-on-white linens, embroideries, crochet, knitting like the finest lace.

'What would Mother think if she could see me knitting little striped bags for Jap soldiers to put their lucky charms in — or their religious medals or whatever it is,' Mavis thought.

Around her the other women sat, each with her own task. Mama-san had decided that it was not good for them to be idle and had arranged for them to have some simple piece work to do which would earn them pocket money. At a table, a group worked on folding and pasting down envelopes from recycled paper. After a month of paper-folding, they were becoming very skilled and quick. Others were knitting bags with the silk cord they had been given. The pile of completed bags had been growing and they all knew that a good number of bags could lead to some concessions for their group. Mavis had earned eighty-four sen for knitting twenty-two bags on the last pay day.

Tootie started counting bags, heaping them up in groups of ten and calling the numbers. 'We've done 1 070 between us,' she announced. 'And 11 000 envelopes.'

'We can fold and paste in our sleep,' muttered someone.

'What I'd like — what I dream of — is an envelope of my own, with my name on it and a letter inside from my mum.'

'Or from a bloke!'

'That'll be the day. . .'

Though they had been in Japan for two months, not one of them had received mail of any kind. Surely somebody's family must be writing letters to her and, if so, where was the mail? And when would they be allowed to write a letter home, even just one letter?

Conversation circled around the room. None of them needed to think about the work in her hands. Kay Parker had a gift for keeping the group cheerful with her good humour and optimism. Even the most pessimistic of them found it hard to resist her confidence that soon they would be released.

'I read it in the leaves in my teacup this morning,' one said. 'I'm to go on a journey — so that must be home.'

Outside the club the wind was rising, rattling the windows. As evening came on, the women put away their work and cleared the tables for their evening meal. Kimora the cook came in with their food, soya bean soup and stew again, and warned them about the wind. 'Lock the windows,' he said. 'A typhoon is coming tonight, maybe midnight.'

As darkness fell, the women heard the sounds of people fixing window shutters in place. Before it was too dark to see, women crowded to peer through gaps in the fence to try to see the harbour. Waves were high and overhead, great clouds rolled over and over, almost seeming to crush the land beneath. Then it was dark, and the women tried to concentrate on their evening relaxation, books or playing cards uneasily in hand. The wind rose and fell, pressing against their window shutters. When it was time to go to bed, women lay restless, wondering what would happen if the heart of the typhoon crossed their area. One by one, they drifted into sleep, lulled by the whining of the wind.

In the morning, the wind had dropped. Over their morning cup of tea, they talked about the big wind which had passed them by.

Dorothy Beale was philosophical. 'After New Britain with volcanoes erupting and regular earthquakes, the edge of a typhoon is just a windy day.'

The mission women asked to have a religious service without much hope that permission would be granted. Dora, like each of them, had clung to her faith in God at the centre of herself, but there had been so little privacy or space since they left the Catholic mission that it had seemed impossible to gather for a formal service of Christian worship. Not all the women in their party would want to be part of it. Dora knew that and none of the mission girls wanted to impose her own needs on others. Nor did they expect their guards, Shinto or Confucian, to be sympathetic. However, a little to their surprise, they were told that a religious service from time to time was permissible.

'We want it, of course, but who is going to lead it?' they asked each other. In their home churches, and working with the mission, there had always been a male minister.

'We'll take it in turns.'

Between the four of them they gathered up everything they had which would held them to prepare. Dora had her treasured Bible. Chris had a New Testament and a book of meditations and readings called 'Come Ye Apart', which her brother had once given her. It was Chris' idea that they try to remember the words of favourite hymns and she began a handwritten collection of them.

'No sermons,' they agreed. 'Sermons won't be appropriate in the circumstances.'

'But if we take time to write our prayers carefully, we can put anything we want to share with each other into the prayer,' Dora suggested.

Dorothy as their leader was willing to lead the first service and, almost with apology, explained to the other groups of women what they planned. As they had expected, not everyone chose to join them in the mission nurses' corner. Among several who came to sit with them were Etta Jones, Mrs Bignell and Cal (Eileen Callaghan).

'You girls are Methodists and I'm a good Catholic, but I don't think God will mind if we pray together, do you?' she said.

At first they were shy. There were so few of them and their singing sounded so embarrassingly loud and exposed. Yet the hymns reminded them of home, and of singing with their families and friends in the security of peace-time churches, and spoke of the God who never abandons his children. For each of them, the prayers and words from the Bible gave a well of strength on which to draw and they knew that they would pray as a group as regularly as they were allowed.

Thousands of miles away, the Catholic missionaries at Vunapope were ordered to move out of their large residences to make way for Japanese use. They were to accommodate their 350 mission staff, mixed race civilians, trainees and children into a smaller section of the Vunapope compound. Many Catholic staff had been brought in from distant mission stations to swell their numbers. Japanese soldiers ringed their area with a barbed wire fence, recycled from their own cow yard. The last Mass was said by the bishop on 3 October in the chapel of one of the convents, and very sadly the priests and sisters stripped the altar of the sacred vessels and cloths and carried them into the area behind the barbed wire.

Allied bombing raids over the area were becoming more and more frequent and, though the missionaries hoped that the Allies had Vunapope clearly marked as a mission on their maps, they knew that they were still in danger from bombs and shrapnel. The sisters made a point of hanging washing lines full of white garments and sheets in the hope that pilots would recognise them as non-Japanese. Using methods learned in Europe during World War I, they began tunnelling into the hillside near their new, crowded accommodation, lining it with coconut timbers to provide a place of escape.

By October, autumn in Japan was cooling the air. Trees were colouring and the women were told that the season of high winds was nearly over. During the summer days, they had been allowed to spend part of the day downstairs in the grounds, sometimes sun-baking or strolling around and on hotter days they had swum in the club pool. But now the season was changing. 'We ought to fix up the tennis court, too, for autumn sport,' they suggested.

Mavis felt the cold as the evenings chilled and cooler breezes curled round her shoulders. For the past three years she had lived in the tropics and had grown accustomed to a hot, humid climate. The thought of a cold winter was alarming. From the grounds and a bathroom window, it was possible to get a distant glimpse of Mount Fujiama, when it was not shrouded in cloud, and they knew that it would not be long before it had a cap of snow. With the other women, she had her nursing uniforms and summer dresses and one cardigan, and Dora did not even have a cardigan. Mrs Jones was the only one among them with winter clothes but, though she was generous with her ample supply, she was so much shorter than most of the women that her things were useless to them.

Then one October day, Mama-san appeared with a big bolt of warm dress material. 'For winter,' she explained, and cut it into four-yard lengths for each woman. Within days a sewing machine arrived — 'for three weeks only' — and envelope making and bag knitting were set aside while everyone sewed a warm garment for themselves. The fabric was thick, coarse and very prickly against the skin, but at least it was warm. 'Must be goat's hair or something!' they complained. Not everyone was skilled as a dressmaker, but Dora was very good at it and found herself in demand to create warm trousers or jackets.

While they were sewing, the ship with the white crosses was seen in the harbour again. It seemed to come and go each month.

'Maybe we won't need to wear these horse-hair things after all — it's spring in Australia and we could easily be home in time for summer!' they said hopefully. They said it with confidence, challenging anyone to deny them their hope. But they went on cutting and stitching the thick fabric, just the same.

Through the months from August till the end of 1942, a deadly duel was waged across the precipitous Owen Stanley ranges that formed the ridged spine of Papua. Wrestling backwards and forwards from the mangroves of the northern coast to within sight of Port Moresby on the southern coast, the young men of the Japanese and Australian armies struggled in mortal combat, forcing their enemy backwards through mud and defiant jungle for a time until, breathless and weakening, they were themselves forced backwards.

The wrestlers fought on, unwilling to surrender, prepared to win or die. They dragged leaden legs up slopes which tore their hearts out and waited endlessly in fear-filled rage in watery green hiding places for a shot at the invisible enemy. They carried the bodies of exhausted and dead friends and gloated over the bodies of dead enemies. A soldier, coming suddenly face-to-face with the enemy, found that he, too, was young, deadly and afraid.

When the fearful combat was over, thousands had died. Port Moresby, Milne Bay and the northern coast of Papua were in Allied hands. The names of Buna, Gona, Imita Ridge and Kokoda were branded on the memories of those who survived and of those who lost their men in those bitter days.

The roses were in bloom in the gardens of Kiama in all the glory of spring. The air was warming gently and the sea spread blue to the horizon. Jean Poole gathered her mail from the letter box by the garden gate as she came home after a day of teaching. She couldn't help it, but there was always a quickening of heartbeat, a tightening of the throat, a brief moment of hope as she opened the lid of the letter box. Perhaps, today. . .

She flicked quickly through the mail. Some letters for her fellow teacher, letters from her family, some periodicals, but. . . no letter from John. Still nothing after months. At least, she tried to comfort herself, she did not have in her hands one of those dreadful letters with her own handwriting on it and an appalling red hand with pointing finger stamped over it and 'RETURN TO SENDER'.

Jean sat on the steps in the sun to open her mail. She smiled as she read her sister's letter. There were only about six weeks of the school term left and then her sister, Joyce, their brother and their parents were coming to Kiama for the Christmas holidays!

They had decided that her cottage opposite the surf beach would make a perfect holiday place for them all. It was more than a convenient holiday place, she knew. Her family was very close-knit and they wanted to be there to support her while John was away.

She tore the brown paper wrapper from the copy of *The Methodist*, dated 31 October 1942 and began to leaf through news of the church in NSW. As she turned a page, her hand began to shake. There was a photo of John on the page, the same photo that she had by her bed. A circle of familiar faces ringed the block of print: Laurie Linggood, Herbert Shelton, Dan Oakes, Dora Wilson, Wilf Pearce, Jack Trevitt, Mavis Green — and John. In large black type, the headline read 'WHEREABOUTS UNKNOWN'.

Quickly she skimmed the article. It told her nothing new. 'Sixteen of our missionaries are prisoners of war. Eight of them from New South Wales. . . We have not had any reliable information. . . The following are the names of the men and women who are now in captivity, and where they are, or how they fare, we know not. . .' and all the names followed — the other nurses and ministers from other states, and the Rev. Mo Pui Sam and Mr and Mrs Thomas Mow. There was a request for continuing prayer for all the missing missionaries, and for the New Guinean ministers, pastors and teachers 'that they remain true to their Lord and be given strength and wisdom to lead the orphaned native church in their land'.

In her mind, she saw the faces of her friends Mikael To Bilak and Louisa, Akuila To Ngaru, Saimon Gaius and the others. Were they safe? she wondered. We'll come back to you, John and I, she promised, when this is all over.

Jean Poole folded the magazine and gathered up her letters to go into the house. Suddenly, the sun had lost its warmth and she felt cold.

'Time for the mannequin parade, girls!' Kay Parker inspected her team and laughed at the sight of them.

Young women who were more at home in nursing uniforms with crisply starched white veils lined up in variations on a theme of coarse wool, stitched with varying degrees of skill. Dora, government nurse Dorothy Maye and Kay Parker were all tall, while Jean Christopher, Etta Jones and government nurse Jean McLelland were short — McLelland's nickname was *Liklik*, the Pidgin English word for small, because of her diminutive frame. (Most of the women addressed each other by surname or nickname: Fud and Tootie, Chris, Cal, Bowie, Whytie, Andy and Mayesie, as well as Kruger, Goss, Oldroyd, McGahan and Green. The two older women were always called Mrs Jones and Mrs Bignell.)

'All we need is a new hat each and we'll be really flash for our Melbourne Cup party. Just look at us! I hope you've all left room to move in these elegant models so we can bow deep enough to satisfy the chief.'

Mama-san opened the door and the women marched downstairs and lined up for their monthly visit by the chief, a gold-braided Japanese officer with responsibility for internees and prisoners in the area. The nineteen were inspected and issues of soap, toiletries and toilet paper were handed over. The line of women bowed humbly to the knee, willing to follow instructions for the sake of the goods.

'Turn — and bow to the Imperial Palace!' they were ordered.

They bent low once more as the flag of the rising sun with its red orb was passed from hand to hand along the line. 'Kiss the flag,' was the order, and the red circle went from mouth to mouth under the approving eye of the officers and then was raised to the top of the flagpole.

When the ceremony was over, they all returned to their room where a morning tea in honour of the emperor and the November Culture Day was set out for them all, with the chief and the other officers, and they found themselves donating ten sen each from their knitting and envelope money towards gifts of sweets for the children of Japanese sailors.

On the surface, it had all been very civilised and polite. But that evening, after the fun of some lively games and a Melbourne Cup sweep, with names of imagined or remembered horses, one of the nurses with an earthy command of language said: 'You know when we were supposed to kiss the flag this morning? I spat on it — and, with a very straight face, said what they could do with their emperor.'

There was such a sameness about their days. Whistles blew to divide the day into precise slices of time for the same preordained tasks each day. Roll call, with the same nineteen women answering their names first thing in the morning and at bedtime. The same room shared constantly with the same people, except for the brief periods permitted in the grounds each day.

Meals, with monotonous fare, the same menus endlessly repeated — rice, bread, soya bean soup, stew and tea, with fruit rare enough to warrant a diary entry. The same piles of papers, folded into the same envelopes, fold after fold. The same little bags, knitted daily, row of plain, row of purl. The same conversations, tedious repetitions of what's for tea, when will the white cross ships come for us, the weather, the mad Matron where I trained, what my father always says.

Almost all the nineteen, apart from Mrs Bignell and Mrs Jones, were women of the same age group: from Mavis Green (who had been twenty-six when they were captured) to Dorothy Beale and Mary Goss (who were in their mid-thirties). And all were nurses, most of them from country towns in NSW or Queensland. But small habits, harmless in themselves or when diluted in a wider and mobile stream of people, gradually become poisonous when concentrated into a stagnant pond of women unable to escape from the sound of each other's voice.

For their own survival, the nurses knew that they must find ways to keep their minds and spirits alive. There was no news coming in from radio, newspapers or mail, and no opportunity to reach outside their group with personal correspondence or phone calls. The nearest they came to news was a few copies of *Nippon Times*, a pro-Japanese propaganda publication in English which usually just made the women cranky.

Sometimes the guards left their own newspapers where the women could see them, but the unknown script defeated them and the marked maps were the only clues to the progress of the war. The Yokohama Amateur Rowing Club had once been well stocked with English language magazines and books, but the old copies of *Time* magazine were all pre-war and, after the women had read them thoroughly, they were used for pictures to decorate the walls. The books in the bookcase were prized, though their range and number was limited.

They were all learning Japanese language but, though useful, most of the prisoners were rebellious about learning the words of their captors. It had been different at Vunapope, when they had begun learning French or German with the nuns, or Kuanua with their national friends, and there had been many women with knowledge of the wider world of Europe. Several of the women, including Mavis Green and Jean Anderson, kept diaries, but Mavis found there was little to record because so little ever varied from day to day.

The parties began as a way of making a ripple in the flat surface of their weeks. Every possible occasion was marked with some sort of celebration. Birthdays, anniversaries, the birthdays of family members at home, church services, the Melbourne Cup, Armistice Day — any excuse was worth a party. Sometimes the women from a particular group — military nurses, mission or government — arranged a small tea party for their friends and persuaded the cook to provide a cake in return for money earned knitting.

Kay Parker's birthday in November was celebrated in style. Though the weather was getting colder daily, it was a fine day and they all trooped downstairs for the regular parade to bow towards the Imperial Palace. Over the past weeks they had been allowed to prepare the tennis court and Kay's birthday was chosen for their first tennis tournament. The women organised themselves into pairs and played with great zest and energy. Many of them came from country communities where tennis was the key winter sport and a number of them were good players. Mrs Kathleen Bignell repeated stories of playing tennis with house parties of young people on her family plantation in the Solomon Islands, set in acres of beautiful gardens.

After the game, the cook produced what Mavis described in

her diary as 'a great tea'. That evening, the small stove in their room was lit for the first time, using coal they had carted upstairs, and they sat around it, hugging blankets around them against the cold, playing party games till they were helpless with laughter. Even when the power failed and the lights suddenly went out, as was happening more and more frequently, they crawled into their beds in the dark with the small glow of the stove to comfort them and the feeling that for a few hours they had beaten back the spectres of enervating boredom and frustration.

Wild wheat and grasses along dusty Australian roadsides shed their seed and whitened in the summer sun. Farmers worked the long hot days of sun-up to sundown harvesting their wheat, a column of dust marking their progress across the paddocks. Farm families welcomed back their servicemen sons, given leave to help with harvest. Heat haze shimmered across open plains, the air seeming to ripple up into a brazen sky. Brilliant red bottlebrush exploded from buds, and acacia trees were hung with curling pods of silvery green and pink like lavishly decorated Christmas trees.

In her schoolroom, heavy with summer heat, Elsie Wilson cleaned the blackboard at the end of the day. She was thankful that the long hard year was over. It seemed an eternity since this time a year ago when she had been interrupted in her end-of-year cleaning at the District Girls' School at Vunairima to be told that she was to be evacuated from Rabaul. There was no-one nearby to whom she could talk about New Britain.

Her close friends were all far away, in Adelaide or scattered across Australia. Her lifeline was the mail, bringing letters from her family and encouraging correspondence from the women of two church organisations in Adelaide with special interest in missionary work, the Young Women's Missionary Movement and the Women's Auxiliary to Overseas Missions. All of them knew about Vunairima and the Girls' School and were concerned for her.

Among the best things to see in her mail was the packet of letters which circulated among her friends from teachers' college days; when the packet arrived it always contained the latest news of her close friends, now teaching across the state, and it was a great support and pleasure to her. She kept in touch with Mary Jenkins, too. Mary had recently written to say that she had agreed to teach the part-Aboriginal children at Otford until it was possible to go back to her beloved Chinese friends in Rabaul. But all these good friends were a long way away and now Elsie was very glad to be going home for Christmas.

In suburban Adelaide, Kath Brown helped her mother prepare Christmas cake and pudding, using their carefully hoarded ration coupons for sugar and other goods in short supply. Little Graham was growing rapidly, crawling around their feet as they worked. Rodger would be home for Christmas, but she was worried about him. For months, since May, he had been travelling from church to church telling his story. The thing which frustrated him was that it was always the same story.

'We were only in New Britain for eighteen months,' he said, 'so I'm no expert and there is no way to learn more up-to-date information at the moment. People only want to hear the story about us escaping from New Britain, anyway. I'm heartily sick of the sound of my own voice telling the same story.'

He had written to the mission General Secretary, John Burton, asking to be transferred to circuit work, but a letter had come back, congratulating him on his excellent deputation work but saying: 'There may be an opportunity during the year for some of you to go back to New Guinea and I think that you should be one of them. In that case, we would utilise you as deputation until such time as there is a possibility of you returning. . .' Kath knew that he was longing to go back. His heart was in New Britain, with those there whom he knew must be suffering. There was a sense in which he felt he had no *right* to be away from them. But when might he return? There was no sign that the Japanese hold on Rabaul was weakening. How long could Rodger live with the frustrations of telling the same story over and over?

In Marrabel on the road running north through South Australia, Daisy McArthur packed suitcases ready to travel. Her older son Malcolm was very excited. He had been talking for weeks about going to his Uncle Don McArthur's farm for Christmas. He had not been very happy at the village school during the year, troubled by all the changes that had happened to their family; the farm, blessed with the abundant love of Uncle Don and Auntie Cass, was a safe, known place in a changing world.

Daisy had mixed feelings about it. Don, when he wore his spectacles, looked so much like his brother Laurie that it hurt, yet she knew that she and the boys were welcome in his home. If her own mother had still been alive, it would have been different, but her mother had died when Daisy was born. Her father was a country man who didn't find it easy to show affection and did not know how to comfort his daughter while Laurie was a prisoner. For Daisy, the one person with whom she could completely share her heart was her husband and, short of a miracle, Laurie was not going to be home for Christmas.

Just before Christmas, Jean Poole waited on the railway platform at Kiama for her family to arrive on the train. John would be missing, of course, and her married sister Sybil would be with her family in northern New South Wales, but the others were coming and she was profoundly thankful for family support. Her dad would be in holiday mood, having put the responsibilities of being headmaster of Bexley Primary School behind him at the end of term.

Gordon would probably come armed with his fishing rod, ready for some rock fishing after an intense year of medical studies and exams. Joyce would tell her all about the work she was doing with her boss at Sydney University, producing the illustrations for a textbook on Australian geology, and they would all go for wonderful walks together, looking for rocks, wildlife or flora. Jean could hear the train coming, traversing the last stretch where the line almost touches the beach. In minutes her family would be with her. But John? John was not coming.

Other women faced the idea of their second Christmas without their husbands. A year ago, they had spent that strange Christmas in transit, sailing south on the *Macdhui* and the *Neptuna*. Now both ships were rusting hulks, sunk by enemy bombs. Helen Pearson was always hopeful; she had dreams of buying a house near the sea where Howard could come home to recover from being a prisoner of war.

Netta Allsop was going to her Pearce family for Christmas and looked forward to the release of being able to talk about her husband Ken and brother Wilf with people who loved them, too. Mel Trevitt had concluded her teaching appointment in Tasmania and was moving to Melbourne and a new job in the New Year. Marion Oakes had decided that she would begin nursing training in 1943, while she waited for Dan, whether her father approved or not, and Nellie Simpson sang Christmas songs for her little girl and the baby boy, wondering whether Tom had ever received any of the letters telling him what a lovely son he had.

Not long before Christmas, many of the women read a poem published in the *Australian Women's Weekly* which moved some of them to tears. An army engineer, writing from the horrors of the jungle battles on the Kokoda track, had written in honour of the native men of the island who were rescuing Australian soldiers. He called them 'fuzzy wuzzy angels'.

Women who had lived in New Guinea thought of men and women they had known, students, pastors and teachers, house servants who had shared their kitchen, neighbours, choirs of singers who had come, black shadows in lantern light, to sing in the warm darkness of Christmas Eve the songs of God-with-us. Were these same friends singing carols for their husbands across a barbed wire barricade?

The poem read in part:

Bringing back the badly wounded
Just as steady as a hearse,
Using leaves to keep the rain off
And as gentle as a nurse.
Slow and careful in bad places
On the awful mountain track,
The look upon their faces
Would make you think that Christ was black. . .

Two days before Christmas in Yokohama, Mavis wrote in her diary: 'Decorated dining room.' The next day, Christmas Eve, she wrote with some disgust: 'Made pull it down.'

'What harm was it doing?'

'Did they think the streamers made the place look untidy or what?' they demanded.

The dining room, for one day, had looked bright and colourful with festoons of fringed paper streamers and illustrations cut from old magazines. On a morning visit to the Club grounds, they had broken off a green branch from the wintry garden, powdered with new snow, and propped it in front of a window in their room. With paper and coloured pencils, they had drawn stars and paper angels and hung them from green twigs. In each corner of the room, women worked to make Christmas cards for each other and tiny handmade gifts.

But a visit from the chief guard crushed some of their attempts at Christmas cheer. He did not approve of the decorations in the dining room and commanded that they be removed. Kay pleaded for the little Christmas tree and, in the end, though the streamers and pictures were grudgingly removed, the pine branch remained.

'This time last year. . .' This time a year ago they had been under threat and the married women had just left, but at least they had been free. There had been Christmas mail from home and gifts, enormous festive meals shared with the mission men, jokes and silly songs, and swimming in the warm sea. It all seemed a world away.

'Where are the chairman, John Poole and the other men spending this Christmas, do you think?' they asked each other. 'They could be here in Japan at one of the camps like us.'

On Christmas Eve, there were two visitors. One was an official from the Japanese Foreign Office who brought them each a towel and underwear. The other stranger filled them with great hope.

'It's the Red Cross!' The message passed quickly among the women and they crowded to the upstairs windows to watch the official visitor leave his vehicle and supervise the unloading of cases of goods identified with the welcome sign of the red cross.

'At last!' they said among themselves. 'We'll see some action now. Look at all those goods coming for us — lovely. And if the Red Cross has found us, then it shouldn't be long before they'll arrange for us to be exchanged and we'll be home — too late for Christmas, but January would be good, too!'

They watched and they waited. But though they saw the Red Cross official, a European who they thought would probably be Swiss, they were not permitted to meet with him or speak with him. They saw him drive away again with a great sense of anticlimax.

'Did he even see us?' they asked each other. 'He must know we are here or he wouldn't have brought the boxes of things. But does he know who we are? Have they told him our names and where we are from?'

'Well, he'll come back again to see us. He must come back.'

It was a very odd Christmas Eve. There was a party in the evening, the women sitting around the fire to sing carols with snow falling lightly outside and a harbour full of enemy shipping lying in the dark beyond the windows. At home, a real, normal Christmas was a time of heat, blowflies and bushfires, with armfuls of gumtips, white daisies, blue agapanthus and pinkish-red Christmas bush to decorate the house. None had ever spent a Christmas as a prisoner. There was an unreality about the giving and receiving of gifts and cards, all carefully handmade; Mavis accepted cards to be given to her younger sister Zelle, and Mrs Bignell was given greetings for her beloved son Teddy. In a way, it made their families seem closer, but they all knew that it was only make-believe.

The individual Red Cross parcels were distributed — '1 chocolate, 1 packet sweets, 1 packet tea, 1 tin jam, 1 condensed milk, 1 packet biscuits' and the rest of the things Mavis recorded — and they were grateful to the Red Cross groups in Africa who had packed their parcels. Sorting through the treasures of the parcel, most of them agreed that they would like to save the contents for special occasions and parties: 'Who knows when we'll get the next one?' they said.

There was the special treat of hot cocoa with sugar in it that night, supplied from the kitchen from the bulk stocks of Red Cross supplies, and some carol singing, but when Mavis and Dora pulled their quilts over them that night they thought wistfully of choirs in New Britain and their families at home.

Their dinner on Christmas Day was an excellent one, with steak and vegetables and cakes, eaten with the company of the chief of the police guards and other men responsible for the internees. They played long, rather dull games of bridge most of the day, but for many of the women the part of that day which they would remember was the church service. Even for women who would not normally choose to attend a Christian church, it seemed good to all of them to worship together on Christmas Day. Strongminded women all had their own ideas of what was appropriate, but they all knew that this was not a time for simplistic images of a pretty baby and cardboard animals. For it to make any sense at all in the midst of war, the coming of the child had to bring the hope of peace.

Against a background of the conversation and laughter of their guards, the women sang carols and took their turn to read a prayer or a passage of scripture. One of them read a prayer for world leaders, discovered in a 1940 Christmas edition of *Esquire* magazine, that 'they may be instrumental in establishing a just and lasting Peace on Earth when men may live free from hate, fear, cruelty, hunger and want'. It was the true prayer of their heart. They had all seen enough to know how desperately the world needed the coming of the Prince of Peace.

As Psalm 46 was read, the women clung to the words:

God is our refuge and strength, a very present help in trouble.
Therefore will not we fear, though the earth be removed, and
though the mountains be carried into the midst of the sea;
Though the waters thereof roar and be troubled, though the
mountains shake with the swelling thereof. . .
He maketh wars to cease unto the end of the earth; he
breaketh the bow and cutteth the spear in sunder; he burneth
the chariot in fire.
Be still and know that I am God. . .

The New Year of 1943 came in with bitter weather in Japan. At the Yokohama Amateur Rowing Club the swimming pool froze over and women huddled around the little stove in their room.

On 6 January, the women watched an air display fly over Yokohama, hundreds of Japanese planes in formation. They tried to count them; some said three hundred, others said five hundred planes. Last year, their guards told them, the air show had displayed a thousand Japanese planes before their people, a mighty show of strength and technology. Now, of course, many planes were in action around the Pacific theatres of war, they explained — 'or shot out of the sky by our fellows!' muttered the women.

On the same day in January 1943, the Japanese Navy Department sent a letter to the Japanese Prisoner of War Information Bureau. It gave details of the sinking of the ship *Montevideo Maru*, 'torpedoed by a US submarine around noon [sic] on 1 July 1942. . . on her way to Hainan Island from Rabaul. . . was sunk immediately. Some of the crew who were in several lifeboats, landed on the following day on the coast in the vicinity of Boeadre lighthouse on Luzon Island. However, all are believed to have been killed on 6 July by the soldiers and Filipinos in the area. . . No record about the POWs on board has been found.' There was also the nominal roll of over a thousand Australian prisoners, 845 servicemen and 208 civilians, who had sailed from Rabaul with the ship and were presumed lost.

A functionary at the information bureau placed the documents among the proliferation of disordered papers being generated by the presence of many thousands of Allied prisoners under Nippon in many camps across Asia, one more set of documents among many. The information was swallowed up in the papery chaos, to vanish for years.

The annual meeting of the Methodist Overseas Mission met in Sydney that January. There was still blackout material on the windows but, over the year since their last meeting, the fear of invasion by the enemy had intensified and then gradually waned. Members gathering to deal with mission business spoke of sons and brothers away in war zones and of the recent battles in Milne Bay and the Solomon Islands. Even so, the very real fear of an invasion of Australia which had shadowed 1942 was lifting.

The question of the missing missionaries was raised. There had been no authentic word since the letters of a year ago, posted from Rabaul on 16 January 1942. General Secretary Burton explained what he had attempted.

'Every smallest clue has been followed up,' he said, 'but no further information is available. Most of the clues proved to be worthless, anyway. We must pray that they are all still safe and well in Rabaul.'

There were murmurs of sympathy and concern around the room, and Burton added, 'It's their families whom I feel most sorry for — a whole year with no news is very cruel.'

When it came to nominations for the positions of the chairmen of the districts, the names of Rundle for Papua, Leonard Kentish for north Australia and Laurence McArthur for New Guinea were brought forward and chosen. They could not have known that within two weeks they would have news that Len Kentish had been captured by the Japanese on the northern coast of Arnhem Land, north Australia, and that he, too, had now vanished.

Dora's January birthday came and went. It marked a full year in captivity under the Japanese for the women. Snow fell during the night and the next day when they went into the grounds to carry firewood for the stove they walked in it, leaving a trail of footprints. Dora was often cold, but she manufactured a jacket for herself from a blanket and wrapped strips of leftover blanket around her legs like leggings and that kept her warmer.

Even with the little stove in the room, it was very cold at night and the women often sat in pairs rubbing their partner's feet or hands to warm them. Too cold to sleep, women combined their bedding, sleeping in pairs with one straw-filled mattress under and another over them and all the quilts heaped up. Since the arrival of the Red Cross supplies, their food had been better for a time, though they were sure that some of the bulk supplies passed to their cook were being redirected to the cook's relatives. With the new year, there were new rules. The women were to take turns to help in the kitchen. This had clear advantages. Mavis particularly enjoyed the chance to cook and from time to time helped make soups, jam and bread.

Despite the cold, there were some compensations during the winter months. The glow of the stove drew them into companionable gatherings around it, playing many long games of bridge or whist with playing cards carefully manufactured by Mrs Bignell. For a short time they were issued with magazines and books through the Red Cross and even, briefly, some records to play on the record player left in the club. Over several weeks, they produced two editions of a handmade magazine they called 'POW Weekly', filled with tongue-in-cheek tales and recipes for delicacies like cooking horsemeat or cabbage 'in washing up water in a rusty tin dish'. Paper folding went on and on and, by the end of March, Mavis recorded the completion of 55 000 small and 19 000 large envelopes. At least two of the guards were kind to them, an old man they called Poppa-san and a very young one with a ready smile whom they called Happy-san.

Through all the cold months there was always the question: when would they be released? The Swiss man had been seen only once in the distance, but they had still not been able to speak to him. They had, more than once, gone through the formality of filling in forms about their personal particulars and had signed no-escape forms. They had been visited by a doctor every few months and a dentist, then a senior man from the foreign office and an official from the POW information bureau as well as the chief of police.

'They come and inspect us,' complained Kay Parker, 'but they refuse to let us send out a single letter and they don't answer any of my questions. They all know that we are here and who we are, but have they let the Australian authorities know? Or is our government just leaving us to rot?'

By the time of Mavis' birthday in April, the worst of the winter was over. The Red Cross supplies had almost all been used up and the food situation was deteriorating again, the stove had been taken out of their room and they were made to work outdoors carrying ashes to put on roads made slushy with the thaw of snow and ice. But Chris gave a tea party for Mavis' birthday, offering the last of the delicacies from her Christmas Red Cross parcel; then there was Easter Day and Anzac Day — all together on the same day.

When Happy-san came in one morning carrying a branch of palest pink double cherry blossom and arranged it with grace in a jar for their pleasure, the women knew that spring had come — and renewed hope with it.

17

May–December 1943

ONE NIGHT IN THE RURAL COMMUNITY of Alstonville in northern NSW, a woman sat knitting and listening to the wireless. Jean Brawn had put her children to bed and now she waited for her husband Arthur to come home from a church meeting. Arthur Brawn was the local Methodist minister and the family had spent a term as missionaries in New Guinea during the 1930s.

Jean Brawn had an active and enquiring mind; she was always eager to explore things which interested her including early Australian history and missionary activity in New Guinea. Though their family had only spent three years on New Britain before ill health brought them home, her babies had been born there and she and Arthur were still part of the network of families who had worked in that island group.

She moved the knobs on her wireless set, listening through the splutter and whistle of static for recognisable sounds. Over recent months, her curiosity had been roused by the voices which travelled by short wave from Tokyo — Tokyo Rose and others. Arthur had said: 'It's only propaganda put out in English to make the Allies upset, you know. Don't take it too seriously.'

She knew that. Often the propaganda broadcast was read by the familiar pre-war Sydney radio announcer Charles Cousens, now a prisoner of the Japanese. They had noticed, she and Arthur, that Cousens altered his intonation according to the material he was reading, a mocking or satirical tone alternating with a serious voice, and they guessed that he might be trying to give clues to his Allied listeners as to the reliability of the news items. Sometimes the program listed prisoners of war who were alive and Mrs Brawn always listened with the greatest attention just in case the names of their missing missionary friends were read.

Across the kilometres which separated her from the other missionary women, scraps of news sometimes passed, including the latest news on where in Australia the women were. Mel Trevitt was back in Sydney doing a personnel course before going to Melbourne to work with the Yarra Falls Woollen Mills where they produced cloth for US Army uniforms. Marion Oakes had begun nursing training at Royal North Shore Hospital in Sydney despite her father's objections. Jean Shelton had not been well for some time, but more recently had been able to get a job with her pre-marriage employers, the Institute of Engineers, and was sharing a house in Haberfield. Helen Wayne was teaching in the Blue Mountains. As to the missing men, no-one had heard a word for at least a year and a half.

The voice of Cousens came through the crackling of the wireless, clear enough to hear every word. Jean Brawn picked up her knitting again. It was always a small triumph to tune in well to short wave. The wool was slipping smoothly onto the knitting needles, plain and purl, when the words from Japan halted her busy fingers in mid-stitch. The voice was solemn, measured, with no hint of flippancy or mockery. The voice spoke of a disaster at sea, of the forces of the United States torpedoing a prison ship off Luzon with almost total loss of life, apart from fewer than twenty crew members who had been on deck at the time. The sober tones continued: the prisoners had been a large contingent of Australians — private citizens and soldiers — being transported from Rabaul. . .

When her husband arrived home later, she told him what she had heard. Could it be believed? It was too terrible to contemplate. Yet, unless it was an immense lie fabricated to demoralise the Allies, it might have happened. Dreadful things did happen. But not to entire communities. Surely not to whole groups of one's friends *at once*. There was no way of knowing what to believe, but they decided to say nothing to others.

Next time Arthur Brawn visited Sydney, he approached John Burton in private and told him what his wife had heard that night on the short wave broadcast.

'We've heard the same story,' Burton said, 'from the authorities in Canberra. They contacted me in confidence to say that this rumour had come to them from Japan, but there is no way of confirming it and they have advised us to say nothing to the next-of-kin of any of our people who were in Rabaul. It could be a hoax. Even if it is true that a prison ship has been sunk, we have no idea exactly who may have been on board at the time.'

Burton looked drawn and tired. The responsibility of doing what was best for his staff (many of whom had vanished months earlier) and their families (who kept up a steady flow of letters asking for any news at all) was weighing heavily. This latest story might well be another groundless rumour, but who could tell?

Arthur Brawn travelled back home to his wife with a confused and burdened heart. These men who were missing were his colleagues during his days in New Britain. Men like Shelton, McArthur, Oakes and Linggood had been his friends. Were they prisoners but alive somewhere in New Britain? Or were some — or all — of them dead? If that was so, how had they died? One thing was certain: until the truth was revealed, nothing should be said to the women who waited so hopefully for their men.

There was a sharp rap on the classroom door. A child entered. 'Excuse me, Mrs Poole, the headmaster is sending this around.'

Jean Poole took the note. A whale and her calf had been sighted in the nearby bay and some of the classes might be interested, he had written.

The lesson in grammar could wait, she decided. With her class at her heels, Jean led them down the stairs, across the playground and along the road to the rocky headland. Below them in the cool wintry waters of the bay were the whales, mother and child. The children were fascinated, astonished at the wonder of the creatures playing, and Jean watched the children's faces as they watched the whales. Her fingers groped in her bag for pencil and paper. She wanted to sketch what she was seeing, to add to her collection of 'mothers and babies'. To her delight, she had been invited recently to illustrate a manuscript being prepared by her former botany teacher, Thistle Harris, for a book introducing young school children to the world of nature. Of all her teaching, this was the most exciting aspect.

As they left the headland to walk back to school, Jean looked around her. To the north lay the long gleaming sands of Seven Mile Beach, where she had walked and played beach cricket with her own family and the Mainstones during the summer. Nearby was the surf beach, over the road from her house, where she swam, and the rocks where her brother Gordon fished; Gordon was now in his final year of medical studies at university and had ridden down to Kiama on his bicycle to do some fishing in his autumn holidays. The primary school was along the road, with the Methodist church and the Anglican church, the shops, the homes of school children and choir members and other townspeople who were becoming her friends.

But nowhere was there anything in that scene which linked her with her husband. They had now been cut off from each other for as long as they had lived together as man and wife — and it hurt.

That weekend Jean joined the people at the Methodist church, as she usually did. She sat with the choir in the choir pews at the front of the church and smiled across at friends in the congregation as they all rose to sing the first hymn. A neighbour beside her gave her a gentle nudge and drew her attention to the back of the church.

The strange men were back again. In a community where everyone knew each other, the two visitors could not hope to remain invisible. They had appeared once or twice before in town, going around asking questions and even coming to church. She had heard in the local grocery store that they were back again.

'Your minister had better watch his step,' the grocer had said, not unkindly.

In the pulpit stood the Methodist minister, the Rev. Dr Collocott. In other circumstances, it would have been her own husband, John, who stood there leading worship. It was hard not to picture John in this place — John's words, John's presence. . . But it was not. Dr Collocott was respected, known as a man of great kindness, but — it was whispered around the town — he was a pacifist. A pacifist, for goodness sake, in these days when any red-blooded man ought to be fighting the enemy, people said. No wonder the government had him under surveillance.

Jean watched him, the knuckles gripping the pulpit, his face pale and intense. 'Be careful,' she found herself thinking. 'You can see them back there. Don't give them anything to use against you.'

With part of her mind she listened to his sermon, to words that were chosen with the precision of one who knows that every word matters. At another level she thought of the times when she and others, including her friend the Anglican minister, had been in the Collocott home for lively discussion groups, when people had explored together what it meant to be Christians in a troubled world and had presented very different ways of understanding the Christian faith. In that setting it had been safe to speak out with honesty. People trusted each other there, even if they did not agree with each other. But not here. Not with those men sitting in the back of the church, waiting to see whether subversion was preached.

On her way out of church that morning, moving out of the cool building into the winter sunshine, she took the hand of the minister at the door. He looked strained and weary as he greeted the people. The poison of war infected everything and everyone, she knew, including those whose strong philosophy rejected everything about making war. No-one was immune.

That afternoon, Jean wrote her weekly letter to John. 'When you come home. . .'

She had used that phrase so often in letters over the months of waiting. So many things were forming an invisible queue, waiting for the day when John would come home; things to show, things to tell and things to do together. It might take years to catch up, it seemed. So few things linked her with him these days. Would he be interested in the whales, or in whether or not Dr Collocott was arrested?

But she had something this time which they had shared and she wrote eagerly, remembering. Beside her on the table lay the slim grey-covered publication. 'Reprinted from *Oceania*, March 1943. Vol XIII. No.3' it read, signalling its academic dignity. 'Still Further Notes On a Snake Dance of the Bainings' proclaimed the title and, under those words and nicely centred, 'By Jean Poole'.

'They published it!' She wrote on, telling John about the excitement of being invited to add her own notes to publications by anthropologists who had observed the people of the Bainings ten years earlier. The publishers had used her coloured illustration of all the dancers in their amazing costumes and headpieces that were like fantastic statuary. She had spent hours reproducing the dancing figures from her rough sketches drawn by firelight there in the mountains, working with her yellow and orange crayons to try to recreate her memory of the glow of the fire, sparks leaping up into the darkness, dancers whirling past — and John close beside her.

'They printed four of your photos of the village people,' she went on. He'll be pleased about that, she thought. We did all those long treks together and collected the sketches, language notes and photographs together — he'll be keen to see the article one day, when he comes home.

There was another piece of news to add which linked her with him but made him seem further away than ever. She wanted to tell him that Kath Brown was expecting a second baby. Kath with a second baby. . . She didn't begrudge Kath and Rodger their family. That wasn't it. But she couldn't help her own private disappointment that she and John had not started their family before this dreadful time of separation had begun. Other women had come back from New Guinea with their children and Beryl Beazley, Nellie Simpson and Eileen Pearce had all been pregnant when they returned and had given birth since. One day, she prayed, she too would have a child.

'When you come home, John. . .'

If it had not been for the changing seasons, there would have been very little to report in the nurses' diaries as the months of 1943 passed slowly by. Snow on the ground of their compound had given way to cherry blossom and now it was summer. Occasionally, they were given cherries. The days and nights grew hotter and hotter — 'like Yass or Junee,' some said, 'cold winters and very hot summers'. One night in midsummer they were given permission to sleep outside. The air outside was just a little cooler than in the heated building, but they were 'eaten alive by mosquitoes!' they complained.

By the time they marked the first anniversary of their arrival behind the walls and gates of the Yokohama Rowing Club on 5 August 1943, the pattern of their lives seemed to have settled into an endless cycle of repetition. There was endless folding of paper into envelopes; '70 000 small and 51 600 large envelopes finished,' Mavis wrote in July, and the number continued to multiply. Endless little knitted bags in gaudy stripes.

There was the rhythm of ceremonial bowing towards the emperor's palace each month and celebration of each other's birthdays, with women now marking their second birthday in captivity. They had heard each other's jokes and anecdotes before, and were condemned to the tedium of hearing them all again. Evening games of cards went on and on interminably. News from the rest of the world was limited to glimpses of their guards' newspapers in Japanese, and many of them had already read most of the books in the bookcase. Food was becoming less plentiful and less varied and the women were losing weight. The last of the Red Cross parcels from Christmas had been used up.

Hope of release had not died. Hope was the thing that kept them going, but it was hard to maintain on those days when they felt that no-one knew where they were, and perhaps no-one cared.

Early in August, they were told they could prepare vegetable gardens for their own use. There were mixed feeling about this. 'It doesn't look as if they are expecting us to leave soon, if it is worth us planting vegetables,' they said.

Even so, Mavis and Dora enjoyed the chance to work in the garden as a change from paper folding. Dora's family owned a nursery business at home in Newcastle and Mavis' family had always grown vegetables, so both felt their spirits rising as they planted seeds with the other women. Over a period of days they saw the first signs of radishes, turnips, cucumbers, beans and spinach bursting through the soil.

The seedlings were still very young when the women noticed that the ship with the white cross had returned to Yokohama harbour. For a week they watched it, taking turns to peer between the slats of the fence which blocked their view of the harbour. This time, perhaps, the ship had come to take them home, they thought.

Kay Parker was called to speak to a Japanese officer on 18 August and came back with wonderful news. 'We've been told to pack up our things, ready to move out!'

'The white cross ship — at last, it's come for us.'

There was not a great deal to pack. The mission women had a suitcase each with their few clothes. So sure were they that they were on their way home that some nearly left behind the coarse winter clothes they had made months earlier, but others urged them to keep everything with them, just in case. Each of them had acquired a few odds and ends with the little money they had earned for knitting and folding envelopes; their woman guard, Mama-san, had done some shopping for them from time to time and every treasured item was carefully packed ready to go.

The next morning they were called together and instructed to bring their bags with them.

'Today is the fourth anniversary of when I left Australia to go to New Guinea,' Mavis said. 'Maybe it will be the day we'll leave Japan to go home!'

For the first time in over a year, the gates into the rowing club grounds were thrown open and they were permitted to walk through them. A truck with guards waited for them outside. As they clambered aboard, hopes were dampened when they saw that the truck also carried mops, brooms and buckets. It seemed that they were to do a domestic task somewhere. Even so, after more than a year behind a fence, they devoured everything with their eyes as they drove along the narrow streets. After a year with no-one but the other eighteen women in their group, a few guards, the cook Kimora, visiting officers and their chaperone Mama-san, it was great refreshment to see ordinary people in the streets.

Pretty girls passed by, many of them wearing Western fashions, women with their children, workmen going by in trams — 'trams like at home!' They passed the restful green elegance of city parks, pointed out the fine buildings that were a major hospital and the court house, stared curiously at the suburban houses. A church spire rose above a city street, overgrown with ivy, the place of an enclave of Christians in Japan.

'It looks so — so ordinary,' one of them murmured. 'Just like any city with ordinary people in it. The people in the street didn't look so very evil.'

The truck pulled up outside the police station and they were led inside. The rowing club was needed for a few weeks for other purposes, they were told, and they were to stay at the police station in the meantime and give the place a complete spring-clean. (They had been watching new buildings going up near the rowing club on the reclaimed land on the waterfront and were aware of troop movements in the area.) Their meals would be brought to them from the rowing club which was not far away. No, the officials told them, there had been no instructions about the women being sent out on a ship; they would do better to obey orders and not dream foolish dreams.

For the next two weeks, they worked at the police station. They were still under guard and there was no opportunity to move from the building, but at least it was a change from the confines of the rowing club and its grounds. While they were there, Mavis was ill with a mild bout of appendicitis. The police officers gave them permission to have a church service, which was only allowed occasionally, and they were thankful to use the chance.

When they were loaded back onto the truck again, they did not drive to the wharves as they had dreamed. They found themselves back at the rowing club. There were some small compensations. The time at the police station had given them a brief change of scenery and a change of people in authority. A few of the women returned to the rowing club with some minor booty, black fabric that looked remarkably like a strip from the lower edge of the blackout curtains and green felt that was reminiscent of the top of the police pool table. The vegetables they had planted were thriving and they hoped to eat fresh greens before too long. The fences that had circled the club with its tennis court and pool had been removed, however, to allow the grounds to be used for other purposes, and they were told that they would no longer be allowed downstairs.

The white cross ship that had been in the harbour was gone. It was no comfort at all to learn later that American women and children had been evacuated on it. 'What about us Australian women? Don't we count at all? Or have we vanished completely from the eyes of the world?'

It was as well that the nurses did not realise that, when the gates shut behind them after their brief excursion to the police station, they would not open again for them for almost another year, and even then it would be to change one prison for another.

Kath and Rodger Brown's second son, Jeffery, was born in September 1943. Kath was not really surprised that Rodger was not able to be in Adelaide near her at the time. Although he had asked for permission to have meetings in Adelaide at the time the baby was expected, he found himself repeating his missionary story far from home while Kath was in labour. Kath tried to be philosophical about it, but Rodger was disappointed and angry.

'Other women have to put up with a lot worse than that,' she said, 'and Mother has looked after me very well.'

Somehow it seemed impossible to escape from the thought that, because Rodger was at home and free while his friends were imprisoned somewhere, there was nothing he could refuse to do for the church. After all, his friends were suffering so much more: why shouldn't he sacrifice something? Repeatedly he had requested permission to leave his itinerant life to transfer to another missionary area or to work in a home circuit. The South Australian Methodist Conference had requested the mission board to release

Rodger for circuit work — 'our need is desperate' — but the reply had been unbending. 'Our need as a board is also desperate. We cannot release him.'

Kath often worried about Rodger. He missed his family desperately, but duty — the duty imposed on him by others and imposed on himself by his misplaced guilt — forced him to be away from them for long periods, including three months at a time in other states. Instead of coming home to his own home and family, he spent many evenings sitting on slow country trains or making polite conversation at yet another parsonage with people he had just met.

Because these kind strangers were his hosts, he never felt that he could pass through their home without offering his time in some practical way; as he chopped piles of firewood or washed up mountains of dishes, he thought wistfully of his own family who had to manage without his help. At every house he would search the host's bookshelves for something worthwhile to read, but after a few chapters he would always have to replace the book and move on to another house with yet another book left unfinished. But it was the futility and repetition of it all that affected him most of all.

'I tell my story,' he told Kath, 'at every school in the district, to every group of women, to little gatherings of people in the evenings or in church services, over and over and over. Even though I've tried to prepare as interesting a presentation as possible, with a good map and slides to illustrate it all, it doesn't help. It gets so bad that I can't stand the sound of my own voice. Sometimes I wake up in the morning, feeling that I'll vomit if I have to say it one more time.

'If I thought I was doing any good, it wouldn't be so bad. But in a lot of places, the people don't really care what might happen after the war in New Britain. It means nothing to them. They know nothing about the people or the place and the only questions they ask are things like, "What do the people eat?" "What's the weather like?" A bloke asked me once, "Are the white ants very bad?" And I couldn't resist it — I looked very serious and told him that a man with a wooden leg hasn't got a chance! They only turn up at the meetings because they think they'll get an exciting escape story — all they want is entertainment.'

His frustration troubled her. If only he could channel all his boundless energy into something that seemed to him to be more substantial. Yet Kath knew that she could not complain. Women all around her were managing without their husbands. Other women's husbands had been killed in foreign lands or were prisoners. Some suffered under the awful uncertainty of the fearful word: MISSING.

Kath thought of the situation of other friends who had been with them in New Guinea. Nellie Simpson's baby John was over a year old and she still didn't know whether Tom knew he'd even been born. Helen Pearson struggled with an exhausting little boy without ever having Howard with her to help. She'd heard that Daisy McArthur had not been well lately; she must be very lonely so far from any of her close friends. Elsie Wilson had been in Adelaide recently to do an in-service course on children with special needs, she'd heard, and was applying for a transfer. Elsie was making the best of a lonely situation and was studying a unit of history through Adelaide University while she waited to go back to New Britain.

There were the families of the missing nurses, too. Kath had been fond of Dora since they were students together in missionary college and she knew Mavis and Dorothy, too. But of them all Jean Christopher was the closest. She was a fellow South Australian and her family had strong links of friendship with the Browns. Chris' sister had been worried about their parents as they waited in vain for news of their daughter, so made a long journey to visit them at their home in Kadina in order to offer some comfort. But she was startled to be received with panic and suspicion: 'Why have you come? What's happened? Is Jean dead?'

No-one was untouched by the poisonous ripples of a war which dragged on. Kath knew that she should be grateful for a good home with her mother, two healthy little sons and a husband who was alive and well, even if he was very unhappy.

Dora looked at the other nurses in disbelief. The guards had just carefully counted every book in the rowing club bookcase, locked the cupboard door on them, and departed with the key.

'What's the problem? Do they think this collection of not-very-good novels and outdated manuals is subversive literature?'

'Maybe they don't want us to escape, even in our imaginations.'

'They didn't count my book,' Dora said. 'I still have my Bible in my things.'

'We'll be glad to borrow it sometimes, if that is all right with you,' some said.

The weather was getting colder again by then and winter was coming on, with wild storms that whipped up the harbour waters. Waves crashed high against the harbour wall outside and the darkening room in which they all worked and slept felt as if it were closing in around them. The summer warmth, their vegetable garden (the produce of which had mostly been eaten by the guards) and the trip to the police station seemed very long ago. The small escapes of travel in imagination through the books in the bookcase had been important to many of them.

Escape was not a realistic idea even in fantasy. When they had been ordered to sign no-escape contracts, there had seemed little point in refusing. How could one or two women slip away without immediate detection when the full group of nineteen was always visible at a glance to Mama-san? The daily roll calls, with the women lined up morning and evening to be counted and then to bow deeply before the guard, were only a formality. Even if they could find a way out of the building, how could one or two shabbily dressed, tall '*Goshu*' pigs' or 'horses' with their Western faces and little fluency in Japanese language find a way to sanctuary in a strange city where they had no friends and where each of them would be identified as the enemy? It would be safer to stay together.

And yet they longed to escape, to leave behind the limitations of their space and the irritations of the deadening sameness of their days. More and more of them were having health problems as their diet became more limited. Kay Parker had become very ill one day and had been taken, with one of the other nurses for company, to a local hospital. She had returned the same afternoon, only a little improved. 'I decided I'd rather come back and die with my friends,' she said, 'if that is going to happen.'

'When we go home. . .' They said it all the time. Some found evidence that soon they would be released when they read their tealeaves, and some had dreams about it. Others planned in detail all the things they would do when at last they were free. Home for the elderly Mrs Jones was America and Mrs Bignell dreamed of the Solomon Islands, but all the others were Australian and each spoke of her own home district as the most prized place in the world. Soon it would be Christmas again and their dreams of being with their families seemed as far away as ever.

Dora was thankful that she still had her Bible. Some time earlier she had set herself the task of reading the whole Bible, the full collection of sixty-six books, from beginning to end. She had always read her Bible as part of her Christian discipline and knew parts of it by heart, but she had never before read it from cover to cover.

Now, as the dull and repetitive days dragged by, she began to read. In one way it was an escape, a movement in thought into the grandeur of the beginnings of things, to see an awesome God creating and releasing his people into the terrors of being free to make choices. Through the great sweep of the history of the people of Israel she read, picturing that ancient people escaping from one bondage under Egypt, but still trapped in the long bondage of their own disobedient wanderings through the wilderness until they could say that at last they had come home.

One book of the Bible followed another — the works of history, law, poetry, allegory, parable, proverbs — and it seemed to Dora that over and over again there was the theme of a people longing to find their way home, generation after generation of wandering exiles, all looking for signs that God was with them. Sitting among her fellow-prisoners, Dora knew that, like those ancient wanderers, they all longed for home. The only thing that sustained her was the knowledge that, while they waited and ached for freedom, God had not abandoned them.

It was after roll call and lights-out that Dora knew that her friends, deprived of their books, were not giving up so easily. 'Dora, come and help us move this thing!'

A small group of women was clustered around the bookcase. With some pushing and heaving, they dragged the heavy cupboard away from the wall. One of them had found something to use as a screwdriver and, lifting away screws from the back of the cupboard, levered the back open until it was possible to pull out some books. After the cupboard was replaced in its former position, maintaining an impression of innocence, the women took their reading matter away to read in private.

'And Dora, put me on the list to borrow your Bible, too.'

Hidden from the eyes of the rest of the world, people continued to live — and die — in the islands of New Britain, New Ireland, New Hanover and the Duke of York group. Thousands of Japanese soldiers replaced the pre-war community. In the earlier months of the occupation, many public buildings including churches had been taken over as warehouses, stables and brothels.

The new Chinese school, with its handsome facade and fine facilities, had been filled with Japanese supplies of food. The families of the Chinese community, who had opened their new school two years earlier with the triumph of a great feast, were now scattered. Some moved out of town to friends along the coast and others clung to what remained of Chinatown, living in partial freedom, though obliged to work as labourers for the army in occupation and to report regularly.

With a tiny group of Australian prisoners still in Rabaul, the former newspaper editor Gordon Thomas noted in his diary, 'We are all getting on each other's nerves after so long a period with no other company.' Monotony, isolation, apprehension: the things that disturbed the Australians were just the same for their Japanese guards. They were discovering, over many months and through a growing facility in each other's languages, that many of the Japanese men they met during their working days were very like themselves: homesick, talking of family and friends, thinking of the civilian lives they had led before war engulfed them, longing for peace to come. Thomas felt sorry for himself and his friends, but also recorded some sympathy for the imported Comfort Women he saw in the community 'looking very tired and coarse — how else with their clientele, said to be thirty to forty per day. . .'

Rumours filtered from one community to another with the few men who were given mobility. Other groups of prisoners were said to have been brought to Rabaul from distant places where they had been captured — British, American, Indian and Chinese servicemen. It was said that there were some seventeen nationalities represented among the people who were behind barbed wire at the mission at Vunapope: missionaries, students, and women and children of mixed race. Stories passed from mouth to mouth of violence and executions, names of former friends or acquaintances being whispered. The group of nine Australian men who had been seen passing Vunapope on a truck at the end of July 1942 had not been seen since; natives said they saw their baggage being buried by Japanese. . . Tom Goss, whose wife was one of the government nurses, and Bill Huntley, who used to work with the Methodist mission, were among them.

For some months through the middle of 1943 there had been a lull in Allied bombing, but late in the year the raids began again with sweeps of planes dropping death and destruction. As the streets of the town of Rabaul were gradually reduced to rubble, tunnels were being gouged from hillsides and more and more of the military used the tunnels for their offices, dormitories and storehouses.

One of the casualties of the bombing raids was the Chinese school which was smashed, burned and gutted. After the fires died down, Chinese men asked permission to salvage what they could from the ruins. There was not much to save. The teacher Mr Mow, with Rev. Mo Pui Sam and the clerk from Burns Philp, Ping Hui, were among those who raked through the twisted remnants of their hopes for the children of their community. Beneath the top layer of destroyed foodstuff they discovered layers of canned food, blackened, bulging from the intense heat of the fires.

'We'll take as many as we can transport,' they decided, 'and use anything that is any good for parties for the children, because food is getting shorter all the time.' They turned away at last, leaving the rubble behind.

It would not be long before the bombing would make Chinatown impossible as a place to live. The Japanese would send them out of town to a place called Ratongo where hundreds of people were forced to create their own camp, begin their own food gardens and find a source of water. It was hard to forget that the Australian evacuation ships had sailed away and had not offered their women and children a chance to escape.

In New Guinean village groups, people mourned the loss of their freedom and their homes. Their land, their gardens and their livestock were no longer their own. In the early months, the army of occupation had assured the New Guineans that they had come to release them from the shackles of the colonial whites, bringing in the dream of Co-Prosperity in their region, but villagers forced from their traditional homes saw little sign of prosperity.

Young village men, deceived by promises of feasts and benefits, left home for Rabaul, only to find themselves taken into distant places of battle as forced labour, many of them not free to return home for years. Men were made to carry heavy loads and were beaten when they fell under their burdens. Old men were stripped of their cherished pigs and chickens without compensation. Family members were made to ask permission before gardens could be planted, but when the food was ripe it was often taken by the soldiers of occupation, leaving village families hungry and distressed. Children were told that they must attend classes in Japanese language, and confused villagers heard their children chanting the words of a people who were hurting and humiliating them.

For many of the people of the villages, Christian faith gave them strength to go on and they did their best to gather often for prayer, the singing of songs of faith and the reading of their Bibles. But these gatherings were an offense to the Japanese. 'You are praying to your god to send the American and Australian bombers to fight against us. It is forbidden to meet in this way!' they were told.

Treasured Bibles and hymn books were carefully wrapped in leaves and buried in secret places and public meetings for prayer came to an end. Searches were made of their simple homes for books, papers and pencils, and anything found was destroyed. In a number of places, New Guinean church leaders were executed, leaving the surviving village groups shocked and grief-stricken.

There were those who lost hope in the Christian God as their world disintegrated around them, returning to the ancient rites of their ancestors, and others who clung more firmly than ever to their faith in a God who would come at last to rescue them.

At the Catholic mission at Vunapope, the community of some 350 people maintained their life behind barbed wire, doing their best to retain the rhythms of worship, study and work. As the bombing intensified, a larger and larger shelter was tunnelled into a hillside, in addition to their bunkers. What had once been a large and peaceful mission compound had become an arsenal of Japanese ammunition and explosives. It was clear that they would be a target of prime importance one day.

Just before Christmas 1943, Jean Poole travelled to Glen Innes in the north of NSW with her sister Joyce. The two sisters went to stay with their married sister Sybil while she waited for the birth of her baby. The women had many family things happening. There were the preparations for the baby, Gordon's completion of his medical studies with the six-year-course concentrated into five years because of the war, Joyce's work on 'Geology of Australia' and Jean's on the school textbook.

'Ask Joyce about the person she brought down to meet me at Kiama recently!' commanded Jean. 'A British lieutenant-commander from an aircraft carrier in Sydney harbour, no less.'

They laughed together, teasing Joyce about her romance, but sometimes it was an effort for Jean to enter into their happiness. She couldn't help it. Joyce in love, Sybil embroidering grub-roses on baby clothes. . . she was herself in a kind of limbo, cut off from her love and with no hope of bearing John's child until he came home.

When they sat together reading the papers in Christmas week, though, she was grateful that her sisters were with her. Newspapers carried stories of Rabaul, told by pilots who had flown over it on bombing missions. Though the south-eastern Milne Bay area of Papua was now in Allied hands again, Rabaul and the island of New Britain were still a strong 'enemy base'. She found it hard to imagine the pleasant tropical town as a major base for thousands of Japanese soldiers. But then these days there were so many things that were hard to imagine. There were stories of continual heavy bombing and the church newspaper suggested that it had probably 'reduced to cinders much of our valuable mission property'.

'Never mind the property,' said Jean. 'What about our men? What about Mikael To Bilak and Louisa, Akuila To Ngaru, and the Chinese community — and John?'

The paper predicted: 'The recapture of Rabaul and other enemy strong points in the Bismarck Archipelago is in progress and will probably result in the bloodiest battles fought south of the equator in this World War. The enemy is heavily reinforcing his troops. . . That our native Methodists will be swept into the maelstrom seems inevitable. . .'

That winter of 1943–1944 was bitterly cold in Japan. Some people said they had never had a winter like it in seventy years. The civilian community beyond the walls of the Yokohama Amateur Rowing Club continued to suffer from the disruptions that war was bringing to their people, as well as shortages and the miseries of harsh and relentless cold.

Snowbound, chilled, isolated, sometimes hungry, sometimes ill, the little group of imprisoned women lived out the endless repetitions of their days. Events to mark the passing of time were valued; two minutes' silence on Armistice Day, an imagined horse race and Cup party for the Melbourne Cup, a table decorated with paper wattle and kangaroos for Christmas dinner, a homegrown minstrel party and drama group for New Year, bridge parties, birthday parties with treasured foodstuff from Red Cross parcels.

The walls of the rowing club tightened around the women, squeezing out news of the rest of the world or any contact with their families, crushing into a confined space all their activities and relationships. Not one letter or message had passed in or out of their prison to their families or employers since they had arrived in Japan. (A secret cable from London to Canberra in those days strongly denied the suggestion that any Australian prisoners of war might be limited to 'only one letter per month'; there were no limits on mail, it declared.)

Even the contents of the large communal Red Cross parcel brought to them for Christmas 1943 depressed them. As they excitedly unpacked the parcel, they were very disappointed. The limited range of clothing and toiletries was insufficient for them each to have an adequate share, and a lot of the items were shoes and clothing for young children.

'They must think we are a group of civilian women and children,' they said in despair. 'Even the Red Cross doesn't know who we are, hidden away here!'

18

January–August 1944

ICY WATER LIKE SHARP DAGGERS stung unprotected skin. Rapid splashes rinsed the last of the soap away and another nurse snatched up a towel to dry herself before she froze. There was no temptation to linger under the cold showers at the rowing club while snow lay on the ground outside. In mocking imitation of the steam from dreamed-of hot showers, the bathroom windows had fogged with condensation when their warm bodies had met the cold water.

'You're getting skinnier!'

'Speak for yourself — so are you. What else would you expect when the food gets less all the time?'

'Being hungry isn't as bad as being cold. When will we feel really warm again? How many months till summer?' Dora pulled her blanket-jacket around her shoulders and sat on her mattress to wind the fraying strips of blanket around her legs. Somewhere, in the fabled warmth of the island of Ulu, she had left a good warm cardigan behind in the mission house long ago on that day when she packed her bag for two weeks in Rabaul.

Warmth and food. Contact with their families. News of what was happening in the world. The dignity of some simple freedoms. It didn't seem much to ask. Yet that winter February in 1944, the interned nurses found that they had to make the most of small happinesses, minor victories. Different women found their comfort in different ways.

The mission women, Eileen Callaghan, Dorothy Maye, Mrs Jones and some of the others found that their informal church services and times of singing songs of faith were a source of strength and peace. Mrs Bignell poured out her feelings in verse and prose, crowding notebooks with ideas, remembered quotations and expressions of sorrow and regret about her family from whom she had become estranged. Several women kept diaries; Mavis Green used phrases in the Kuanua language when she wanted to keep a diary entry confidential.

Three of the women, including Kay Parker, had decided to shave their heads to avoid problems with headlice to the fury of their guards; the women enjoyed their small act of defiance. Some read books, others played cards for hours, some filled time by bringing back to memory the details of cooking recipes, others sketched or embroidered.

The endless folding of paper into envelopes went on during the official hours for work. There were two advantages in folding envelopes, they discovered. For one thing, they were paid in Japanese currency for their work and with the money they were able to arrange for the purchase of small items through the woman guard. The other advantage had been discovered by accident. One cold day, while working with the warm thick paste made daily on the stove to stick together the folded paper, one of the women licked her fingers. To a hungry woman, the mixture was not unpalatable, and when they experimented with the addition of a little sugar or salt, they decided that the paste was quite filling and not unlike arrowroot. When Kay Parker made the next batch of paste for the envelopes, she had to disguise the fact that they needed greater quantities than before, because the workers were dining on it.

Members of the Methodist Overseas Missions Board gathered from various states of Australia for their annual meeting in February 1944. It was not an easy series of meetings. Whole segments of the work in the Pacific and north Australia were disrupted or silenced, and had been for the past two years. Two of their chairmen of mission districts, Kentish and McArthur, had vanished somewhere in the obscuring fog of the war and another, Rundle, was an army chaplain in north Australia instead of leading his district in the islands of Papua. Instead of the rhythm of annual reports from each of the mission districts, there had been no word from missionaries or people of New Britain for two years and, apart from the observations of fighter pilots returning from the islands with news of widespread destruction, there was nothing at all to put in the minutes.

Board members demanded to know what steps had been taken to discover the whereabouts of the missing people. It seemed unacceptable that no-one could find any clues at all, and each of them came on behalf of wives and relatives of the missing in their home state whose pleas for information came with such pain.

General Secretary Burton outlined the steps he had taken, through government channels and the Protecting Power, Switzerland, to the Japanese Foreign Office and through them to the Prisoner of War Information Bureau, as well as through the world YMCA and the Red Cross. A letter had been received from a New Guinean student who had been at Vunairima with the missionaries when the Japanese arrived; after several years and many adventures as one of the many New Guineans who were conscripted as forced labour to carry Japanese cargo in the invasion of the New Guinea mainland, he had finally escaped to Port Moresby where he worked with the Australian troops. The last time he had seen the missionaries was in February or March 1942, and who knew what had happened since then? Gradually, several areas of New Guinea and the western end of New Britain were being taken back by Australian and American troops.

'A letter is being prepared in the vernacular,' Burton explained, 'to be copied and distributed through the areas that have been released by the American Red Cross. Mrs Shelton and retired missionary sisters Miss Woolnough and Miss Mills are doing the translation. We are hoping that someone reading the letter might have some news. As soon as we hear anything, relatives will be informed by urgent telegram.'

It didn't sound very promising. Yet at least it gave the feeling that some sort of action was being attempted. The group had more confidence in the decisions about north Australia. As soon as military permission was granted, Miss Jessie March would be able to return to the north, to Croker Island, and take a party of older Aboriginal boys and girls back with her.

On the day that the meetings of the Methodist Overseas Mission concluded in Sydney, 11 February 1944, the bishop, missionaries and people emerged after Mass from the small grassroofed church of the nuns behind the barbed wire fence at Vunapope, New Britain. It was still very early in the morning, but the heat of the day was already beating down on the cluster of temporary buildings which formed their camp.

'There are rumours,' the word passed among them, 'that the Allies may plan to bomb the mission. They think it is an arsenal of Japanese explosives. There may be some truth to it, but our bishop thinks not — he says he has visited all the main buildings and they are so crowded with people that there is no room left for storing explosives.'

Beyond the barbed wire which surrounded their area, the mission buildings where once they had lived and worked were now filled with some 1 500 Japanese people, with several large buildings being used as military hospitals.

'Surely the Allies won't bomb Vunapope,' nuns tried to reassure each other. 'They'll know we missionaries are still here, won't they?'

'Maybe. . .'

Some of them placed hope in the Latin inscription 'Salve Mater', written in huge letters made by a dark red border plant grown outside the large grotto they had built in honour of Our Lady of Lourdes on a nearby hillside. Airmen would realise, they hoped, that Catholic missionaries, not Japanese soldiers, would use Latin. Others placed more confidence in the sets of tunnels they had built into the hill not far from their houses, shored up with coconut palm logs, or the slit-trenches dug near their houses and covered with several feet of earth and iron.

An air-raid alert sounded. Some of the young schoolboys were the first to see the long lines of bombers and fighters streaming through the clear morning air. At first, it seemed that the planes would sweep by Vunapope and drop their cargo of bombs over the harbour or airfields, as they had done so often before. Then they realised that the whole gleaming formation of planes was swinging back and that the target was Vunapope.

Nuns ran for the tunnels with crowds of children. Other Sisters dived into covered slit-trenches near their small temporary convent. As the last of the missionaries, including the bishop, sprinted into the shelter of the tunnels, machine-gun bullets were spitting around them. Then the bombs began to fall.

In the suffocating heat and darkness of the narrow tunnels and the slit-trenches, missionaries crouched, nuns clung to each other and children clustered tightly. The earth shook like the vibrations of a violent earthquake with the impact of falling bombs and, as soil sifted down over them, they knew that there was the danger that the tunnel would collapse. Sisters in a slit-trench felt the thud of a bomb falling close by, and were half-smothered by falling earth from the shallow roof of their trench.

As a counterpoint to the whining, whistling, screaming, crashing, smashing, rattling of instruments of death, voices blended in the hot dark of the shelters, whispering and chanting the words of ancient prayers. With the flavour of the sacred wafer of the Body of Christ still in their mouths from their morning Mass, they knew that their last hour might have come. 'Lord have mercy, Christ have mercy. . .'

And then it was over. The last throb of departing engines faded and the missionaries and people of Vunapope emerged to see the carnage that surrounded them. It was horrible. Many of the large buildings on both sides of the barbed wire fence were smashed beyond recognition or severely damaged. Bombs which had just missed the buildings had fallen directly on slit-trenches which each had been sheltering over a hundred Japanese men. A former convent building which had been the home of the New Guinean Sisters, later the Australian nurses and now housed two hundred Japanese airmen had been blown out of existence. The small building where a sick Brother had rested had become a gaping bomb crater and several other missionaries who had not been in the tunnels were severely injured and later died.

Yet, when the shaken and distressed missionaries counted the cost of the raid on their community, they realised that in fact they should be deeply thankful that most of the 360 people of their group were alive. Five hundred Japanese people had died within metres of them.

The horrors of the aftermath of the raid almost outdid the terrors of the raid itself. When the Sisters returned to their convent which was not far from the Japanese quarters, they were appalled at what they saw. Bombs and bullets had torn living human beings into fragments, scattering the remains widely through the mission compound.

'I can't do it. . .'

'We must do it, with God's help. . .'

Australian, German, Irish, Dutch and Italian nuns, hardy and compassionate women who steeled themselves to the task, walked through the grounds to return the lost Japanese to their own people for burial, bearing bits of bodies in buckets.

That was only the first day. Every day until the end of February, the bombers returned. Day after day, the Vunapope people crowded into the unventilated, stifling darkness of their tunnels. No-one trusted the slit-trenches any more. The Japanese survivors did not stay at Vunapope, but moved away with soldiers, nurses and hospital patients to safer places hidden in the bush. The electricity had been lost when their powerhouse was bombed. Water tanks were gone and daily water had to be collected from waterholes near the beach. Food supplies had been destroyed and livestock died from machine-gun fire and shrapnel. A rough shelter to provide a new cookhouse was bombed the day after it was built and a feast of machine-gunned fowls, pigs and goats was destroyed just before it finished cooking.

Buildings which had survived the early days of bombing fel as the month went on. As a variation of aerial bombing and strafing, they were also shelled by naval destroyers from offshore leaving the former Fathers' and Brothers' three-storey house ablaze. The grotto of Our Lady of Lourdes was totally destroyed, perhaps because it appeared to be an air-raid shelter entrance. Sick and wounded priests and nuns were lovingly cared for in the narrow safety of the tunnels, but day by day people died, seventeen of them during February. Malaria, dysentery and typhoid attacked very old and very young alike.

In the tunnels, Mass was celebrated by the priests each day, but funerals had to be accomplished with haste and the minimum of dignity, their friends being buried in their blankets near the entrance to the tunnels; no coffins were available and the cemetery had been desecrated by bombs. When many buildings had been bombed, an air-raid showered Vunapope with incendiaries which set fire to several other buildings which still stood and set ablaze the dried coconut palm fronds which they had dragged across the entrances to their tunnels as camouflage, filling their hiding place with thick, choking smoke.

The nuns did what they had to do every day — washing the soiled linen of the sick, caring for the mixed-race children, nursing and cooking. The chemist Sister worked on a method of making soap for the whole community using their own coconut oil, ingredients and containers salvaged from the ruins and potash from the ashes of their mission buildings.

As they watched the destruction of the place they loved, the nuns prayed, 'Lord, deliver us from our friends!'

It seemed that the Americans would be sending in a landing force any day, having heavily bombarded the area daily for so long. Yet they did not come. By the end of March, orders came from the Japanese authorities that the mission community must move from the embers of Vunapope.

After negotiations, a site was chosen at Ramale in a steep hidden valley, thick with virgin timber and scrub, suitable for building new tunnels for safety, not impossibly far from their food gardens in the bush and with an excellent spring and stream for water. A period of time was permitted for new tunnels to be built and shelters erected at Ramale, as well as transporting loads of everything they could salvage from the ruins of Vunapope.

'When we go back to New Britain, after the war. . .'

'When the Allies finish the job and take Rabaul again and we can find out what has been happening in the lives of our New Guinean people. . .'

It was a relief to hear others echoing her own thoughts. Jean Poole was glad that she had accepted the invitation from Kath and Rodger Brown to visit them in the May school holidays. It had been a long tiring journey, hundreds of miles from Kiama on the south-eastern coast of New South Wales all the way to Adelaide in South Australia. But it had been worth it.

For two years there had been a strong need to be with people who understood, people who had been there with her and John, who knew just what she meant when she said, 'Out at Kalas. . .' or 'Do you remember, at Vunairima. . .?' Her own family were a great comfort and support, but New Britain was only a place of story and photograph for them. Her new friends at Kiama were very kind, but they had never met John and New Britain was a completely unknown world.

Now they sat together at Kath's mother's house and it was almost as if John sat there with the three of them. Name by name, they thought of their friends who were missing as John was: Mr Mac, Laurie Linggood, Jack Trevitt, Howard Pearson, Herbert Shelton and the others.

'I keep thinking about Dora,' Jean said. 'I like Dora. She was at our wedding with the two of you and she came on that first bush patrol with John and me. Do you think the nurses are in the same camp as the men, somewhere near Rabaul? And Mavis and Chris — we always had Wednesday lunches together when the girls were at Malabonga and we were at Kalas, and Mavis did a long patrol with us.'

'We've known Chris for years. It is very rough on her family, waiting for some news — on all their families, for that matter.'

They were silent. Each of them pictured people who were important to them: husband, close friends, work colleagues. For more than two years they had waited with no word. Other people in their communities had received the bitter news of deaths in battle or from illness, but at least they knew. They prayed, each of them, earnestly, persistently, pleading for the lives of those they loved. But it was hard to know how to combat the deadly seeping poison of uncertainty, a daily not-knowing. It contaminated their thoughts with anxiety and took the gloss from the happiest day.

There were so many of them in the community, just waiting. Thousands of families waited for men and women lost somewhere after the fall of Singapore or the fall of Ambon. They had heard that the names of some of the army nurses missing since the fall of Singapore had been passed through to their families as prisoners of war, but there was still no news of many of the others.

The families whose men had been in Rabaul were only some of the many who waited. Everyone was familiar with the big coloured poster which urged the waiting women to join the workforce in that 'Victory job'. A young woman was pictured slumped miserably alone on a couch and the caption read: 'Lonely? The place is darn lonely without him. The best way to make time pass and help bring him back again is to take a war job. . .'

Different women responded to what was happening to them in different ways. Some threw themselves into work, filling their days so that they were exhausted by bedtime and had little time to think. Some, like Elsie Wilson, chose to use the time of interruption to their work for study; Elsie had been transferred to a larger school and community in South Australia's Riverland. In Adelaide, Helen Pearson had the support of her own and her husband's family; she had organised the purchase of a house in the Adelaide hills where Howard could recuperate and was unfailingly confident that he would come home to enjoy it.

Nellie Simpson had her two small children to care for, but she also needed to support herself and had found a clerical job at a garage where her intelligence and charm made her a valued staff member.

In the case of some, the stresses of waiting for missing husbands and brothers had sent them to their churches with a great need to find God's strength and comfort. But for other women, there was a sense of profound betrayal. They resented what they saw as the neglect of the church to help them or take positive steps to locate their husbands, and had turned their backs on the institutional church, preferring to count on their own inner strength rather than what they saw as the feeble impotence of their church communities. If God could let this happen to her husband, said one or two of the mission women, a man who had given his full energy and everything he had to serve as a Christian missionary, then what sort of a God was he?

Rodger had met several of the waiting women as he travelled around Australia. Whenever he visited Melbourne, he saw Essie Linggood, who was living with her family and continuing to use her initiative and energy in many voluntary ways through her home church, never losing her strong commitment to missionary work. On a visit to Perth, he had seen Beryl Beazley, with the little girl her father Syd had never known, and in Tasmania Eileen Pearce had appeared at a series of talks he had given in a number of churches: 'She didn't seem to care that she had heard the talk several times already,' he said. 'It just seemed important to her to be near someone who had known her missing husband Wilf in New Britain and could talk about him.'

Rodger had a disturbing story to tell of his time in Queensland. 'This waiting for news is terrible for everyone,' he said, 'and some thoughtless people can make it worse. I was in Brisbane earlier this year at a big public church meeting. In the middle of the program, someone came rushing on stage with urgent news. He said he'd just heard that our north Australian chairman, Len Kentish, had been found alive and safe.

'Well, everyone jumped up, all excited, and started to sing "Praise God, from whom all blessings flow". But it wasn't true. The information was not true at all — someone had misunderstood some news and it was all a mistake. The worst thing was that Mrs Violet Kentish was in the audience. . .'

Jean was shocked. 'That's dreadful. False news would be worse than no news. I want to know that John is alive, but it has to be the truth!'

The woman stood in front of the mirror staring at her reflection. Her eyes were shadowed and tired. It was not easy to sleep these days, with the thoughts that went round and round in her mind, endless lines of questions with no answers. Where was Laurie? Was he ill? Was he starving? Was he being treated humanely?

Daisy McArthur picked up her plain felt hat, settled it firmly on her head and anchored it with a hat pin. It was time to go. She had agreed to speak to a group of women while she was visiting Adelaide, to tell them about missionary work in New Britain. It was something which she had done before and would no doubt do again. At one level it was something she loved to do. Without being proud, she knew that she was a competent speaker and her audience would be interested and responsive. She would speak of things she had seen and learned during her years as a missionary, and would share stories of the goodness and faithfulness of God.

With a deep breath to steady herself, Daisy gathered up her handbag, her notes and Bible and pulled on her gloves. She must go. The mirror had told her that she was neat and her hat was straight. The women at the meeting would not notice, she hoped, the weariness around her eyes, the grief, the questions. Perhaps, over their tea and scones after her talk, she would be conscious of women leaning over to whisper to each other, 'Mrs McArthur's husband is a prisoner of war, you know. . .' They would know that.

Daisy pulled the door shut behind her. Once more she would go and speak of the faithfulness of God. She believed it — she did believe it — but it was a struggle. Why could she not feel the comfort of her faithful God in the deep places of her own spirit?

The words of the blessing Laurie had written in her Bible all those years ago, in those happy years before separation, went with her as she set off to go to her speaking engagement: 'The Lord bless thee and keep thee. . . and give thee peace.'

On 6 June 1944, a community of 350 people from seventeen nations of the troubled world, hidden deep in their subterranean refuge at Vunapope, waited with their bundles packed as priests moved quietly along the narrow passageways.

'The body of Christ given for you. . . The blood of Christ. . .' they murmured. To each one, the living presence of Christ was nourishment, security and peace.

Moving out into the open air, the long procession began to move away from the mortally wounded remains of their mission compound. There was no need for further bombing by the Americans or Australians. As they set out to walk the nine kilometres to Ramale, they passed through a cratered wilderness of desolation and ashes. Any building that had not been bombed had been burned, with at last the twin towers of the cathedral collapsing. They still had to carry their things through heat, weariness and fear to Ramale, with Japanese guards following them and Allied planes flying across their track with the threat of strafing.

In silence, they turned away from Vunapope. There was nothing left.

When change came for the nurses in Yokohama, it was almost without warning. For months their life in the confines of the rowing club had been like an almost stagnant pool, with very little that was fresh entering and nothing flowing out to escape to a wider world. Winter had passed and guards had brought them branches of cherry blossom with spring. They later distributed seeds of tomatoes and cucumbers to plant in the warmth of summer but, though they were warmer they were hungrier, more discouraged and more frustrated.

In the dull repetition of days, high moments became events, like trips to see the dentist for a few of them, a Mothers' Day party with white paper flowers and the crude and painful attempts by several girls to pierce their ears — 'for something to do'. From time to time there were the wailing of sirens, warnings of air raids, fires glimpsed on the far side of the harbour, earth tremors, wild winds and blackouts.

But the immediate things of their world remained the day by day business of following routine and living with eighteen other women. An amiable guard offered them some English language newspapers and they learned that Rabaul and the area around it were still in the hands of the Japanese, but there had recently been heavy attacks by the Americans.

'Are any of our mission men still in Rabaul? What about our Catholic friends at Vunapope?' they wondered. The silence was hurtful.

Red Cross parcels arrived from time to time, as well as a large selection of first aid and medical supplies and a gift of library books through the YMCA. These were all greatly valued, but since Christmas 1942 they had received no visits from any International Red Cross workers or any other members of the international community who had responsibility for internees or prisoners of war. News filtered in with the guards that other groups of civilians from other nations had been exchanged for Japanese civilians returning to Japan but, despite their hopes through the past two years, this had not happened for them. They still had received no mail, nor had they been permitted to send any letters home.

(The women would not have been encouraged if they had seen an official statement from the Postmaster General's Department in Melbourne during 1944: the route taken by airmail from Australia to Japan travelled from Melbourne to Karachi in India, north-west through Baghdad and Teheran, north to Moscow then east on the Trans-Siberian railway into Manchukuo, through Harbin and at last across the Sea of Japan to Japan. The note added: 'These routes are subject to interruption. . .')

'Are we too small a group? Is Australia not influential enough to get us out on the exchange scheme? Or does nobody know where we are, anyway?' None of them knew the answers.

Then early in July 1944, the order came. 'Prepare to move out. Pack your things.'

Even the most hopeful among them did not really expect that they would be exchanged this time. They gathered everything they had made, been given or had scrounged — the books, the handmade playing cards, the secret diaries, the tiny cards and gifts they had made for many birthdays, left-over silk from knitting, empty cans. If they were going from one prison to another, they would need everything they could lay hands on. When they were ready to go, the women left the rowing club with anything that was moveable.

'We're turning into the biggest thieves,' they said unrepentant-ly.

'Because food is getting short here in Yokohama, you are going to the country, to Totsuka, where there will be more vegetables. Also, you will be safer from bombing in the country than here in Yokohama,' they were told.

On the morning of 9 July, the nineteen women and their guards left the Yokohama Amateur Rowing Club after two years behind its walls, apart from their one brief respite at the police station. Their one regret was to leave behind half-grown vegetables they had planted. It was nearly five years since Mavis had left Australia and she gazed at the unfamiliar sight of trams and trains carrying the population about their business. They passed by city parks and private gardens, each with air-raid shelters, and saw some signs of bomb damage.

During the journey, which took nearly an hour, they moved from city streets to the outskirts of Yokohama and watched as city housing gave place to thatched cottages, canals and boats, and open country with rice fields and wayside summer flowers. Beyond the pine forests and the patchwork of fields with their farmhouses, Mount Fujiama rose, lovely with a veil of cloud swathed around its shoulders.

They were taken along a main highway and then turned off it at Totsuka along a lane beneath chestnut trees. A large farmhouse waited for them, comfortable, bright and airy, set among gardens and trees. It had formerly been a hospital for tuberculosis patients and there were separate bedrooms for groups of four women. As the women walked through the building and the grounds, they felt their spirits lifted by the beauty of the countryside and the new space and comfort. The four Methodist nurses, Dorothy Beale, Jean Christopher, Dora Wilson and Mavis Green, were grateful to be able to have a room of their own together.

The early weeks at Totsuka were unexpectedly pleasant. The weather was warm and summery. Their surroundings offered beauty which their spirits had been craving. For a time their meals improved as promised, with vegetables available from the local rural community. The furniture in the house was reorganised to suit their needs and a doctor came to see them all, providing medication for those who were ill. More vegetable seeds were planted in the garden immediately and they hoped there would be enough warm weather still to come for the plants to mature.

After the restrictions of the rowing club, there was the new freedom of walking outdoors in the garden and along the lane, with the sight of Fujiama framed between pines and chestnut. After the lack of privacy of the open room at the rowing club, only slightly lessened by a few dividing panels, it was possible to retreat to a room with close friends. The original groupings of army, government and mission women were retained and the women took their meals into their rooms, inviting other groups or individuals to join them as occasional guests.

The mission women chose to have a period each day when they offered each other the gift of silence in their room, to give time and quietness for personal prayer and meditation: they understood each other's needs.

It was not all easy. They knew it could not be. Though the house in the country was pleasant, many of the women were ill and all were underweight and weakening. Eileen Callaghan was seriously ill — they recognised the signs of tuberculosis. Others suffered from bouts of malaria, dysentery and worms. Though their health and strength had deteriorated, for the first time they were expected to do heavy manual work. The walks in the countryside were always with a purpose: carrying heavy loads of coal along the lane from the main road to the house, collecting firewood from the woods, carrying buckets of water for the kitchen from an outdoors pump and kitchen duties. Within days of arriving at Totsuka, the women were ordered to begin digging a deep trench as an air-raid shelter, then later another and still another.

'It's hard enough digging over a garden bed to plant tomatoes,' they complained. 'Digging a great hole in the ground is wrecking my back.'

'You could be glad to crawl into the hole if the Allies start bombing around here — if they ever let us use the trench.' It would depend on who their guards were at the time, they knew. Some were much more concerned about their safety and comfort than others.

As she was their leader, Kay Parker arranged rosters of workers, trying to share the load so that the weaker and more debilitated women were supported. Kay Parker was becoming more and more the person on whom others leaned; even when snakes were discovered lurking in the dry summer grass it was Kay who despatched them. Yet Kay herself, who had always been a tall and imposing woman, was driving a body weakened by undernourishment, encouraging others with her humour and commonsense at times when she might have given in to discouragement.

'We might as well make the best of it, girls,' she said. 'Bean-curd and stew of those everlasting chunks of white daikon radish are not my favourites, either, but this house could be a whole lot worse — we're not behind barbed wire or high walls and we've got a great view of Fujiama!'

19

September 1944–
January 1945

A LAST GLOW OF RED AND GOLD gleamed beyond the pure lines of Mount Fujiama. Lights were beginning to shine from farmhouses on the slopes, as farmers and their families ended their day of work harvesting grain in the fields. Some of the women prisoners came back to the house with their guards, their arms loaded with firewood for the kitchen and a bunch of bluebells, autumn berries and daisies balanced on top.

Dora walked in carrying a spray of leaves tinted with the palette of autumn. She laid the delicate foliage out on her bed, arranging the leaves into a pleasing pattern.

'I'm going to draw these. I found them down in the woods when I was getting wood,' she said. 'The colours are lovely.'

'Look what I've got.' Mavis held up a bundle of skeins of wool. 'Old Poppa-san has asked me to do some knitting for his daughter.'

Now that the women had come to Totsuka, the knitting of little silk bags and the making of envelopes had finished. As well as manual work in the grounds where they lived, several of them had been asked to knit garments for the guards and their families. Mavis was pleased to knit for Poppa-san's daughter. The girl was a medical student and a pleasant young woman. After the boredom of knitting hundreds of little silk bags, there was much more satisfaction in producing a cardigan.

Not all their guards were as kind as the elderly retired police officer whom they called Poppa-san. Some had been given the lowly task of guarding interned white women because they were sick men, unable to manage more demanding work. The nurses recognised signs of tuberculosis and other diseases in men set to guard them. The cheerful young guard, 'Happy-san', had been left behind in Yokohama; he had completed some studies, passed his exams and moved to other work.

Now the women did their best to enjoy the beauties of autumn. Winter was coming.

Dust swirled up from the parched land as the convoy of military trucks rumbled through the tiny town of Marrabel on the long road towards Darwin. Daisy McArthur heard them coming before they crossed the frame of the open post office doorway. She had come, without much hope, to ask her sister-in-law behind the counter whether any mail had come for her. Beside her, her three-year-old son clung to her hand and stared at the passing convoy.

Inside the building, it was hot and dim behind drawn blinds and, outside in the full glare of the sun, the heat was unbearable. More trucks passed, more soldiers. Some of them would probably stop in the town at the shop, to get drinks or to fill their water bags before they drove on. She watched them pass with a knot of tension twisting painfully inside her. After they had gone, there would be more stories.

Up and down the road the stories travelled, scraps of information — torn fragments of news — tossed along on the hot winds of rumour, half-truths and propaganda. Everyone picked up their own collection of odds and ends and tried to make some sort of a picture of it. It rarely made much sense. Daisy knew that after this convoy of trucks had gone on their way, people would come into the post office to pick up their mail or buy a stamp. They would offer the latest bits of news and urge her sister-in-law to pass it on: 'You should tell Mrs McArthur about that, her husband being a prisoner of war. . .'

There were only a few people in the town with whom she felt

really close and Daisy valued those special friends. Yet she knew that other people tried to be kind.

She turned her back on the bright frame of shimmering heat and dry plains beyond and went back to her rooms. Sooner or later, someone would come and tell her some story about prisoners of war somewhere, some dreadful tale of brutality — the stuff of nightmares. In November, there had been the first appalling stories published in the papers of torture, slave labour, starvation, disease and death of Australian prisoners under the Japanese. The first stories had come with the survivors of prison ships sunk by the Allies, the *Rokyo Maru* and the *Tamahoko Maru*, of the horrors of prison camps in Asia and on the Burma-Thailand railway. Someone would come to chat about it again and she could not bear to listen any more.

Where was Laurie? Was he safe? Had he been injured, damaged in body or spirit? Could he even be dead or was he suffering somewhere? Why had he not been able to write to her in all the years he'd been away? Other women had received letters from their men who were prisoners, not frequently and sometimes with a delay of over a year between the time the letter was written and the time it was received, but they had something, some word to say their men were alive and in camp in this country or that. She had not had one letter since that paper cut-out dropped over Port Moresby two-and-a-half years ago. Nor had any of the other women whose husbands had stayed on in Rabaul, so she heard. Dear God, her heart cried, why? What is happening?

The dark cloud of depression settled more and more bleakly into her mind. Sometimes she wondered whether there was something very wrong with her. Surely she should be trusting God. . . she was a Christian after all. . . shouldn't she be able to be peaceful and cheerful and confident. . . that's what all the hymns said. But she couldn't.

I haven't got enough faith, she decided; it's my own fault. . . if I prayed harder, if I were a better believer, then I wouldn't spend my days wrapped in this horrible smothering blanket of despair. She tried to sing, her own way of remembering the promises of

God, letting the sound of her voice singing the melody of hymns remind her that God loved her. But the sound quavered a little and carried a hint of tears.

In her Bible, she returned time after time to the story of the disciple Peter out in the fishing boat in the dark before dawn. Wind-driven waves washed up in the darkness and, through the gloom, he saw Jesus Christ walking towards him over the waters. Terrified, he and his companions thought they were seeing a ghost, but they heard the voice of Christ above the noise of the storm: 'It is I. Don't be afraid.' Christ held out his hand to Peter and said, 'Come.'

Peter took all his courage and, with his eyes fixed on his Master, stepped out of the boat into the water and began to walk. But the waters lapping around his feet were insecure, bottomless, and he looked down, feeling himself sinking. In terror, he cried out for help and Jesus grasped his hand and lifted him, helping him into the fishing boat to safety. 'How little faith you have! Why did you doubt?' Jesus said.

Daisy heard those words echoing in her own mind over and over again. She knew herself to be sinking through a storm into the depths of a bottomless despair and, though she tried so hard to stretch out her hand to find the strength of the supporting hands of Jesus, she could never quite reach. It's my own fault, she thought, I haven't enough faith. . .

There were steps on the verandah outside and her older son came in from school. For the children's sake, I must be strong, she said to herself. Perhaps, when we move from here soon to the place in Wilmington, I'll be able to manage better, she thought. In Wilmington, we'll be part of a bigger community and closer to more family members; perhaps my son will be happier at school there. Yet, even as she tried to reassure herself, Daisy knew that her depression was not a simple matter of geography.

The conversation had begun calmly enough. Mel Trevitt was visiting Jack's parents and began to speak about plans for the future.

'If Jack comes home. . .' she began.

'How can you say that?' Mel Trevitt's father-in-law demanded an answer, his face revealing a mixture of anger and fear. 'You mustn't talk like that. You must never question that he's coming back. *When* Jack comes home, you and little Bruce will be able to get back to normal as a family.'

Mel hesitated, words ready to say. Then she decided to be silent. It was no good. Dad Trevitt would only be upset if she told him that, for a long time, she had sensed that she would never see Jack again. He would accuse her of giving up. He might even think that she didn't care, that her efforts to be strong, independent and increasingly skilled in her profession were because her life with Jack didn't matter.

There was no point in arguing. The older man loved his gifted son so dearly — but so did she! Nor did she feel she could tell him about an encounter she had recently had with a senior Methodist minister who had spoken to her with great confidence: 'I have information that you will be seeing your husband again very soon,' he had said. Mel had listened politely. If only she could hope, she thought, that he knew what he was talking about.

Yet it seemed to her that there was no hope, that her beloved Jack had gone forever.

In his Sydney office, Methodist General Secretary John Burton sighed and picked up another letter from his correspondence. The year 1944 was coming to an end and still there was no sign of relief from the anxieties which had haunted him and his organisation for the years of the war. There were still pathetic letters from the families of the missionaries who had been missing for years: Mrs Green from Maitland asking about Mavis, Mrs Wilson of New Lambton asking about Dora, Mrs Marion Oakes backed by her father, who was now the President of the NSW Methodist Conference — asking hard questions about what they were doing about Dan.

Despite all their efforts, there was no real news to offer and his contacts in the Commonwealth government said that they were as much in the dark as he was.

In Melbourne, Essie Linggood was ill and in hospital for surgery. The mission had offered financial help, but she had assured them that she could manage. Essie Linggood was a very practical person who had been throwing herself wholeheartedly into the work of her church and community, as well as being a leader in the Victorian Women's Auxiliary for Overseas Missions and writing and editing material about New Britain. She lived with her parents and sister and had good support through her family, her home church and the New Guinea Women's Association. In some ways, she was better off than some of the other women whose men were missing.

Mrs Daisy McArthur was ill. Though John Burton had not been in regular touch with all the wives of the missing missionaries, he was in contact with people from South Australia. Mrs McArthur had moved to Wilmington with her children, but she was now in hospital. It seemed that she might be there for some time: she had suffered a nervous breakdown. The pain of separation, the isolation, the depression had taken their toll on her spirit. Her children had been sent to live with aunts.

It had been possible, finally, to arrange for Rodger and Kath Brown to spend some time together as a family. They would be coming to the Sydney circuit of Chatswood just before Christmas to stay for some months. The news from the Australian government was that it should be possible to send chaplains with troops to New Britain soon and Brown was keen to go. American and Australian troops had landed on the north and south coasts of West New Britain by March 1944 and had the large Japanese army contained on the Gazelle Peninsula of East New Britain. Surely, it would not be so very long before the ground forces moved east to relieve what was left of Rabaul after the Allied bombing and then perhaps their captured missionaries would be freed.

John Burton made some notes. He would send letters of condolence to some people connected with the mission who had just heard news of the deaths of their men and, while he was about it, he should also write to the wives and families of the missing missionaries. It was a grim job as it was impossible to know what to say to women who had already waited in vain for almost three years.

There was a tap on his door.

'Excuse me, sir, but there is an urgent telegram from north Australia.'

Burton opened the envelope with a sinking heart. Chaplain Rundle, one of the three chairmen of mission districts who, with McArthur and Kentish, was absent from his work because of the war, had been working as an army chaplain in the north until it was possible to return to his battle-scarred district in the islands.

He would not be returning now. Rundle had been killed in a road accident.

'Do you know what I miss more than anything?' Eileen Callaghan sat propped on a bed with the group of women who gathered on a Sunday morning for a simple church service. It was cold again and one or two of the nurses had stayed in bed to keep warm.

'What's that, Cal?'

'Mass. Going to confession on a Saturday evening, getting things off my chest and then early Mass on Sunday morning. Sometimes, I try to remember all the words — the Kyrie, the Gloria, the Sanctus — all the parts in Latin that I only partly understood, but there was this wonderful sense of the mystery of it all and Jesus being there offering his body and blood, for me — for us all. I try to remember the smell of the incense, the sound of the bell and that feeling that you were all caught up in something immense and healing, and forgiving. . .'

She paused, interrupted by a bout of violent coughing. The others waited until she leaned back, exhausted.

'Even just to be able to go to confession again and be sure that I'm forgiven for all the things I've done, said and thought in these years as a prisoner — I think about it a lot, these days, since I've been sick. What if I die and I never get the chance to go to Mass ever again?'

Someone started to say, 'You're not going to die, Cal,' but their words faded. All of them were determined not to give in, not to let things beat them, but Cal was a sick girl. A Japanese doctor visited from time to time and brought medicines, but they had nursed TB cases themselves and knew that, despite their best efforts, they were not able to give her the help she needed.

'We'll just have to do the best we can by ourselves.' The Methodist women understood their friend's sense of loss. They had never been familiar with the Mass that Cal described, but they knew that her memories of things that mattered for her were matched by their own. It was so long since they had sat quietly before a table covered with white linen and heard a minister say, 'We do not presume to come to this Thy table, merciful Lord, trusting in our own righteousness but in Thy manifold and great mercy. . . The Lord Jesus, on the night in which he was betrayed, took bread and when he had given thanks he blessed it and said, This is my body, given for you. . .'

There was no bread, no wine. There was no priest or minister. And yet, as the group of women sat crowded together in the small bedroom, singing songs they had written in Chris' book of songs: 'Peace, Perfect Peace', 'What a friend we have in Jesus', 'O Love, that will not let me go' — and hearing the words of hope read from Dora's Bible, they knew that they were not alone. The symbols of Christ were not there, but *he* had come, himself.

The day the circus came to Kiama was like a bright rainbow of colour and excitement in a drab and austere land. Across NSW, it had been a very hard year for farmers. In the Riverina and the west of the state, a very long drought had continued through the year, with a winter of hard, clear skies and bitter frosts which shrivelled vegetation. There were no rains in autumn or spring to enliven growth and the wheat harvest would be half the normal yield.

Along the coast around Kiama, dairy farms lay dun-coloured and herds were being hand fed. In the mountains, the bush was tinder dry and bushfires leapt through the tops of eucalyptus forests, the smoke boiling up like a dark bruise against cloudless skies and drifting across the coastal cities. Inland there were no bushfires. There was nothing left to burn, only dying stock, bleaching bones, kilometres of parched earth eroding in hot winds which whipped dust up into choking dust storms.

'The worst drought in Australian history. . .' they said.

Then the circus came. Jean Poole watched from the classroom

window as the trucks pulled in and parked on the empty paddock just below the school. She looked across the heads of her class, bent over their work. It was not long till the end of the school year and the days had been hot, windy and tiring. Windy days always made the children irritable and silly and she could not blame them.

She did her best to make the classroom interesting and pleasant, but at the moment it was crowded with salvage — all the bits and pieces of ironmongery, bottles, old newspapers and other things so earnestly collected by her class for the war effort. They had brought in so much stuff, in the hope of winning the weekly pennant for the class which had collected the most salvage, that they had all been tripping over it and would have to wait until Friday for someone to come with a truck to cart it away.

There were times when being a teacher was a burden, but she knew that, even in the tiring times, teaching was what she loved to do. If she were not teaching, Manpower regulations would pick her up and she might find herself in a munitions factory, picking fruit as a Land Army girl or building bombers. At least, of recent days, it had become a very rare thing to have to obey the air-raid siren and hurry the children out into the shelters in the school playground; the threat of a Japanese invasion had faded and the air-raid shelters were used for children's games.

Just outside the school grounds, the brightly painted circus trucks were beginning to unload. There were not many excitements for country children, she thought, even these boys and girls who lived in such a lovely part of the country where the drought conditions were tempered by living so near to the sea.

'Pens down,' she said. 'All stand.'

There was a clatter of wooden seats flapping up.

'We are going to go downstairs and, when we come back, you can all write a composition about what you are going to see.'

They filed outside, open-mouthed. Sitting on a grassy slope under a tree they had a ringside view as the circus people began to erect their tent and bring their animals out to graze, tethered in the wide paddock. The children were enchanted.

A lion in a cage, an elephant, bears. . . few of them had ever seen such creatures except on the silver screen when they went to Saturday matinees at the local cinema. A great tent began to rise, ready to be filled with magic. Children chattered among themselves, excitedly promising that they would surely come to the circus performance that night.

Jean listened and was happy for them. For children like these, the austerities of war were normal life. They were too young to have clear memories of the time before rationing and clothing coupons, of the time before it was illegal to have more than one pocket in a shirt or frivolous embroideries of women's underwear, or of the time when the icing on birthday cakes came in colours other than red and white.

It was accepted that there was little petrol available for civilians and people were discouraged from travelling far unless they had a good reason. They didn't remember the time when the evening news on the wireless did not include the latest news of the war in Europe (the latest news of Europe was that France had just been taken back from the Germans). It seemed natural to see people in uniform, for the fathers of many children in the school to be away at the war and for mothers, aunties and grandmothers to be the stable centres of their homes who carried home the family groceries in homemade string bags.

'It wasn't always like this!' she wanted to say to the children. 'This is just the time in between, the waiting time. . .'

But the wriggling children, absorbed in the sight of a man leading a circus pony across the grass, would not have understood. To them, she was Mrs Poole, a woman teacher who lived with another teacher in the town, but who seemed to have no husband.

We grown-ups are all waiting, she wanted to say, waiting for peace to come in the end, waiting for our men to come home, waiting to go on with our lives that have been interrupted. She thought of older men who went silently through their working days, unable to speak of their sons who were away and perhaps would never return, just waiting. There were so many mothers and wives who filled their days with volunteer war work through groups like the Red Cross, the Australian Comforts Fund and the

Country Women's Association: reconditioning army uniforms, making camouflage nets, sewing and mending, sorting old clothes, endlessly knitting, anything to fill the waiting time.

But the waiting seemed to go on and on. None of the promises of politicians or generals of an early end to the conflict had been fulfilled. Year after year went by and there was still no sign of peace. There was still no reply to any of the letters she wrote to John, week after week. It was hard to carry on a conversation with someone who had not answered her in nearly three years. Other women occasionally received letters from their men who were prisoners and she believed that one day she, too, would hear something. If anything had happened to him (she would not even think the words 'if he is dead'), she would have had a telegram, she reasoned.

The activity around the circus vehicles was slowing down. The tent was up and most of the circus people had disappeared into their caravans to rest before their performance. Jean called the children to attention. It was time to go back into the classroom where they could begin to write their compositions. It was still very hot and dusty, but the children were in good spirits. Jean followed the children up the school stairs. She had been waiting this long and she would go on waiting for as long as it took.

Food and warmth. As autumn chilled into the winter of late 1944 in Japan, the need for food and warmth filled the minds of the women, narrowing their world. Rumours and Japanese English-language papers reached them from time to time, but they had learned to be cynical: they never knew whether they were reading truth or crumbs of truth with a thick icing of propaganda.

There had been no mail or Red Cross visits to give any sense of perspective. Their world shrank to the scale of the house, the ups and downs of personal relationships with the other women, the secrets, the hidden business of trading for food, the little parties for birthdays of themselves and all their relatives.

Behind the farmhouse stood another house where a Japanese woman lived with her children. Through Oba-san, or Biddie as the nurses often called her, they had second-hand contact with the local community. She was a woman of influence in the area and used that influence to control, for good or ill, many things pertaining to the imprisoned women. From time to time, they were able to witness Japanese customs because of their proximity to her family. It did not take the women long to realise that their lives could be made more comfortable, and they could be better fed, if they cultivated a good relationship with Oba-san.

During autumn, things were not quite so bad for them. They were able to pick some of the vegetables they had planted and, though tomatoes and cucumbers were not very filling, they all hoped that the fresh food might be supplying some much-needed vitamins. Sometimes, working under guard in Oba-san's autumn gardens, they managed to bring home vegetables. Scrounging, they called it; stealing really, Mavis thought, but she didn't care — it was take what you could get or you would never survive. The nurses sometimes produced pumpkin, cut in slices like cake and handed it around for afternoon tea; no-one enquired too closely where they had found it. The chestnut trees in the lane ripened and they were permitted to go to pick up fallen nuts. If a guard's back was turned, they would give the trees a furtive shake in hope of gathering more nuts, but even then they didn't get enough to satisfy them.

Sometimes women on kitchen duty would report to the others, 'There should be a good meal this evening. We saw people bringing good vegetables to the kitchen door for sale.' They would describe the bundles of carrots, turnips, parsnips, leeks and onions, sacks of potatoes and sweet potatoes, oranges, apples and eggs. Later, they would smell the food cooking in their kitchen but, when it was time for their own meal, they were disappointed. The fresh food had been taken around to the back of the building to the guards and Oba-san, and their own dinner was bean curd and soya beans again, with rice or bread if they were lucky.

'When will we get some of the sweet potato?'

'Not now, tomorrow.'

It was always the same. The women dreamed of food and talked of food, adding more recipes to their collections. Roast pork with crisp greasy crackling, steamed date pudding, jam rolypoly with hot custard and cream, leg of lamb with mint sauce and baked potatoes, thick slices of ham and chicken with potato salad and finely shredded lettuce drowning in rich mayonnaise, chocolate sponge cake and coffee. . . They knew that these were only the stuff of fantasy; but real, satisfying food was surely within their grasp if only they could find a way to have their share of the sweet potatoes.

One night, Mavis lay awake. She had gone to bed hungry, as they all had, even though they had saved most of their ration of food until the evening. The bean soup with daikon radish through it had been thinner than usual and it did not even have any of the mysterious fragments in it which could have been rabbit, but they suspected of being cat. She stared sleeplessly through the window, watching the branches of a cherry tree silhouetted against a silver moon. There was snow on Fujiama now, and the sky was so clear and star-filled that she was sure there would be frost. Though they had recently been issued with new futons, collecting the bundles at the main road and carrying them gladly up the lane to the house, she was still cold. Cold and hungry.

How could they get some of those precious sweet potatoes, extra rice or peanuts which they knew existed? She thought of the methods they had already tried. Mavis, Dora and Chris, among others, knitted for Oba-san for payment in potatoes but, even with skilled and rapid knitting, they needed a quicker way. One of the other women tried exchanging a pair of children's shoes left over from an earlier Red Cross parcel, suitable for Oba-san's child, for a big bag of sweet potatoes; this produced some potatoes, but then the shoes were returned and the potatoes withdrawn.

As she lay sleepless, Mavis remembered a passage from the Bible which she had once learned by heart in Sunday school. The words repeated a pattern in her mind:

'Ask and you will receive; seek and you will find; knock and the door will be opened to you. . . Would any of you fathers give his son a stone when he asks you for bread? Or would you give him a snake when he asks you for fish? As bad as you are, you know how to give good things to your children. How much more, then, your Father in heaven will give good gifts to those who ask him!'

It seemed almost impudent to ask God for food. She had always thought that one could pray about being patient, to ask for forgiveness or to pray for healing. But it seemed trivial to pray about sweet potatoes. Even so, the words kept echoing: 'Ask, and you will receive . . . how much more will your Father in heaven give. . .'

A simple prayer formed in her mind. 'God, you know how hungry we are. Please help us to have some of those sweet potatoes.'

She must have dozed because when the knocking began she almost missed it. Chris was whispering from her bed near the door. 'Green! Wake up. Oba-san wants to talk to you.'

Mavis groped her way to the door. The Japanese woman had a proposition to make. Sweet potatoes for cigarettes from the Red Cross parcels. She herself was a chain smoker deprived of a ready supply of cigarettes and she had noticed that Mavis was not smoking her Red Cross supply. Very soon, with Chris acting as lookout and Dorothy and Dora helping, cigarettes and potatoes had changed hands and the satisfying roots with the delicious flavour had been cooked in Oba-san's kitchen and then devoured in the privacy of their room. That night, they slept with stomachs full and the knowledge that they had found a way to supplement their diet.

(So discrete was each group of women that few of them realised that Oba-san was dealing privately with each group. Her need for cigarettes and other items was supplied from the Red Cross parcels which arrived in October and December — boot polish for potatoes as their shoes were worn out and they were wearing wooden clogs, cakes of soap for two eggs, a packet of tobacco for potatoes or soya beans — even the empty cardboard boxes for plates of food. Intrigues, secrets, whispered plots to exchange things for food without the other women knowing about it: these all became part of the pattern of life.)

As the year chilled towards Christmas, there were few days when it was pleasant to walk along the lane to collect the loads of coal and firewood. Bitter winds blew off the snow on Fujiama and the last of the autumn leaves dropped and turned to dark slush. Hard frosts froze the water in their buckets of washing water, and froze the water pump. There was no heating in the house, no hot water except in the kitchen. Many of the women chose to stay in their beds under their futon as long as possible, to share their beds with a friend for extra warmth and to take turns to rub some warmth into friends' chilled hands and feet by vigorous massage.

When snow started falling in December, they all knew that it would be months before they might feel warm again — 'If we live that long,' some of them were heard to mutter. Waves of United States Air Force Superfortresses had begun sweeping overhead on their way to bomb Tokyo and the docks and shipyards of Yokohama; new bases had been established in the Mariana Islands, bringing the Allies within striking range of Japan.

For the women in the farmhouse at Totsuka, it was hard to know whether to be glad that the Allies were coming to bomb Japan, or afraid that an Allied bomb might smash their own house and them. They realised that life was hard for their Japanese neighbours, too; they, too, were increasingly short of food, bombs were falling on their homes, the same earth tremors that shook the ground beneath the feet of the nurses made the Japanese farming families tremble as well, the same cold chilled their bones. Sometimes, the women watched Japanese families gathering around little bonfires in the snow, trying to keep warm in the blaze of fragments of fallen timber and leaves raked together.

In the darkness of that hard bleak winter, it was hard to remember that it was Christmas. Had the Christ, the Son of God, truly been willing to leave the beauties of heaven to come to live in such an unwelcoming world as this? Even so, the women prepared tiny gifts for each other and hung up their stockings on Christmas Eve. On Christmas Day, they decorated the tables and Dora spread out her delicate placemats, a memory of warmer weather, the fine detail coloured and cut from paper in a tracery of serrated autumn leaves, each leaf unique.

In an extravagant gesture, they used up most of the delicacies of their Red Cross parcels for one grand Christmas feast and Oba-san offered sweet potatoes. In the darkness, they were determined to make Christmas Day a sign of hope.

Mavis made a note in her diary that evening: 'Very nice Christmas dinner. Sweet potatoes.'

Christmas 1944 in Australia. . .

In the eastern states there were heatwave conditions, temperatures climbing up and up to unbearable heights. Bushfires blazed on Christmas Day in Sydney, destroying some homes in the suburbs of the northern beaches.

The New Guinea Women's Club held their annual Christmas party for the children at the Feminist Club. A Father Christmas handed out gifts to 150 children whose fathers had been captured in Rabaul, while their mothers talked among themselves of their missing men, prisoners somewhere, and the trials of keeping going alone. Surely, this coming year they would all come home again.

The children of Daisy McArthur came to see her in hospital for Christmas. She watched them come through the door — shy, hesitating, with their aunts, not certain how to greet her.

'Mother is not very well yet, dears. . .' Her big boy was ten now, a sensitive child, very bright, anxious without the stability of his own home, despite the care of his relatives. 'I thought I saw Daddy one day, from a bus window,' he said, 'but it wasn't him.'

It was Christmas Eve 1944 and the people of the internment camp in the deep jungle gorge at Ramale, New Britain, prepared themselves. Since the group of Catholic missionaries, students and mixed-race children had left the ashes of Vunapope behind in June, they had established themselves in their hidden valley under a canopy of spreading trees which hid them from aerial view. Lines of huts had been built for the various communities with bush materials and salvaged bits of corrugated iron, and a network of protective tunnels had been cut into the steep valley wall.

It was very possible, they realised, that the Allies had no idea that a large group of assorted missionaries had lived through the destruction of Vunapope and was gathered under the layer of treetops.

Down the steep and slippery track descending into the valley came a line of New Guinean nuns, baskets of sweet potato, tapioca roots, greens and bananas balanced on their heads. Every day the women came with food for the community in the gorge from the mission gardens some distance away.

To their grief, the New Guinean women were excluded from their fellow-Catholics because as indigenous people they were not interned; they were kept outside the fence, never allowed to come close enough to speak or touch, and never able to participate in the Mass which the others celebrated every morning. The daily journey with vegetables brought them in sight of their friends, but each day they laid their basketloads of vegetables down near the office of the *Kempei-tai*, part way down the hill and, after they had gone, schoolboys were allowed to go to collect the food for the camp.

On this morning, Christmas Eve, the long line of native Sisters moved down the slope, erect under their loads, and then climbed away again. After they had gone, and the schoolboys brought in the vegetables, a parcel of cooked bananas was delivered from them as a gift to the bishop. Unwrapping the wilted banana leaves, the bishop found hidden among the bananas a message from the women.

'Dear Bishop and Father,' they had written. 'We want to let you know that we are in distress. For days and nights we have been crying and unable to sleep for sorrow. Christmas is so near and we know there will be no Mass and no holy communion for us even on our Lord's birthday. Can you help us, dear Bishop? Your Little Sisters.'

Bishop Scharmach did his best. He tried to persuade the Japanese authorities that the Sisters could be safely allowed to enter the camp under guard for a Christmas Mass, or that a priest could go outside the camp to serve them, but was refused. At last, it was agreed that the New Guinean women could stand outside the fence very early on Christmas morning and watch and listen from a distance while their friends received holy communion. The bishop made one other request.

It was customary, he explained, on this festive day, for all his people to come to him, one by one, to kiss his bishop's ring and shake his hand in greeting. This would be permitted, he was told.

That Christmas morning under the protective canopy of trees in Ramale Gorge, Mass and holy communion was shared with the group who lived their life there as a large and international family. Beyond the fence, chased well back up the slope by soldiers, were the Sisters Immaculata, the New Guinean women who listened with longing to the words of adoration, forgiveness and blessing and the beautiful singing of the community. When the last of the community within the fence had been served and the service was over, the bishop moved among them, shaking hands and allowing his people to kiss his ring.

In the splendour of purple and flowing robes of his soutane and bishop's surplice, he moved at last away and walked up the slope to the *Kempei-tai* office where he shook hands with the Japanese officers. In the good humour and friendliness of the festive occasion, he said, 'Major, I would like to shake hands with the native Sisters.'

Permission was given and the women filed forward, each one kneeling before her bishop, and bowing her head over his ringed hand. Close by, the Japanese major and the leader of the *Kempei-tai* began a loud argument, the noise filling the air around them, but the kneeling women seemed unperturbed and the bishop greeted each one. As the women turned to go, the bishop was allowed to speak to them briefly.

'My dear Sisters, you have wept for days and nights. . . Our Lord has not forgotten or forsaken you. This morning he himself came to your hearts and offered himself to you as your Christmas present. . .'

The women began to cry and, weeping, climbed the steep track back to their own camp, walking without words until they were safely back in their own place. Only then did they speak the post-communion prayers together and tell each other what had happened. As each woman had knelt before the bishop, his hand had slipped into the folds of his robes. To each bowed nun in secret, from the ciborium hidden under his garments, he had offered with his ringed hand a sacramental wafer, the body of Christ.

On a freezing evening at Totsuka, when several of the women had already crawled under their quilts for warmth, the three who had been on kitchen duty returned with a prize. The kindly cook had given them a brazier full of hot coals to take to the communal room. The women were delighted. Some had saved slices of bread from their meal and they crowded around, warming cold hands and cooking bits of toast over the coals. A door flung open and a guard stormed into the room.

'Where did you get that? Who gave you permission to have the brazier in here? The cook? He is nothing — I have the authority here. Take it out immediately!'

The man seemed to be outraged at the challenge to his power. He insisted that the girls who had gone to bed get up again and made them wait, shivering, until eight o'clock before he lined them up for evening roll call. They filled the time with chatting and loud singing. A long time ago they had agreed that they would never let their enemy see them in tears or defeated. But when at last he called for roll call, they rushed to stand in line and bowed very deeply.

It was no better the next day or the next. The little man seemed to have become very dangerous. He shouted and he roared; he kept them at work longer than usual, threatening the women if they paused. Sometimes, he treated them like children, to be humiliated by standing in line reciting phrases in Japanese. Mary Goss was feeling sick and lay down, but he struck her for disobedience. Bowie tried to intercede, but was knocked to the floor. Mavis was among a small group pulled out of the line of women while he stood on tiptoes to reach up in an incongruous display of power to slap the face of their tall leader, Kay. The others watched, unable to move.

For days the tension was high. Among themselves, they named the guard 'Basher'. When the women caught the eye of one of their friends, it was to ask the silent question: Was the man unhinged or was he plain evil? It was hard to guess what might offend him or cause him to rage at them. Basher wore his ceremonial sword at his side and, one evening as they lined up for roll call, he tore the sword from its scabbard and brandished it in their faces. In earnest or in horrible theatre (they could not be sure), he suddenly lunged at one of the nurses, swordpoint gleaming towards her body as she staggered backwards.

Don't let him see we are scared. . . Don't cry out. . . Look him in the eye. . . The wordless messages passed from one to another. Basher strutted before them still, sword in hand.

'This is how I have killed a man,' he said with relish, 'and how I have beheaded him.' The sword wove an evil arc through the air before their eyes. 'Now go to bed.'

After he had gone, the women lay in the darkness, tearless and sleepless. Terrible images refused to leave their minds. They whispered together, looking for comfort, and most of them found themselves shaking. Several nurses quietly murmured prayers for themselves and others, begging God for protection and for the grace of dreamless sleep.

In the morning, Eileen Callaghan asked Jean Christopher to add another hymn to their notebook of remembered songs.

'The words came back to me in the night,' she said, 'but I don't know if you girls will know it.' She began to sing softly, and several other women nodded in recognition. Words sung long ago in the peace of summer Sunday mornings in Australian churches took on new depths of meaning:

> Faith of our fathers, living still
> In spite of dungeon, fire and sword. . .
> Our fathers, chained in prisons dark,
> Were still in heart and conscience free. . .
> Faith of our fathers! Holy faith!
> We will be true to thee till death.

Before the winter was at an end, Basher had gone. Someone with higher authority had transferred him away from duties with the women and sent other guards who were more balanced. The women were relieved.

During January 1945, the wife of an army captain who had been serving with the 2/22nd in Rabaul received a letter from her husband. Mrs Mollie Nottage knew that her husband Stewart was a prisoner of war in Japan — he had travelled to Japan in July 1942 on the *Naruto Maru* with other officers and eighteen Australian nurses. From time to time, she had received postcards and very brief letters and so she had been able to send regular letters, six a year, to him in Zentsuji camp.

As always, the letter was marked 'Opened by Censor', the Australian censor, and resealed. For those first dreadful months, before she knew that he was in Japan, her letters to him had come back with the label 'Returned to Sender'. This time there was a whole typewritten page of news and even some photographs of Stewart and his fellow-officers at Zentsuji.

Within days, Mrs Nottage received a letter from the Australian Military Board. They had heard from the Australian censor, they wrote, that her husband had referred to the missing men from Rabaul:

> Although the Commonwealth government has made repeated requests to the Japanese authorities for information, the Japanese have failed to supply particulars. . . [Your husband's letter] is the first news that has come to hand regarding them and is naturally of great interest to the Australian Military Authorities.

The letter concluded with a request that she send them the letter and the photographs, which she did on 30 January 1945.

Before she sent on her husband's letter, she re-read the section which had interested them so much. His letter was written months earlier in April 1944 and he had just received her letter of September 1943. He had commented: 'Ralph and approximately 830 other lads, plus 300 civilians left Rabaul on 22 June 1942. That's the last we have heard of them.'

During the same weeks in January 1945, secret cables passed to and fro from one side of the globe to the other, crisscrossing between London, Canberra, Washington and Geneva. The Australian High Commission in London had been given at last, after years of trying, some slight clues about the whereabouts of some of the many Australian nurses missing from Rabaul and Singapore. The Delegate of the Protecting Power, Switzerland, was able to tell them that eighteen Australian women had been transferred from Yokohama to Totsuka in Japan but, despite repeated requests, he had not yet been permitted to visit.

The messages which arrived in Australia were frustrating and disturbing. The Japanese insisted that many lists of prisoners of war had been lost in transit through the misfortunes of war. Though the Australian authorities knew of a number of prison camps in Japan, they did not have reliable lists of who was in them, and had never heard Totsuka mentioned. Now eighteen Australian women had been mysteriously discovered in Japan at Totsuka. But who were they?

Dora stumbled as she came back into the house. Snow was thick on the ground and she had been out in it sweeping paths clear for the Japanese caretakers, Oba-san and Morli the cook. Her feet were wet and chilled, she ached with cold and her knees and ankles were swollen with beri-beri as a result of vitamin deficiency. It was getting painful to walk and climbing steps was cruel. There were times when she wondered, in her increasing weakness, whether she would ever be fit enough to earn her living as a nurse again, when they were freed. Though she had just had her thirty-second birthday, the fourth in captivity, she felt thirty years older.

'Dora, you're freezing. Sit here and let me rub your feet.' Chris helped her off with her damp jacket and wooden clogs. The jacket she had made from a blue cotton blanket padded with cotton wool was not waterproof and hung from her thin shoulders as a sodden weight.

Her friends helped Dora into dry clothes and wrapped her in her futon, chafing her icy feet till the circulation began to move again. Mavis recalled her own sense of shock when she had helped Dora in the bathroom not long before; she had washed Dora's back, the wet cloth moving over the corrugations of exposed ribs and backbone under slack skin.

'We have to do something about this. This girl is going to freeze without something thicker to wear in the cold.'

The idea came to them in pieces, each one adding something to it. Instead of always knitting for their captors, they should knit a cardigan for Dora. But how? There were only a few small balls of wool left over from other work which they could scrounge.

'We'll make our own knitting yarn,' said Chris, 'like the New Guinean women — you remember — like this. . .'

She searched among her things and produced some of the corded knitting silk they had once used for knitting thousands of little bags and a handful of cottonwool saved from gifts from the Vunapope nuns and Red Cross parcels. With a swift tug, she pulled the loose end of the thin silk cord and it unravelled into a long fine thread.

Plucking pieces of cotton wool, she hitched her skirt aside and began to roll the cotton wool around the length of silk thread with long massaging strokes between palm of hand and the side of her leg. Dorothy and Mavis joined her, remembering the hours they had watched women in the islands rolling string from vegetable fibres, and their fingers began to pick up the rhythms of the work, bonding Japanese silk to Australian cottonwool with New Guinean techniques. Mavis offered to knit the cardigan, bamboo knitting needles were produced and the first stitches cast on with leftover wool.

One of the women left the room later that evening. 'I'll be back with a treat if I can do it without being caught,' she said. Dora was still shivering when her friend returned in triumph. Very carefully she set down a large milk tin on the floor between the beds. She had filled it with hot coals from the kitchen stove after the cooks had gone to bed.

With the flourish of a magician, she then produced two large potatoes, hidden in the hollows of her scrawny armpits, and prodded them down among the hot coals. Crouching over the warmth of the tin, taking turns to fan the coals into enough life to cook the potatoes, the women were determined to make the best of things. With something creative to do for a friend, a tinful of warmth and the prospect of a bit of stolen potato baked in its jacket for supper, they knew they could go on for another day.

20

February–6 August 1945

'WHAT'S WRONG?' DORA COULD SEE the gloom on her friend's face.

'Nothing. Everything.'

Mavis found it hard to say just what was making her so miserable. It was so many things. Hunger — it seemed to be constantly with them all, leaving them preoccupied with every crumb. Hopelessness — it seemed that they were never to be part of an international exchange of civilian prisoners. Fear — sometimes the guards were unpredictable, given to bursts of face-slapping and threats of worse. Health problems — none of them were well.

Homesickness for her family. *That* was the worst.

She didn't know how to say it, but all day she had carried an imprint on her mind, the shadow of a dream that had come to her in the night. Something was very wrong at home. At significant moments in the past, she had known special insights, dreams, perceptions — and they had always meant something important.

It was nearly three years since she had received any news of her family, but today she was sure something had happened. Her mother, that strong, accomplished woman who did everything she put her hand to so well? Her brother in the air force? Her father, much older, gentle, sensitive, who always had a special closeness with his first-born, 'his little girl'? Something was wrong with her father — she knew it.

He had been with her at all the turning points of her life; when she completed her schooling, began nursing, went to Sydney to do obstetrics. But that day in 1939 when she had gone home to collect her things before sailing for New Guinea, she had urged him not to come. 'Don't come to Sydney to see me off at the boat,' she had said. 'You'll be too upset and then you'll have a long train trip home again — let Mum come.' She could still see his face at the country railway station, saying goodbye, and feel the shock of a father's tears. Had he known that they would not meet again?

'I don't know what it is, but I'm feeling really down. I've been as flat as a penny all day. I can't explain it.'

Dora knew that it was not the answer for whatever private fears troubled Mavis, but it was all she had. 'I know it's pretty dry — knock off the corner with the mould on it. When they gave us bread last week, I put it away for a treat to have later. But you have it. It might cheer you up a little bit.' She held out her hand and in it offered a slice of bread, a gift of love and sacrifice from one hungry and lonely woman to another.

A hot westerly wind whipped her skirts around her as Jean Poole walked along the beach. The summer was fiercely hot and, now in February 1945, the heatwave conditions which had begun before Christmas still assaulted them. It was bushfire weather, the hard, hot wind relentlessly forcing trees to bend, daring pale, dried-out summer grasses to burn.

Jean trudged along the water's edge. It had been a mistake to try to walk along the beach today, she decided. The water rushing around her ankles was cool, but wind-driven sand stung her skin and irritated her eyes. She walked more quickly, climbing away from the beach over rocks and up towards the headland. Norfolk pines stood like sentinels above the rocks of the headland and offered a little shade.

The sensible thing to do was to go home. The house would

be heavy with heat, but at least there would be shade. There were things to do at home: school compositions to mark, classroom preparation to do, a meal to prepare, a garden to weed. She had begun a new task, too, which fascinated her, of reorganising the Kuanua-English dictionary which Laurie Linggood and Jack Trevitt had published in 1940, so that potential new staff in New Britain could work from English to Kuanua.

It was hard to admit it, but she didn't want to face going home to write another letter to John. She turned along the path to the Kiama Blowhole and argued with herself as she walked. What could she write? He wouldn't be interested in the gossip of Kiama. There was no more news of his parents and sister since she had last written, though she kept in touch with them regularly. She had included something about one sister's romance and the other sister's toddler in all her recent letters, and she had already written about her brother completing his residency at Sydney Hospital and being accepted for the air-force.

No, that wasn't the real problem. She could always chat in a letter.

But who was John these days? Had he changed in the years since she had given him that last farewell hug? Had he been wounded, tortured, starved, demoralised, psychologically damaged? She had spent all these years dreaming of going back to New Britain but, if John had spent those same years imprisoned and under threat in those islands, would he be longing to stay home in Australia? Was there any point of contact between them?

Earlier, walking along the beach, Jean had seen engraved in smooth wave-washed sand a heart shape, and the initials of lovers. Would it be honest if she were to print in big letters in the sand 'J.P. loves J.P.'? She knew that she loved the man she had married. But who was John now?

Every day for years she had looked at his photographs, formal in clerical collar and precisely groomed hair, or sitting on a rock in the Bainings with his face shaded by his hat. Never once had his expression altered, never had the wind rumpled his hair, never had he pulled off his wide hat so that she could see his grin without the shadow. Had he become a stranger, changed beyond recognition? When he came, would he recognise the woman she had become?

There were women whom she knew who feared the return of their men; in the years of loneliness they had found comfort in another love. No other man had come to take John's place in Jean's life. Even so, the man she had married seemed so remote as to be no longer real.

Below her the waves of the ocean pounded in, plunging through the gap in the rocks that people called the Blowhole. Successive waves would wash harmlessly in below a shelf of rock, worn by millennia of waves, filling the hidden space with increasing energy until the water could no longer be contained. She could hear the sounds of splashing and sucking, wave upon hidden wave driving under the rocks.

So many times she had stood here, watching the explosion of water, calmly discussing the science of it with her geologist sister or laughing as she was splashed in the spray. Today, she stood waiting with a sense of foreboding. Forces beyond control were building up, bringing violence, bringing danger. . . With a roar, a tower of water exploded, bursting up through the narrow gap in the rocks, powerful, threatening anything in its path. Jean stepped back, but even in the safety of her place well back on the path some of the salty driven waters fell on her.

She turned away. It was no use standing around brooding, letting her imagination get out of hand, she decided. There were things to do at home. To the west, the sky was bruised with smoke and dust and the orange glow of fresh bushfires. The smell of burning was on the wind and soon bits of burnt ash would float down over her garden. It had not been an easy summer.

Bright sunshine reflecting from snow dazzled the eyes of the women as they worked out in the fields at Totsuka. Mavis had woken one morning to see the cherry tree outside her window heaped with snow so that it seemed to be covered with white blossom and, from then on, there seemed to be snow almost daily through February. Now the snow was deep and the guards had told them that this had been Yokohama's coldest winter for thirty years.

The women tugged and strained at a tree stump bedded in snow. Fallen branches for the kitchen fire were becoming scarce and they had been sent out under guard to grub up some dead stumps. It was heavy work and none of them had any strength. A little fire of twigs and leaves burned nearby and the women found excuses for taking turns to move near to the small warmth.

Chris caught her breath in pain as she dragged against a tree branch. 'I've done my back,' she muttered. It wasn't the first time that one of them had injured herself while they had struggled with heavy manual work.

A siren sounded in the distance. The women looked up, but it seemed they were to continue work. Far away the first sound of planes approaching came through the clear air and they watched the gleam of aircraft coming nearer.

Someone whispered, 'It's the Americans,' and they watched, fascinated. On other days they had watched flights of planes pass over on their way to attack cities and industrial areas. It seemed unlikely that the Americans would choose to waste their bombs on minor rural communities.

This time the planes passed much closer than usual. Mesmerised, the women stared up, their stump-grubbing forgotten. Other planes darted into view, Japanese fighters coming to fend off their enemy. Before their eyes, an aerial battle was waged, man against man, aircraft against aircraft. Even as they watched, they realised there was a nearer enemy. Their guard was shouting at them, angrily kicking snow over their little fire and ordering them back to the house.

'Signals!' he yelled, brandishing his sword. 'Signals to the airmen,' and herded them back into the house.

The women looked at each other in confusion. How could they have made signals to the Americans? What special skills were they supposed to have? 'If only we could. . .' they said.

Even so, they were not sorry to be in out of the snow. Their feet were wet and chilled, the rags they had wrapped around their hands had not protected them from damage on the tree stump,

Chris was in pain with her back and all of them were very weary.

In the weeks that followed, the bitter winter continued. When it was not snowing, gales of rain and sleet dashed against the windows. Women fell ill with respiratory disorders, colds, flu, pneumonia, as well as chilblains and rheumatism. Food supplies seemed to dwindle still further and they realised that the local villagers were also very hungry.

In the shelter of their room, the mission women continued to knit and sew. The cardigan for Dora was growing and in some ways it was a symbol of hope. Despite the dangers, despite hunger and cold, despite the hints that were becoming stronger that any enemy prisoners should not expect to survive an Allied invasion of Japan, they continued to work on a garment to keep their friend warm. Not only was it to be functional, but Mavis had decided that this garment should be ornamented and had designed a simple pattern to be knitted into its fabric. The scrounged wool was finished and the handmade yarn, laboriously spun between hand and thigh, was knitting smoothly into the garment. There was not an endless supply of cottonwool and the women began to wonder whether there would be enough to complete the job.

With the ingenuity of countrywomen, they thought of another source of wool to be spun for Dora's cardigan. Although none of them had menstruated for several years because of their deteriorating health, they had from time to time been supplied with sanitary napkins. 'We don't need these!' they decided, and they pulled them apart to tease out the cottonwool centres to be transformed into yarn. Chris created buttons by cutting small rings of bamboo in cross-section and enclosing them in blanket stitch. It was going to be a beautiful gift for Dora.

Winter was still dragging on when they saw, across the plain from their place on the lower slopes of Mount Fujiama, distant fires. Sirens had been wailing all day. Flights of Allied planes had been pouring across the skies and now the sky was darkened with dense clouds of smoke haze, black and grey reddened with the flames of a thousand fires.

Looking across the plain that day, 10 March 1945, Mavis Green noted in her diary: 'The big city badly raided. Big fires seen here.' Though the Australian nurse did know what she was watching, the city on the plain was Tokyo — desperately wounded and ablaze — and one hundred thousand men, women and children were dying.

By the time Dora's cardigan was finished and she was able to wear it, it was almost spring and Eastertime. That Easter was a curious tangle of beauty, fear, creativity, depression and hope. Snow melted into streams, cherry blossom burst from tight buds on the branches outside their bedroom window, young green tinged the rice paddies and, through the clear blue of spring skies, silver planes flew to destroy. On the newly warmed breezes that touched their skin, the women heard the sound of exploding bombs. Wildflowers spread across the fields and white cranes stood gracefully by streams while the people of the place watched their children slowly starving. Imprisoned women mingled despair and hope, kindness and pettiness, rage and humour, physical weakness and spiritual searching.

Dora helped prepare a church service which recalled the Stations of the Cross, the painful progress of Christ towards his death and the people he encountered on the way. 'Remember when we did this with the nuns at Vunapope and with Chaplain John May, in 1942?' they asked each other. That time and place was a world away.

There was no way of knowing whether John May was still alive somewhere in Japan and there had been no hints of what had been happening in the Rabaul area; perhaps their friends the nuns were dead. At that other Easter, there had been some fear and some anger, but nothing like this. Now they knew what it was like to feel despised, damaged bodies falling under their burdens, mocked by their captors, abandoned by their friends and even, it sometimes seemed, forsaken by God. This was Easter; the Son of God had walked this path before and walked it with them still.

For Dora, reading again the story of death and life in the Gospels, it had never been clearer. It was as if her spirit, living in a body that was being reduced daily in a slow starvation, was free to feel and understand things of the spirit with a clarity she had never known before. Even the darkness of Good Friday, with its backdrop of air raids, sick colleagues and hunger, was made luminous by a longing for peace and a sense that the Christ who was dying was also the One who was wonderfully alive.

Preparing a prayer to offer, Dora considered the women who shared the house with her and their Japanese neighbours whose lives were also being torn apart. In the end she prayed, 'Oh most gracious Father, we bring before thee again this morning the desire that is uppermost in the hearts of everyone in this time of waste and war amongst all nations, the desire for peace,' and was moved when a woman not noted for her piety in normal times asked to copy the words into her own notebook.

When the mission women gathered in their room after singing the joyful songs of Easter Day, Chris announced a treat. 'I've been saving this up for you all!' she said, and produced little Easter eggs made with sugar and raisins saved for months from her last Red Cross parcel.

During the school holidays in May, Kath Brown travelled from Sydney to visit Jean Poole in Kiama. Kath and Rodger were the only ones from New Britain with whom Jean had kept in touch. Many of the women who had been on the mission staff were now scattered across Australia and had little contact with each other.

'Some people think it is really strange, at this stage,' Kath said, 'but Rodger is enlisting. The church has finally released him and the idea is that he will be able to get back into New Britain before most other missionaries if he goes as a chaplain to the Australian troops.'

Rodger had attended the annual meeting of the Methodist Overseas Missions, so Kath knew far more than Jean about what was happening in relation to New Britain. Though the war was not yet over, it seemed to the leadership of the mission that the time had come for planning and vision for the post-war reconstruction of their mission areas. It was decided that they needed additional staff to go to New Guinea. It was recognised that the team of men and women who were prisoners of the

Japanese would need a period of recuperation once they were finally released and would not be ready to return to work quickly, if at all. In addition to rebuilding their former work, the board had a new dream; during the years of war, military pilots flying over the Highlands of the mainland of New Guinea reported large populations of previously unknown peoples in the mountains and they planned to send missionaries to them as soon as possible.

As far as New Britain was concerned, Rodger would not be the first one to return. An experienced Methodist missionary, the Rev. Con Mannering, had returned to Victoria with his family in 1939. He had already gone to work with the troops in the western part of the island, as they prepared to attempt to win back Rabaul and the Gazelle Peninsula. Mannering had sent news of the people of Nakanai where Rodger and Kath had worked pre-war; the New Guinean people had been suffering a hard war. Any mission staff returning to the areas where battles had been waged and people had been under enemy occupation for years should expect to find great changes and many difficulties.

Kath described Rodger's entry into the army. It had not been easy, particularly as it may have seemed to outside observers that he had waited until the war was almost over and Germany had surrendered before enlisting. However, when men discovered that this new chaplain was one of the few among them who had been under enemy fire and had travelled back from the dangers of New Britain with men of the 2/22nd early in 1942, they saw things differently.

While the two women played with Kath's two little boys, they caught up with news of other mission staff. Of the South Australians, Elsie Wilson had been transferred to a school at Mount Gambier near her parents and was much happier, though she was still very eager to get back to work in New Britain as soon as she could.

Daisy McArthur was still not well and her boys were in the care of relatives — 'That would be the worst part,' Kath said, 'not being well enough to have her children with her.'

In NSW, Marion Oakes and Jean Shelton had both been given church assistance to send their sons to a church school, Wolaroi

College in Orange, NSW; Marion was nursing and Jean was housekeeper for a widowed missionary from China and his family in the provincial city of Bathurst. Essie Linggood was very busy and her latest of many tasks was writing a booklet about New Britain.

'And you, Jean, you've filled your life with school and church, and many other things you've been doing while you wait for John to come home,' Kath said. 'Now your name is on this book. You must be delighted. Won't John be proud!' Thistle Harris' new book, *Nature Problems: A Book of Natural History for Australians*, lay on the table between them, with the title page crediting the illustrations to Jean Poole and A. Turnridge.

'Surely, it won't be long now.' Jean had been following every clue in the newspapers describing the progress of the war and knew that the Japanese in the islands were being forced into a tighter and tighter place. 'Then John will come home and, as soon as they let us, we can all go back and get on with our work.'

There were several pairs of bleary eyes and a lot of yawning at the morning tea for Mavis' birthday. No one had had much sleep. Sirens had begun wailing soon after midnight and the sounds and vibrations of an air raid had gone on until not long before dawn. The raids were becoming more and more frequent and much more intense.

'What does it mean, do you think?' they asked each other. 'Are we winning?'

'Must be. It can't mean anything else, not with all those American planes going over every few days. But what else is happening in the world?'

They had very little news, but it seemed to them that the pressure was mounting on their Japanese neighbours. Not only were they being subjected to attack from the air, but many of their men were away from home, fighting in other parts of the world. The latest rice harvest had been the poorest for over ten years and many people were malnourished and under stress. There were frequent fights in the farmhouse kitchen between the woman Oba-san, Morli the cook and the guards, and the women knew that tempers were short and quarrels quickly ignited.

Though the nurses had been told, with delight, that President Roosevelt of the United States had died, very little other news was passed on and they took this to be a hopeful sign. If the war news had been favouring the Japanese, surely they would have been told, they reasoned. As it was, Morli told them that they should be ready to move out to some other destination at a moment's notice. Even Totsuka was becoming dangerous.

In the narrow world they inhabited, food and survival were central. None of them were in good health. As well as being very underweight, Dorothy was one of several who had regular bouts of malaria, a number had swollen and painful legs with beri-beri, and everyone knew the miseries of infestation with tapeworm and dysentery. Cal was bedridden, very ill and needing medical help. 'I have to stick it out long enough to die at home,' she told them.

Trading in food continued, often done in secret, each group hoping to take advantage of any food that might be available. Morli's wife was willing to trade — milk for cigarettes, homemade donuts for sugar — as well as Oba-san from her house at the back, and occasionally local villagers left small gifts of vegetables on the back steps.

Dora was asked by Oba-san to sew a suit for a man in the neighbourhood. All transactions passed through Oba-san.

'A suit for the hot weather,' Oba-san explained, 'like this one,' and she showed trousers and simple jacket. 'For this sewing you can have twelve eggs.'

'Anything for twelve eggs!' Dora told her friends later.

Dora had to begin by drafting a pattern based on the garments she had been shown, a complex engineering feat, and then cut out the thin, slippery fabric and stitch it, every stitch made by hand. For many days she worked, bent over the fabric passing through her bony fingers, almost tasting in her mind the eggs she was earning — fried, scrambled on toast, poached, or perhaps a little omelette, shared with her friends, of course. . . When at last the suit was finished, she took it to Oba-san.

'Very sorry, but I have not many eggs, only three.'

Dora was disappointed and annoyed, but not really surprised.

All that work for almost nothing. She might have known. Either Oba-san had never intended to pay her so well or other people had used greater trading skills to win the precious eggs. The constant need for food gave some people extra cunning, strong bargaining skills and, on occasions, power over others. I'm not tough enough, she decided; people tell me I'm too lenient.

In the uneasy quiet after a night of air raids, some of the women met around the bed of Eileen Callaghan for prayers. Not all the women among the nineteen prisoners chose to turn to Christian faith in those days of stress and anxiety. In their attempts to find answers to the questions for which there are no clear answers, each woman groped for her own path.

Some said: 'Look at what is happening around us! How can you say that there is a God? Either there is no God and never has been or, if God exists, he must be totally evil or uncaring to let this happen to the world. What sort of a God is this, who could create a world, then turn his back and let it destroy itself?'

Others were not sure what to think. Though they had never been interested in the church before, it seemed that perhaps now was a good time to make contact with things of the spirit, just in case. Anyway, this wasn't like going to church — best clothes, hat and gloves, rituals and all that — this was trying to understand the most elemental things about being alive and human at a time when they were acutely aware that life might end suddenly.

For Dora, Mavis, Chris and Dorothy, sitting with Cal, Mrs Jones, Dorothy Maye and others, the belief that God was in control gave them strength to go on. Dora's Bible was passed from hand to hand and they turned to the words of the ancient psalmist in Psalm 46. It seemed that humanity would never learn; even so long ago people were at war in a troubled world.

'God is our refuge and strength,' Dorothy read, 'a very present help in trouble. Therefore will not we fear, though the earth be removed and though the mountains be carried into the midst of the sea. . .'

Chris read on. 'The heathen raged, the kingdoms were moved; he uttered his voice, the earth melted. The Lord of hosts is with us; the God of Jacob is our refuge.'

There was hope in her voice as Mavis went on. 'He makes wars to cease unto the end of the earth; he breaks the bow and cuts the spear in sunder; he burns the chariot in the fire!'

Somewhere in the distance they could hear Oba-san and the cook fighting again. Cal was trying to catch her breath after a bout of tubercular coughing and Maysie looked a dreadful colour. The insistent voices of some women in the next room, going over and over the same conversations, buzzed with the irritation of mosquitoes. From the window, they could see a sky stained with the smoke and ash of shattered cities on the plain. At some unmarked moment, sooner or later, the sirens would begin again and the Allies would return to bomb them.

Dora took a deep breath before she read to the end of the psalm. She knew the words by heart, but in the many layers of stress in which they lived it was hard to make them real. But if she could not cling to God and believe that he could bring peace at last, what else was left?

'Be still, and know that I am God,' she read. 'I will be exalted among the heathen, I will be exalted in the earth! The Lord of hosts is with us; the God of Jacob is our refuge.'

In a strange and confused way, through April, May and June 1945, the Australian women at Totsuka in Japan were both an audience for the global drama that was being played out before their eyes and also members of the cast. It was not possible to separate themselves from what was happening around them and, knowing so little of what it meant, they were caught up in the action in a way that was out of their control. The earth tremors, the violent spring rainstorms, the shortage of food and the danger of being bombed and burned-out were common to them all.

Though they lived within the bounds of the farmhouse, its closest fields and the lane out to the main road, and went nowhere without their guards, they saw other Japanese, mostly at a distance — farmers, workmen, women — gathering firewood like themselves, and they saw children on their way to school. In some cases, the lines between enemies and friends were becoming blurred.

When the squadrons of planes came over, splitting the air with their speed and noise, carrying death in their bellies, the Australian women wanted to watch the show from the dress circle. They could be bombed any moment by their own people. They knew that. No-one had any idea where they were, so why should they expect invading pilots to avoid Totsuka? Anyway, if the Americans did invade, their guards had warned that prisoners should not expect mercy, so it wasn't going to make a lot of difference whether or not they watched the battles and cheered for their champions.

Perched on their window-sills in the dark, Mavis and Dora looked out past the branches of the cherry tree. For weeks there had been raids every few days, some midday strikes which sent farm workers scurrying to shelter and other attacks after dark. Tonight, the first shrilling of the sirens had come after ten o'clock and, as the cacophony built up, they knew that they would not sleep.

'Do you want to go out to the dug-out?'

'There's not much point. If they drop a bomb on us, we'll have caught it in the neck whether we are in the house or in the shelter.' They knew that the dug-outs they had prepared were not deep enough or shielded enough to protect them from bombs or shrapnel. In any case, they tended to think that they were less vulnerable to attack in their country farmhouse than they might have been in the thickly populated harbourside area of Yokohama at the rowing club.

The orchestration of wailing sirens, the sonorous throb of engines, the wild timpani of machine-gun fire and percussion of anti-aircraft guns and explosions beat upon their ears. Searchlights slashed across the sky like the rapier of a cosmic swordsman in pursuit of an elusive enemy. Moonlit midnight clouds reflected the flash and glow of a myriad blazes far across the plain, a storm of tracer fire.

'Thirty-nine, forty, forty-one. . . fifty-five, fifty-six. . . sixty-eight, sixty-nine. . .' The chant went on, the women counting off the planes that passed in view of their windows, the ones that had come in from the sea and their enemies who had just taken off from the huge Japanese military air base at Atsugi further along the road which ran past their front gate. Later, they would count the planes back in, keeping score of losses.

'Not there! Get down — aim to the left — miss him, miss!' they yelled into the violent night to the anti-aircraft gunners who sent endless arrows of death into the sky.

Their shouts made no more sense than the shrieks of ancient onlookers watching gladiators in mortal combat, or screaming spectators urging on their favoured sporting team striving for mastery. No-one could hear them. No-one heard their gasps as distant planes exploded in the air and plummeted to earth. Only their companions understood the painful pounding of their hearts, the extreme tension of watching one of many battles which would decide their own fate, the sense of reckless bravado of those sitting on their windowsills through a major raid. Each woman knew that, sooner or later, she would be snatched out of her place as a spectator in the dress circle and would be thrust unwillingly onto centre stage. They knew that, whichever way the battle went, the end would not be long.

By the time summer was warming the countryside, they heard that much of Tokyo and Yokohama was in ruins. They had watched four hundred planes go over on one day, the immense clouds of smoke hanging in the air through the long hours of another day of battle. The violence was coming closer and closer. The nearby bakery was bombed and they were told that even the uncertain supply of bread would no longer be available.

In one week, Mavis recorded in her diary: 'Yoshida and Fuji's houses burned;' 'Morli's house burned;' 'Streets in Yokohama burned. No shops open.'

Morli brought his daughter to the farmhouse. Their family home was gone and the distressed girl was taken into the house with the Australian women. A few weeks later, another of their guards, Seiko, arrived from Yokohama looking unshaven, dishevelled and shocked. His house and possessions had just been destroyed in the latest raid. Yokohama was devastated, he said, thousands of citizens had been killed in the raids and those who had survived were taking shelter in large sheds and warehouses. He had come to collect some clothing and food from their Red Cross supplies.

A flight of US army planes flew over, dropping leaflets onto the fields. The first time it happened, the nurses saw villagers scouring the fields to collect them, but were not told what the leaflets said. At the end of June, the nurses were working in the fields when another shower of pamphlets fluttered to earth. This time, slow as many of them were, some were able to snatch a few of the papers up.

'It says, "Surrender or expect invasion",' they read.

The women thought about it with a mixture of hope and despair. 'Surrender? The Japanese will never surrender. It would be against everything they've ever been taught. They'd choose an honourable suicide every time. So how could they surrender as a nation? They are trapped in an impossible place.'

'What about us then?'

'I don't want to be pessimistic, but I don't like our chances.'

They felt even more dubious when old Poppa-san came to tell them that he was resigning. At first, he explained that he needed to return to Tokyo to deal with property of his which had been damaged in the raids. He had always been kind to them and they had grown fond of him. With other former police officers, he had been more civil to the women than guards who had previously been in the army.

Mavis had among her things the elegant black and gold lacquered bowl Poppa-san's daughter had given her in thanks for her knitting. But now the old man said, with his usual courtesy, 'You have been like my daughters. Now that things are going badly for us, I wish to go away from here. I do not want to hurt you, but I could not disobey an order. . .'

If the Japanese were forced to a national suicide, it seemed that they did not intend to leave any prisoners behind.

Rodger Brown, still becoming accustomed to wearing his army uniform, was given the honour of attending the meetings of the Methodist General Conference at the end of May, which met as a national body every three years. There was much in the agenda which interested him, as the members tried to plan for the possibilities of a nation at peace at last, with all the complexities of reconstruction. Everyone felt sure that it was only a matter of time before Japan, like Germany, would finally surrender.

The time came for the vote for the next President-General, the man who would be responsible for steering the Methodists of Australia through the hazards of a post-war world. It did not come as a great surprise when the overwhelming vote was given to John Burton. He was a vigorous man of seventy and had just retired as the General Secretary of Methodist Overseas Missions. He was highly respected overseas, a skilled writer, a man with significant links with other church denominations and a wise leader.

When the official visitor arrived on 1 July 1945, it came as a surprise. The imprisoned nurses had been visited by officials from the government from time to time, but here at last was someone from the Japanese Red Cross. The last time they had seen anyone from the Red Cross was when the Swiss delegate arrived with their Red Cross parcels on Christmas Eve 1942.

'No-one knew where you women were,' they were told. 'Now a cable will be sent to the International Red Cross Committee in Geneva to let your people at home know.'

There was so much to try to say in a limited time. The Red Cross representative asked many questions about the conditions under which they had been living, and answered their questions about what ought to have been the conditions for civilian internees.

'Just think what they've got away with!' they said after he had gone. 'We should have been having a monthly allowance, no manual labour, warm clothing and bedding, a decent daily rice ration, no clouts — and mail! Now we find out that we should have been able to send and get letters and cables every month. Every month. . .'

'And just think what it must be like for the men in the big camps. At least we've had Oba-san to help us get a bit extra, even though she's cheated us — the old girl has probably saved our lives.'

The visit gave them hope. Somebody must have always known their whereabouts because the Red Cross parcels had continued to come through occasionally, though the last ones had been early in May and were long gone. Yet their isolation from the rest of the world had been as complete as if they had been kept in a dungeon or behind high prison walls. Not only did the Red Cross visitor take news of their existence out to others; he also brought them news of the world. For the first time they discovered, to their astonishment, that the war in Europe had been over for two months already and that Hitler was dead; there had been whispers that Germany might be getting close to surrender, but the rumours had always been denied by their guards.

'If Germany is finished, then the Allies must be concentrating on beating Japan now. That explains all the raids we've been having lately,' they said. 'It should be over soon, and we'll be out of here and off home.'

'Or dead.'

A secret cablegram arrived in Canberra from the High Commission in London on 19 July. Under the heading 'Prisoners of War Far East Australian Nurses', the message told of a series of connections through the British, Swiss and Japanese which led to news of nurses missing in Japan. They were at Totsuka, the message read, and 'M. Suzuki added that a complete list of those persons had been sent to Swiss Legation and that a delegate of the Legation would be able to visit them shortly.'

The Australian authorities were grateful for the news, but there were still no names available and they knew that at least forty Australian army nurses were still missing as well as civilian nurses. There was still nothing to report to the families of the missing women.

If anything, the weeks that followed the visit of the Japanese Red Cross representative were even worse than those that went before. The tension in the local community was palpable. For some there was anger and for others despair and hopelessness; people expected to fight to the death, but for those who survived they expected slavery and the abuse of their women by invaders.

When a party of dancers came from the nearby temple to dance for a festival near their house, they danced in a frenzy of emotion which raised clouds of dust and left the gardens trampled. Guards were on edge and aggressive and the Australian women found themselves swinging between deep depression and wild excitement.

Raids of B-29 fighters and Flying Fortresses came in waves, sometimes surging over the battered countryside from early morning until dusk and sometimes filling the nights with the glow and smell of burning. Women who knew more about aircraft than others suggested that they were beginning to see planes which were not capable of very long-range flights: 'they must be flying from aircraft carriers or even land bases within easy reach of Japan — the end must be getting very close.' Guards spoke about the wreckage of their city of Yokohama, families trying to build themselves shelters with the twisted iron from bombed buildings, wandering orphaned children, women anxiously seeking food for their families and finding little.

The days were very hot and humid and the women dreamed of iced water or cool slices of fruit dripping with juice. In common with the rest of the community, the women were constantly hungry. The rice ration was becoming more and more watery and, though the women picked a few beans and cucumbers from the gardens they had planted, their diet was very deficient; the last time they had seen any meat protein through their stews of radish and soyabean, the meaty fragments had some fur on them — 'looks more like cat than rabbit to me!' they said.

Most of them were ill — Dorothy Beale with another bout of malaria, Jean Anderson in such pain with beri-beri that she could barely walk up two steps, Mavis with an attack of appendicitis, another woman vomiting a tapeworm — but they knew that if Cal didn't get help soon, she would not live to see Australia again.

'They'll have to give up soon, surely. Can't they see they are beaten?'

'They won't give up. They can't.'

(The imprisoned women did not know that on 27 July six key Japanese leaders, the Supreme Council for the Direction of the War, met to consider the proclamation which had been sent from a meeting of Allied nations at Potsdam. It declared two options: Japan was offered an opportunity to end the war by an unconditional surrender or it could choose annihilation. The six were divided. To the military leaders, it was unthinkable to give up; Japanese soldiers were not permitted to surrender and lay down their arms, therefore as a nation they must fight to the end with courage. Others believed that surrender was the only way Japan could survive as a nation. Stalemated, they chose to ignore the proclamation.)

As August began, hot, muggy and hungry, Mavis was feeling better again. When the mission women had a little party in their room which Dora arranged to try to keep their spirits up, Mavis showed them a verse she had found in the Bible.

'I'm not sure that I achieve this, but it's what I want to aim for,' she explained, and read aloud the words, written centuries earlier by St Paul from prison to his friends the Philippians. 'I have learned, in whatsoever state I am, therewith to be content. . . everywhere and in all things I am instructed both to be full and to be hungry, both to abound and to suffer need. I can do all things through Christ which strengtheneth me.'

And then it was 6 August 1945.

In Sydney on that day, the new General Secretary of Overseas Missions, the Rev. A.R. Gardiner, received letters from the wives of several of the missing missionaries. They were hoping that the end of the war was in sight and very soon their husbands would be home again.

In London that day, another cablegram was sent around the world to Canberra, Australia. Among other things it stated: 'Eighteen nurses interned Totsuka were captured at Rabaul with Australian soldiers and are in good health. Swiss delegate will be authorised to visit them. Names are as follows. . .' For the first time, the full list of women was transmitted: 'Kathleen A. Parker, Marjorie Jean Anderson, Daisy C. Keast, Lorna Whyte, Eileen M. Callaghan, Mavis C. Cullen, Joyce O. Harris, Joyce O. McGahan, Alice M. Bowman, Mary E. Goss, Jean M. McLellan, Grace D.M. Kruger, Dorothy L. Beale, Jean Christopher, Mavis F. Green, Dora

E. Wilson, Dorothy M. Maye, Kathleen Bignall.'

In Japan that day, a B-29 bomber flew over Hiroshima at a very great height. After months of waves of low-flying bombers carrying destruction, the distant speck in the sky was ignored. A parachute was seen falling towards the city. At 8.15 am there was a blinding white flash. In a single unspeakable searing blow, 64 000 human beings — mothers and their babies, schoolchildren on their way to school, workmen starting work for the day, young girls and elderly men — were dead or dying.

The Japanese leadership were given an ultimatum. If they refused to accept the terms of surrender, 'they may expect a rain of ruin from the air'.

21

7 August–31 August 1945

THE YELLING WOKE MAVIS AND DORA. A guard was shouting for Kay Parker. The women had gone to bed, but it was too warm and muggy, the long summer dusk was too light and they were too hungry for sleep to come easily. The sound of agitated voices disturbed the others and they lay waiting. Something was happening.

After a pause, a gale of laughter nearby drew them into the corridor. 'What's going on?'

'The guards called me out,' Kay said. 'They are very upset. They say that they've just heard the news that the Allies dropped one bomb on Hiroshima today, just one, and it practically wiped the whole city out — killed thousands and thousands, nearly all civilians, too, they said. Well, I tried to keep a straight face and said, "We've got plenty of those, so you'd better expect more."'

'Poor silly fools — fancy thinking one bomb could do all that!' The group rocked with laughter.

Two days later, a second story was told them of a single, mysterious new bomb and its victim this time was Nagasaki. They could not imagine what might be happening. The guards described this strange bomb as running along the ground, consuming everything in its path, but neither they nor the guards understood what it might be. They only knew that it might not mean good news for anyone who was a prisoner of the Japanese.

They remembered that only a week earlier they had been set to dig deeper into one of the air-raid dugouts. Now they were told: 'In the next three days, all prisoners are to be killed.'

In the deep valley of Ramale, on the island of New Britain, the missionary prisoners and their people watched the beginnings of a new tunnel being dug into the hillside. Schoolboys who were ordered to help the military police with the digging reported that the new tunnel did not appear to link with the existing network of tunnels and was very deep.

The priests and people ignored the tunnel most of the time. They had been spending the months of 1945 busy with conferences on mission work, taking advantage of the presence together at Ramale of Catholic missionaries from widely separated areas of the Solomon Islands, Manus Island, New Britain and New Ireland, working together on agreed catechism material and translation work. For recreation, they had formed choirs, produced skilled handcrafts and enjoyed long and lively evening conversations. Nothing had been said to give them any direct message about the progress of the war, but the clues suggested that the end was getting nearer.

Just occasionally someone would look at the new, deep blind tunnel and ask, 'Do you think they might plan to do away with us all in that hole?'

Pits were being dug in other parts of the islands in those months, with puzzled villagers obeying orders to dig, as they had been forced to obey orders to provide garden food for the invaders or cut down their sago palms to feed troops. New Guinean people were very weary of the war. As bombing became more and more severe, their homes were destroyed and it became dangerous to stay in their village areas. Villagers hid in the bush, living in caves or building humpies to protect them from the elements. They had lost the freedom to travel between villages or to meet for Christian worship, and the food in their gardens was being used by the invaders. Their pigs and fowls had all been eaten and they were discouraged, dispossessed, ill and afraid. It had been whispered from area to area that some of their own men had been executed. Some leading men had dreams which gave them hope, but it was so hard to know who could be trusted and the dreams were rarely shared.

The newspapers lay spread on his desk, headlines black and shocking. 'Atomic Bomb on Japan. Huge Blast Effect' read one and the next day, 'Atomic Bomb May End War' followed by 'Victims Were "Seared To Death" — Tokyo.' John Burton read the articles with pain. The irony was that the name of a dear Japanese friend, Toyohiko Kagawa, was there describing the horror of this destruction.

Burton tried to imagine what had happened in Japan a few days earlier. The *Sydney Morning Herald* of 7 August quoted a Washington correspondent describing a weapon more powerful and deadly than any which had gone before. It said that the atomic bomb 'with more power than 20 000 tons of TNT and producing a blast 2 000 times greater than the largest bomb previously used, was dropped on Hiroshima (Japan) today. This was the first of many which will be used to complete the destruction of Japan. Hitherto on the secret list. . .' The article went on to list other air attacks over Japan using thousands of tons of incendiaries and high explosives bombs, including 'airfields and targets of opportunity in the Tokyo area'. The first news suggested that, though this new weapon was bigger and stronger, it was just one of many deadly weapons.

The true story only began to become clear after a few days, when the boiling dust had settled and photographers flying over the devastated city brought back their film of utter ruin. Burton read the chilling words of the newspaper of 9 August. From Tokyo Radio, it was reported that the bomb 'seared to death practically all living things, human and animal. The dead are too numerous to count. . . burned beyond recognition. . . Sixty per cent of the city, which is bigger than Brisbane, was completely destroyed. . . Even the men who worked for years on the perfection of the bomb and the crew of the *Enola Gay* which dropped it have no conception of the weapon they are using. They. . . prefer to take comfort from the fact that Japan brought this destruction upon herself. . .'

Perhaps that was true enough. But Burton could not separate the military decisions of the leadership of the Japanese aggressor from the effect those decisions were having on the civilian population of their own land and those who were prisoners there. Only the previous day, there had been news from the Australian military to say that they hoped to have news of the missing nurses any day now. They could be among the group discovered in Japan. If the four missing mission women were in Japan, perhaps the mission men might turn up there, too. If, of course, they were not to be among the victims of the new brutal technology which destroyed everything in its path, not merely military targets.

And Toyohiko Kagawa? A few years before the war, the respected Christian Japanese had toured Australia. His messages had drawn huge crowds, 115 000 people in meetings over two months in 1935, and continually pointed his hearers to Christ, Son of God, Prince of Peace. Burton had been his host around Australia and had come to love and honour this godly man. A letter of appreciation from Kagawa after his visit was among Burton's treasured possessions: 'I sincerely hope that through my testimonies for Christ I may have been some help in the furtherance of the kingdom everywhere I have gone and for promotion and continuance of international friendship between your country and Japan.' Now Kagawa was quoted on Tokyo Radio, speaking about the injustice of such total destruction of the civilians of Hiroshima.

Would the devastation of this new bomb force the Japanese leadership to surrender and bring the war to an end? Would the Americans fulfil their threat that this bomb was 'the first of many'? Would his friend Toyohiko Kagawa and the mission staff survive such a holocaust?

Burton had no answers, but he knew that the only recourse he had was to plead with a sovereign God for his friends, and for the world. The mission board was to meet the next day and he knew that they would continue to pray for their friends in such great danger.

All that day there had been anguished meetings in Tokyo, of divided Japanese leaders trying to find a path between the desire to surrender and their inability to surrender. Close to midnight on the night of 9 August, in a deep bomb shelter in Tokyo, the leaders took the unheard-of step of requesting the emperor to cast his vote to release them from the impasse: to choose to surrender and survive or to fight on with honour to annihilation. With grief, the emperor said that the time had come to bear the unbearable and gave his sanction to the proposal that the Allied proclamation from Potsdam be accepted, that Japan capitulate to their enemies' demands.

In the dark before dawn of 10 August 1945, the Japanese cabinet made their bitter choice and began the process of preparing for a surrender. Coded messages were sent to Sweden and Switzerland to be passed on to the Allied powers, but it was decided that the people of Japan would not be told yet.

On the day that the Japanese leaders came to their decision, far to the south, in Sydney, Australia, a group of church leaders met for their regular meeting of the Board of the Methodist Overseas Missions. They gathered around the big table, greeting each other warmly. Through the years of war these people and others had struggled to make wise decisions about the work of missions under their responsibility. It had never been easy.

Many of the members of the board had known their own family griefs because of the war and each of them cared deeply about their friends, the missing missionaries. Now they talked before the meeting began about the latest war news. Could the force of the two atomic bombs dropped that week bring Japan to the point of surrender?

The meeting was called to order as John Burton entered. There was something in his face which demanded attention.

'We have just received this telegram from our Melbourne office,' he said. 'It reads: RED CROSS MELBOURNE ANNOUNCES OUR FOUR RABAUL NURSES WELL YOKOHAMA.'

'Thank God!'

The group were on their feet. At last. . . thank God. . . Sister

Beale. . . Sister Christopher. . . the NSW girls, Dora Wilson and Mavis Green. . .

A single voice began to sing and they all joined in, voices strong with joy and wavering with emotion, singing with eyes filled with tears. Mrs Cheetham, whose special care the mission women had been, John Burton, Percy Clark, R.H. Doust, Stanley Bowyer-Hayward, Richard Piper, Bert Wyllie, G.W. Cocks, F.W. Kitto, Dr McClelland and the others, all singing and startling the office staff outside the Board room:

Praise God, from whom all blessings flow,
Praise him, all creatures here below,
Praise him above, ye heavenly host,
Praise Father, Son and Holy Ghost.

They sat down, at last, overcome with the implications of the news. 'Now it shouldn't be long before we'll have news of our men, too.'

In her home in Kadina, South Australia, Mrs Christopher was having a morning of baking. She had just put a tray of apricot slice in the oven when the telegraph boy rang the doorbell. The baking was forgotten as the mother who had tried to hide her terrible grief through the long years of silence ran out into the street, shouting to her neighbours, waving the telegram.

'Jean is alive! She's safe. . .' When at last she came home to her own kitchen, the apricot slice was blackened charcoal, but who cared: her daughter was alive!

In Brisbane in Queensland and Maitland and New Lambton in NSW, families heard that Dorothy, Mavis and Dora were safe. At Maitland, the telegraph boy was sent posthaste to make the delivery. The whole community knew that Mrs Green had a daughter away as a prisoner but that all her letters had been returned to her. Now, when the message reached the post office, the lad ran all the way to bring the good news.

Across Australia, families were already welcoming home men who had been the prisoners of Germany and soon, they hoped, the war against Japan would also come to an end. Then the twenty thousand who had been prisoners of Japan would be released and join their families once more.

'It makes no sense.' The nurses at Totsuka were puzzled. 'If they really expect to kill us, why are they letting us write our first letters home now? They've never allowed us to write home before.'

Not much made sense in those days. It was so very hot, and the guards were so much on edge. It was over a month since the first visit from the Red Cross and several weeks since they had heard that their names had been forwarded on through the Swiss Red Cross. But nothing else seemed to have changed. They were still hungry and sick, the air raids still stormed over their heads and they still did not know what was really going on in the world.

'No more than one hundred words in our letters! How can they expect me to tell my family over three years' worth of news in one hundred words? I've got at least a hundred questions I want to ask, just to start with!'

Each woman sat over her letter, writing on the special note-paper, selecting and discarding words. Their letters were dated 11 August and, although they knew nothing of it, in Australia on that day the newspapers shouted with their largest headlines: 'Japanese Government Seeks Peace — Japan has informed Britain, USA, Russia and China that she is ready to capitulate.' It was not yet quite a surrender, just an intention, but the listening world began to hope that the end of the long horror had come.

Over the next three days, invisible to the world, messages passed to and fro between Japan, USA and Britain; negotiations, questions, coded cables and translations. The emperor had decided to take the unprecedented step of speaking to the people of Japan in a wireless broadcast, to tell them that their battle was lost. Though the ordinary people of Japan had never heard the voice of their emperor, it was felt that such an announcement could only come from the mouth of the one who symbolised their nation and for whom so many Japanese had already died.

Even as the emperor and the leaders of government and military in Japan wrestled with the bitter task of accepting defeat and taking practical steps to bring the war to an end, some within Japan who caught wind of what was happening were determined to resist. Retreat and surrender were so dishonourable that they could see no other way than a fight to the death or an honourable suicide. A group of young officers in Tokyo was convinced that the emperor was being manipulated against his will to agree to surrender and that the nation was being betrayed by senior advisors; they began to plan a coup to protect the emperor and to prevent the formal announcement of surrender being made. Further along the road which ran past the farmhouse at Totsuka was the largest air base in Japan, Atsugi; it was well equipped, well defended and with a very large complement of men and aircraft, so some officers plotted to refuse to surrender.

Without knowing it, the women at Totsuka balanced on a knife edge that week. They were told that cables had been sent to their next-of-kin and their letters to their families were taken for posting on 14 August. Other things seemed to be as usual. Oba-san and Morli were having another of their famous fights in the kitchen and an air raid went on for most of the day.

They could not know that in Tokyo that day there was an entanglement of plots and counterplots, revisions and further revisions of the formal Imperial Rescript which was to be the wording of the announcement of surrender, slow and reluctant signing of the Rescript by the cabinet, murders and suicides. Nor could they see the tall column of smoke and blackened fragments of papery ash floating above a fierce bonfire of files and documents which blazed behind the War Ministry, as soldiers continued to toss official records into the pyre; there was talk of destruction of all records and then a mass suicide as an apology to the emperor for failure to win the war. Infernos of documents were to blaze for days. American planes dropped leaflets over the countryside, but the only scrap of news the women heard was that the USSR was now at war with Japan.

For yet another night the women watched waves of planes going over on their way to bomb Tokyo, Yokohama and other nearby cities. They cheered as a Japanese plane was hit and plunged to earth in the distance and then tried to sleep while the raid went on through the night. Across the plain in Tokyo at midnight, the emperor was carefully guarded as he recorded the Imperial Rescript for broadcast the next day. Through the hot summer night, Imperial Guards, palace chamberlains, officials, men of high authority and young conspirators wove their way through a final intricate dance in the darkness of the city, meeting and parting, circling and confronting, a choreography of rage and despair.

When the sun rose, red on another hot day, Mavis noticed the date.

'Today is 15 August,' she commented to her friends. 'It is six years today since I left home for New Guinea. I expected to be home three years ago!'

At noon that day, the people of Japan paused in every city and hamlet. They had been instructed to listen to a broadcast by the emperor and people gathered wherever a radio was available. The women at Totsuka had no radio and their grasp of Japanese language was limited, but they heard the sound of weeping.

The voice of their emperor brought a message of great anguish. Japan was surrendering. He spoke of the gallantry and sacrifice of the men who had fought and died and the service of the millions of Japan. But their enemy had begun to 'employ a new and most cruel bomb. . . Should we continue to fight, not only would it result in the ultimate collapse and obliteration of the Japanese nation, but also it would lead to the total extinction of human civilisation.' The quiet voice went on, speaking of the hardships before them all, but 'we have resolved to pave the way for a grand peace for all generations to come by enduring the unendurable. . . Unite your total strength, to be devoted to construction for the future. . .'

The Australian women did not hear the broadcast, but they saw the face of Morli the cook as he told them that Japan was surrendering and heard the sobs of their neighbours.

It was hard to believe that soon they might be free to go home. They had not been told officially that they were free and in fact their guards were suddenly increased from three to five to 'protect them'. Even now, it might be too late for Eileen Callaghan who was very ill.

On the same day, 15 August, the NSW Methodist church paper published a centre spread. Surrounded by photographs of the four mission nurses, the large headline read, 'The Silence Breaks'. Jean Poole read it and fresh hope filled her. Her friend Dora was alive and well in Japan — and Mavis, Chris and Dorothy! She stared at the photographs. They had used old pictures, of course, because the women were still somewhere in captivity but, after all these years of silence, at last there was news.

Later that day, the news of the surrender of Japan was broadcast and Australians everywhere laughed and cried with relief and thankfulness. Bells rang in every town, and newspapers prepared their banner headlines with the best word, 'PEACE.' Waiting women ran to talk to neighbours, to tell their children. At their boarding school in the country, the young sons of Dan Oakes and Herbert Shelton ran wildly around their school playground, beating a tattoo of joy on garbage bins.

Jean Poole was jubilant. Soon, very soon, John would be coming home.

Waiting at the locked gate in the fence that surrounded the tropical valley of Ramale a few days later, the group of Catholic mission internees grew impatient.

'Where are the guards?' they complained. 'Have they forgotten to unlock the gate so that we can go to work in the gardens?'

Someone went to the *Kempei-tai* office to ask. He returned with the key in his hand and a curious message. 'They said, work as long as you like, no restrictions. And they all look very upset.'

Then they remembered that it was now several days since the walls of their tunnels had vibrated with the impact of bombs over Rabaul. They could not help trying to guess what might be happening, and when, a few days later, the bishop and his people were told officially that the war was at last over, they were not surprised.

The local Japanese official, Seiko, visited the women at Totsuka. It was true. Japan had surrendered.

'The war is over, peace is here,' said the guards and one old man wanted to shake their hands. Guards became very careful of their welfare, anxiously asking that the women give a good report of their guardianship to the Allies.

'It might be over, but we're not free,' the nurses complained. 'We've been told to stay inside the farmhouse boundary for our own safety. They are expecting paratroops to arrive any minute and someone might decide to get rid of us before they get here. We won't feel safe till we are home again.'

The food, when it came after the long hard months of hunger and deprivation, came in an excess that was almost ludicrous. First an entire side of raw beef, perhaps twenty-seven or more kilos of it, and vegetables. Morli, the cook, announced that they could take charge of the cooking now and he had been issued with 1 000 yen to buy food. Within a week, the Japanese Red Cross brought two boxes of food and a few days later each woman was given butter, two pounds of sugar, two bottles of beer and no less than twenty-two tins of salmon. And that was before food began to rain from the skies.

They all knew that it was foolish, that their long-starved bodies should have taken small amounts of food, carefully prepared, till they could tolerate the new diet. But they found they couldn't help themselves. For so long they had lived on the smell of handwritten recipes. Now women ate sugar and butter in spoonfuls and took turns to cook a sequence of meat meals in an orgy of frying, baking and stewing, ringing a bell to call the others to eat as soon as each meal was ready. In a kind of madness, they ate and ate, vomited and ate again, ate till they were bloated and in pain with mouths tasting foul, nineteen women devouring half a beast in three days. 'We have to eat fast or the meat will go bad in this heat.'

Eileen Callaghan was very ill. Dora and Mavis and the others went to see her in her bed from time to time, but everyone knew that, despite Kay Parker's careful nursing, their rescue would probably come too late for Cal. Kay's pleading for medication for

Call had gone unheard and even now, when a German doctor appeared, it seemed that little could be done. When the Red Cross representatives visited on 23 August, they sent the message to Geneva: 'General health of party is fair, rapidly improving since recent increase in rations, with the exception of: Eileen Callaghan aged thirty-two years who is suffering from advanced bilateral tuberculosis aggravated by lack of medical care.'

The others sent a general message that they were well and would be home soon, but Cal's message read: 'Not very well, do not worry.' The next day a priest came to Cal and her Methodist friends were thankful that her wish had been granted and she had once more received the sacrament of the eucharist, even if it might be for the last time.

Near the end of August, the women began to lay large canvas sheets on the ground outside the farmhouse with the markings 'PW' The US military would be making parachute drops of food over prisoner of war camps, they were told by the Red Cross representatives, but they would have to identify themselves as no-one had known they were there. There was excitement now as they spread the cloths and every passing plane was watched with hope. The sky was still busy with American aircraft, but they were no longer dropping bombs.

It was a strange time. Free and yet not free. They were still among the people who for so long had been the enemy, yet felt an unexpected friendliness with some of these people who had shared their lives. They were free to roam on long walks around the countryside, but were aware that they were still the foreign *Goshu*, even though village children no longer threw stones at them. The rumours among the local people were that the US forces under General Macarthur had taken over Atsugi air base and the US fleet had entered Yokohama harbour. Very soon, they hoped, some Allied people would come to rescue them, but for the moment they had to wait.

Walking through beautiful countryside, Mavis, Dora and some others went with Oba-san to visit her brother. Though the Japanese woman had sometimes cheated them, manipulated them and involved them in intrigues among themselves, they were all grateful to her; without her help and intervention their lives at Totsuka would have been more difficult than they were. As they walked with Oba-san now, they saw the first signs that autumn was coming. They had never been able to walk so far before.

Soon the first falls of snow would whiten the top of distant Mount Fujiama and trees would turn red and gold on the lower slopes against the green of pines higher up. Orchards of mandarin oranges grew in stripes and the distinctive roofline of Japanese houses ornamented the landscape. For most of their time in Japan, the women prisoners had been kept within walls and fences and their picture of the country of their imprisonment was limited to the views from windows. Now there was a grudging admiration for a beauty which transcended human war and enmity.

As they walked back to the farmhouse, a plane circled overhead. It seemed that the crew had seen their signal with its big 'PW' on the ground. Suddenly, objects began to fall through the air, dangling from parachutes, then crashing to earth. The women ran to the site. Drums had burst open on the ground, scattering tins of food everywhere. They gathered everything up, tins bent and buckled by their fall, but holding food they had not tasted for years.

'All this food will keep us going for ages!' they said.

In Sydney, women gathered from many parts of the city for a big party. Women who had been waiting for years for the return of their men from battle fronts and prisoner of war camps met at Paddington Town Hall for a grand celebration. Not only Germany had surrendered, but now Japan had capitulated as well and their men would soon be released. Members of the New Guinea Association like Netta Allsop and Helen Wayne were there, talking of the men of the 2/22nd and the community of Rabaul. They had supported each other through the years of waiting and now the waiting was almost over.

Jean Poole did not attend the party. She had never been a member of the Association because she lived too far out of Sydney to attend meetings, but she sensed the euphoria which lifted her and women around Australia. The women whom she had not seen since they left the ship *Macdhui*, women like Daisy McArthur, Essie Linggood, Helen Pearson, Nellie Simpson and the others, would be like her, she was sure: anxious, excited, thankful and a bit apprehensive.

It was impossible not to feel a little anxious. Stories were beginning to come back from prison camps just contacted of dreadful things which had happened in other parts of the world.

In South Australia, the coming of peace opened a new door for Elsie Wilson. After the years of chafing at her separation from the work she had always wanted to do, the years of loneliness in communities where she did not really belong, at last she could move. During the war, it had been impossible for women teachers to transfer from the teaching service to other employment. Now Elsie took immediate steps to apply to be released from the Education Department of South Australia. She had already written to the General Secretary of the Methodist Overseas Missions. As soon as she was free, she would be available to go back to New Guinea.

August 1945, a month which had seen such a turmoil of grave decisions, was nearly at an end. In Yokohama harbour, fleets of the world were gathering for the formal signing of the documents of surrender by the Japanese. The first of waves of American troops had begun to land unopposed on Japan's home islands and the rescue of prisoners of war had been ordered. General Macarthur landed at Atsugi airfield and drove to Yokohama to set up headquarters.

At the end of the month, an Australian officer, Major H.S. Williams landed in Manila, Philippines. He was on his way to Japan on behalf of the Australian forces, charged with the task of locating the thousands of Australian prisoners of war who were missing. Major Williams had spent many years in Japan before the war and spoke the language fluently; he knew that he would need all his skills to begin to uncover the mysteries of the missing people. Among many groups of missing men was the large crowd from Rabaul.

In the Rabaul area, New Britain, joyful New Guinean villagers came flooding into Ramale to greet the Catholic missionaries from whom they had been separated for so long. Other groups of prisoners of whom the missionaries had only heard rumours came to visit them. For the first time, they were face to face with troops who had been captured in various parts of South-East Asia and brought to Rabaul through the war years, men from Indonesia, India and elsewhere who had suffered greatly and were the remnant of their people who had survived. Large numbers of former prisoners came to Ramale to celebrate survival and freedom, bringing musical instruments into the camp to offer joyful concerts. They were still surrounded by a hundred thousand Japanese troops and papers of peace had still not been signed in their region, but at last they had confidence that there was a future.

From the farmhouse at Totsuka, the Australian women watched and waited. In their long walks they had seen the US Army transports on the road passing from Yokohama to Atsugi, always in the distance. Mavis counted 250 lorries loaded with troops in full battle kit, but they were never near enough to make contact, though they tried. The women went on cooking and eating, attacking the surfeit of food that had fallen at their feet, daily putting more weight on their bony frames.

Then on the last day of August, another load of food was parachuted to the ground and the women went out to collect it. Two nurses decided to walk out as far as the main road in the hope of being able to hail an American truck which might pass by, while the others returned to the house with the food. When they were not really expecting it, the women in the house saw an American jeep come driving up their chestnut lane with the two nurses on board.

'This is Major Morley of the 11th Airborne Division!'

Two men in the uniform of the US Army stepped from the jeep. The major said, 'We saw these two ladies racing up the road, waving their arms and shouting, so we thought we'd better be gentlemen and stop to pick them up.'

The women did not know whether to laugh or cry. Help had come at last.

'Get packed up tonight,' the major said when the excitement had eased a little. 'We'll send out a field doctor straight away to see Sister Callaghan and in the morning a truck will come out to pick you all up and take you to Atsugi. Will you be okay to spend one more night out here?'

One night? Only one? After waiting three years and seven months in captivity and with three plane loads of foodstuffs for their next two or three meals, what was one more night?

22

---

31 August–13 September 1945

ONCE THE DAM WALL WHICH had kept them from any contact with the rest of the world was breached, everything flooded in at once. Totsuka, invisible to the Allies for so long, was suddenly the destination for an influx of visitors. American personnel officers, the doctor and war correspondents all appeared along the lane that first day. Women, who had waited for so long to explain their story to someone, at last had an audience.

That evening, preparing to leave Totsuka the next day, each woman packed her bag. Dora folded the cardigan handmade with kindness by her friends, a tiny knitted silk bag with a Japanese coin inside which Chris had given her for a birthday, her delicate papercut tablemats and her Bible. Mavis collected her little black diary, and the matching book of recipes, as well as the handkerchief Sister Columba had given her long ago at Vunapope on which Mavis had embroidered the names of all her companions in imprisonment.

Each one had their own treasures: handmade playing cards, diaries, little gifts like buttons and earrings crafted from scraps, Chris' handwritten collection of remembered hymns, each thing with its own part in the story of their captivity. These objects had meaning as expressions of their survival.

When they woke on that last morning at Totsuka, they knew

it was the first day of autumn. They would not have to face the bitterness of another winter in Japan; in their weakened condition they knew that a number of them would not have survived it.

With their bags ready, they waited impatiently all morning for the promised truck. They were so close to freedom now that it was frightening to think that something might have gone wrong and they could be forgotten once more. At last it came, hours late — 'Sorry, we broke down and had to go back' — and it was time to go. Each woman farewelled Eileen Callaghan and promised to write; Cal was to go home on a hospital ship as she was not well enough to face the journey with the others.

Clad in the new summer dresses and shoes the Red Cross had brought them, the women lined up on the doorstep outside the farmhouse. A photographer waited by the truck.

'How about a smile and wave, girls,' he called and captured an image of laughing faces and thin arms aloft against the entrance decorated with Japanese script.

None of them could help smiling. 'We're going home!' they said as they scrambled on board the truck, waved goodbye to their Japanese neighbours and travelled without regret for the last time along the avenue of chestnut trees.

The journey to the great air base at Atsugi passed in a blur of dust and excitement. Few of them cared to watch the passing scenery. They were on their way home. The air base, head-quarters only a week earlier for thousands of Japanese men and aircraft, had been taken over in the last few days by the US Army and, as they arrived, processions of US planes were taking off and landing on the one runway which had survived Allied bombing.

After the simplicity and isolation of their life at Totsuka and at the rowing club, they felt they were being bombarded with impressions, information and news. The atomic bombs. . . the death of Hitler. . . the election defeat of Churchill. . . the thousands of other Australians who had been imprisoned in Japan and South-East Asia since 1942. . . it was overwhelming. Since their last sight of the officers from Rabaul back in 1942, the women had seen almost no Caucasian men and now they were sur-rounded by healthy young Americans in uniform — Mavis noted in her diary that night: 'All Americans have beautiful teeth.'

That evening, they were taken to the mess where a substantial meal was set before them. There seemed to be so much food, and yet they could not help the habit of years. Several women surreptitiously slipped portions of the food from their plates onto their laps — 'to eat tomorrow'.

'Hey, you don't need to do that. There's plenty more where that came from, ladies!' The Americans were amused, but to hungry women it had not seemed funny, only sensible.

The news that a party of Australian nurses had just been recovered somehow reached a few Australian men who had also been rescued. The men and women exchanged stories; it had been wonderful to be rescued by the Americans, who could not have been kinder, but to have a chance to talk about their experiences of captivity with fellow-Aussies. . . ! All of them had known hunger, isolation, fear, depression and boredom, but the stories the men told were far more chilling than anything the women had experienced. Later that night, when they were all together, too excited to sleep easily, they talked about some of the stories of brutality they had been told, cruelties inflicted by both sides.

'After hearing all that, I guess we all have a lot to be thankful for,' one said.

'The treatment we've had has been marvellous by comparison,' said another.

Early on the morning of 2 September 1945, at Atsugi air base where just over two weeks earlier Japanese officers had plotted to reject the emperor's decision to surrender, Australian women ate a large breakfast of bacon and eggs. By the middle of the morning they were all aboard a troop transport plane and were airborne. Below them lay the home island of Honshu, Japan, where they had lived for so long without seeing it. Mount Fujiama rose below them, wearing its summer colouring of reddish-brown volcanic ash and lava, draped in wisps of cloud and surrounded by lakes and long, crinkled green mountain ranges.

Somewhere below lay Totsuka, among rice paddies, pine forest and mandarin orange orchards. Hidden by the miniature houses were Morli and Oba-san, still quarrelling, perhaps, and the people of the neighbourhood who used to stare at the *Goshu* women so curiously. Almost immediately, the battered patterns of the streets of Yokohama and Tokyo were passing below them.

'It looks like a carpet square,' remarked Mavis; a worn and faded carpet square with damage to much of the design. The thunder of the engines of their plane made it hard to talk, but women looked down and then at each other with unspoken messages: Could we have survived if we had stayed at the club in Yokohama?

They had been an audience for the deadly theatre of the Allied attacks on the cities of the plain and now they witnessed the scene for the final act. Looking down on the expanse of Tokyo Bay, the women identified Yokohama harbour where they had lived on the harbour shore. Now the harbour was filled with the might of the world's shipping, line upon line of submarines, the fleets of the Americans and the Japanese Navy, gigantic stageprops for the scene which would ring down the curtain on a global tragedy.

The planeload of women flew on across the sea, with six hours of flight ahead before they would land on the island of Okinawa. Behind them on the harbour, the spotlight of the world fell on the great battleship *USS Missouri*. In a ceremony of dignity and deep significance that day, representatives of the nations who had warred together signed documents of surrender on the deck before many witnesses. General Macarthur concluded proceedings with the words, 'Let us now pray that peace will be restored to the world and that God will preserve it always.'

Leaning against the wall of the plane as it flew south, Dora closed her eyes. The words of a psalm sang across her mind:

> If it had not been the Lord who was on our side,
> when men rose up against us,
> then they would have swallowed us up alive. . .
> We have escaped as a bird
> from the snare of the fowlers;
> the snare is broken,
> and we have escaped!
> Our help is in the name of the Lord. . .

It was almost impossible to concentrate on her work, Jean found. Around her, rows of children bent over their desks, painstakingly copying an exercise in handwriting into their books. As she paced between the desks, she absently noted that a child had dropped an inkblot on her work and pointed out a wobbling loop which did not follow the classic line prescribed by the Education Department. Only half aware of the familiar odour of chalk dust and ageing bananas in battered leather schoolbags, and the sound of squeaking pen-nibs and heavy breathing of children who laboured earnestly over their writing, Jean Poole let her thoughts run far from the classroom in Kiama.

The news had it that within days, the surrender of the Japanese forces in Rabaul would be signed. Many thousands of Japanese were still in the Rabaul area, but the surrender documents would be signed on board the ship *Gloria* in Jacquinot Bay, New Britain, which was already in Allied hands. And then, so they said, the Australians and the Americans would move in and occupy Rabaul once more. Only that day, a newspaper had carried the headline: 'Likely to recover number of European captives at Rabaul.'

Maybe in the next week or two news of John would come. In the pit of her stomach was that tightening, almost as if she could be ill, which was becoming a familiar feeling in these days when the waiting must surely be nearly over. Was John well? Damaged in mind or spirit? What had he suffered during these years of silence? How soon would he come to her?

The sound of a clanging bell shook her from her thoughts. It was playtime for the children and they were busily pressing blotting paper to their finished work and laying steel-nibbed pens down in the grooves on their desks. They were watching her, waiting until at last she gave the sign that they were free to move outside into the spring sunshine to the simplicities of marbles and hopscotch.

For the first time in over three-and-a-half years, the close-knit group of nineteen women was beginning to separate. It felt very strange to see a space where a friend had been. Cal had been left behind in Japan to travel home by hospital ship and, after they arrived on the island of Okinawa, Jean Anderson collapsed. They had known

22. *Interned nurses after release, Manila, Philippines, September 1945*

23. *Some of the interned nurses after release from Japan*
Back l to r: *Dorothy Beale, Dora Wilson, Joyce Oldroyd Harris, Mary Goss*
Front l to r: *Jean Christopher, Dorothy Maye, Etta Jones, Mavis Green, Lorna Whyte*

that Andy wasn't well, weakened by malnutrition and beri-beri and exhausted by the long plane flight, but an attack of malaria was the final straw and she was sent to hospital in Okinawa.

'Wait for me to catch up in Manila,' she begged. 'I'll be wild if you go on home without me.' But they knew that they had no control over their movements and would travel when they were told.

After an overnight stop in Okinawa, they travelled south once more, this time a further eight hours of flying to Manila in the Philippines. Flying over ocean and cloudbanks without landmarks, weariness competed with excitement. 'We have escaped. . . we have escaped. . .' they thought, but home was still many kilometres and ten days away. It was easier to close their eyes and try to avoid thinking about it. Soon enough they would be on their own, having to make their own decisions without the support of their group. For the time of travelling they would trust their weakened and tired bodies to the care of the crew of their plane and try to sleep through the no-man's-land between captivity in Japan and whatever the future held at home.

Once they arrived in Manila, they were gathered into the competent hands of the US Recovered Persons' Program and the Women's Replacement and Disposition Centre twenty-nine kilometres out of the city. Little more than a week earlier, Major-General Uhl had instructed the military staff assigned to the task of processing and caring for the thousands of former prisoners who would pass through their care: 'You will all be hosts to honoured guests who have suffered. . . welcome them back to a world at peace. . . give full measure of courtesy, kindness and cheerfulness.'

When the weary Australian women arrived and the Red Cross and nursing staff discovered that the American, Mrs Etta Jones, was with them, the kindness and hospitality was boundless. Mrs Jones was the first American woman to be recovered and the other women were the first of the Australian nurses.

'There are quite a few Australian nurses missing somewhere,' they were told, 'but you are the first to make it back.'

For ten days they remained in Manila. There was so much to

do and to learn. There were forms to fill in, interrogations, statements to be taken; they discovered a security and sense of identity as at last their names and personal particulars were recorded and filed, after years of being invisible, placeless and nameless to Australian authorities. There were medical examinations, inoculations, clothing issues, dental appointments, newspapers and books to read, a hairdressing salon ('hairstyles have changed!' they marvelled, eagerly accepting stylish haircuts and perms), interviews with war correspondents, newsreels and entertainments to see, visiting dignitaries to meet, photographs to be taken.

Piece by piece, they were putting together the missing parts of the years that had gone; the stories behind the fires of Allied airpower they had witnessed over Tokyo, the vast cemeteries of the recently-dead seen on Okinawa, the bay full of sunken shipping as they approached Manila, with signs of war damage and overturned trains.

And food — at every possible moment they were being plied with food and they could feel themselves getting heavier every day. Special orders for favourite foods were taken — 'Pancakes!' said some, and pancakes appeared — and oranges were flown specially from California.

'They are killing us with food!' Tootie declared, but no-one complained. After years of dreaming about flavours and aromas and the texture of food on their tongues, satisfying their bodies, they kept on eating everything put before them, even though they knew that it was probably not good for them.

In the avalanche of food, health care and entertainment, the chance to send and receive mail was one of the greatest privileges. Both Dora and Mavis received cables from home and sent messages. For Mavis, the cable was a mixed blessing. Though it was wonderful to have her first word from her mother — 'Everyone is looking forward to having you safe home' — she was puzzled that her mother signed it with her own initials instead of her usual custom of using the initials of her husband.

What about her father? Was this the confirmation of her premonition that something was wrong at home? Each of them began writing letters home, trying to tell some of the story without alarming their families too much.

Each of them was questioned minutely by Major H.S. Williams and other staff of the 1st Australian POW Contact and Enquiry Unit. The unexpected arrival of the party of Australian nurses gave the officers their first eyewitness accounts of the period in Rabaul between February and July 1942.

'Were any of your group executed? Tortured? Raped? Did you witness any atrocities or hear of any?'

Atrocities? They searched their minds. Occasional face-slappings and threats hardly counted as atrocities. They told the story they had heard in Rabaul in 1942 of the torture and execution of Captain Grey and passed on everything they knew of the boys of the 2/22nd, the men of the town, plantations and missions. They explained that they had heard that a large group of Australians had sailed for Japan, they thought, two weeks before themselves, but they had no direct news. It was disturbing to discover that the investigating officers did not know where their friends had gone.

'They should ask the Rabaul officers who travelled with us on the *Naruto Maru*,' they agreed among themselves. 'We know the officers are somewhere in Japan, and they saw the men leave camp. The men won't be still in New Britain, but they'll probably turn up in one of the big camps. No-one has heard from us all these years either, and we are all right.'

Remembering the things they had heard while they were still in the Rabaul area, and the graphic stories they had heard from other recovered prisoners, the women began to realise that in fact their own imprisonment, for all its grim reality, had been generous and courteous compared to the experience of others. Their hunger, cold and the threats from bombing had been shared by their Japanese neighbours.

Mavis Green wrote a letter while they were in Manila to Mrs Cheetham, the senior woman on their mission board at home. 'You may be wondering about our treatment by the Japanese. We have been wonderfully protected all through and we know you have been praying for us and your prayers were truly answered. Our chief complaints are that we were not allowed to communicate with our home folks. We were starved, and many nights we went to bed hungry. In winter time we suffered extreme cold and had very little clothing, no fires etc., otherwise we had nothing to complain of, but much to be thankful for. . . Our faith has been strong all through, although at times it has been hard. . . At our last camp we were in a very beautiful area among the paddy fields and pine forests. . . We had no work other than domestic duties. I have kept a diary so will tell you all when I come home. . .'

The first short list of recovered prisoners was published in Australia on 8 September and, after that, almost daily there were more names. For women searching the papers for the name of the man they loved there were also the lists of those who had died. Telegrams like this arrived at one house and another, randomly: 'Safe Allied hands home soon.' Across the country, the agony of uncertainty was something that women woke up with every morning, and took with them to bed every night.

For many, those weeks and months when men and women were being recovered slowly, group by group, were more stressful than the years that had gone before. Then, one just went on stolidly, one day at a time, believing that one's son or husband or lover must surely be alive in a prison camp somewhere, but knowing that no end was in sight and one must just do the best one could in the meantime. Now, every morning women woke with the thought: 'Today might be the day! Today I might hear that he's on his way home.' And then came the enemy thought: 'Today I might hear that he is dead.'

In many homes, women had learned to hold their tongue about the beloved son who was missing, daily swallowing the poison of silence. 'It upsets his dad so much to talk about it,' they whispered to women friends, 'that I can hardly even mention my boy's name.'

There were women who feared the return of their man. For some, the new freedoms of being able to travel, work in a challenging job or live independently had been relished; when the men came home, they knew that they would have to retreat to domesticity. For others, the wait had been too long and they knew that they would have to face telling a man, broken by years of imprisonment, that it was too late for them: she had left him for someone else.

Girls who had married three, four or five years earlier in the excitement of a boy's last leave before going overseas, now wondered whether the handful of letters exchanged through the years had been enough to sustain the commitment to marriage to an almost-stranger for either of them. Other girls, who had worn engagement rings for years, waiting for a missing fiance, prepared for weddings planned for within days of their return with a mixture of delight and panic: Could they be making a terrible mistake, after all this time?

News came through that warehouses full of undelivered mail to Australian and other Allied prisoners of war had been uncovered by American troops in Yokohama, Japan, letters dating back to 1942 and lovingly prepared packages from families which had never reached their destination. Women who had heard nothing for years agonised over whether their men thought that they did not care and had forgotten them, never bothering to write or send a parcel.

While so many waited hopefully for their men to come home, Kath Brown prepared for her man to leave. Rodger had been waiting for so long to go back to New Britain. It had drawn him through the years and he had always been sure that the day would come when he would be able to go back to the work he had begun. Every fragment of news about Rabaul was important. Each new stage took them closer to the moment of parting.

First, they heard that the peace documents had been signed on board the ship *Gloria* on Jacquinot Bay, New Britain on 6 September and then the first reports came through that the Allies had re-entered Rabaul on 10 September. It was not until later that they learned what a dangerous gamble that had been; although the peace had been formally signed, it had been tempting fate to send in 2 700 Australian troops to take control of about 100 000 Japanese troops with little air or naval support for the first six days and no artillery, tanks or transport. But it had been done and the news came back that the former town site of Rabaul was in ruins.

24. *Mavis Green and Dora Wilson, Manila 1945*

25. *Mission women welcomed home at Mascot, Sydney, 14 September 1945*
Left to right: *Dorothy Beale, Jean Christopher, Mrs Wilson, Dora Wilson, Miss Green, Mavis Green*

Rodger could hardly wait to begin his journey, travelling to Rabaul to his posting as chaplain to the 118th Australian General Hospital.

'How long do you think it might be before they'll let Australian women back into Rabaul?' Kath wanted to know. Though she was accustomed to Rodger being away for three months at a time, it did not become easier. Now he was leaving for an indefinite period and once more it would not be right for her to complain.

'It will be quite a while before they let civilian women back into Rabaul, I expect. They say that the place is wrecked and there are thousands of Japanese soldiers to send home. It might be only six months, but it could easily be years.'

In the final days before they left Manila, the nurses rested in the safety of the well-ordered arrangements of the Americans for recovered prisoners. They were among friends, and guards were no longer in control. They needed to make no decisions, take no responsibility. They were fed to the point of satiation and, when Mavis was weighed the day before they left, she was startled to realise that, in the four weeks since food had become available, her weight had increased from less than six stone to over eight stone; it was the same for everyone. They had been pampered by the American nurses (such beautiful healthy girls with the latest in hairstyles!) and befriended by returned soldiers, all going out for long walks together into the town and feeling young and carefree again.

There were even chaplains and the mission girls had been able to attend church in Manila and receive holy communion in the Red Cross rooms.

Yet, after three-and-a-half years as a group, sharing everything whether they liked it or not, they knew that very soon they would all be parted. Already Eileen Callaghan was somewhere on a hospital ship. Jean Anderson still had not arrived from Okinawa, though till the last moment they hoped she would come in time. Mrs Etta Jones, who had been a comfort and support to the younger women for three years, had been repatriated to America, though she promised to come to visit them one day. Soon they would all be scattered and that would feel very strange.

Few of them slept well on that last night in Manila. At 4.00 am on the morning of 12 September, they were woken to eat breakfast before driving to the aerodrome. Excited, tense, they stumbled around in the half-dark, gathering the last of their things and farewelling staff. It all seemed unbelievable.

Their plane waited and as they climbed on board they learned that this was a special flight to Darwin, Australia, by the B24 Liberator and crew detailed to take the Australian women home. Everyone was buoyant, exuberant. They had waited so long for this moment. The plane stood on the tarmac, engines roaring with such power that the shell of metal cabin shook and thundered. At last they began to move, rushing across the ground, on and up. They were on their way.

It was a very long day. The Red Cross had made arrangements for their food and they would not be landing along the route. The aircraft had been converted from its earlier life as a bomber over New Guinea, they learned, and was not designed for great comfort. They talked and dozed or gazed from the windows over cloudscapes, anonymous islands and sea. Little by little, women fell silent. Between the years of exile and the longed-for return to family and home, there seemed to be nothing important enough to say and women allowed each other the privacy of their thoughts.

They wanted to get home. Of course, they did. They had dreamed of walking back through their own front gates, running up on to the verandah and in at the door. Sometimes they saw themselves at the front door and sometimes the kitchen door, whichever path they had followed as a schoolchild or student nurse coming home for days off. They had imagined the family dog leaping up against their legs, panting and trying to lick their face, or the old tabby cat still sleeping in the sun by the hedge of rosemary and lavender, as if it had not moved a whisker in all the years they had been gone.

All these years they had pictured their family around the kitchen table, laughing, handing out plates of Mum's cooking, at peace with each other. There was always food in their dreaming, wonderful, aromatic, delicious food, and some of them had already sent orders for the dinners they dreamed of in letters to their families. Faces of friends, women and men, drifted across their mind's eye.

They looked forward to returning to hospitals where they had trained and worked in Australia. Each place had been described in detail to their companions, with the staff names, like the names of all their relatives, recited as a faithful litany so often that each nurse knew all about all the significant people in the lives of each of their companions. These would be the people who would welcome them home.

But now it was nearly time to re-enter a world they had left long ago. Sitting through long hours on the flight home, often too cold in the cabin, cramped, stiff, uncomfortable, they knew that the limitation of a long plane journey was not the only reason for their discomfort. Tangled in among the hope and excitement and delight of going home was anxiety. Prickles of fear, uncertainty and grief scratched at their thoughts when they tried to grasp the lovely thought of going home.

The newsreels of the impact of the war in Europe and the Pacific were beginning to teach them that years of war had not left their home country untouched. Things would not be the same, could not be. They would have to learn, lesson by lesson, what had happened to the people and places who had inhabited their thoughts for so long.

Some women had already had letters saying that their family had moved house, moved to another city. 'Moved! But I wanted to go home to Smith Street. . .'

Few families would be as they were left; people had aged, little sisters or brothers had grown up, brothers were scattered across the world with the air force, the navy or the army and, in moments of honesty, the women remembered that there had been few times when their family had sat round the table in complete peace.

What of their old friends — were women friends now married and moved away and were men friends even still alive? The hospitals where they had worked would have gone on without them and now, out of touch with their profession, they would need to learn new techniques and new drugs before they were employable again.

Even their dreams of food were perhaps unattainable. 'Did you realise that some things have been rationed in Australia for years, and some imported foods have disappeared from the grocer's shelves altogether?' they had been asked in Manila.

Late that afternoon, they watched with pounding hearts as the crew pointed towards land in the distance.

'Australia,' they shouted, over the beat of engine sound.

With faces pressed close to the windows, they watched the distant line come closer. The orb of the sun, dropping slowly towards the western horizon, polished the sea to a high sheen, burnished the wide-spreading ripples of land and scattered gold dust across purple shadows. It did not matter that most of them had never visited north Australia. This soil rushing up to meet the wheels of their plane was part of the ancient whole, the beautiful southern land that was their home. Turning to each other, women recognised in the eyes of their friends the glisten of tears.

When at last the plane shuddered to a halt on the tarmac and the door was opened onto the heat of Darwin, it was almost too much to move their stiff limbs and take the first steps down onto the earth of the country of their dreams. Emotional and shaky, they were quickly surrounded by a welcoming party of officials and Red Cross ladies with cool drinks and biscuits. The voices around them were Australian voices, accents of home, and somewhere a magpie was singing. One of the returning nurses lingered for a moment to place a kiss on the side of the plane which had carried them safely.

In the welcoming crowd, Dora felt someone tap her on the shoulder. 'Dora!'

She turned. A man in air force uniform was beaming at her. She had not even known if Keith was still alive, yet here was her own brother standing with arms outspread, the first to welcome her home. Sister and brother mingled laughter and tears at the top of their home country, in a place they had never been before, in a miracle of meeting.

For a brief time there was a conference between Kay Parker and some officials. It was suggested that the women should immediately board another plane and continue their flight to

Sydney. Kay Parker, in one of her final acts of leadership for their group, refused to let the weary women, after twelve hours of travel, face another thirteen hours before they had a chance to rest. Cars came and they were all taken to the hospital for the night. Journalists came to talk to them, looking for sensational stories, and assured them that their story would be in all the newspapers the next day before they even arrived home.

Later, when they were being given hospitality by the hospital staff and the Red Cross, there came a message for Jean Christopher.

'There is someone here to see Sister Christopher.'

Chris went to investigate and came back clinging to the arm of a man in RAAF uniform. 'One of my brothers is here, too!' she cried. 'Mick, come and meet the girls.'

Later, a young Methodist chaplain arrived to greet them, and there were cries of recognition from the mission women. Wilbur Chaseling was known to some of them as one of the young ministers they had known in NSW and to others as Mel Trevitt's brother. Chaseling brought greetings directly from their mission Board.

'The General Secretary sent me a cable specially to tell me to come out to meet you four girls,' he said. 'You probably don't even know that we have a new General Secretary, Rev. Gardner, but Mr Burton is also very anxious to see you.'

There were so many questions they wanted to ask. The lack of news had been one of the most difficult things about their exile. People, events, church news, deaths and marriages: the long silence was suddenly being filled with a deluge of information.

Chaseling turned to Mavis. 'You wouldn't know that I've been working in your area quite recently. I know your family. They've been very good to me. With food rationing so tight, your mother always gave me vegetables from her garden, or beautiful homemade butter and fresh cream. . .'

He talked on about her mother, her younger sister, her brother overseas with the forces and, as Mavis listened, she had a strong feeling that there was something he was not saying. The conversation flowed on, about the local farms, the town, the church.

Listening, Mavis knew that none of that was as important as the one name he had not spoken.

Her voice was very small, but she forced herself to speak. 'Do we still have Dad with us?'

He looked at her gently and shook his head. She rose from her chair and walked blindly from the circle of friends, looking for a place alone. She had known, somehow she had known, but that didn't ease the shock of grief. Some time later the chaplain came to sit with her.

'I was there,' he said quietly. 'I was with your family when your father was dying and conducted his funeral service. The mission people contacted me here in Darwin, when they knew that you were coming through, to ask me to tell you about your father if you seemed strong enough to hear it.'

They talked for a long time. Through her weeping, she was grateful to hear all the details of the story of the passing of her father. She needed to know. Over and over she thought, God has brought this man here so that Mum doesn't have to break the news to me. It seemed that God had given each of them some miracles — the chaplain who had known her dying father, Dora's brother, Chris' brother — to remind them that he loved them.

The last day of the journey home passed for many of them in a blur of exhaustion, emotion and an overwhelming sense of distance. It was long before dawn when they woke to prepare to travel on and they knew that even after they landed in Sydney at dusk, most of them still had long train trips in front of them. Their journey was not only across landscape, but also from a threatening to a welcoming place, and through time, a returning through lost years.

Mavis had left home in 1939 before war was declared in Europe and Dora was wearing a floral dress, carefully saved through the years for just this moment, which she had bought in 1940, in another life. Hundreds of miles of Australian landscape unrolled below them, hour after hour. It was a very long way.

On that day, 13 September 1945, in Kiama, Jean Poole opened her newspaper to see an article about the mission nurses. They had been interviewed in Darwin, it seemed, and would be back in Sydney by evening. She imagined the excitement of their families. Dora and Mavis, Chris and Dorothy, safe home within hours; the girls first, and then John and the men would be home.

That day, as the nurses flew south, Kath Brown wandered around her mother's house in Adelaide with a sense of new loss. Rodger had left for Sydney to attend the meeting of the Board before he travelled on to Brisbane and Rabaul with his unit. She could still feel the strength of his last embrace and see his head thrust out of the window of the train, straining for a last look at his family as the train carried him away. With her two small boys, she had come home to mother's place, to begin another long time of waiting.

It was nearly dark when the Dakota touched down at Mascot in Sydney. Stepping down into the unexpected coldness, the women were dazzled by the flash of camera bulbs. Arms were thrown around them as mothers, fathers, sisters and brothers hurried forward. In the excitement and confusion, hands draped coats around them and hurried them into the light of the terminal.

Mavis saw the strain on the face of her mother and said, 'I know about Dad, Mum.' They clung to each other and then she turned to hug her younger sister, so grown-up after six years, and her cousins. Dora's mother, her hair whiter than Dora remembered, could not bear to let her daughter go and kept a hand around her shoulder as she greeted others.

Chris and Dorothy did not expect to see their own families in Sydney — they would have to wait until they finally reached Brisbane and Adelaide — but even so there were familiar faces waiting. From the crowd of friends from the mission board, all eagerly waiting for a chance to give a welcome, Rodger Brown stepped forward.

'Chris! I've been in touch with several of your family in the past week and they are all so thankful that you are safe.' She gripped his hand tightly. Rodger was like a brother, a friend of her family.

Dorothy turned to find another well-known face smiling at her. Jessie March hugged her. The two women had worked together for some years in those long-ago days when Vunairima was a beautiful campus with schools and hospital. Jessie had spent her war years caring for the Aboriginal children at Otford near Sydney, after their epic journey across the continent.

'Oh, Dorothy, your hair is still so pretty!' she said, and Dorothy was touched to think that, despite everything, despite feeling tired and older than her years, her wavy fair hair could still be seen as beautiful. Each of them had tried to do her best with her appearance, to show their families that they had not given up their self-respect.

In the noise and intensity of the moment, the mission nurses were aware of other reunions around them. Great armfuls of flowers were being offered and a little nephew thrust a bunch of sweet boronia into the hands of one of the women. Mrs Bignell was leaving on the arm of her daughter, the army girls were explaining to Andy's family that they had left her behind in Okinawa, and women who had shared their lives so intimately were saying quick goodbyes before being whisked away by their families or the Red Cross. After so long together, the end was very sudden and almost unmarked.

The four mission women were surrounded by family members and excited members of the mission Board and staff. For years they had been waiting and praying and now their prayers had been answered.

'How soon can I go back to New Britain?' demanded Dorothy Beale. 'You'll have to take four years off my age, though, because I'm not counting the last four.'

And then they were parted. For three-and-a-half years, the four had rarely been out of sight or sound of each other. Now the whole party was driven to Central railway station and, in the seething multitudes hurrying along the concourse, following blindly as they were led along to the platforms where trains were waiting to take them far away from each other, the women said goodbye.

Dora, Mavis and their families boarded the train for Newcastle and Maitland, travelling north together, talking all the way with those who loved them. Hours later, after midnight, they would both fall with thankfulness into their own beds in their own homes.

Chris was settled into the night train for Melbourne and Adelaide, a very long way and a journey she must make alone. Mission people had thrust gifts into her hands before the train steamed away from the platform. Now she was by herself on that long route back to a normal life. More than a day would pass before her train would pause at a station on the border between Victoria and South Australia at 2.30 in the morning and her brother Clem would board the train to find her, sleepy and seemingly shrunken, wrapped in a blanket. With Clem's company, she would travel on to Adelaide and the wonder and confusion of the reunion with parents and relatives, friends, mission staff and the demands of the press.

On the train heading for Brisbane, Rodger Brown tossed his own kitbag up onto the luggage rack and helped Dorothy Beale with her things. They would be able to travel together. Though their friends from the mission had loaded them with food for the journey — gifts, magazines and books — Rodger and Dorothy did not expect to have time for any reading during the long hours on the train. There were far too many questions to ask and stories to tell.

At last, each of them had met a colleague from New Britain, someone who had been there in those last weeks before Rabaul fell. This travelling companion knew and loved the people and the place as they did, and perhaps might have news of those who were missing. They both knew that they were likely to talk and listen all the way to Brisbane.

After the trains had all gone, the remaining mission staff met in Wesley Chapel in the city for a short service of thanksgiving. They had waited so long for this moment. Tears flowed as they sang, 'Now thank we all our God. . . Who wondrous things hath done. . .'

As they thought of the women restored to them and the missing men still to come, they read together the words of Psalm 40: 'I waited patiently for the Lord. . . He brought me up out of an horrible pit. . . He hath put a new song in my mouth. . .'

23

15 September–November 1945

IN THE CONFUSION OF THOSE WEEKS, it was impossible to see any pattern. In the same towns, in the same streets, some families hung a celebration of bunting outside their front doors and children inscribed signs proclaiming 'Welcome Home Dad', while others sat in silence, staring at a malign telegram propped against the teapot.

Old women reached out to touch young men with kitbags on their shoulders, joy transparent through tears, and old men choked on their grief, transmuting it into gnawing rage. Newspapers published maps of staging points for released prisoners on their way home and families pored over the maps, hoping against hope that their child was among the travellers now circling the world.

Yet, though families like those of Mavis and Dora were rejoicing, thousands of missing people were still unaccounted for; twenty thousand Australians had been in captivity under the Japanese and records of many of their names were missing, withheld or destroyed. For some, there had been miracles of survival. For others, there had been no miracle. There was no neat sorting of threatened humanity into the good and the bad, the deserving and the undeserving, the useful and the useless.

Caught in the grinding wheels of global evil, the remorseless turning cogs of violence and selfishness, greed and unforgiveness, hatred and pride, men and women were being destroyed. People blamed God. Why didn't he make the machinery of death stop?

On 15 September 1945, just two days after the nurses arrived home safely from Japan, nuns, priests and people in the hidden valley of Ramale, New Britain, heard the sound of a loud 'coo-ee' echoing from the top of the gorge. They had known that very soon the Australians would come and had made plans to welcome them with a formal ceremony and a choir. But when they heard the shouts and saw their rescuers running, leaping down the steep winding track towards them, no-one waited for formal speeches. In their old clothes, habits stained with vegetable dyes to disguise their whiteness, decorous manners forgotten, nuns took to their heels and ran, laughing, weeping, calling each other, snatching the hands of the Australian men.

When the first wild greetings subsided, the camp choirmaster called the people together. Later, there would be time for questions, to ask and to answer. There would be prayers of thankfulness and memories of those among them who had died in captivity. The survivors of Vunapope and Ramale clustered together, women and men of seventeen nationalities including nine Australian nuns, tears running down smiling faces, and sang in harmony, 'Advance Australia Fair': 'Australian sons, let us rejoice, for we are young and free. . .'

Australian journalists with the party who visited Ramale also travelled to see other communities of internees. One commented that it was like moving through an international exhibition, passing from one national group to the next; Indian, British, Indonesian, Chinese. Of the Chinese community, the journalist wrote with great admiration; despite many difficulties, the people had maintained their family life, protected their women, provided food in large plantings of rice and vegetables and hundreds of happy children played among their makeshift shelters and tunnels.

Nothing seemed to be quite what the Australian army and the journalists had expected. The large group of Australian men of Rabaul town and the 2/22nd whom they had expected to find in the area had disappeared. Chinese and New Guinean witnesses said they had sailed in 1942.

26. *Catholic community in Ramale valley, New Britain, after release from internment by Australian troops, 16 September 1945*

27. *Catholic missionaries and New Guinean friends at Ramale, New Britain, as first nuns are evacuated to Rabaul, 16 September 1945*

Disturbing stories began to circulate about what might have happened to them. An Anglican missionary who was presumed to have died, along with his women colleagues who had been executed at Gona, appeared at Ramale, alive and well after many adventures. No outsider had expected to discover a large party of Indian servicemen in Rabaul, brought in from Asia and badly treated, or British servicemen brought from the rout of Singapore. Indeed, after the total destruction of the Catholic mission at Vunapope by Allied airpower, no-one had expected to find about three hundred survivors living with dignity in a cosmopolitan Christian community.

On the same day as Ramale was contacted in New Britain, a rescue party set out from Singapore for Sumatra, convinced that there could be some Australian nurses still alive in a prison camp somewhere. Men who were being released from Changi prison had told the terrible tale of the deaths of nurses through enemy fire on their ship the *Vyner Brooke* — by drowning when it sank, and by shooting in the surf off Banka Island. There had originally been sixty-five Australian army nurses in the group but, when the searchers located their camp the next day, they found only twenty-four survivors. They were emaciated, ill, filthy and odorous, but they were undefeated and alive. Disease and malnutrition had taken eight who had survived sea and firing squad; some had lived until 1945 and at least one did not know that peace had been declared before she died.

The first days at home were wonderful, upsetting, delightful, overwhelming. For Mavis, those first days passed in never-ending waves of voices and visitors. All day there were people at the door, friends ringing up, and the boy from the post office was run off his feet delivering telegrams to welcome her home. Everyone was so pleased to see her. Everyone stared, as if she was a curiosity. Everyone wanted to feed her, bringing garden produce, homemade cakes, fresh eggs, treats. And everyone was wide-eyed, wanting to hear her story.

It seemed that she was the heroine of the biggest adventure drama they had ever heard and every detail was exclaimed over.

Her little treasures which she had brought home — her diary and recipe book, the embroidered handkerchief, some little knitted silk bags — were fingered curiously, and stories were told over and over to gasps of amazement: 'Just imagine, eating the paste from the envelopes!' they said, 'and having to bow to the Japs. . .'

Watching their faces, she knew that none of them could ever understand what it had been like. No-one who had not been there could know that. The stories she told were like a succession of strange and astonishing pictures, the images of a magic lantern show, entertaining and even educating for a few minutes, and then dismissed and forgotten when something more interesting offered. In the six years since she left home, she had missed the life of her home community and it was as much a mystery to her as was her experience in Japan to them. She would keep on trying to explain the meaning of those lost years, but even then, in that first week, she knew that only Dora, Chris, Dorothy and the others would understand the truth of it.

Tears were never far from the surface. Her mother and sister had had months to accustom themselves to the absence of her father, but everywhere she turned were reminders of Dad — his chair by the wireless, his spade in the garden.

'Don't mention her father,' she heard her mother whisper to guests. 'She'll burst into tears if you do.'

She knew that she couldn't help herself. The silence which hid her father's name was as difficult as the tears, but she tried to control her feelings for her mother's sake. When she had been home several days, she was taken to the cemetery to see her father's grave. The place was tidy and she and her mother took fresh flowers to replace the dead ones, but as she stood there, desolate, it hurt so much that the earth covering her father's grave had been there for months. She had not been there when the grave lay open. She had been cheated of the privilege of being with her family, weeping with those who wept, able to talk of him with those who gathered for the ritual of meeting after the funeral. The silence which hid her father denied her the freedom to grieve.

'She's still weak — she'll just get upset,' they said, trying to shield her, but it seemed that this was one more thing which had been taken from her by her years of imprisonment.

It was during the first week at home that news was published of the massacre of the nurses at Banka Island and the deaths that followed. Mavis was thankful that Dora's home was within reach.

'We thought it was bad for us,' they said to each other, awestruck by the news. 'When we met POW men in Japan and Manila, we knew that they had had a worse time than us, far worse, but we thought maybe it was because they were men, soldiers. But these girls were nurses, just like us. Compared to them, we were very lucky indeed. . .'

The pieces of puzzle were at last coming together. For years the jigsaw pieces had been scattered, held in isolation from each other. Some elements of the picture were held in the memories of sixty officers of the 2/22nd battalion who had been imprisoned in Japan; they knew the men who had been under their command and saw them marched out of the camp for an unknown destination on 22 June 1942. Chinese, New Guinean and Australian people in the Rabaul area knew that there had been a large passenger ship, and some had recognised men among the hundreds who boarded it.

The Catholic bishop at Vunapope, New Britain, had been told long ago that the ship had been lost, but he did not believe it and had been given no evidence to prove it. A Japanese shipping company had known for a long time that one of their ships, the *Montevideo Maru*, carrying prisoners, had been sunk by the Americans, but they did not know who was on board. The crew of an American submarine knew that they had sunk a large nameless ship on 1 July 1942 and believed it to be carrying enemy troops. The officials of the Japanese Prisoner of War Bureau knew that they had scores of records, of sorts, of Allied prisoners held across the world but, with no clear recording and indexing system, they felt that it would be impossible to locate specific information; in any case much material had already been destroyed by bombing or in the conflagration of records immediately before and after the surrender on 15 August.

Now, with the new freedom of movement in Rabaul, people who held small pieces of the puzzle began to compare their segment with the piece held by someone else. Questions were being asked of prisoners being released from Japan as well as Rabaul, and the authorities did their best to lay out the gathered information into a picture. It was not easy. By the end of September, though lists of names of recovered men were being published every day, the fate of nearly five thousand missing Australian prisoners across the world was still unknown and over a thousand of those were the missing men from Rabaul.

As the picture began to take shape, despite its shadows, blank spaces and uneven edges, journalists and others began to describe what they thought they could see emerging.

That afternoon, when Essie Linggood boarded a Melbourne tram for home, she was tired. She had spent the day working at a local refuge for unmarried mothers, one of a number of practical kindnesses which were a natural part of her life. Essie balanced her shopping basket on her knee and moved up to make room for someone who sat beside her and opened up an afternoon newspaper. For a time she sat, staring unfocussed at the passing streets and at the plain felt hats of the other women passengers. Soon they would begin to see pretty new hats, she thought; only the day before the news had come through that the wartime restrictions on fashion had been repealed.

The passenger beside her rustled his newspaper and refolded it to the front page, catching her eye. Under an advertisement for Rosella tomato sauce was a headline in heavy black type: 'Rabaul Men Lost at Sea Is Fear.'

She looked up. Around her, women sat unmoved, string bags and baskets on laps, waiting patiently for their tram stop, while her world crumbled. Her eyes were drawn back to the newspaper:

Canberra: Carrying between 700 and 1 000 Australian prisoners-of-war, a Japanese prison ship may have been lost at sea, early in 1942. This may be the solution to the mystery of what happened to the majority of the garrison which was overwhelmed by the Japanese at Rabaul. . .

After that, the print became too small to read over a stranger's shoulder without seeming rude, but fragments of the story seemed to enlarge before her eyes. She saw the words, 'grave fears. . . it had not been possible to trace the movements of the ship. . . most urgent prisoner of war enquiry now being conducted to determine the whereabouts of the men of the Rabaul battalion'.

Had Laurie been with the soldiers? Was he still somewhere on New Britain? Was he dead? Essie did not know the answers. She sat on the tram looking blankly in front of her. The stranger with the afternoon edition of the *Melbourne Herald* for 26 September 1945 left the tram and innocently went home to tea.

Essie grasped her basket and prepared to leave the tram. If the news was in the papers, she wanted to go to the school to meet her children at the gate. If she could avoid it, her children would not discover that their father might be dead through school playground gossip. She must tell them herself.

When she first heard the rumours, Jean Poole did not believe them. John drowned? How could that be? Where was the evidence? All they were able to say was that no-one knew where the Rabaul men were. With thousands of missing men still to be located, why were they pinning their theories on the idea that there had been a ship, with all their men on board, and that the ship had been sunk with total loss of life?

No, she would wait for more information before she let herself give up hope. All along she had been so sure John would be coming home. Yet she could not deny the weight that settled on her heart, the feelings that were not unlike nausea.

Across the country, families heard the suggestions that the Rabaul men were lost. Some were listening to the evening news on the wireless, peacefully sitting with their knitting after they had finished the washing-up, and heard that perhaps their men might be gone. Others had a phone call from a friend who had heard.

Members of the New Guinea Association, all of them women whose men had been in Rabaul, set in motion their own network, contacting friends and trying to offer support and hope in the face of this dreadful rumour; surely, they tried to reassure each other,

28. *Australian troops with children in Chinese civilian internment camp after surrender of Japanese, New Britain, 18 September 1945*

29. *Mission house, Raluana, New Britain, newly built of pingpong tables and other army disposals scrap; Thomas Mow and Mary Woolnough on verandah, November 1946*

this was nonsense and the truth would come to light soon enough. People began to write letters to the papers, demanding more information, and questions were asked in parliament.

Under a few sheets of corrugated iron supported by a rough bamboo framework, a Chinese man sat writing a letter. There was just room under the shelter for two stretchers and a small table and he was thankful to have it. For the first time since the Australians had re-entered Rabaul and come to relieve their community of over 800 Chinese at Ratongo, there was an opportunity to write a letter. Rev. Mo Pui Sam had already completed a letter to his wife; he had last seen her in China before he left to travel to his missionary appointment six years earlier and there was no way of knowing whether the years of war in China had spared her.

Now he pulled another page of notepaper towards him and headed it 'Chinese Internees' Camp, c/- ANGAU, Rabaul, 27 September 1945'. This time he wanted to write to the leaders of the Methodist mission in Sydney. He began with greetings and explained how many of the Chinese had moved to the mission plantation near Vunairima before the Japanese invasion.

He went on: 'Rev. Trevitt, Rev. Pearson and Mr Beazley were at Vunairima; two days after the Japs landed, they were taken prisoners. We also met Rev. McArthur and Rev. Poole at the wharf while unloading cargo for the troops. A few months later, we saw them all walked on a Jap steamer, after that, we could not hear anything about them. I am very sorry that they would be met by the worst things. . .'

It was hard to express what those years had meant. He wrote of the prohibition on holding Christian services, 'but our faith in God had not failed'. There were all the children running around, wasting their time for years because there was no school. There was the hunger among his people and their hard work in making gardens to feed themselves. It was hard to write of the bad memories of air raids and machine-gun attacks, the illness and deaths in the camp, despite his efforts to offer medical help with very limited resources.

While Mo Pui Sam wrote his letter, his colleague and headteacher Mr Thomas Mow also wrote to the mission. 'Thanks be to God that Rev. P.S. Mo, my family and I are all liberated. . .' He sent his greetings to Miss Mary Jenkins who had worked with him and his wife in the Chinese school for many years and added, 'Kindly let me know something about the Revs McArthur and Pearson and the other ministers.'

At the same time as Mo Pui Sam was writing his letter in Rabaul, an Australian officer was beginning his complex and demanding task in Tokyo, Japan. Thousands of Australians were still missing, even though large groups in prison camps were being released and sent home, and Major Williams was determined to follow any trail which would lead to the whereabouts of the missing men. High on the list of missing groups was the puzzle of the men from Rabaul and he had been particularly asked to watch for information about a group of missing missionaries: the names of McArthur, Trevitt, Linggood, Pearson, Poole and others were on his list.

In the ravaged remains of Tokyo, Major Williams set about his quest. At first, it seemed impossible. The maze of organisations who might have known the answers seemed to twist and turn, always presenting dead ends. The Recovered Personnel Division GHQ set up by the United States military in Tokyo had little experience or expertise in POW matters. The Japanese Prisoner of War Information Bureau seemed incapable of informing, being understaffed, disorganised and buried in papers to which no-one had easy access.

When Williams visited the Japanese Navy Ministry, he found that many of their records had been lost in Allied bombing raids over Tokyo and other POW documents had been deliberately destroyed; the only clues they could offer were from memory.

The Japanese army records had not been bombed but, when Williams enquired, he was told that perhaps what he was seeking might have been burned; the confusion and fear of the time of surrender had meant that when orders came from 'higher authority' that certain secret documents should be destroyed, no-one was sure what had been hurled onto the bonfires of blazing papers. The Japanese Red Cross presented a fine facade to the world, but very little practical effort appeared to have been put into caring for prisoners.

The postal service to which Australian women had entrusted letters to their men for more than three years, under the stamp of the Japanese Red Cross, had been handed over in bulk and left to lie unread in warehouses. The Japanese Foreign Office could not help, they said, because many of their records had been destroyed, but someone remembered questions being asked of the Bureau about a large party from Rabaul, but they could not recall ever having an answer.

Though he was faced with such a mountain of obstruction, Major Williams persisted. People from the Swiss Legation and the International Red Cross were very eager to help, but they were discouraging.

'We've been trying to get information out of all these organisations for years,' they said, 'on behalf of POWs, and have met nothing but obstructions, excuses or stories which don't ring true — such as being told that the Japanese have never had charge of a lot of Australians out of Rabaul. They all escaped to the hills, we were told. Nobody has any information, they tell us, and get very angry when we keep trying.'

Major Williams, with the new power that came with being an officer of the victorious nations, returned to the Prisoner of War Information Bureau. He demanded to be allowed to make a search of their records himself. The staff, now eager to be helpful, showed him through the chaos of their record system and tried to offer clues. Using his skill in Japanese script, he searched through the day, fearing that he could be trapped in the labyrinth of paper for months.

Perhaps it was a miracle. Perhaps the information had always been available. Before the first day of searching was over, 28 September, Williams knew he had found something important. The record was a very long one, a list of names that ran on and on, 1 053 names in elegant brushstrokes, with age, occupation, nationality and place of work set out. Part of the nominal roll appeared to be of servicemen, identified by name and serial number, and the rest seemed to be civilians. Even as he lifted it up and spread it out before him, Williams knew that he held in his hands the lives and future of many families, whoever they were.

He began to read the civilian roll. Translating from the Japanese, he identified the first name on the list.

'Page, Harold Harris, age 52, Deputy Administrator, Australian. Place of capture — Rabaul. . .'

During the following weeks, when the search went on for many other groups of missing men, Major Williams would find the report of the sinking of the *Montevideo Maru* made to the Japanese shipowners by the Navy on 26 July 1942. He would also find documents which the Navy Department forwarded to the Prisoners of War Information Bureau on 6 January 1943 with the nominal roll of those who left Rabaul on the *Montevideo Maru* and notification of the loss of the ship, from which only seventeen officers and crew escaped and 1 053 prisoners and 133 crew and guards lost their lives.

On the morning of Friday, 5 October, Rodger Brown stood on the deck of *m.v. Ormiston* as it came into harbour, and stared at the ruins of Rabaul. Five years earlier, he had stood on such a deck looking for the first time at the lovely town of Rabaul. Then Kath had been beside him, his bride, and they stood with their friends John and Jean Poole and Dora Wilson, all of them excited, happy, with no premonition of what the years might bring.

Now the town, with streets of buildings set among tropical trees along the shore and up the hill slopes, had disappeared. Not a building was left standing. Rusting wrecks of ships and barges lay beside damaged wharves and along beaches. Jagged poles poking up along the water's edge were the leafless remains of palm trees, and the avenue of rain-trees had been blasted out of existence. A plume of volcanic dust hung over Matupi volcano on the harbour edge, with the odour of sulphur, a fitting background for calamity.

Barges came alongside the *Ormiston* and carried the newly arrived men to the shore. They were warned that the harbour still hid an unknown number of mines and to beware of unexploded bombs and mines left across the battered landscape. The advance party of Australians had entered the area less than a month earlier and the Japanese soldiers, a hundred thousand of them, though disarmed and surrendered, still far outnumbered the Australians. They would find that the 118th Australian General Hospital, set up on the north coast, was merely a collection of tents: very rough, they were told.

Rodger Brown did not care how rough it was. He had been waiting for this moment for years. Through all the long hours in country trains travelling to meetings across Australia, through endless repetitions of the story of New Britain, he had dreamed of the day he would come back. Even before he had set foot on land, Rodger had begun calling greetings to New Guinean people, joyfully using the local language which he had begun to learn five years earlier. To his delight, one of the first people he encountered on the road, before they reached the hospital site, was one of the New Guinean ministers. Quickly, the word went around that a *talatala*, a missionary, had come back.

The next day, after making initial contact with his senior chaplain and the hospital staff and patients, Rodger walked through what had once been a scenic colonial township, the former capital of New Guinea. The jungle, forced back by successive generations of German and Australian residents, tamed into flamboyant gardens among shaved lawns, had seized the advantage while people's backs were turned and taken back its land.

He followed narrow tracks between encroaching jungle where once he had walked along tree-lined streets. Among the bomb craters and piles of rubble were acres of gardens planted as food gardens by the Japanese, tapioca, corn, millet, tobacco, pineapples and pawpaws competing with jungle growth. Where colonial gentlemen had sat in comfort in hotel lounges, sweet potato and climbing beans flourished. Only the concrete foundations remained of the elite New Guinea Club, and bits of blackened frame of the big warehouses which had served the major trading company of Burns Philp.

When he searched for the buildings which had been the Methodist church in the town and the Cox Memorial offices newly opened in his first months in the area, he found the front steps of the church and some foundations, and the historic foundation stones of both church and offices lying among the grass. The church building had gone; he supposed that the village churches had also been lost. They could be rebuilt.

More importantly, where was the church, the believers? Where were his friends, Mr Mac, John Poole, Laurie Linggood and the others? In this desolation, where might a large party of prisoners be held? What of the New Guinean ministers and pastor-teachers? All of them must, he thought, have been subjected to the onslaught from the air which had laid waste the town of Rabaul.

After his Sunday morning church parade, Rodger travelled with the senior chaplain by jeep to nearby villages for church services. Groups of villagers gathered and a loincloth was spread over a board set on a forty-four gallon drum as a pulpit. Despite their great difficulties, these Christians had survived. In one place their village pastor had died and worship had been forbidden, but they had hidden their Bibles and hymnbooks and Methodists and Catholics had combined to pray and sing hymns together. Now villagers sat around on the ground with their tattered books, resurrected from hiding places, still experiencing the new freedom of worship which had only been theirs for the past few weeks.

In another village, where Rodger was welcomed with beautiful singing, the pastor told him that they wanted to rebuild their church building soon, but pointed out the mission land which was stacked high with a great dump of live bombs and strewn with shells and live ammunition: 'We'll wait and build when it is safe,' they explained apologetically.

That night Rodger made his way to the tent which was the officers' mess, the only place with a table and a light. He wrote first to Kath and then to the mission at home:

From the few sources available so far I have learned nothing about our missionaries, but Rev. Mo Pui Sam is somewhere in the district. . . Rev. Akuila To Ngaru is still alive and working. The Japanese did not favour Christian worship and destroyed many Bibles and hymn books. Teachers were sent

away from their work and the people lived in the hills and
worshipped secretly through the years. Sickness, sores, ulcers,
fear, hunger and bombs have combined to kill hundreds,
perhaps thousands of our people. . .

When the *Ormiston* sailed on Monday 8 October, it carried
Rodger Brown's letters home and also a large party of missionaries
from Ramale, free at last and going home to Australia for a holiday
before taking up their missionary work once more.

On the same Friday that Rodger Brown arrived back in Rabaul, the
Minister for External Territories rose to speak in the Australian parliament in the city of Canberra. The many rumours and theories
about the whereabouts of the missing men of Rabaul had come to
a point where the evidence seemed clear.

The House of Representatives was very quiet as he began to
speak, reminding them of the quest for the missing men:

> The Minister for the Army has asked me to announce the
> result of these enquiries. Investigation in Japan by Australian
> Enquiry Officers working with General Macarthur's Forces
> has confirmed the government's fears that the majority of the
> Australian prisoners of war and internees, captured in Rabaul
> and still missing, lost their lives at sea. . . A roll which it is
> understood contains the names of the personnel aboard the
> *S.S. Montevideo Maru* at the time is now being translated in
> Japan in order that the information may be transmitted to
> Australia for notification of next of kin. . . As there is a total
> of 1 053 persons involved, it is anticipated that some time
> will elapse before all names are available. . . So far no authen-
> tic information has been obtained as to the names of the
> civilian internees on the vessel.

Lists and lists of names were being prepared. In Japan,
translators worked over the lists in Katakana script of the nominal
roll linked with the *Montevideo Maru*. Many of the names were
clearly recognisable as possible Australian names, but other names
had been twisted out of shape in the process of translating from
English to Japanese and back again. Translators tried to imagine

what the Japanese scribe had heard on that day in May 1942, at the camp in Rabaul, as he worked with his brushes — could 'Saamee-Ru' be Samuel, and what of 'U-Vu-Su' or 'Sinsiedel E.R.'?

Handwritten lists were offered to interrogating officers in Rabaul or Lae, recorded in pencil in 1942 by Gordon Thomas, or remembered by McKechnie, Creswick and Ellis, men who had been among the handful of Australians left alive in Rabaul. There were names dredged up from the past of men known at the New Guinea Club or the Cosmopolitan Hotel or names listed by the nurses who had seen men at Vunapope early in 1942. There were names of young soldiers known to the officers who had been questioned in Manila on their way home from prison camp at Zentsugi, Japan and a list prepared by the Department of External Affairs of Australian men from Rabaul 'reported to be missing since 1/7/42 and for official purposes presumed to be dead'.

'When did you last see this man?' survivors were asked. 'Was he in the camp in Rabaul? Did he leave with all the others?'

There had been so many men, over a thousand in the camp, and all those who had escaped from Rabaul, some of whom had left Rabaul but had not arrived safely in Australia. In some cases, the survivors were sure that there had been an execution. In others, there had been no witnesses to deaths, but small parties of Australians had been seen, under guard, being led away into the jungle without their luggage. They had not come back.

Lists were compared with lists; names, occupations and places of work were checked. Some names appeared on one list and not on others; was it because they were men who had lived and worked out of town, on an island plantation or as a missionary somewhere on New Ireland or New Hanover, and so were not known to the survivors from the town, or had they never been with the men of the *Montevideo Maru* at all? By the time the translated roll, with the other lists, was sent to Canberra late in October, everyone knew that the work of determining the details of the nominal roll was truly a task of life or death.

It was as she had imagined so often, when their little group had met to worship God at the rowing club at Yokohama or at the farmhouse at Totsuka. Dora had tried, in those prison days, to hear a choir in her mind, or an organ, or to imagine that she was part of a great crowd of Christians singing together. Now, in Wesley Chapel in the heart of Sydney, a pipe organ pealed, filling the high space with rich resonance. A light shone through the jewel colours of stained glass and people were all around her, singing songs of thanksgiving. The Methodists of Sydney had gathered to welcome the nurses home, surrounding them with love in the celebration of a Thanksgiving Service.

Dora felt tears flowing. She couldn't help it. She was safe, alive, home. She could feel the emotion and love of the crowds surrounding them, men and women who had prayed for them through the years of separation. Mavis was beside her. They had travelled down to Sydney on the train together and had talked about the strange business of coming home; it was wonderful, exciting — and lonely. They both missed, more than they could have imagined, the company of the women who had shared their years and were now scattered all over Australia.

A woman from the mission board had presented them with the imaginative gift of a bound set of missionary magazines for the years of their absence, but much of the Australian experience while they had been away remained a mystery. Nor could anyone understand what those years of captivity had meant.

The last hymns were sung, the last prayers spoken. 'Answers to prayer,' they had been called. The two of them were surrounded by kind-hearted people, all wanting to speak to them, to ask questions — all talking at once, looking at them as if they were curiosities.

'You girls are so wonderful. . . so brave. . . we're so proud of you. . . just fancy all that barbed wire,' people said, and the two nurses gave up trying to explain.

'Have you heard,' people said, 'that Dorothy Beale and Jean Christopher have already applied to go back to New Britain? And Elsie Wilson wants to go back to the school as soon as possible — but, of course, the army is not letting any women in yet.'

It was exhilarating, confusing and overwhelming. After the isolation of years spent with the same group of women, a battering flood of strangers was almost enough to drown them, leaving them gasping and exhausted. Former missionaries, board members, women from the Women's Auxiliary for Overseas Missions and church members queued to speak to them.

Then Dora saw a woman who had been waiting quietly to speak to them both. The woman, tall and dignified, held out her hand and clung to Dora's. After all the words that had been spoken, there were no words for this. The last time they had seen each other, Dora had been at the wharf near the plantation on the island of Ulu, watching this same tall woman say farewell to crowds of weeping islanders: 'You're not to cry. . .'

Dora remembered waving goodbye to the older woman as she took her small children and went reluctantly but obediently with her husband, Herbert Shelton, to face evacuation in 1941.

'Mrs Shelton. . .'

There was no need to say it. They both knew that Jean Shelton was one of the many who was waiting for news. Was Herbert Shelton's name on the list which was being translated? They had all been saying, with jubilation, 'Our prayers have been answered for our missionary nurses!'

What about the men? Where was God in the fate of the men?

Five days after the thanksgiving service in the city chapel for the nurses, Jean Poole was interrupted in her country classroom by a knock on the door.

'Mrs Poole, could you please come to the headmaster's office?'

She left her children with instructions to read their School Magazine and set out for the office. It is nothing, she said to herself, nothing special. But even then she knew that she was deluding herself. It was already too late. She had caught a glimpse of the telegraph boy pushing his bicycle away from the school steps and pedalling away. A class was chanting their seven-times-table — the worst one — as she passed and another was singing a patriotic song slightly off key.

And then she was in the headmaster's office. A telegram marked 'Urgent' was placed in her hands. It was very hard to open the envelope with hands that fumbled and shook, somehow detached from her mind, but the paper was unfolded at last.

It was addressed to her. 'It is with deep regret. . .'

Jean shut her eyes. The lines of block lettering had blurred and the drumbeat of her heart pounded in her ears. Somewhere nearby someone was asking, anxiously, would she like a cup of tea. She took a deep breath and forced herself to read on, although she knew what it was going to say:

> It is with deep regret that I have to inform you that the translation of the nominal roll of the Japanese vessel *Montevideo Maru* which was lost with all personnel after leaving Rabaul in June 1942 shows that Rev. J.W. Poole was aboard the vessel and I desire to convey to you the profound sympathy of the Commonwealth Government. Minister for External Territories.

Across the nation, one thousand and fifty-three telegrams went into homes and workplaces. Mel Trevitt was delivered her telegram at work at the Yarra Woollen Mills, Melbourne, telling her what she had known in her heart for a long time, that Jack was gone. Helen Wayne was in the classroom in the Blue Mountains when she heard about Ron. Nellie Simpson in Adelaide learned that her beautiful children would never know their father, and he would never know he had a son.

Beryl Beazley wept for her little girl who had never seen the daddy who would have loved her so much. Helen Pearson, received a telegram but refused to believe it. Marion Oakes turned her grief into anger, a rage against the church which had left her beloved Dan in danger when he should have been at home on furlough. Netta Allsop was dealt the double blow of the loss of both her husband and her brother. Hannah Huntley was left in pain and confusion as there had been no telegram nor any news of Bill.

At Wolaroi College in Orange, NSW, a headmaster was faced with giving the news to the sons of Marion Oakes and Jean Shelton, lads who had so recently turned metal garbage bins into jubilant percussion when they had thought their fathers were coming home.

The nightmare which had haunted Daisy McArthur for years had become a reality. She could no longer accuse herself of letting her imagination run away with her, or of wallowing in a bottomless pit of depression which was all of her own making. The telegram said plainly that Laurie was gone. It was real. What it all meant she could not bear to think, but she knew that she was wounded to the heart.

'I can't tell Malcolm — that is beyond me at the moment,' she said, and so it was the headmaster at her son's school, Scots College in Adelaide, who called the young boy to his office to be told that his father had been dead for more than three years.

Essie Linggood, in Melbourne, found it hard to believe that her Laurie had drowned. He was gone, she was sure of that, but she had always feared another end. When she felt ready, she went to her private papers and found the letter. Years earlier, before the war, Laurie had written a letter for her and sealed it. It had waited through the years of silence and now she knew that the time had come when she would hear his voice once more.

With hands that shook a little, she unfolded the pages and saw the familiar handwriting. Laurie had written in 1938; what had he known? He was writing, he said, 'as a message of love to you after I have passed on to higher service. There is no premonition of impending disaster in my mind or anything of that sort. It is just that for years I have felt I would like you to be able to read a happy note of love should I leave you first. . . Perhaps I may pass on without being able to give you those loving words of farewell. . .'

He went on, with a beautiful expression of thankfulness for the richness and delight of their married life — 'eight glorious years of life and love'. Among his final words of blessing and peace, he spoke of Essie's 'common sense and wise judgement' and she knew that he trusted her. 'As to the future, I leave that to you. . .'

Memorial services were held almost immediately in several states. There was a rush of valedictories in church papers and people wrote of 'supreme sacrifice', 'the blood of the martyrs', 'the nobility of their passing'. The men were named, honoured, eulogised. A church leader wrote that 'the greatest calamity of our mission history has befallen the Methodist church, in the mysterious and tragic fate of the ten missionaries from the New Guinea District.'

People who had grown up with the men, studied with them, had joked and had fun with them in youth camps, had attended their weddings and farewelled them when they left home for the mission field, struggled with the thought that these men — these happy, young, gifted, enthusiastic and very human young Christians — should be taken in a catastrophe which made no sense at all.

The men were gone. Their wives knew that they had to go on living. The bayonet thrust of dreadful grief would wound deeply, but they would not die of it. For their children, for themselves and for the men they had loved and lost, they would have to find a way to go on.

The waves swelled and fell away, rising and falling with a strength that lifted her. The sun was going down beyond the western hills and Jean let the water carry her as she looked back towards the beach, gleaming in the golden light beyond the foam of the breakers. On that beach she had been happy, waiting with confidence for John to come home. Along those sands she had walked so often, remembering, looking forward, praying for her husband. She had played there, been part of Sunday school picnics and family holidays, dreaming of the time when John would join in the fun.

On school days, after stormy nights, she had taken her pupils down to the beach to see what wonderful treasures the sea might have washed up on the sand. They had danced along among the piled strands of seaweed, exploring all the small marvels — seahorses, cuttlefish, conjevoy, crabs and sea urchins — which had been cast up from the ocean. From the depths of the ocean. . .

She kicked against the water, turning her back on the beach and staring out to sea. All this long time, in the depths of the ocean. He was not coming home. All those years of waiting — and he had been dead all the time. All those letters she had written, which he had not answered, had been stacked in bags in a Japanese warehouse through the years. All those stories she had told him, thinking that, though he did not reply, surely he would be glad to hear about Joyce's British naval officer, Sybil's little boy and the publication of the book with her illustrations. But he had known of none of these things.

Swimming alone, she let her tears flow. Her mother used to call her the 'girl who was afraid of nothing' and it was true that she tried to be strong. But now she wept for all that she had lost, all that could now never be. No-one would hear if she wept aloud and her salty tears became part of the great salty ocean.

What was God doing now? she wondered. Perhaps she was swimming in the endless tears of a God who wept.

'God, are you listening? Does all this hurt you, too?' She felt free to ask him, there buoyed up by his waves, with tears flooding. He had made a world that was so beautiful, she thought, and made creatures, men and women, to live in it in peace and harmony. Of course, he was grieved. His wilful children were determined to destroy what he had made, in their arrogance and greed, quarrelling over the world until everything was in ruins.

It was not his plan that millions should die. It was the choice that humans had made and until he chose to put an end to history, he would watch and weep. Jean felt God's tears, weeping with her for John, for the loneliness of a future without him, for John's children that she would never bear.

She had made up her mind. However much it hurt, the only thing she could do was to go on and rebuild her life. Perhaps she had always known that this was what she would do. Within days of the news that John had gone, the school at Kiama had offered her a permanent position. As a married woman, she could not have a permanent teaching post. As a widow, she could.

Jean swam back through the surf, letting the waves wash over her, washing away the day's tears. It was flattering to think that the headmaster respected her teaching skills and wanted to keep her on.

'Thankyou,' she planned to say. 'It's kind of you to offer it. But I won't be able to accept. I'm going back to New Britain.'

24

November 1945– November 1946

THERE WAS A TELEGRAM, but no tombstone.   A name on a list, but no grave where she could take flowers.   A series of events seemed to add up to the death of her husband, but there had been no funeral, no rite of passage to help her face the finality of his passing.

Jean Poole, like the many other women in the same position, found it very hard that she could never know what had happened. She had not been there to say goodbye.   There had been that moment as the *Macdhui* had eased away from the wharf in Rabaul and John had run with the other men to follow to the limits of the wharf, diminishing in the distance until she could see him no more.   Even then, they had not thought that it would be forever. A few months, perhaps, at the most.

It was nearly four years since they had last held each other close and now, without the precious pain of being there at the end, she would have to go on without him.

There were so many questions she wanted to ask, even though she feared the answers. Had the end been quick? Had John been asleep when the torpedoes struck?   Had he been close to his friends in those last minutes? Had the voyage to that point been like the horror journeys described by some other returned prisoners, or reasonably civilised like that of the *Naruto Maru* with the nurses and officers? She knew it was no use asking. No-one would ever know the answers. The end for John and his friends would always remain unknown.

Yet there were some small clues. Chaplain John May, who had been in the prison camp in Rabaul with the men, had arrived back in Australia from captivity in Japan at the end of October. In reply to a letter from Marion Oakes' father, he wrote that he had known Dan Oakes and saw him among those marched out of the camp on 22 June 1942; as an Anglican chaplain, he had known and shared many things with the Methodist ministers and missionary laymen, as well as with the Salvation Army bandsmen and other Christian men. Chaplain May wrote to the General Secretary of Methodist Overseas Missions and his letter was published later. Jean read the letter with care, trying to picture John in those last hours when there were eye-witnesses.

John May had written:

On 22nd June, very early — about 4.00 am — the camp was roused and all the civilians and OR.s were ordered to get ready to move. The officers were confined to their hut and the only contact we had was through the windows and the sides of the hut. There was no opportunity for a service, even though it was a Sunday, but I had discovered that Psalm 107, set for the 22nd Day in our Prayer Book, had some verses which might be of help to the men, so I read it to a few and sent the references as far among the various parties as I could. That was practically all we could do, except for a few prayers with a few who were nearby.

Shortly afterwards they were all marched away (a few were cot cases and were carried) and the Japs told us about a week later that they had gone on board a ship which had safely reached its destination. . . not one of us saw them after they left the camp; the wharf was out of sight behind trees. That, I think, is about all I can tell you of their movement, except that their spirits were high and they went off with laughter and great courage.

The letter from the mission, when it came, was courteous but discouraging. 'Dear Mrs Poole,' it began, and thanked her for her offer to return to New Britain. 'However, at present the Department of External Territories is unable to approve of the return of any white women to Rabaul.'

Not even the women on the staff of the 118th General Hospital had gone back into Rabaul yet and were waiting at Jacquinot Bay further around the coast until conditions were safer. The mission would not be sending any women back for quite some time, the letter said.

(The mission did not mention that they had received a rush of offers to go back from former mission staff, both men and women. To send women yet was out of the question, they decided, particularly women with children. Any men would have to be experienced, very fit and prepared to live without their wife and family for what might prove to be years. Rodger Brown had already gone as a chaplain, with the understanding that as soon as he was demobilised he would continue his missionary work. Gil Platten, who had escaped from New Ireland, was going back before Christmas and Con Mannering, who had returned to Australia in 1939 because of family health, had been appointed acting chairman of the district and had been in Nakanai in the western end of New Britain for some time.)

Jean Poole was disappointed. Now that the long silence had at last been broken and she knew that she must travel into the future alone, the one clear goal seemed to be to go back to the islands. She was a good teacher, she didn't mind roughing it, there were no children to consider and they would need teaching staff in the islands once things settled down again. She knew that she would not give up, even if it took time to persuade the mission to let her go.

There had been the letter from her friend Kath Brown, too. Kath had written a letter of sympathy as soon as she heard the news about John and the other men; Kath was determined to join Rodger when it became possible. Jean tried to imagine what the news of the loss of nearly all his former colleagues would mean for Rodger.

'We always said we'd go back,' Jean thought. 'And if John can't come, I'll go by myself.'

The letter from the mission weighed heavily in Rodger Brown's pocket. As the army jeep in which he was travelling passed through the ruin that was the Rabaul area, the news that had just arrived was the most crushing blow of all.

All of them? Mr Mac gone? Laurie Linggood? John Poole, his new mate and Howard Pearson, his old friend? Dan Oakes with his vitality and passion, big shy Tom Simpson and Herbert Shelton, a calm and understanding host to a mob of unruly young missionaries at that last synod? All of them, all those who shared Christmas dinner with him, and New Year's Day 1942 fun at the beach and around the dinner table — Jack Trevitt, Syd Beazley, Wilf Pearce and his brother-in-law Ken Allsop, Ron Wayne, Bill Huntley — all gone?

And not only them. What about the men from the stores and the banks, the men from plantations, the heads of government departments, the doctors, the men met in the street? What about all the boys from the 2/22nd whom he had met at church and the Salvation Army blokes with their great choir — he had crowded into friends' houses with them all, eating cakes and drinking tea, swapping yarns. Would none of them ever come back?

How could he tell the New Guinean church leaders? In the weeks he had been in the area, he had travelled around to a number of places, asking everywhere if people had any news of the missing missionaries. He had met Rev. Mo Pui Sam, Mr and Mrs Thomas Mow and the Chinese communities as well as the New Guineans. So far, no-one had been able to tell him anything. They had told of their own tragic losses, though.

Bit by bit, he was piecing together a sad story of people who had seen the fabric of their lives ripped and shredded by warring strangers. Church leaders had been executed, tortured, imprisoned, forbidden to lead their people in worship. Some leaders had abandoned their people and their faith. Others had died of disease or left their work because of illness, hunger and fear. Groups of Christians, meeting in remote places, had been strafed by Allied planes. How could he tell people who were battered and bruised by the wounds of someone else's war that almost none of their Australian Christian friends could return to them?

Now it was Sunday again, and he had sent messages to the pastor-teachers and their families from the Raluana and Baining areas to meet him in the afternoon for a service of worship and a meeting at what had once been the beautiful mission station of Raluana, across the bay from Rabaul.

When the jeep pulled up in a cloud of grey pumice dust, it was hard to identify the place. If it had not been for the New Guineans hurrying to greet him, Rev. Akuila To Ngaru looking older and more worn and teacher Mikael To Bilak and others, he might have missed it. School, house, church and printing office had vanished. The terraced clover lawns which had flowed to the edge of the ocean, and the great mango tree, were gone. The little beach had vanished under a tangle of vines and creepers and the lawns had become a moonscape of bomb-craters and crisscrossing trenches, overlaid with wild undergrowth and sweet potato runners.

The handshaking and excited greetings subsided and the group found a place to sit on the cement floor that was all that was left of the school. There were some forty of them; two ministers, a number of pastor-teachers and their wives, as well as some villagers from the Raluana area. There was so much to talk about, so much that had been lost and which they wanted to find.

Mikael To Bilak had a question. 'What was the date of Easter this year? What about 1944 and 1943? I remembered what you once told me about working out the date of Easter by the moon and each year of the war we remembered Easter — did I get the dates right?'

'Yes! You were right.' Rodger was moved to think of the villagers sick, under threat and very discouraged continuing to find strength in remembering the death and resurrection of Christ, and doing it in company with Christians around the world from whom they were completely cut off.

After years of no schools, they talked of beginning again — but how? There were no buildings, too few teachers, no blackboards, chalk, pencils or books. A teacher bravely suggested that they could gather the children outdoors and write on the ground until supplies could be found. Church membership rolls were all lost and the people scattered, the few surviving Bibles and hymnbooks were tattered and stained after years of being hidden, often buried, and the spirits of the people were fragile after years of fear, disease, tyranny and confusion.

With great reluctance and sorrow, Rodger took the letter from his pocket. He had to tell them.

'I have a letter from the Methodist mission people in Sydney. It is very bad news. I will translate it.'

And he began, sentence by sentence, watching the concentration and shock on the faces of his friends sitting cross-legged on the cement floor. Before he finished the sad litany of names of the men who had been their teachers, fathers, brothers and friends, he realised that several were shaking their heads.

'No!' they said. 'That story can't be true.'

'But. . .'

'Not true.' Several leaders were dismissive of the message. Some even laughed. 'Some of our people saw some of the missionaries on the back of a Japanese truck only months ago. They said that they heard a white man call out in our language as they passed and, though he was very thin and bearded, they were sure that it was Mr Linggood. Very few white men speak our language.'

'When the Japanese arrived in 1942, John Poole, Mr McArthur, Mr Linggood and Mr Pearson were with us at Kalas,' said Mikael To Bilak. 'Early in February, the missionaries left to go to Rabaul and met the Japanese at Taulil. One of them tried to ask for permission to go on with their mission work, but they were beaten, their watches taken from them and they were made to change into the clothing of prisoners. I saw them later at Gaulim, before they were taken to Rabaul and later to Vunapope. Much later, when the fighting became worse, they were taken to Bitagalip and they made them work in various places.

'Some of our people gave them food in secret. We thought that they stayed at Bitagalip until near the end of the war. In fact, a Japanese officer told me that they were there till the end and he said that by now they might have started their missionary work again or have gone back to Australia.'

They talked among themselves, confirming their conviction that some missionaries had been seen long after July 1942. They were all very sure, and spoke of one or another who said they had seen them. One remembered leaving a bunch of bananas for the missionaries to collect when they were working outside the camp. Someone said that the wife of one of the New Guinean ministers had said that she had smuggled chicken to one of the missionaries through a fence at a camp in the Duke of York Islands.

'Do you think that any of them would still be alive, then?'

The men and women looked at each other, and at the ground in silence for a long time. Heads were shaken. 'No. We think they are dead. You say they did not go back to Australia, and we know that they haven't begun their work again, here. But we don't know how they died. Perhaps some of them went on that ship. But we think that some of them stayed in these islands.

'We don't understand this story about a ship. We don't have faith in that story. But what really happened is a mystery — we must wait until the end of the world before we know the truth of this thing. . .'

Later, driving back towards the hospital camp on the north coast in a cloud of dust, Rodger was confused and disturbed by what he had heard. The loss of all those men was horror enough. But what if some of their friends had not gone on the ship after all? Could that be true? The group of people who had met at Raluana had spent the war in many different locations, in the mountains and on the coast, and only now were free to travel and hear each other's stories. They brought together the knowledge of many communities. The New Guinean leaders, men he trusted like Mikael To Bilak and Akuila To Ngaru, had been so sure that Linggood, at least, had been on a truck going up Malmaluan hill, only months ago. If that were true, how had he died? Or had he died at all?

Riding through obscuring dust, Rodger tried to decide what he should do about this information. Rabaul was a very long way from the offices in Sydney and even further from the widows of the men who had been lost. Already in Rabaul, authorities were gathering to conduct a War Crimes Commission and former prisoners, villagers and Japanese were being questioned about executions, atrocities and suspected mass graves. The story he had just been told would surely come out in their investigations, and if any of the missionaries had been the victim of a long imprisonment and then death in the islands, it would be revealed. Should he write to the General Secretary about it?

He thought about the women involved, Mrs McArthur, Mrs Linggood, Helen Pearson, Jean Poole and the others. They had just been told that their husbands were dead, drowned at sea. Would it be even more cruel to say to them that perhaps he drowned, or perhaps he spent years working in slave conditions, ill, lonely, desperate, until he was shot or beheaded? For the moment, he decided, let it remain a mystery. He would say nothing yet. When the other stories came out in the investigation, and their graves were discovered somewhere in the islands, then it would be time enough to say, 'Some of our New Guinean people knew this.'

It was three days before Christmas 1945 before Jean Poole could bring herself to fill in the 'Information of Death' form for John. She would attend to it in due course, she had said to herself — when she wasn't so busy, when school broke up for the holidays, when she went back to Sydney for Christmas, when one of her parents could go with her to act as witness. Somehow it did not seem quite real.

She had not realised how hard it would be. Some of the questions were straightforward: name, date of birth, date of marriage and to whom. But then it moved into the realm of the unknown.

Date of death? 1 July, they thought, but who really knew? Cause of death? Lost at sea. . . lost. . . Name of doctor who attended at death? Her pen marked a dash. Place of burial? Again her pen marked the place with a sign that said: this is unanswerable. Name of clergyman — name of undertaker — names of witnesses to the burial. . . nobody, not a soul. She felt like writing in huge block letters: I DON'T KNOW!

There was a space to write the names and ages of her children.

Another blank. How could an inanimate piece of paper full of questions hurt so much? She slid the form across the desk to her father for him to sign as witness.

All over the country, a thousand families were filling in the same papers. None of them had the answers to the official questions, the same questions which gnawed at their spirits. Where? How did this happen? Was my man really there or somewhere else? Most urgently, they asked: Why?

Letters began to arrive in Australia in the homes of former missionaries. The links of friendship which had been strong before the war were being renewed and strengthened. Retired older single women, Maggie Harris and Mary Woolnough, had invested long years of service in the islands and now their love for the people and skill with the language was repaid with letters from the hearts of New Guineans.

Mary Woolnough shared with others the sad letter from one of the New Guinean ministers from New Ireland, Aminio Bale, after he had seen a copy of a vernacular church paper circulated from the Allied forces early in 1945. 'I was sorry when I saw the enquiry about our New Guinea missionaries and nursing sisters. We here in New Ireland know nothing about them and enquire with sorrowing hearts concerning their whereabouts. . . My fathers, we wait for your coming again. . .'

A later edition of the church paper prompted a letter to Miss Harris. The New Guinean writer told of his excitement when he first saw a copy of the church paper, 'but when we started to read it, we came to the great disaster in it. Our hearts were filled with sadness and sorrow and our joy departed, because we expected to meet again our missionaries — but no — we were waiting to meet them again and take them by the hand and laugh with them — but no! the dear souls, the young men, the missionaries, and the chairman. Where are they now? We send our love to their wives and children, who are fatherless, may God stay with them in their loneliness and give peace to their hearts. . .'

Women whose husbands had been lost, as well as the recovered nursing sisters, received letters of love and sympathy from the people of the islands and learned something of the trials which the islanders had suffered. Jean Poole was not the only one who offered to go back to these wounded people. Helen Pearson and Eileen Pearce, both widows of missionaries and with a young child each, offered to return, but their offers were refused because of the children. Dorothy Beale, Jean Christopher and Dora Wilson hoped to return when women were accepted. A number of older men, retired missionaries and ministers, also offered. Among them, Ben Chenoweth and Walter Davies were accepted and planned to travel north during the year.

As for Elsie Wilson, as soon as she heard the news that teachers were no longer obliged to stay at their teaching posts, she resigned from the South Australian Education Department. So eager was she to return to her work in the islands that it did not occur to her that she ought to work through official channels and the church leaders in her state. Elsie caught a train east to Sydney and presented herself at the mission head office, to the astonishment of the General Secretary.

'But Miss Wilson, you can't possibly go straight to New Guinea now!'

Faced with a young woman who had left her job to come to Sydney, the mission officials decided to appoint her to work with other staff at Otford near Sydney, with the part-Aboriginal children who were still waiting to return home to north Australia.

By March 1946, a new group of prospective missionaries had entered training at George Brown College in Sydney. Mary Woolnough, in her sixties and a strong-minded veteran of New Britain since 1914, had just resigned as Matron of George Brown College and was already agitating to go back as soon as any women were permitted. Among the group of trainees was Jean Poole.

'There are no permits available for any women to go to New Britain yet, and may not be for a long time,' she was told.

It was strange to be back in the college. In this panelled dining room she had come as a visitor, shyly sitting with her new fiance John and meeting for the first time Dora Wilson and Rodger and Kath Brown. Though she had been neither student nor resident in those days in 1940, she had often visited and sat in on some lectures with John in the sunlit lecture room lined with bookshelves. Now there were moments when it seemed that John might come in unexpectedly through the doors from the garden or come hurrying up the long corridor, as he had done in those days. He never did. Nevertheless, Jean threw herself into the business of study and in her spare time worked on an English-Kuanua version of the dictionary done years earlier by Laurie Linggood. To go back, to offer to teach in the country where she and John had gone with such high hopes, seemed to be one path to follow. She had no doubts about it.

In April 1946, with a party of sixty-nine part-Aboriginal children and six staff, Elsie Wilson boarded the ship *Reynella* in Sydney Harbour to sail for Brisbane and Darwin. The children who had trekked across the continent early in 1942 were going 'home' to Croker Island. Croker Island had been home for the group for such a short time before the war that it had become a place of vague memories, but it was north and closer to their scattered places of origin. A number of the older boys had returned some time earlier to help prepare buildings for the group. Elsie's mentor and friend, Jessie March, who had been with the children for much of the war period, was retiring from that work, but Elsie knew that they would keep in touch through their mutual interests.

The crew of the *Reynella* seemed happy to have a cargo of children and had set up rows of beds like a big dormitory. The sea voyage promised to be very pleasant, as the ship's crew were to take responsibility for meals for the boys and girls, and the whole party was very excited.

Before they sailed, a group of people from the mission office came to the wharf to farewell them. Among them was the redoubtable Miss Mary Woolnough, tall and grey-haired, single-minded in her lifetime focus on the people of New Guinea. Elsie did not know Miss Woolnough well, other than by reputation, as the older woman had retired following a serious accident only a month after Elsie arrived in New Britain in 1939.

'I'm still doing my best to convince them that I should go back to New Britain,' said Miss Woolnough. 'The people will need a lot of encouragement and comforting after all they've been through — and that's what I could do.'

Elsie listened to her with very mixed feelings. Though she was willing to travel with these children to Croker Island, it still felt somehow that she was failing to fulfil her first commitment, that even now she was being frustrated in her hopes of beginning her real work again.

As the *Reynella* began its voyage up the east coast of Australia, Elsie had the feeling that she was going the wrong way. She had not forgotten the work she had begun in the islands. She would not let the mission officials forget. One day she would travel north again, and next time she would go back to the islands of New Guinea.

It was much harder than they had imagined to settle back into their home communities, the returning mission nurses discovered. For one thing, they missed each other. For so long they had shared the same space, day in and day out. There had been moments of irritation, or times when the moods or mannerisms of one of their friends had been hard to bear, but there had always been a friend nearby, someone who knew how you were feeling, someone who cared about you. Now, when faced with a problem and the need to talk to one of the other girls, each one found it hard to accept that their friends were not there.

The people at home did their best. Families made all kinds of sacrifices to try to make up to their returned girls something of what they had missed. They tried to be understanding when it was impossible to understand, but it was often not easy for any of them.

For Dora and Mavis, one special homecoming gesture meant a lot. The hospital where they had both trained, Newcastle General Hospital, held a thanksgiving service for them and presented them each with copies of their original nursing certificates — 'in case yours were lost'. Through all the years of isolation, they had not been forgotten and, as they walked through a guard of honour of nurses and saw the faces of staff, friends and former patients, they knew that they were being received back with honour.

Not all of the women who had been prisoners were well again. The long debilitation of malnutrition had not been easily healed by large quantities of food. Even after they had had dental work done and other health care, their bodies still carried the long-term effects of deficiencies in their diet.

Any hidden impact of trauma on their minds was offered no medical or other help; of the women and the thousands of returned men prisoners of war people said, at first, 'Don't let them talk about it — they're all mad as hatters after what they went through — change the subject from the war and talk about things that won't upset them.'

Dorothy Beale was very ill in Queensland with malaria and Dora Wilson failed her medical when she re-applied for missionary service in New Guinea, partly because it was suspected that she had contracted tuberculosis. People pointed out that it was probably not a wise thing for women who had just been through years of captivity to attempt to go back to the islands so soon.

Mavis Green knew that it would not be right to return and leave her widowed mother. When she was offered a position at her local hospital, Maitland, NSW, she accepted gladly and began to rebuild her life in her home community, with family, fellow-staff and church. People began to invite her to come to their churches or community groups to speak of her war experiences. Armed with some of the objects she had brought back from Japan, she discovered a flair for public speaking and found that telling the story was a helpful part of the healing process. There were times, later, when she found herself nursing men who had been prisoners of war and the things she had learned from her own experience helped in her approach to their care.

Though the return to an ordinary life, without the strength of the constant support of friends, was often difficult for all of the women, they were often reminded that they had not been forgotten throughout those long years of capitivity. Wherever they went, they met people who had cared about them, including many who were strangers.

While on a holiday in the Blue Mountains with her sister, in the period of recuperation, Mavis attended a church service. The minister welcomed them publicly and after the service was over an elderly man, who had been sitting next to them, leaned over to take her hand. His eyes were full of tears. 'Thank God that you are here, alive and safe,' he said. 'You don't know me, but I am one of many people who prayed for you nurses every day while you were missing.'

As the year went on, women around Australia did their best to regenerate their lives. For most of them the long time of waiting was over. Either their man was back, often damaged but alive, or he would never come home again. The mission women were very conscious of the situation of Mrs Violet Kentish whose husband the Rev. Len Kentish had been captured by the Japanese early in 1943 off the coast of north Australia; she still had no news. In Rabaul, Mo Pui Sam was still without news of his wife in China; there had been no contact for years.

When the lists of names of men lost with the *Montevideo Maru* were published in the paper early in 1946, Mavis and Dora realised that their co-prisoner, Mrs Bignell, had lost both her son and her son-in-law. The lists of names of the dead included the boy soldiers who had visited them at Malabonga, all the doctors and medical assistants, the butcher, the baker, clerks, policemen, planters; the men of an entire town and district were gone.

For some of the women, however, there was a continuing unease. How could they be sure that their husband or son was on the ship? Could some of them have been marched away from the Rabaul prison camp, not to the invisible ship but to a massacre? Was there a mass grave hidden somewhere among the rubble of Rabaul?

Later, it was learned that the husband of nurse Mary Goss had been in the same small party of Australian men as Bill Huntley, former Methodist missionary and husband of Hannah; these men had hidden in the bush for months, but had been captured late in July 1942 and finally executed. News of individuals filtered through, men seen occasionally around Rabaul by the four Australians who had been kept to run the freezer; short lists of names were added to, altered, matched against the nominal roll from Japan. Every memory was mined for the smallest grain of information, but it seemed that, apart from the large group at Ramale, the freezer four and groups of prisoners from other nations, no other Australians had survived in the Rabaul area. Women said to their friends, 'I just feel that my husband was never on that ship,' but there was no way of knowing the truth.

Those were the months of obituaries and the dedication of memorials, stained glass windows, brass plaques or church furniture in memory of men who had died. The Methodist church launched their new fund-raising program in memory of the lost missionaries, with the goal of providing funds for replacing the education, health and church facilities lost in New Guinea during the war years.

Yet despite stained window memorials, many women found great difficulty in persuading various authorities with power over their access to funds that their husbands were indeed dead. A year after women had been told that their husbands had been lost on the *Montevideo Maru*, many had still not been provided with a death certificate. Without the certificate, pensions were held up, insurance money was unavailable and it was not possible to apply for a grant of probate on their husbands' estates. Social services offices refused to pay a war pension on the strength of a name on a list of casualties in the newspaper and insurance companies would not pay out, even with a death certificate 'for official purposes presumed dead', because they demanded proof that in fact the person had been on board the *Montevideo Maru* at the time it was sunk.

Women were outraged that, after years of struggling to survive, living in a single room separated from their children so that they could go to work, paying taxes, now their pension was dated from January 1946 instead of from July 1942. Some women fought their own battles for justice and others had the help of family or church.

In addition to the entanglement of red tape about their financial affairs, many of the bereaved women felt very hurt that it seemed that no-one cared to investigate the full story of the fall of Rabaul and the loss of civilians as well as the men of the 2/22nd.

One woman wrote to Prime Minister Chifley: 'No inquiry into the tragedy of Rabaul has been allowed. You yourself have expressed the opinion that no good can come of it but, as a widow of one of the men, I hope the inquiry will be made. . . We women were kept in ignorance far too long. To us have been the years of anxiety, loneliness and sadness. . .'

Women who had always had the security of living in a church parsonage now had to find a permanent home. Many of them needed to find employment now that they were no longer receiving a portion of their husband's stipend. Mel Trevitt, Essie Linggood and Daisy McArthur returned to teaching. Jean Shelton went to work at Frensham School in Bowral and others continued in their former work.

In a way which she had not expected, Daisy McArthur discovered that it was possible to go on. The dreaded thing which had hung over her for so long had become a reality and yet she still lived. Her sons still needed her. Her own family and Laurie's still supported them. The storm which had broken in all its violence over her head was as terrible as she had feared, but she was making new discoveries.

In the back of her Bible, she added some notes. The story in Mark's Gospel of the storm on the Sea of Galilee described the power of a storm which lashed the little fishing boat, terrifying the fishermen disciples of Jesus. They thought they were lost. And yet, at the darkest moment, they realised that Jesus himself was with them in the boat, sharing the danger. He was there in the storm beside them and, when he spoke, there would be peace and safety at last. He had been there beside her all the time, Daisy was discovering, even when she was at her most despairing.

Kath Brown wrote to Jean Poole at the missionary college. The months were passing and there was still no sign that either of them would be able to travel to Rabaul. 'We won't give up,' they agreed.

In New Britain, Rodger Brown had been demobilised by April 1946 and was throwing himself wholeheartedly into his original missionary work, working beside the new chairman Con Mannering. Their friend from Adelaide, Chaplain Gordon Young who was married to Kath's old friend Grace, was also offering to join them in missionary work as soon as he was demobilised. Rabaul was very much a man's town, with military and ANGAU staff, a Japanese army being repatriated over the months and a War Crimes Commission doing its work of identifying, trying, sentencing and in some cases executing convicted war criminals.

As the superstructure of an army at war was being dismantled, Rodger and Con were busy bidding for and accumulating all manner of useful war surplus material, everything from a boat to a typewriter, lamps, spades and loads of khaki shorts. Gordon Young was rescuing truckloads of army dry rations before they were disposed of. Rodger and Con were living with other men in a rough dormitory, but they were doing their best to scrounge enough war surplus materials to build something at Raluana. It could be a long time before it was possible to invite Kath to join them.

The New Guinean villagers were so worn down by the rigours of war, disease and malnutrition that they had no energy left for hard physical work. The two missionaries had begun the back-breaking work of filling in the bomb craters and open trenches on the church property at Raluana.

'The village people stand and watch us anxiously,' Rodger wrote to Kath, 'and in church they pray earnestly that we two ministers will be given strength to do all the hard work!'

There were still so many unanswered questions and mysteries. Nellie Simpson in Adelaide learned from Con Mannering that he had visited her island home at New Hanover. The New Guinean teachers there told how, early in 1942, both Tom Simpson and Dan Oakes were together at Ranmelek, the mission station on New Hanover, waiting with three other white men for the arrival of the Japanese. The Japanese came, and the villagers saw the missionaries walk to the wharf to meet them, knowing that on that island they could not hide forever. The next day they were taken to Kavieng, where church members saw them in the gaol. After that, no-one could tell Nellie anything further.

Because Tom worked on such a remote island, he was not

known to Rabaul residents and his name did not appear on the lists made up by Gordon Thomas and his mates at the freezer.

Then one day in her home suburb in Adelaide, Nellie was walking with her children, pushing her little boy in his stroller and with her small daughter running beside her. Standing on a street corner was a tall woman in black, a stranger. As they came nearer, Nellie recognised her.

'Sister Maye!' She was the nursing sister in Kavieng before the war. 'You were taken to Japan with Jean Christopher and the others, you poor thing!' The two women greeted each other warmly. In those pleasant pre-war days, Nellie had visited Sister Maye's clinic before the birth of her first child and they had often met at Kavieng social functions.

'I heard that you were in Kavieng for some weeks after the Japanese arrived — did you see anything of my Tom?'

Dorothy Maye hesitated. The young children at their feet were demanding their mother's attention and the nurse said, 'Why don't you take the children home now, and come round later to my brother's house, where I'm staying, and we can talk about Kavieng. This evening?'

That evening, after the children were settled, Nellie went to the address she had been given. There were the politenesses of the offer of a cup of tea, the passing of a flowery plate of homemade biscuits, and the verbal circling of near-strangers saying nothing which mattered. The weather, the recipe for biscuits, anything but Kavieng and Tom.

At last, Nellie could wait no longer. She had come to talk about her husband. 'Sister Maye, *please*, what can you tell me about Tom?'

The nurse went very white. Her mouth opened, but no sound came. With a sudden burst of movement she jumped from her chair, watching Nellie with eyes that held unspoken horror. Knocking the teatray and spilling the flowery plate as she went, the nurse ran from the room, the sound of her screaming trailing behind her.

When at last Nellie found the strength to get up and walk home through the darkness, the echo of the anguished scream still hung, invisible and appalling, in the air. Sister Maye had not come back. Nellie would never meet her again.

For Nellie, the long silence had been broken. It had been replaced by a scream. That was all.

A tug-of-war, hidden but full of energy on both ends of the rope, was going on between the men in Rabaul during 1946 and the women in Australia who wanted to join them.

'It's far too soon for women to come here,' said the men. 'There are no houses, little transport, no comforts, no equipment. It is not as they remember it. They don't realise how rough it is.' It was not that the men did not miss their wives and children. There was a great longing to be together again. But they saw the disintegration of the society around them, the loss of morale among the local people, the impact of illicit alcohol distillation and the multiplying of brothels, the inversion of many former values and behaviours which were resulting in high numbers of villagers in gaol. They thought of their children playing on beaches still sown with mines, or their wives trying to make homes under sheets of iron or huts of thatch.

'We're going to get there, anyway,' said the women. 'We're not looking for comfort.'

The married women, Kath Brown and Grace Young, said: 'A year apart is quite long enough. As soon as we can get a passage, we'll be on our way.'

The nurses, Dorothy Beale, Jean Christopher and a new staff member, Joyce Walker, were all keen to get back to work. They were sure that there must be years of neglect of health in the villages. Dorothy and Chris had passed their medical examinations and, though some church leaders were dubious, the women were eager to travel north. Miss Mary Woolnough also was determined to return to the people she had loved since her youth in the days when it was still a German colony in 1914; she had presented her lean, ageing frame to the medical examination with confidence and had passed: 'I want to go to encourage the people,' she insisted.

Jean Poole continued her studies at the missionary college

through the year and waited impatiently. By August, she had been given an official permit to go to New Britain, but there was no transport. Also, the mission had received a discouraging letter from the chairman, Con Mannering. Jean had never met Mannering. She read with disappointment that he had written that 'no more than three Sisters should be returned to the field and these must be nursing Sisters. . . the position in this district regarding education is so uncertain that no policy can be framed until after synod in November. . .'

Then one day in September an excited Grace Young called to see her friend and neighbour Kath Brown. Through the contacts her husband had in the forces and her former work with the AWAS, she had made a discovery. 'The army is sending a ship, the *Duntroon*, to visit all the New Guinea towns that were battle sites, to do with the work of army disposals. It's not a passenger ship, but I'm sure we can wangle berths — they are going to be landing at Rabaul!' The two friends sat at the kitchen table with a map spread in front of them, tracing the route the ship would take — Brisbane, Port Moresby, Samarai, Finschhafen, Lae, Madang, Rabaul, Kavieng — while Kath's mother watched them with distress.

'Are you girls sure you know what you are doing? Wouldn't it be much nicer to stay here in Adelaide, where it's safe?'

'We're going, Mum.'

Before the *Duntroon* sailed, early in November, the group of women gathered in Sydney. Assembled were Kath Brown and her two little boys, Grace Young, Miss Woolnough, Dorothy Beale, Jean Christopher and the new nurse Joyce Walker. Jean Poole was there, too, ready to sail. Despite the General Secretary's misgivings, she had been persuasive — she had already arranged for her berth on the *Duntroon*, she insisted. The General Secretary had written a letter to Con Mannering on her behalf, assuring him that 'Mrs Poole would be quite willing to fit into any plans the chairman might have in regard to her work'. She didn't mind what she was asked to do; she just wanted to go back and be part of the work of reconstruction.

In those final days before they sailed, they were farewelled at a service in Wesley Chapel in the city. The chapel, which had been the scene for the thanksgiving and welcome home when the nurses came home from Japan and also for the mourning of the memorial service for the ten lost missionaries, now saw the team of women embraced by the people of the Methodist churches across the city.

In the close network of people linked with the mission, news was passed on. In shocked undertones, people said, 'Have you heard about Len Kentish?' Kentish, chairman of the north Australia district, had been missing since early in 1943. When his wife, Violet Kentish, had still heard nothing by September 1946, in desperation she sent letters to major newspapers pleading for any clues that might be available. She had just had several responses and had learned that her husband had been beheaded on an Indonesian island on 4 May 1943.

The other news was of Helen Pearson. Helen, widow of the Rev. Howard Pearson, had applied to return to New Guinea with the Methodist mission and had been rejected. Now she had applied to go with the Education Department of the Territory of Papua and New Guinea and had been accepted as a teacher. She was to travel to Rabaul in the new year, with her young son.

'We are worried about her,' some of the Board commented. 'Helen is going back, we think, because she is convinced that Howard was not on the *Montevideo Maru*. She wants to get to Rabaul to find him, dead or alive.'

There was the strange feeling that she had done all this before. Last time Jean Poole had left her parents' house to drive to the wharf to sail for New Britain, she had been a new bride. John had been beside her and her wedding dress, worn three days earlier, had been hanging in the cupboard.

Now she was alone. As she walked from the front door for the last time, hands full of the last-minute gifts her family had been thrusting upon her, someone captured a photograph of a smiling, confident young woman. The loss of John still hurt deeply and she would never forget her life with him. Yet she knew that she must go on.

Last time, she had gone to board the ship for New Britain with great excitement and anticipation, but she had gone because she had married John, and that was his plan. This time she was going as an independent woman.

She knew that there would be difficulties, though she was not sure what they would prove to be. She was choosing to go back, without hesitation, because this was where she felt she must be — the place where God was calling her.

25

November 1946– November 1947

THE LAST OF THE STREAMERS were torn in two, papery fragments flying in the wind as the *Duntroon* was drawn away from the wharf. The last embraces and handshakes could still be felt, phantom pressure on cheeks and fingers. Jean Poole could still see her parents, her sisters and her friends from Kiama waving.

It was hard to say goodbye, yet she had no hesitation about going back to New Guinea. She looked along the line of profiles of the women who were her travelling companions. They leaned on the rail, watching the hills and cliffs ringing Sydney harbour flow by as the *Duntroon* moved on towards the open sea; the nurses Dorothy and Chris, the new nurse Joyce, Kath and Grace determined to rejoin their husbands, the ageing Miss Woolnough and herself.

'We're a strong-minded lot,' she thought. 'None of us is willing to take no for an answer, despite being told we shouldn't come at this stage — pigheaded, maybe! Anyway, we're on our way now, and they'll just have to put up with us.'

The *Duntroon* sailed north. Jean was still a poor sailor, she found. Once the ship reached the coast of the Territory of Papua and New Guinea, the women saw the debris and ruin left by war in each of the tropical towns they visited on War Disposals business. In Port Moresby harbour, Jean and Kath saw the rusting carcase of the *Macdhui*, the ship which had carried them south away from their husbands nearly five years earlier. The small colonial island of Samarai was still scarred by the torching of most of the commercial and government buildings in 1942 by the Australians, exercising a scorched earth policy before the Japanese came to Milne Bay. At Finschhafen, Lae and Madang they stepped down onto bare wharves on the edges of hot, dusty one-time towns. As a group of Australian civilian women they were a novelty. American servicemen still serving in the islands offered enthusiastic hospitality, driving them around by jeep to see the sights in townships which had borne the heat of battle.

'You wouldn't call this a pleasure cruise, would you?' They all agreed. There was little to commend any of the towns they had seen. Everywhere they had gone land was cratered and pitted by bombs, and buildings were pocked, as if diseased, with the marks of bullets and shrapnel.

'Do you think Rabaul will be like this? Or worse?'

Two days before the *Duntroon* was due to land at Rabaul, the women helped to celebrate young Graham Brown's fifth birthday. As a tiny month-old infant in a woven basket, he had been carried from Rabaul with his mother in the evacuation and now he was going back.

Crew members asked the women: 'Are you ladies sure that you know what you are doing? You're a game lot! And did you know that the blokes in Rabaul are calling this the "bride ship"? If you don't like it once you get there, it could be months before another ship comes up to take you home again.'

The sun was rising on the dawn of 22 November 1946 when the *Duntroon* sailed at last into harbour. During the long progress from the open ocean to the inner, sheltered Simpson Harbour at Rabaul, Jean Poole stood at the rail watching. Her bags were ready and she needed a few moments alone.

Five years ago she and Kath Brown had farewelled their husbands on a wharf in this harbour. Now the town as she remembered it was gone. The long wharf was gone, too, one of a jagged fringe of wharves, broken, twisted, partially submerged,

30. *Mission group farewelling Rev. Mo Pui Sam (centre) from Rabaul, 1948*

31. *Postwar staff of George Brown College, Vatnabara, New Britain, 1947*
Rear: *H. Linge, W. Davies, K. Virginga, S. Gaius.*
Front: *A. To Gogo, Jeane Poole, L. Ne Male, V. Ia Vaninara, W. Valdima*

of a piece with the frieze of wrecked shipping and barges along the shoreline. And John was gone. Kath would meet Rodger very soon and was combing and re-combing the little boys' hair, ready to meet their daddy, and Grace Young was as excited as a bride. Miss Woolnough was delightedly pointing out landmarks to the new nurse and sharing anecdotes with Dorothy and Chris.

But John was gone. 'I always said we'd come back together, after all those years of waiting,' she thought. 'And now it's just me. But here I am. . .'

The *Duntroon* eased in beside the wreck of a bombed ship, half under water, and the crew instructed the passengers to disembark onto its deck and walk to shore across it.

'We warned you, didn't we, ladies? There are no wharves left. Welcome to Rabaul!'

The women stood clustered together on the rusting deck of a victim of war, suitcases and two young children beside them. There was no sign of anyone from the Methodist mission. Others came to welcome people connected with town and army camp, and Gordon Young came for Grace. Then they heard the reassuring sound of a work boat chugging towards them. There were shouts of welcome, and they saw Rodger waving with three other white men and a group of New Guineans.

'It's the ministers! The native ministers have come to meet us.'

A rope ladder was slung from the wreck down to the mission boat and one by one the women scrambled down it, Kath into the arms of her husband. The men were all together in Rabaul because they had just concluded the 1946 synod meetings and were ready to return to their appointments. The Australians were strangers to Jean — the new chairman Con Mannering, Walter Davies, a senior minister who had worked in the region twenty years earlier and Gil Platten who had escaped from New Ireland in 1942. Jean found herself turning to the New Guinean men. Among several who were strangers stood a tall man whose hand was stretched out to her.

'Akuila — Akuila To Ngaru. . .'

His large dark hand grasped hers and his eyes melted with tears which brimmed over and ran down his lined face. He was

32. *Methodist women preparing to return to New Britain, 1947*
Rear: *Dorothy Beale, Joyce Walker, Dora Wilson*
Front: *Kath Brown and sons, Jeane Poole, Jean Christopher*

33. *Aquila To Ngaru and Rodger Brown, Duke of York Islands 1947*

34. *Synod at Vatnabara, Duke of York Islands, 1947*
Centre row from second left: *Jean Poole, Jean Christopher, Elsie Wilson, Con Mannering, Dorothy Beale, Mary Woolnough, Masori Flentje, Grace Young*

silent. He had no trite words of sympathy, no neat formula to offer in the face of grief. But he did not release his grip on her fingers or turn away the direct gaze which looked into her face with such compassion. Of all the ministers, only Rodger and Akuila still lived who had known both Jean and John. Akuila had welcomed them as newlyweds to the area, come to them when earthquake had shaken their home, travelled with them on long walks through the mountains, advised, encouraged, taught them his language, prayed for them and with them. He had been their friend. Though she did not know the stories of Akuila's war, she knew that he, too, must have his own griefs.

She had thought that her tears had all been shed. There had been enough tears, it had seemed, through three-and-a-half years of dark silence and she had known for over a year that her husband was gone. People hinted that she ought to be over it by now. But with the strong hand holding hers, Jean wept as she watched tears splash down from Akuila's dark weathered cheek onto his shirt.

The mission boat turned away from the half-submerged wreck and set off across the harbour towards the mission station at Raluana. Everyone was talking at once. Rodger Brown was gazing at his wife and sons, reunited after fourteen months apart — 'This is the third time in young Graham's life that I haven't recognised my own son when we've met again!' Miss Woolnough, Dorothy Beale and Jean Christopher were talking with high excitement to the New Guinean ministers, who were all well-known to them.

'You've brought your own beds and saucepans and things, I hope. You realise that you've come to very rough conditions.' Con Mannering was polite but honest. 'We've done our best, but there is so much to do everywhere in reconstruction that there has not been enough time to spend on making things comfortable for ladies.'

They were eager to reassure him. They didn't expect luxury, they said; anything would do, just so long as they could come back and be useful. Mannering continued to look dubious. Later, Jean would learn that he and his wife had accepted the discipline of a long separation in order for him to offer his considerable energy and practical skills to the reconstruction of the Methodist mission in New Guinea while his wife raised their sons alone in Victoria. It must have been hard, Jean thought, to accept that a party of other women had insisted on coming against his better judgment and now he would be responsible for their well-being.

She would not have guessed, moving across the water towards a point on the coastline, that this was Raluana. A single building stood where once there had been a whole community, great trees were shattered stumps and. . . 'Don't go walking along the beach — it is still sown with landmines.' But a great welcome was waiting for them, smiling villagers crowding at the water's edge to watch the women clamber from the launch.

Moving through the crowd, shaking outstretched hands, trying out once more her fluency in their local language, Jean had the feeling that the wordless message of the coming of the women spoke more loudly than any work they might do. If an older woman like Miss Woolnough, a young woman with small children like Kath Brown, the nurses who had been imprisoned and even herself as a widow had come back to them, then the long years of trouble must at last be truly over and they had not been forgotten.

'We were going to paint the house for you but ran out of time — Mannering had us working till midnight last night, anyway!' Rodger Brown was leading the way to the house. 'No proper kitchen, of course — you'll be cooking on a couple of primus stoves to start with and then we should be able to organise a bush oven out of a cutdown forty-four gallon drum. . .'

It was not as bad as they had feared. The house looked like an oversized child's cubby house, patched together with bits and pieces of material left over from army use and bought or scrounged by the mission. Odd sheets of iron on the roof, bush timber uprights, walls made of table tennis tables salvaged from the Comforts Fund and floorboards recycled from other places; the women looked into the small rooms and the wide breezeway between the rooms which would serve as communal living room.

Set like statuary around the house were five large Japanese anti-aircraft guns, pointing at an empty sky. It was to be the

Brown's family home, but for the present it was also the only accommodation for five single women as well, with the help of a tent pitched nearby.

(Chaplain Gordon Young had arranged a place for his wife Grace at the army camp; this mayor's daughter from a wealthy Adelaide home set up housekeeping with great good temper in a former army store with walls of open arcmesh and the small privacy of a bedroom enclosed within sheets of coarse black tarred sisalkraft.)

Con Mannering said: 'It will only be for the first few weeks. Synod has decided to send Sister Beale and Mrs Poole over to Vatnabara in the Duke of York Islands before Christmas — Sister Beale will recommence medical work there. Our plan is to relocate the teacher-training at George Brown College over at Vatnabara instead of at Vunairima, with Rev. Walter Davies as principal and Mrs Poole on the staff.'

There was no doubt about the welcome they received. In those first weeks, while they were all at Raluana, there were streams of visitors. Mikael To Bilak and other teachers and students who had been with Jean and John Poole at Kalas came to see Jean, always with tears. 'When we see you, *Marama*, we remember John Poole and all the other missionaries who are lost. . .'

Jean did not know that To Bilak and other New Guineans questioned whether all the missionaries had been on board the *Montevideo Maru*. The men were gone and they were grieving for them all; it would be even more cruel, they had decided, to suggest to their widows that some of their husbands might have suffered long and cruel imprisonment and then died under an enemy sword. What she did learn was that the people of the Bainings had had their traditional lives dislocated and damaged as war had sent the men of two armies through their villages. The people of the mountain villages where she had once sketched the bird dance had seen their populations decimated by violent death, abuse, malnutrition and disease.

Akuila To Ngaru and the teachers had continued to move around the villages to conduct worship, but as time went on Christian worship was forbidden. There came a time when To

Ngaru and others were captured because they still led the people in worship, imprisoned in a cave and beaten with canes. To be a Christian had been a dangerous thing.

The leaders of the Chinese Methodists came to visit them. Mo Pui Sam and Thomas Mow shared the stories of the Chinese people as they did their best to rebuild in the Rabaul-gothic of salvaged scrap iron and army disposal remnants. Australian men serving with the army sometimes came to visit, though most of the troops had now been demobilised and repatriated. There were also visits from men who had come back without their women to try to rescue abandoned plantations.

One morning the women were sitting on the open verandah area having morning tea when a party of six men walked up towards the house from the beach. Their conversation died in mid-sentence. Even at a distance, the women could see the distinctive caps and uniforms of Japanese soldiers. Four of them had never set eyes on a Japanese soldier before, though the existence of the Japanese military had so profoundly affected their lives. Chris and Dorothy looked shaken; just like this had men walked up from the beach only a few miles further along the coastline at Vunapope in 1942. The soldiers stepped up close to the verandah and bowed courteously.

'Excuse me, please,' one said, 'have you seen an Australian sergeant? We've lost our guard. We came from the camp with him to help move the mines from the beach.'

The women shook their heads, then noticed a lone Australian coming. He had gone further along the coastline to make sure that they had missed none of the mines left with wicked noses protruding. There was an exchange of greetings and then the party of men departed, leaving the women nonplussed by their odd encounter over morning tea with Japanese men waiting for trial as war criminals.

The jeep hit another bump and Jean and Chris bounced yet again into the air, landing on the seat with a thud. Rodger Brown at the wheel was unperturbed. He had been driving on the ruins of the east New Britain road network for a year now and knew most of the craters and corrugations well.

'I don't know which is worse, the jeep or the three-ton truck,' Jean said. 'You feel every jolt and bump, either way. I could almost prefer travelling by water.' She was not seriously complaining. If rough travel conditions had worried her, she would not have come. Now she clutched the movie camera she had brought from home, excited by the opportunity to see things that few white women would have the chance to witness. In any case, it was good to escape from the overcrowded house at Raluana where Kath Brown was left to try to keep the peace between too many strong-minded individuals in too small a space.

Dust rose around them as they travelled, settling thickly on vegetation and the dead army of abandoned trucks and lorries lining the roadside, left to rust where they had fallen victims. Dark gaping mouths of miles of underground tunnels leered from the sides of hills as they passed, sinister and unwelcoming — 'I wouldn't want to explore in any of those,' they agreed. Where once the road had passed through the formal aisles of coconut plantations, the mature palms had been smashed and the young growth was often smothered under vines and weeds.

Many villagers were still living in very temporary shelters while the villages were being re-established. Rodger explained that the authorities were trying to discourage village groups from rebuilding churches before they built their own houses, but the need for a focus for their community had often outweighed other considerations. As they drove past a sequence of villages, Rodger commented on the loss of morale among the people, with a rising crime rate, illicit brewing of potent 'jungle juice', the appearance of brothels where there had been none before and the way villagers who had received large payments of war compensation were literally throwing the money away in endless gambling games.

'Things are much the same out on the other side of Raluana,' Jean Christopher remarked. Chris had taken an opportunity to revisit the nuns at Vunapope and had come back from a wonderful day of reunion with stories of the nuns' experiences under bombardment. There were not many things of value which the war years had brought to the islands, but for Chris one thing she cherished was the understanding and affection which had grown between Methodist mission nurses and Catholic nuns who had offered them refuge. Like the Methodists, the Mission of the Sacred Heart was rebuilding its work from the ashes of Vunapope, though many of the staff were still living in tents.

Jean Poole had seen and filmed the new Rabaul, a confusion of temporary buildings of scrap-iron and timber, thrown together wherever there was a space between bomb craters or ruins. The original streets had vanished under rubble, food gardens and jungle growth and if ever the town were to be rebuilt it would need to be resurveyed. As it was, the authorities had decided to abandon the town site because it was so close to the volcanoes and rebuild further around the coast at Kokopo, so any buildings going up had an air of impermanence.

That day they had also driven out to Vunairima on the north coast, but all that was left of the beautiful mission education campus were cement stumps which had once supported fine buildings, now vanishing under a tangle of vegetation, and a row of poinciana trees. Dorothy Beale had been with Jean that day and had grieved over the loss of the hospital where she had once trained medical workers. It was the same everywhere they went: ruin, loss, grief and the many post-war problems for villagers struggling to throw off the lethargy of years of poor health, danger and oppression.

The jeep bounced and jolted on, climbing the road towards the Bainings. Last time Jean had travelled this road, John had been beside her and the back of the utility truck had been piled with her luggage and the abundance of fruit and vegetables the villagers had showered on her in farewell. Within weeks of that journey, the same road had seen many Australian troops of the 2/22nd, escaping from invasion and about to disappear into the hidden tracks over the mountains. The people of the Bainings had seen a lot of trouble since then.

As they rounded a corner on a rise before they began the descent into the valley where once Jean Christopher, Mavis Green and Dora Wilson had run a health centre at Malabonga, they came upon hundreds of villagers gathered for an open-air market. The sound of the jeep made heads turn. Very few vehicles travelled the road these days. Someone shouted and then there was a sudden rush of people running towards them. 'Sister Christopher! *Marama* Poole!'

The jeep was surrounded and brown hands reached out to the two women, grasping hands, touching with outstretched finger-tips, weeping, shouting, calling their names, speaking rapidly in their language. Jean and Chris were shaking hands with both hands at once, while people who could not reach a hand leaned across to shake an arm or an elbow in their excitement. At Raluana, these two women were just a pair of unknown white women. Here, in the community where they had worked, they were known, remembered and loved. The welcome they received was overwhelming. When at last Rodger was able to edge the jeep slowly through the crowd, the people ran down the road behind them, shouting their names and calling their welcomes till at last the sound faded in the distance.

'They remembered us. . .'

'Of course. We lived with them. We haven't forgotten them, have we?' Chris was not surprised. 'In all that crush I could see women whose babies I've delivered, patients I've treated, lads who have helped in the Sisters' house.'

'Yes.' Jean had seen familiar faces, too, people who had come to Kalas, former schoolboys, villagers who had helped her when she had walked on patrols with John. She brushed a hand across her face, smearing tears through dust. No, she had not forgotten. Nor would she forget.

Before they reached their destination of the village of Gaulim, the jeep approached a point that she knew well. Just at that place there had once been a road turning off through the tall timbers. As a bride, with her husband at her side and her wedding gifts in boxes in the back of the small truck, she had turned at that corner, following the road to the clearing that was Kalas and home.

'Just here,' she started to say, 'this is where. . . there used to be. . .' No longer. A great log lay across the place where once a road had turned towards Kalas. The road that once was had been swallowed up by jungle. There was no way back.

When some of their lost possessions began to reappear, the women were amazed. Kath Brown was delighted to discover that a box of her things, including some wedding gifts with the silver teapot her mother had been so distressed to lose, had been located at Nakanai and brought to Rabaul. The New Guinean minister who had spent the war under Japanese occupation in the Nakanai area had kept the box for them in his own house, passing it off as his own when questioned by Japanese soldiers; it could have meant his death if they had opened the box and found a crystal jug, silver teapot and china.

Then one day villagers from the hills behind Raluana came to the house with a battered trunk which looked as if it might have been buried for a long time. Shyly, they explained that they had been hiding the contents of the box from the Japanese through the years of war, first in a remote village church and later buried, for the sake of the missionary family who had lived with them for so many years.

The lid was lifted off the box and Kath Brown gave a cry of recognition.

'These are Essie Linggood's things! Her best cups and saucers — her coffee set. . .' They lifted out each piece with care. Everything was coated with dust and the last fragments of wrapping paper left by insects. 'I remember this pattern on the china, Jean, from all the times we washed it up during synod here at Raluana in 1940.'

It was odd but, as they washed the rescued china and wrapped each piece in discarded khaki army trousers for the journey back to Essie Linggood in Melbourne, the cups and plates became a visible link with a world that had been lost. Laurie and Essie Linggood, host and hostess to their colleagues, had offered afternoon tea in the garden under the mango tree, with the gracious mission house beyond, edged with scented flowering shrubs.

The house was gone. The men were gone. That world had vanished on the night when an army had come shouting cries of war as their landing barges scraped on the sand at Raluana Point. In their place was a house built of scraps and table tennis tables, edged with bomb craters and Japanese guns.

But the cups and saucers had somehow survived. So had the team of missionaries who now crowded around the table to eat the meal Kath had prepared. There were many times when they wondered why some of their colleagues — more experienced, cleverer, with better language skills or gifts of leadership than themselves — had been lost, while they themselves had been spared.

Rodger often struggled with this; why was he still here in New Britain, young and comparatively inexperienced as he was, and not Mr Mac or Laurie Linggood or one of the others? Was it all as random as the survival of a coffee set, treasured by a woman as a wedding gift, when so many other treasured things had been lost? They had no easy answers. Whatever the meaning of the puzzle of the tragedy which had touched all of their lives, each of the group knew that they had been given the chance to be part of beginning again.

'You realise, Mrs Poole, that you will be starting with nothing?' Con Mannering had looked at the young woman before him that day, before she set out for her new appointment. She was not sure whether the expression on his face meant disapproval or anxiety. 'Less than nothing, because those small islands of the Duke of Yorks have still to be cleared of war damage. Our mission wants to re-establish teacher training on Ulu Island, but you do understand, I hope, that there is nothing there — no building, no blackboard, no books?'

'I know.' She had smiled at him, she remembered now, confident that nothing need deter her from her goal.

That was shortly before Christmas 1946. Con Mannering might be unconvinced about the wisdom of sending Jean Poole to a non-existent school, but if Dorothy Beale were to begin her medical work again, she would need a woman companion. They were only filling in time at Raluana, adding to the crowded conditions for those living with the Brown family.

So they had come, crossing the waters from Raluana on New Britain to Ulu in the Duke of York Islands. Jean saw the beauties of the scattering of small islands with the bulk of New Ireland beyond, bright green against the vivid blue of sea. Some islands were large enough to support several villages and coconut plantations and some were tiny outcrops above the water with space for a single clump of palms. Ulu Island, their destination, had been set aside for mission use many years before. Seventy years earlier, in 1875, pioneer Methodist missionaries had chosen these small islands as a strategic location to begin their missionary work because ships passed through them on a northerly route between the island groups.

When the mission workboat anchored at the site of the mission at Vatnabara on Ulu, and Jean found herself clambering down the rope ladder into a waiting dugout canoe below, she began to discover what Con Mannering had meant when he said there was nothing to work with. There was no jetty at Vatnabara and women, suitcases, mattresses and bedsteads were manoeuvered from the workboat onto dugout canoes for the final part of the journey to the shore. Rodger Brown and Akuila To Ngaru had come with them to help them get established and they all walked over the coral rock to be greeted by some villagers and retired minister Walter Davies who was already in residence.

'It's all gone.' Dorothy was shaken. They had known that everything would be changed, as it was at Raluana and Vunairima, but that did not make it easier to accept the desolation. In earlier years the mission chairman had lived here, with key institutions and a large staff under his care. Many Japanese had lived here over the past few years, digging trenches and dugouts for protection. Australian bombers had pounded the island from above, and the ground was cratered, with no sign of the gracious tropical houses which had once stood among gardens.

They were shown to a small hut of folded palm fronds, roofed with kunai grass.

'We have built this for the mission women,' the villagers explained. Rodger and Akuila put their heads through the space that was the doorway and then made way for Jean and Dorothy. Inside it was dim, with patches of sunlight pouring through the small, uneven holes which formed windows, with their edgings of round timbers; it was divided into a living area with two little bedrooms. Above their heads danced dust motes falling from the grass roof and rough sapling rafters. The whole stood on a concrete floor which was all that remained of a pre-war building.

Rodger shook his head. 'Number ten,' he said. On a scale of excellence, in Pidgin English, 'number one' was the pinnacle and 'number ten' the least.

Akuila pulled a doleful face. 'Number ten and a half!' he declared.

Jean and Dorothy were unperturbed. By the time their two beds were set up inside the house, with a table and chairs, a bench for their primus stove and food preparation as well as some rough shelving for pots and plates, there was little room left for the other things they had brought, so most of their linen and crockery was left in packing cases under their beds. (When it was possible to unpack the boxes a year later, it was discovered that silverfish, whiteants and cockroaches had dined on their things in the meantime.)

Two sheets of corrugated iron were propped up as water catchment over a pair of forty-four gallon drums for their water supply and the people pointed out a delightful beach not very far from the hut where they could bathe. There were no food gardens planted, but the army was still supplying the local people with rice while they rebuilt and replanted, and the women had been given quantities of dehydrated vegetables salvaged from army stocks, so they wouldn't starve.

'We'll be fine here,' they assured the others. 'As it is, we have the only house on the island, and in this warm climate we can manage without a door or a bathroom!'

Sitting in the narrow canoe, Jean Poole narrowed her eyes against the glare of sun on water. The palm-fronded island in front of them was not very far distant and she was discovering the pleasures of canoe travel. She and Dorothy Beale had been invited to go with Walter Davies to visit one of the larger islands in the Duke of York group for the opening of two church buildings in island villages.

'When I was at Vunairima, we had a canoe,' Dorothy began.

'The last time we used it was at the picnic with the men on New Year's Day 1942. . .'

Her voice trailed away. It was often the same. She would begin to speak of the missionaries who had gone and then would stop. Whether it was that she found it too painful, or whether she was afraid to upset her companion, she rarely spoke of them. Yet Jean waited, always hoping to hear John's name, to be reassured that he had lived once and that other people remembered him, too.

'We didn't know. . . we had no idea, then, how soon. . . how close. . .' Dorothy's voice was almost inaudible. 'I remember that we were all playing around, having fun. . . I was tipped out of the canoe by one of them because I'd pushed someone else in. All those men. . .' There was silence for a while. 'We don't forget, you know.'

The canoe sliced on through the sun-sparkled water, resting at last on an island beach. Jean scrambled out behind Dorothy and followed their village hosts to the cluster of buildings which had been erected again since the departure of the Japanese. A new building, fragrant with fronds and grasses still drying and vivid leaves and flowers tucked into the walls, was surrounded by people of the village.

After a formal ceremony to pronounce the new church open, everyone crowded inside to sing and pray. Despite the evident happiness of the people at the new building, there was something a little pathetic about the occasion. Jean knew that for these people, too, there were the missing faces who should have been with them. The singing, so joyful and harmonious in the past, was uncertain; only one or two hymnbooks, dug up from wartime hiding places, were being shared among the crowd.

Later, sitting in the shade with the village women, Jean and Dorothy listened to their story. Their experience of the war, even in those lovely islands, had been full of violence.

'We were forbidden to worship and our pastors were forbidden to preach,' they explained. 'Our Bibles and hymn books were burned, but a few of us were able to hide them in the ground. But it was not possible to sing aloud, so we have forgotten the words of the songs and our children have never learned them.'

'Perhaps in other places it was possible for people to hide from the Japanese, and worship. But our islands are very small, and there was nowhere safe to hide. So we would pray together in the dark, in our houses. . .'

'They arrested all our pastor-teachers and our ministers, Beniamin Talai and To Golo, and put them all in prison because they would not stop leading us in the worship of God. Our church buildings were torn down and our leaders were tortured. . . Talai and his son were beheaded and nine other church leaders. . . To Golo survived because he was blinded with cataracts and they let him go. . .'

'We saw them digging great holes in the ground, in the last months of the war, and we thought they were graves for us all. . .'

Jean listened, deeply moved. Dorothy in her imprisonment and she in her loneliness and loss were part of a world of women and men who had been profoundly hurt by the years of war. On remote coral islands, in captivity in a Japanese house, separated from old friends and husbands in Australian country towns and cities, women had waited, prayed and wept.

'But we did not forget God,' the village women went on. 'Our church buildings were torn down, but we still worshipped God in our hearts.'

'God didn't forget us, either. Remember the crabs?' Women chuckled and nudged each other. They could see that God cared about them, they explained, because in the worst times, when the invading army had stripped their villages and gardens of other food, their fruit and nut trees in the bush bore well in season and out of season — 'and swarms of little crabs came on the beaches, plenty of crabs, and we knew that God sent them for us!'

Jean caught Dorothy's eye. There was a gleam of tears. She touched a nearby brown hand. 'Yes. . . yes, God looked after us, too.'

Rain fell in drowning torrents, in the sudden violence of the tropics. Since Christmas and New Year 1947, they had had many weeks without rain and had almost run out of water. Now trickles of water were leaking through the bundled kunai grass which formed the roof of the hut and splashing onto Jean's work, while gusts of water sprayed in through the wide doorway. Jean pushed her papers to one side and jumped to her feet to snatch up the hammer and a tarpaulin. If she was not quick, her bed would be saturated. She was still nailing the tarpaulin over the open window space when Dorothy ran in, shaking water from her umbrella.

'We've got our wish, anyway!' They stood at the door watching water stream down their corrugated iron sheets and fill the empty water drums. 'If it hadn't rained soon we wouldn't have had water for a cup of tea or anything!'

They laughed. Jean was thankful to see how relaxed Dorothy was. It wasn't always like this. Dorothy was so glad to be back at work, after the years of inactivity and imprisonment, and threw herself into her task with all her strength. She had begun to make regular contact with women and children who had had no maternal or infant welfare clinics for years and to assess the medical needs of the people. Many of them were in poor health, the result of years of malnutrition, stress and no medical help.

Dorothy worried over the large numbers of people suffering from ulcers, respiratory diseases and yaws, and malaria was a constant problem. A small hospital was being built of bush materials for her work, and each day they watched women and children carrying in bundles of kunai grass for the thatched roof. But the older woman was not always as at ease with herself as she was today. There were the times when she retreated into morose silence. She had told Jean enough stories of her years as a prisoner for Jean to catch a glimpse of the hurts of those years, and Jean tried to give her time without intrusions until she felt able to respond in a friendly way once more. The time of war had hurt both women, but their experiences were so different that it was almost impossible for either to fully understand the other.

'I've been working on a new curriculum for the teachers,' Jean said, 'and I'd just started a letter to the mission board in Sydney when I had to stop to cover the window. Now I think of it, I wonder if the board will think I'm complaining — I just described our house, and the leaks in the roof, and the millions of hungry mosquitoes here, and having our bath at our lovely little beach. Perhaps I should make sure they understand that it is all in the fun.'

Dorothy began to prepare their evening meal. The dehydrated vegetables from old army rations which formed the bulk of their diet were flavourless but filling. 'You didn't say anything about our cardboard vegetables, did you?'

'No. I just wish I had more to say about our school. Though I hate to admit it, Con Mannering was probably right when he said I had come too soon and there would be no teaching to do for a while. I'm not much use helping Mr Davies and the pastor-teachers build a school building for us to work in.'

Jean packed away her papers for the day. She was in the strange position of having too little and too much to do. Too little, because there was still no school building, nor even the simplest of school equipment. Yet in a sense there was so much to do that it was overwhelming. She had been working on the outline of a school curriculum to use for re-training the teachers, but it was slow work. Nothing had survived the bombs and devastation of war of all the excellent work done by previous generations of teachers in the islands nor had she herself any experience of teaching New Guinean children. Jack Trevitt and Laurie Mc-Arthur, both gifted educationalists who would have advised her, were dead. Now she was the only trained Australian teacher working with the Methodist mission, the Australian administration had never taken an interest in village education before the war and the Catholics at Vunapope were also beginning again from nothing.

Five good New Guinean men had come to Vatnabara to build a place where George Brown College could begin again but, though they were all leaders who had carried their people through the troubles of the war years with heroism and great strength of spirit, their education and teaching skills were limited. So she was alone, slowly finding her way without a map. Still, there were some new signs of hope; she had been invited to attend a series of meetings of the handful of Australian teachers from Catholic, Administration and Methodist school systems and she hoped they would be able to rebuild something together.

The rain eased and the two women walked to the beach for their daily swim. In the swift dusk of the tropics, the aroma of citronella insect repellant drifted around them as they armed themselves for the nightly onslaught of mosquitoes. Later, after the meal of reconstituted vegetables and their portion of army rice, Jean picked up her pen again. In the pool of lamplight, Dorothy was reading, her curly head bent over her book. Once, the one who had shared her lamp on tropical evenings had been John. . . She dipped her pen in the ink and continued writing her letter, speaking of the sadness of the island people as they tried to gather their lives together again after years of such pain and grief.

'I hope this letter doesn't sound like a tale of woe,' she wrote. Glancing back across the pages, it seemed to her that much of it was telling of troubles or inconveniences. That would not give a true picture, she knew. There was such a sense of privilege to be with the island people, sharing the challenges of the time of rebuilding.

'Really,' she went on, 'we are quite happy and we make fun of these things. Miss Woolnough at Raluana is having the time of her life — she talks away to the people like a long lost friend!'

Kath Brown stepped to the edge of the verandah and looked yet again out into the dark. The only sounds were the rustlings of wind through palm fronds, the surge of waves on the beach and sometimes the noise of the passing of flying foxes through the trees. It was late. Every evening it seemed to be later before Rodger came home. It worried her.

She pushed open the door into the tiny room where her sons slept, safe under their tent of mosquito netting. They both lay sprawled on their sheets, tossing a little in the heat. It seemed a long time since Rodger had been home in daylight with time to talk to his boys. Kath was tired herself after another busy day teaching her little boy his correspondence lessons and taking charge of all the household needs of family and house guests with very primitive facilities.

Somewhere in the distance, at last, she heard the sound she had been straining to hear. The throb of an engine came along the coast road and stabbing headlights cut through the night. They were coming at last. Kath carried the lamp to the kitchen table. Two plates of dinner waited forlornly hidden under tea-towels. That was a nice meal once, she thought with regret. She took pride in the food she offered her family and house guests, but it was very disappointing, night after night, to see Rodger's dinner dried up and spoiled because he was so late home. One of these days, she thought, she would tell him how she felt — wasting her time, it seemed, on cooking good dinners for people who always seemed to come in too late to enjoy them — but not tonight. Tonight it was too late, and he and Miss Woolnough would be too tired to think.

By the time the jeep rocked to a halt outside the house and Rodger and Miss Woolnough climbed stiffly to the ground, the primus stove was lit. The pungency of methylated spirits and kerosene scented the air around the primus flame as Kath reheated the dinners. Miss Woolnough was still talking as the travellers stepped up into the circle of light, giving instructions about her expectations for the next day.

Kath gave Rodger a kiss of welcome. He looked exhausted and dusty and, when she held him briefly, she realised that he was shaking. She looked a question and he shook his head. They had become skilled at communicating wordlessly. There was rarely a time in their own home when they were without the presence of other missionaries or guests.

'You've had a long day,' she said mildly as she put the food before her husband and the senior woman.

'Yes. Some news — Helen Pearson is back in Rabaul.'

'Is she really? I thought the mission had said that they wouldn't take her because of her little boy.'

'She's been able to get here through the government education program, to work with women. Helen has come mainly because she is convinced that Howard was not on board the *Montevideo Maru*. She believes that he is still somewhere around New Britain, dead or alive, and she's come to search for him.'

'The poor thing! How terrible for her if she thinks she's going to find him wandering around with amnesia, or hidden away in the bush somewhere with the local people. Surely she knows that anyone who has survived will have been found by now.'

'Helen thinks that there is a big cover-up, some sort of conspiracy to keep the women from finding out what really happened. I think,' Rodger said wearily, 'that she is determined to find him or his grave and won't give up until she does.'

Kath made a fresh pot of tea for Rodger and Miss Woolnough while they talked of their day. Every day they brought home tales of journeys to Vunairima, to Rabaul, to Kabakada or Gaulim where Chris and Joyce Walker were re-establishing the medical work. Miss Woolnough was prepared to travel many miles to meet with the village people, encouraging them, listening to their tales of the war years, telling her own stories of memories of their parents and grandparents over a span of thirty-three years. She ran clinics for the women at a number of locations and the people knew that she loved them. Her strength of will drove her on when she was weary, forcing her to keep going as long as she could see tasks to be done.

Her philosophy of relating with the New Guinean people had been moulded by generations of colonial missionaries. 'Be firm, be fair and be kind — and never mix the order!' was her advice to younger missionaries. Miss Woolnough was a wonderful woman, respected, loved, admired — and she exhausted those around her.

Later, when at last Kath and Rodger were alone with their door shut, Rodger dropped thankfully onto the bed. 'At least I sleep in my own bed every night,' he said. 'But it seems so long since I have seen our boys when they've been awake. There is just so much work to be done, everything to be rebuilt or begun again — Con Mannering and I are both working as hard as we can and there won't be any relief till the new staff arrive later in the year. And Miss Woolnough has such high expectations of what should be done. We'll be off again first thing in the morning. . .'

Kath extinguished the lantern. 'You can't keep going like this,' she murmured. 'You're one person — do you think you have the strength of ten?'

There was no reply. Rodger's breathing had deepened and she knew that he was already almost asleep. Kath lay in the darkness praying for him. It was not just the stress of satisfying the demands of Miss Woolnough which sometimes made him begin to shake with tension. Certainly the eccentric older woman was not easy to live and work with. Kath herself found it hard when she wanted to keep her chickens in her room — 'so that I don't risk losing the eggs' — and there were those times when nothing pleased the older woman and Kath was made to feel that everything, even an unexpected rainstorm, was somehow her fault.

But that was not all that was driving Rodger. It occurred to her that though he did not have the 'strength of ten', in fact, he was trying to do the work of ten men. He had survived the war and ten colleagues had not. He did not understand why. There were times when the burden of survival with all its responsibilities and demands seemed unbearable.

For the rest of his life, he would drive himself on to work as hard as he could, pouring all his great energy into his work because, after all, he was alive. Kath knew it and knew that, because he was alive, she would live with it, thankful to have her husband beside her.

'There is something wrong with Helen Pearson,' people started to say. 'She's not well.'

Every time she could find an opportunity and transport, she was travelling around the district following any clues she could find in her quest for her missing husband. Little by little she was giving up hope that Howard might be still alive, but she questioned everyone she could find — New Guinean Christians, Australian officers working for the War Crimes Commission, Chinese friends who had been interned in Rabaul — for any small hint about Howard's fate. During those months, the trials of war criminals were going on in the town and she imagined Howard as a victim of one of the acts of violence for which men were being sentenced to years of imprisonment and to death.

The horrors of some of the stories being told by witnesses filled her mind. No-one had said that they had witnessed Howard's execution, but the more she searched, clambering desperately through tangling bush looking for a secret grave, the more sure she became that her husband had died terribly. Her little boy trailed behind her, confused and distressed as his mother became more and more a frightening stranger, not like the happy woman he loved.

There came a day in June 1947 when friends found the child wandering alone, searching for his mother. The dark floods of not-knowing had engulfed her. Friends and medical staff took responsibility for her welfare and Helen Pearson left New Britain for the last time, her child beside her, strapped to her seat on the plane for her own safety as she travelled under care to Sydney and hospital. With medical help and the arrival of relatives to take care of her, Helen began to regain her balance and was able to travel home to Adelaide with her family to begin to rebuild her life.

In time, a letter arrived in Rabaul from the Sydney office of the mission. The General Secretary wrote to let the missionaries know that Mrs Pearson was greatly improved after a week in hospital, but that when she arrived from Rabaul 'she was in a terrible state, poor soul. It is tragic when you remember her story. . .'

It was not only the white ants in the church pews or the houses devised from the debris of conflict. There was something insecure, insubstantial, about the whole community spread across the Gazelle Peninsula during 1947. The certainties of an earlier era were gone. Planters and missionaries, business people, New Guineans and government officers all knew that things would never be the same again. The rebuilding of a society and a region could not be simple.

The end of hostilities had not meant the end of wounding. The poison from years of enmity would continue to infect relationships between individuals and nations for years to come. For Jean Christopher, a letter from Japan caused some comment from her co-workers. One of the Japanese, Morli, who had been part of the life of the interned women for several years, wrote begging for some financial help. He and his family were hungry and in great need in post-war Japan.

'You won't send him any money, surely?' Kath asked, shocked.

'I suppose not,' Chris said, yet she remembered how hungry they had all been and could feel again the bitterness of living in a starving body. But Morli had had his moments of cheating them of food, too. Should she forgive now that she was free and he and his family were hungry?

Rodger found young Australian soldiers, stationed in Rabaul to work with the War Crimes Commission, who were faced with questions they found impossible to answer. One young man, a regular attender at church services, confided that he had become friends with a young Japanese officer who was on trial for a war crime which had been committed reluctantly but under orders.

The two young men — the Japanese and Australian — were both Christians and talked together about faith in God, and courage to face death with the hope of eternal life. Despite doubts about the case, the court condemned the Japanese officer to death and his Australian friend was appalled to find himself detailed to the firing squad. His only hope was that he had drawn the one weapon with the blank ammunition, so that his friend's blood was not on his hands. Rodger talked with him and with other men who faced similar questions, yet he knew that some of the actions of the courts in Rabaul that year would haunt men for years.

As for the nurses Chris and Dorothy, Con Mannering was worried about them. He wrote anxiously to head office: 'We often wonder whether the situation up here is really appreciated down south. Of our three nursing Sisters, two have borne the stress of those years of captivity in Japan and it is unfair and unwise to expect them to carry the heavy burden that they are. . .' They were both such skilled workers, so well respected, but so stretched physically and emotionally.

Mannering wondered whether perhaps a mistake had been made in letting the women return so soon. If more help did not come soon, he feared that the pressures of trying to re-establish medical and infant welfare work would be too much for them, and the women themselves would be damaged in the attempt.

And yet, despite everything, a slow rebuilding and healing was going on. None of it was easy. The building of houses was hard enough, with endless correspondence to Australia to arrange for the import of caneite and hardwood for flooring to build even one mission house to replace the many that had been destroyed. On Ulu Island, the bones of an army hut, recycled, were being erected for Jean Poole and Dorothy Beale and they were delighted to think that soon they would have an iron roof to keep out the rain and catch fresh water.

New staff were arriving and, as each new worker came to share the load, some of the burden was lifted from the others. Army chaplain Gordon Young joined the mission staff after he was demobilised from the army and he and wife Grace went to Ulu. Former mission staff were being drawn back by their affection for the people of the islands and a sense that there was still a place for them to be useful.

Slowly the people of the place were regaining their strength and optimism, though the troubles of the past years could never be forgotten.

Elsie Wilson, far from her former colleagues, went on teaching at Elcho Island in north Australia. Other women had already gone back to New Guinea, she was told, but though she was told that permission had been granted for her return as early as January 1947, she was still waiting for further instructions. To her own surprise, she discovered that she loved Elcho Island. She found the island beautiful and the children a pleasure to teach. For the first time in years she was part of a happy team of mission staff who had become good friends. Yet there was still that strong feeling that she ought to be somewhere else. She had expected to make her mission teaching a life work and had committed that effort to the people of New Guinea, so that anything else seemed to be failing in her duty.

There were times when she thought they had forgotten her, but at last the message arrived. She was to make her way to Sydney and be prepared to travel on to Rabaul. When she planned her route, to travel from the off-shore island of Elcho to the coast of Arnhem Land and on in an immense arc tracking across the centre of Australia to Adelaide and then curving east and north through Melbourne to Sydney, her co-workers reminded her that she was retracing their steps. Her friends Jessie March and Margaret Somerville and the Aboriginal children had made the same journey in 1942.

It was indeed a long journey and Elsie was sad to farewell her friends on Elcho. But at last she reached Sydney, where she stayed with Mary Jenkins who was still disappointed that her health would not let her return to her former work among the Chinese people of Rabaul. The magnet of the people of the islands drew them both, as it was drawing others, but Mary knew that for her it was impossible.

When at last Elsie left Sydney for Rabaul on the final stage of her journey, many things were different from her first trip to New Britain in 1939. That first time war was to break out within days of her departure, but she had not known it. Now in 1947 the terrible floodtide of war had washed over the islands and retreated, leaving a changed land in its wake. That first time she had travelled by sea with other new mission staff, very young, very innocent, very hopeful. She was returning by plane, as a mature young woman whose earlier determination and sense of purpose had strengthened.

The journey seemed to have taken forever, but at last she looked down from the plane on the crescent of Blanche Bay, the offshore islands and the curves of the ring of volcanoes. The green of the vegetation was as she remembered it, and the blue and aquamarine of the sea. Tears were not far away as she felt the thud of wheels touching down and the plane roared to a halt. A cluster of people waited, waving and smiling. She could see the Browns and the angular lines of Miss Woolnough. As she stepped down into the heat of Rabaul, her friends hurried forward. Miss Woolnough hugged her, welcoming her with delight.

'I'll never forget the look on your face,' Miss Woolnough said, 'that day I saw you off on the *Reynella* for north Australia. You looked so forlorn. Your face said, "I'm going in the wrong direction." But now you're here!'

They had been watching for the mission boat since quite early in the morning. Today the boat would bring everyone from Rabaul for the synod meetings in October 1947 and the people at Vatnabara on the island of Ulu were to be hosts. Everything was ready for their guests.

'Well, it's as ready as we can manage,' Dorothy said. 'After the long dry spell there is not much in the way of vegetables except sweet potato, corn and snake beans. They'll all have to put up with tinned fish and rice and some native greens. It's not like the last time we had synod here at Vatnabara in 1941, just before the invasion. It couldn't be. The gardens were beautiful, then.'

Of course, it could not be the same. Jean knew that as well as anyone. Nor was it the lost gardens that she remembered. It was the people.

There was a shout at last, and they knew the mission boat was in sight. Canoes went out from the beach and brought back the visitors, a few at a time. The ministers were there, New Guinean and Australian, and Jean hurried to shake the hand of Akuila To Ngaru as he stepped from canoe to beach. Rev. Mo Pui Sam had come for his last synod with them; he was soon to return to China to try to find the family he had not seen for nearly ten years. Jean waited for the women; their new house was ready to receive Miss Woolnough, Jean Christopher and Elsie Wilson and she and Dorothy looked forward to their company.

In the days that followed, plans were made for the future. Energy was returning, new work could be planned, new staff had come and several experienced staff had come back to help. Senior New Guinean men who had borne the weight of leadership through the war were being ordained to the ministry, a sign that one of the new marks of the church in the islands was the emerging national leadership. New Guinean and Australian people shared the planning and the discussions and mourned together for the death of one of that first group of men trained for ministry by Howard Pearson; Aminio Bale had survived imprisonment and torture on New Ireland, but his health had been broken.

News was passed on about mutual friends. 'Dora Wilson is coming back in the new year,' they said, 'as soon as she has a medical clearance. Mavis Green is nursing at Maitland Hospital, near her home. Daisy McArthur is well again and both she and Essie Linggood have gone back to teaching.' Other names were mentioned, former mission staff, women who had lost their husbands and widows who were remarrying.

Though many of them were little more than names to each other, there continued to be a sense of belonging to a larger group of people who had been touched by the same events and bound by invisible links to a shared drama.

The group clustered together under the trees. Someone had insisted that there should be a synod photograph — 'We have always had a group photo,' they said. Brown faces and white mingled, laughing and teasing as they arranged and rearranged their positions around Con Mannering as chairman in the centre with the white women on either side.

'Can you wait a moment? I'd like to take a picture, too.'

Jean Poole moved quickly to face the group. Within the frame of the lens, they looked very small and distant. Every person in that frame had a story of what the past years had brought; for some imprisonment, for others isolation, grief, persecution, dislocation and loss. Men and women who had once formed a close community had been scattered across the globe, hidden from each other, out of touch apart from the unseen linking of their prayers. Now they had been drawn back together, a broken and wounded community reaching out to each other with hands that welcomed and comforted. For a brief moment, she imagined that she saw other faces among them. Australians, Chinese and New Guineans. . . faces of the missing, the bereaved and the dead. Faces of friends.

Jean blinked. The scene had blurred, memories overlaying the day's truth. Those other faces faded. John was gone. The home at Kalas was gone. She had stood one day beside the cement steps in the undergrowth, steps rising up to nothing, and the mockery of cement foundation stumps with nothing left to support. All of that world had gone.

Through the narrowed vision of the lens, she looked again. The group waited, solemn or smiling, those friends who represented the many who were starting again. She was one of them.

It was time to move on. The pressure of her finger captured the picture, a gathered-together group crystallised in time.

Afterword

The years that followed

THE YEARS OF WAR were, of course, only one part of the long lives of those whose story has been told.

Jean Poole remained at Vatnabara on Ulu Island for several years, teaching with the New Guinean staff at George Brown College. Her interest in botany, linguistics and photography continued, and she also undertook work in the field of vernacular literacy, using modern methods. Another interest was the task of translating from the Kuanua language the 1951 biography of Methodist minister, Hosea Linge. During her years on the island of Ulu, she bought a local four-seater canoe and had an arrangement with the New Guinean staff that, if they needed to use her canoe to travel to another island for church services, she and her nursing colleague Dorothy Pederick could go for the ride; this meant that she was able to visit most of the area.

When George Brown College was moved back to Vunairima on New Britain in 1952, she went with the others. In 1953, she resigned from the mission to travel to England to spend a year with her sister.

The former chairman of the mission, Rev. Con Mannering, had returned to Australia and his family in 1948. His wife Beatrice Mannering died in 1954 from a heart condition. After Jean Poole returned to Australia, Con Mannering made contact with her and in due course a romance developed. Jean Poole and Con Mannering were married in 1956 in Jean's home church of Rockdale, where she had married John Poole sixteen years earlier.

Con and Jean Mannering returned to New Britain in 1959, initially working in Ulu Circuit and then at Vunairima with George Brown College. It was the third period of missionary service for each of them. Among other work, Mannering was the founding principal of Rarongo Theological College which began in 1962. The Mannerings returned to Australia in 1965, living in Dromana, Victoria, on a large block where Jean grew Australian native flora. Now widowed again, Jean Mannering has returned to her original home area and lives in retirement in Hurstville, Sydney.

Dora Wilson returned to New Britain in 1948, but found that things had changed, both for the area and for herself. She returned to Australia after two years, due to health problems. In 1958 Dora married George Dunn and continued in the life of her church and community, giving generously of her nursing skills to those in need. Now widowed, Dora lives in the suburb of New Lambton, Newcastle, NSW, where she was born and grew up. She and Mavis Green have kept in touch with each other and with other women who shared their war experience, particularly the army nurses.

Mavis Green remained in her home district of Maitland, NSW, working at the Maitland District Hospital through a long career. Over the years, she has often been invited to speak to groups about her experiences during the war, and has cherished a range of mementoes of that time, including the hand-knitted cardigan which Dora gave back to her, now in the Australian War Memorial, and her war diary.

Mavis has retained a strong interest in the work of missions, participating in many activities related to missions overseas through the Methodist and now Uniting church, and was delighted to revisit Papua New Guinea with a missionary cruise group in 1967. She continues to correspond with several New Guineans first met over fifty years ago.

Dorothy Beale moved from Ulu Island at the end of 1947 and

went to work on New Ireland at Kimadan setting up nurse training for the district, starting with two students. Her work was much respected by medical workers in the Australian administration and in 1952 she was chosen to attend a conference on nursing education in Taiwan, under the auspices of the World Health Organisation. On her return, she recommended the establishment of a central school of nursing in a centre of high population; this concept came to fulfilment five years later when a school of nursing began in Port Moresby. In January 1952, Dorothy Beale was awarded the MBE in recognition of her services to nursing. She retired from the Methodist work in 1954, and continued nurse training with the Anglican mission in the Northern Province of Papua from 1955 to 1957. Dorothy Beale retired to her home state of Queensland, where she spent her last years.

Jean Christopher worked in New Britain from 1946 till 1949, re-establishing the health service which had formerly been at Malabonga but was now moved to the large village of Gaulim on the border of the Baining Mountains. On her return to South Australia, she joined the nursing staff of the Mothers and Babies Health Association and was known as a fine nurse and a devout Christian. When she became ill with cancer years later, several friends from the war period, including Dora (Wilson) Dunn, Joyce Walker and Rodger and Kath Brown, gathered from around Australia to be with Chris, counting the last celebration of holy communion at her bedside as one of the most moving experiences of their lives. Jean Christopher died in Adelaide in July 1973.

Elsie Wilson taught in the islands from late 1947 until 1951, establishing a new middle school at Kimadan on New Ireland. She was then asked to undertake a new challenge. In 1950, the Rev. Gordon Young and his wife Grace had been invited to pioneer a new missionary work in the Southern Highlands of New Guinea. Gordon Young first walked into the remote mountain valley with his companions and a government exploratory patrol in November 1950. Grace Young, nurse Joyce Walker and teacher Elsie Wilson, together with the Rev. Roland and Miriam Barnes, joined the first small party in the middle of 1951, as soon as a rough airstrip had been carved from the valley. Elsie Wilson was responsible for establishing the first school in the Southern High-lands of New Guinea at Mendi, in very challenging circumstances and among a people who had never before encountered the concept of literacy or a world beyond their high valley.

She retired from missionary work in 1959, greatly loved by the people she had served, and returned to teaching in South Australia. In 1991, she was delighted to be visited by one of her early schoolgirls from Mendi, now the matron of the large Mendi Hospital forty years after Elsie first went to begin her bush school. (An aside: I followed Elsie Wilson as head teacher of the Methodist Mission School in Mendi in 1961, where the name of Miss Wilson was held in high regard.) Elsie Wilson lives in retirement in Adelaide.

Kath and Rodger Brown worked in New Britain until 1954, when they returned to South Australia because of illness. Kath was able to revisit Malalia where she had lived pre-war; all that was left of their pre-war home was a cement pad, as everything else had been bombed, but the mountains were the same as ever, reminding Kath of the eternal faithfulness of God through all that had happened. The Browns have never lost their enthusiasm for the area and people of the New Guinea Islands, revisiting several times, retaining their ability with the language and keeping in touch with friends.

Rodger spent many years serving as Overseas Missions Secretary for the Methodist church in South Australia, continuing regular relations with the church in New Guinea islands. They have never forgotten their friends and colleagues lost during the war and the questions raised by that calamity have influenced them ever since. Kath and Rodger live in retirement in Adelaide and celebrated fifty-three years of marriage early in 1993.

Of the mission women widowed during the war, Jean Shelton, Mel Trevitt, Eileen Pearce, Marion Oakes, Helen Pearson, Netta Allsop and Nellie Simpson re-married. Others, like Daisy Mc-Arthur, Essie Linggood, Helen Wayne and Beryl Beazley rebuilt their lives, caring for their children and in many cases returning to or continuing their earlier professions. In the first few years after the war, in company with over a thousand families who had a man on the nominal roll of the *Montevideo Maru*, they had to face a sequence of encounters with government, legal and insurance agencies where they were required to produce proof that they were indeed widows. Civilian widows were being offered the possibility of making claims for assistance from the Civilian Internees Trust Fund as late as 1953.

A number of these women have found it very difficult, through the years, to express what their experience of loss has meant, preferring not to speak of it and to put it behind them. In the case of some of the mission women, the experience led them to withdraw from the institutional church for many years, feeling that they had been let down by the church leaders and, perhaps, by God. For some, the years have brought continuing pain, bitterness, anger and emotional breakdown. Others saw the poison of the uncertainty and grief of the loss of their husbands infecting their children, now people in mid-life whose childhood memories still have power to hurt them.

Daisy McArthur recovered her health. In the years after the war, she developed her gift for preaching and used her intellect as a fine teacher and Christian laywoman, with particular involvement in the Womens' Auxiliary of Overseas Missions. Her faith was always central and she continued to explore and grow in things of the spirit all her life. Stories filtered back to her that some of the New Guinean Christians who had known her husband well were sure they had seen him — thin, bearded and passing along a road on the back of a truck with Laurie Linggood — late in the war years.

When her elder son Malcolm went to work in Papua New Guinea in the early 1970s, he met Mikael To Bilak who spoke to him of it. Daisy was suspicious of the story that her husband had died with the *Montevideo Maru*; it seemed to her that the church leaders were trying to cover something up in order to make the widows feel easier. Though she was convinced that her husband was dead, she always carried an uncertainty about how he had died, hoping only that it had been swift and merciful. Daisy McArthur died in Adelaide in 1977.

Marion Oakes completed her nursing training and went to

work as school nurse at her sons' school, Wolaroi College, Orange, NSW. While there, she met a visiting Member of Parliament; they were married in 1947 and Marion bore a second family of four children. A very capable woman who combined homemaking skills with business acumen, nursing, public speaking, sharing her husband's political career and leadership in the Girl Guide movement, she chose to separate herself from the church for a number of years. She felt that the mission authorities had been at fault in delaying her husband Dan's furlough and then in failing to recall their staff before they were captured.

In the 1950s, Marion's son George returned to the islands as a patrol officer, continuing the family link. Marion did not forget the people or the place, visiting Papua New Guinea in 1972 and 1975 and supporting New Guinean students, but the memories have never ceased to hurt. She prefers not to discuss that experience, feeling that the matter should be left to rest. Marion (Oakes) Hearnshaw lives in retirement in Sydney.

Nellie Simpson said of herself, in her old age, that she had had a 'life of starts and stops'. Before her marriage to Tom Simpson, her first fiancé had died during their engagement and, after Tom's death, she had two further marriages. Nellie worked at a number of jobs, including a long period as accountant/bookkeeper, and began teacher training at the age of fifty, a new career which she loved.

In the 1970s, a family connection told Nellie a story which he had heard from a sea captain who had plied between New Ireland, New Hanover and New Britain before the war. The story was that Tom Simpson had been killed, probably beheaded, by the Japanese early in the war before the group captured in the area of Kavieng had reached the camp in Rabaul; Tom had tried to protect a young soldier who was being threatened. The last time Tom Simpson was named by witnesses as having been sighted was in Kavieng in the early months of 1942, but his name appears on the nominal roll of those on the *Montevideo Maru*.

Nellie felt that the story she had been told fitted other clues which had come to her earlier about Tom's end; she was also impressed by the fact that the man who told her the story had done so under a sense of compulsion and had died only weeks later. Nellie (Simpson) Thirkettle, widowed once more, lived to see Tom's children's children grow up and died in Adelaide in 1992.

Essie Linggood returned to teaching, working at the Church of England Girls' School, Glen Iris, Victoria. The New Guinea Scholarship, provided by the organisation of women who had lived in the islands before the war, made it possible for her son to attend Wesley College and her daughter to attend the Methodist Ladies' College in Melbourne. Essie maintained her strong interest in missionary work and in New Britain in particular, expressing it with great energy through her local church at Malvern, as a member of the central executive of the Victorian Women's Auxiliary for Overseas Missions and as editor of a mission magazine *The Link* for twenty-five years.

In 1964, her son Bill returned to New Britain to work, as his father had done, as a Methodist missionary. Essie visited her son and his wife Caroline and was received back with great joy by the older people of the community at Raluana where she had worked with her husband before the war. Essie's family was a great source of joy to her. She died in Melbourne in 1975.

Helen Pearson, who had been so certain that her husband would come home, recovered from her breakdown in New Britain in 1947 and returned to teaching at Unley High School, South Australia. However, the trauma of the loss of her husband had affected her deeply. Though she had strong support from her own and Howard's families, the rest of her life was burdened with continued searching along a range of religious paths, with personal griefs, with serious health problems, with anxieties and confusion. The intelligent young woman, full of a zest for life, was a victim of war as much as was her husband, though for Helen the war did not end in 1945. In her later years, Helen Pearson endured a minimal quality of life and died in 1992.

Mel Trevitt, following her work during the war in personnel and welfare in Melbourne, decided to return to teaching after the war as this suited her young son's pattern as a schoolchild. When a stained glass window in memory of Jack Trevitt was unveiled in his home church of Eastwood in Sydney, she flew from Melbourne with her son for the unveiling. In later years, she was to marry and be widowed twice more. A very able woman, she travelled widely and used her gifts in both the work sphere and in voluntary service such as Lifeline. In the 1960s, she revisited the islands with a missionary cruise organised by the Methodist church and was able to see places and meet people who had been part of her earlier life. Mel (Trevitt) Walker died in Sydney in 1992.

The New Guinean minister, Akuila To Ngaru, retired from his appointment to the Bainings circuit in 1952 and died in 1953. The pastor-teacher Mikael To Bilak, who with his wife Louisa had been at Kalas with John and Jean Poole in 1940–1941, became a candidate for the Methodist ministry in 1950. To Bilak was a much respected minister for many years, taking positions of church leadership and among other tasks making a major contribution to the translation of the Bible in his own language. Saimon Gaius, who as a young student made a welcome speech to the new missionaries in 1940, as well as being among the New Guinean staff who worked with Jean Poole at the post-war George Brown College, also became a Methodist minister. In later years, he became the first New Guinean bishop of his area, in the period after the former Methodist mission became part of United Church of Papua New Guinea and the Solomon Islands. Bishop Saimon Gaius was knighted by the Queen.

The United church in the islands of New Britain, New Ireland, New Hanover and the Duke of Yorks has been responsible for its own local leadership for over twenty years now, employing Australians and other overseas staff for specific roles when they choose to do so. As well as taking charge of their own affairs, the Methodist/United church of those islands has also provided staff for the post-war pioneer missionary work in the Southern Highlands of New Guinea, from the time when two of their pastor-teachers went with the pioneer team to Mendi in 1950.

The Chinese minister, Rev. Mo Pui Sam, returned from Rabaul to China in 1948. By the time he finally returned to his home area, he had been away for ten years, for seven of those years having no contact with his wife because of war in both China and Rabaul.

He discovered that his wife, thinking that he must surely be dead, had remarried. Mo Pui Sam now lives in Canada. The teacher Thomas Mow remained in Rabaul until the 1950s, teaching at the post-war school begun for the Chinese children and acting as a lay leader in the Chinese church. A number of members of the wartime Rabaul Chinese community now live in Sydney and retain strong links of friendship.

Of the staff who travelled across Australia with the Aboriginal children in 1942, Margaret Somerville remained for many years in north Australia and her name is linked with continuing, though very different opportunities for Aboriginal children in the north in the 1990s; she now lives in Sydney. Jessie March, who first went to New Guinea in 1925, returned there to teach at Gaulim Teachers' College from 1967 to 1971, and was noted for riding her motor scooter at the age of 70; several generations of mission staff celebrated her ninetieth birthday with her in Adelaide in 1990.

The mystery of the last days of the men who were lost from Rabaul and neighbouring islands in 1942 has continued to trouble a number of the families, with alternative stories of what may have taken place being told through fifty years to the present day. Women who had accepted that their husbands were lost with the ship were very disturbed when Bishop Leo Scharmach of the Sacred Heart Mission, Vunapope, published his story of the war years in 1960. He stated that in his opinion 'it is highly probable that a *Montevideo Maru* never existed' and suggested that the men had been machine-gunned and tossed into a mass grave on New Britain and, 'to put investigators on the wrong track, [the Japanese] assiduously spread the story of the *Montevideo Maru*'.

Australian visitors to New Britain also brought home stories told by New Guineans of sightings of the missionaries towards the end of the war. The sons of both Laurie McArthur and Laurie Linggood were told by New Guineans many years later, in the 1960s, that their fathers had been seen by villagers as late as 1945. A number of people, including the Rev. Arthur Brawn and his wife Jean Brawn, and the Rev. Neville Threlfall, have tried to establish the truth over the years, gathering evidence from many sources but the complete picture remains unclear. (Arthur Brawn had been a missionary colleague during the 1930s of a number of the men who were lost and the tragedy was to haunt him and his wife, leading to a lifelong search for information and great persistence in bringing the story to the attention of the community until their deaths in 1993.)

From US and Japanese records it seems clear that the US submarine USS *Sturgeon* torpedoed and sank the ship *Montevideo Maru* on 1 July 1942 with almost total loss of life. A nominal roll of 1 053 Australians from Rabaul was recovered in Japan by Major H.S. Williams in August 1945 and translated back from the Japanese language; it included the names of all the Methodist missionaries who were missing as well as former staff Allsop and Wayne. The name of Bill Huntley, another former staff member, was not on the nominal roll and this meshes with the information that Huntley and a party of others were seen by the Catholic mission doctor at Vunapope at the end of July 1942 being taken in a Japanese truck towards Rabaul; it is understood that the party were later executed.

Of the men of the community of Kavieng, New Ireland, many of their names appear on the ship's nominal roll, however other evidence suggests that at least some of them were not on the ship, having died earlier by execution or disease. It seems certain that a very large party of Australian soldiers and civilians was lost with the ship, yet perhaps this question will never be answered: Was every man listed on the roll in fact on board the ship when it sank?

The mystery will always remain a mystery. As a New Guinean wrote many years later, 'We must wait until the end of the world before we know the truth of this thing.'

By 1955 a plaque in memory of the Australian Methodist missionaries who died during World War II was placed at the George Brown Methodist Missionary Training College at Haberfield, Sydney. The names included ten men from New Britain (McArthur, Shelton, Linggood, Oakes, Simpson, Pearson, Poole, Trevitt, Pearce, Beazley) as well as the two other missionary chairmen who died in the period, Kentish and Rundle. Other names which do not appear on the memorial are also remembered as members of the same mission family; they include Rev. Don

Alley, a New Zealand Methodist working in Bougainville, whose name appeared on the *Montevideo Maru* nominal roll, with the names of former mission staff Ron Wayne and Ken Allsop, as well as former staff member Bill Huntley and Chinese mission carpenter Leong Tim, who were both executed. When, in time, changes meant that the Haberfield property was to be sold, arrangements were made for the memorial plaque to be re-sited at the Uniting Church Centre for Ministry at North Parramatta, Sydney.

On 2 July 1988, more than 300 people gathered at North Parramatta to honour those remembered on the plaque as it was unveiled in its new location. The guests included missionary widows Mel (Trevitt) Walker, Jean (Shelton) Stuart and Jean (Poole) Mannering, as well as mission nurses Dora (Wilson) Dunn and Mavis Green, Rodger and Kath Brown, Arthur and Jean Brawn who had made sure that the community did not forget, with special guest Bishop Sir Saimon Gaius and his wife Lady Margaret. The gathering listened to a taped message and memory from former chaplain, now Canon John May, who was among the last Australians to see the troops and civilians before they left Rabaul.

To remember the loss of the community of Rabaul and wider district at the time of the fiftieth anniversary of the sinking of the *Montevideo Maru*, a large crowd met on 4 July 1992 at the Centre for Ministry, North Parramatta. Among the group who met over a meal and for a service of remembrance that day were people representing almost every part of the story of what happened fifty years earlier. There were the widows, adult children and grandchildren of the soldiers and civilians whose names were on the nominal roll of those lost on the *Montevideo Maru*; and the families of planters, missionaries, government agents, commercial enterprise, medical staff and the young soldiers of the 2/22nd Battalion. There were men from among the 400 soldiers and civilians who escaped from the scene of battle and made their way home, through many adventures and stresses, in 1942.

Among the women were some who had been evacuated from Rabaul and had spent Christmas 1941 at sea on the *Macdhui* and the *Neptuna*. One of the nurses who spent the war interned in

Japan was present as well as two of the women who had escorted the large party of part-Aboriginal children across the continent in 1942. A Chinese couple was there who had been married in Rabaul fifty years earlier as members of the interned Chinese community; they remembered the privations of their internment under Japan and the bombing raids of the Allies. Bishop William To Kilala represented the New Guinean people who had suffered so terribly through those years from a war that was not their own. A former RAAF bomber pilot who had bombed the area was there, as were representatives of the Seventh Day Adventist Church and the Salvation Army who had lost men with the sinking of the ship, and a former missionary doctor who had travelled on the *Montevideo Maru* in its earlier years as a passenger vessel in the waters of Asia.

The opportunity for so many people to remember the events of the war as it touched the islands of New Guinea was valued by the people present. Those events have had a profound impact on the families and friends of those who died and those who survived, whether they died in battle, escaped, were lost with the ship, or were interned in Rabaul or Japan. For many of those present, it was a great relief to be able to speak with others who understood the power of their memories of that place and time, and the way those events had shaped their family.

This part of the Australian story has not become legend, in the way that some other war events have become part of the national landscape, even though twice as many Australian men died in the loss of the *Montevideo Maru* as died during the whole of the Vietnam War. This has angered people who feel that there were major failures on the part of the Australian government and military at the time which left both the civilian communities and the army garrison in Rabaul unprotected and ill prepared for what happened. The long silence and the unresolved mystery associated with the loss of the *Montevideo Maru* have left deep wounds for many Australian families, wounds which even now after fifty years have not been fully healed.

Appendix

Methodist mission personnel and associates referred to in the book

Australian mission staff:

Beale, Dorothy; nurse; 1934–1945, 1946–1954
Beazley, Sydney; carpenter/teacher; and Beryl; 1937–1942
Brawn, Arthur; minister; and Jean; 1932–1935
Brown, Rodger; minister; and Kath; 1940–1942, 1945–1954
Chenoweth, Ben; minister; and Ruby; 1923–1941, 1947–1960
Christopher, Jean; nurse; 1937–1945, 1946–1949
Clark, Percy; minister; and Dorothy; 1935–1941
Davies, Walter; minister; and Rita; 1924–1927, 1946–1948
Green, Mavis; nurse; 1939–1945
Harris, Margaret; nurse; 1918–1941
Holmes, Dorothy; nurse; 1941
Jenkins, Mary; teacher; 1933–1941
Jones, Stanley; minister; and Hazel; 1936–1939
Leong, Tim; carpenter; 1920–1942
Lewis, Frank; minister; and Catherine; 1932–1938, 1950–1955
Linggood, Laurence; minister; and Essie; 1930–1942
Mannering, Con; minister; and Beatrice; 1930–1939, 1945–1948
Mannering, Con; minister; and Jean; 1959–1965
March, Jessie; teacher; 1925–1939, 1967–1971

McArthur, Laurence; minister; and Daisy; 1931–1937, 1939–1942
Mo, Pui Sam; minister; 1940–1948
Mow, Thomas and Wai Yin; teachers; 1934–1947
Oakes, Dan; minister; and Marion; 1933–1942
Pearce, Wilfred; accountant; and Eileen; 1926–1942
Pearson, Howard; minister; and Helen; 1936–1942
Platten, Gilbert; minister; and Isabel; 1927–1934, 1937–1942, 1945–1949
Poole, Jean; teacher; 1946–1954
Poole, John; minister; and Jean; 1940–1942
Shelton, Herbert; minister; and Jean; 1935–1942
Simpson, Thomas; minister; and Nellie; 1936–1942
Trevitt, Jack; minister; and Melville; 1936–1942
Walker, Joyce; nurse; 1946–1951
Wilson, Dora; nurse; 1940–1945, 1948–1949
Wilson, Elsie; teacher; 1939–1941, 1947–1951
Woolnough, Mary; nurse; 1914–1932, 1936–1939, 1946–1948
Young, Gordon; minister; and Grace; 1946–1950

Former mission staff, still connected with the Methodist church in Rabaul in 1942:

Wayne, Ron; lay missionary; 1924–1938; court interpreter; 1939–1942; and Helen
Huntley, William; agricultural worker; 1932–1940; postmaster; 1941–1942; and Hannah
Allsop, Ken; Chairman's Assistant; and Netta; 1933–1934

New Guinean ministers:

Akuila To Ngaru; minister
Mikael To Bilak; teacher/minister; and Louisa
Saimon Gaius; teacher/minister; and Margaret
Aminio Bale; minister; and Rubi Ia Margat
Beniamin To Golo; minister
Beniamin Talai; minister; and Idi

Bibliography

BOOKS

Adam-Smith, Patsy, *Australian Women at War*, Nelson, Melbourne, 1984

American and Allied Personnel Recovered from Japanese Prisons: Pictorial History Recorded by Replacement Command, AFWESPAC, Manila, 1945

Aplin, Douglas A., *Rabaul 1942*, 2/22nd Battalion AIF Lark Force Association, Melbourne, 1980

Australian Parliament, Canberra, *House of Representatives: Statement concerning loss of Montevideo Maru by Minister for External Territories*, 5 October 1945

Benson, James, *Prisoner's Base and Home Again: The Story of a Missionary POW*, Robert Hale Ltd, London, 1957

Brown, Rodger, *New Guinea Methodism in War and Peace: a Personal Record*, Uniting Church Historical Society (South Australia), Adelaide, 1989

Clarence, Margaret, *Yield Not to the Wind*, Management Development Publishers Pty Ltd, Sydney, 1982

Clarke, Hugh V., *Last Stop Nagasaki*, George Allen and Unwin, Sydney, 1984

Connolly R. & Wilson B., *Medical Soldiers, 2/10 Australian Field Ambulance 8 Division 1940–1945*

Coulthard-Clark, C.D., *Action Stations Coral Sea: The Australian Commander's Story*, Allen and Unwin, Sydney, 1991

Dexter, David, *The New Guinea Offensives: Australia in the War of 1939–1945*, Australian War Memorial, Canberra, 1961 [Series 1 (Army) Vol.6]

Goldsmith, Betty & Sandford, Beryl, *The Girls They Left Behind: Life in Australia during World War II — The Women Remember*, Penguin, Melbourne, 1990

Japan's Longest Day: The Story of Japan's Struggle to Surrender — August 1945. Told By the Japanese Themselves, Pacific War Research Society, 1968

Johnson R.W. and Threlfall N.A., *Volcano Town: the 1937–43 Rabaul Eruptions*, Robert Brown and Associates, 1985

Kenny, Catherine, *Captives: Australian Army Nurses in Japanese Prison Camps*, University of Queensland Press, St Lucia, 1986

Kettle, Ellen, *That They Might Live*, F.P. Leonard, Sydney, 1979

Linge, Hosea, *An Offering Fit for a King: The life and work of the Rev. Hosea Linge*, told by himself, translated by Neville Threlfall, Toksave Buk, Rabaul, 1978

McCarthy, Dudley, *South West Pacific Area — First Year: Kokoda to Wau*, Australian War Memorial, Canberra, 1959 [Series 1 (Army) Vol.5]

McCarthy, J.K. *Patrol Into Yesterday: My New Guinea Years*, F.W. Cheshire, Melbourne, 1963

Nelson, Hank, *Taim Bilong Masta: The Australian Involvement with Papua New Guinea*, ABC, Sydney, 1982

Nelson, Hank, POW *Prisoners of War: Australians Under Nippon*, ABC Enterprises, Sydney, 1985

Pictorial History of Australia at War 1939–1945, Vol.1, Meeking, Charles (ed.), Board of Management of Australian War Memorial, Canberra

Scharmach, Most Rev. Leo, *This Crowd Beats Us All*, Catholic Press Newspaper Co. Ltd, Sydney, 1960

Selby, David, *Hell and High Fever*, Currawong Publishing Co. Pty Ltd, Sydney, 1956

Simons, Jessie Elizabeth, *In Japanese Hands: Australian Nurses as POWs*, William Heinemann, Melbourne, 1985 (Originally issued as *While History Passed Them By*, 1954)

Somerville, Margaret, *They Crossed a Continent*, privately published, Darwin, 1991

Threlfall, Neville, *One Hundred Years in the Islands: The Methodist/United Church in the New Guinea Islands Region 1875–1975*, Toksave Buk, Rabaul, 1975

Threlfall, Neville, manuscript of 'From Mangroves to Frangipani: the story of Rabaul and East New Britain Province', 1988 (In publication, Robert Brown & Associates (Qld) Pty Ltd, 1993)

Wigmore, Lionel, *The Japanese Thrust: Australia in the War of 1939–1945*, Australian War Memorial, Canberra, 1957 [Series 1 (Army) Vol.4]

NEWSPAPERS

Melbourne Herald, 1/9/1945 — 30/11/1945; 26/9/1945

Missionary Review, Methodist Church of Australasia, 1940–1946

NSW Methodist, 1940–1945

Sydney Morning Herald, 1941–1945

JOURNALS

'Did a Ghost Ship Sail From Here?', *Pacific Islands Monthly*, October 1960

Drain, Dorothy, 'Hunger, privation did not subdue their spirit', *Australian Women's Weekly*, 29 September 1945

Nelson, Hank, 'The Troops, the Town and the Battle: Rabaul 1942', *Journal of Pacific History*, 27: 2, 1992

Poole, Jean, 'Still Further Notes on a Snake Dance of the Baining', *Oceania*, XIII: 3 March 1943

Sweeting, A.J., '*Montevideo Maru* — Myth or Merchantman?' *Australian Territories*, 1: 2, 1961

ARCHIVES AND RESEARCH MATERIAL

Private Papers

A Nilai Ra Dovot (Voice of the Truth), Methodist paper for New Guinea Islands, July 1972 (galley proof)

Brawn, Jean, statement concerning shortwave broadcast from Japan telling of loss of Rabaul prisoners, heard in NSW during war

Green, Mavis, Diary of Rabaul, Yokohama and Totsuka, 1942–1945

Harry, C.O. (Bill), manuscript recorded, 29/9/1971

Harry, C.O. (Bill), 'New Britain 1941/1942: the Japanese invasion and thereafter as recorded by VX24.800'. Manuscript.

Harry, C.O. (Bill), personal communication, 3/9/1992

May, Canon John, personal communication describing events at Vunapope, Malaguna and on board the *Naruto Maru* during 1942; written 11/2/1992

May, Chaplain John, letter of 26/11/1945 to Rev. G.E. Johnston regarding last contacts with interned men before sailing from Rabaul.

Oakes, Dan, personal letter to father-in-law G.E. Johnston, 8/12/1941

Poole, Jean, photograph album, New Britain, 1940–1941

Record of speeches made by representatives of key groups and eyewitnesses of events, at commemoration service for prisoners on the *Montevideo Maru*, held at Rabaul, 22/6/1972

Shelton, Herbert, personal letters to wife Jean, December 1941 – 14 January 1942

Shelton, Jean, photograph album, New Britain 1935–1941

Thomas, Gordon, letter to Mrs Jean Brawn regarding theories about loss of *Montevideo Maru*, 24/2/1965

Wayne, Ron, personal letters to wife from Rabaul 23/12/1941 – 16/1/1942

Australian Archives, Canberra

Cable from Australian Prime Minister's Department, 12 December 1941: A816/1 14/301/255

Correspondence from various widows inquiring about death certificates and other legal problems post-war: A1066/1: IC45/55/3/19

Correspondence concerning difficulties of obtaining information about prisoners in Japanese hands, 1945: AA1973/362/1: P26/9: PT13

Defence of Rabaul, 1941-1942: A816: 14/301/255

Nurses at Totsuka and Yokohama: A816/1: 37/301/277A; A1066/1: IC45/6/1/17; A1066/1: IC45/55/3/14/2/1

Australian War Memorial, Canberra

Account by Major D.I. Figgis of events leading up to Japanese invasion of Rabaul, evacuation and escapes: AWM54: 607/7/1

American and Japanese accounts of sinking of *Montevideo Maru*, including War Patrol diary of US Submarine *Sturgeon*, 30 June-1 July 1942: AWM54 779/1/26

Captured documents Nos 58 and 74, diaries of members of Japanese Kure No.3 Special Landing Party, March-August 1942. Reference to Rabaul, Coral Sea Battle and Kavieng: AWM54 253/5/7

Information obtained regarding the murder of Capt. Gray at Vunapope Catholic Mission, February 1942 [recorded in 1945]: AWM54 1010/9/32

Knickerbocker, H.R., Despatches from war correspondent concerning mail dropped by Japanese from Australian prisoners-of-war in Rabaul 1942: AWM54 773/4/65

Letter from Japanese forces, Rabaul, 1945: AWM54 779/1/5

Nottage papers, concerning the fall of Rabaul, prisoners-of-war on *Naruto Maru* and at Zentsugi, comments about missing men: AWM (PR 83/189)

Plans for evacuation of civilians from Rabaul, Department of Army Military Board, 1941: AWM60 611/41

Rabaul personnel reports of events before and during evacuation of Rabaul: AWM54 607/9/7

Reports of conditions, action and withdrawal from Rabaul, January–March 1942 by 2/22nd Battalion, by various officers: AWM54 607/8/2; AWM73 1; AWM54 779/3/76

Reports on investigation of loss of *Montevideo Maru* by Major H.S.Williams, 1945: AWM54 779/1/1; AWM54 779/1/5

Mitchell Library, Sydney

Correspondence and papers from New Britain, Methodist Overseas Missions, 1926–1947: ML MOM 501; 1931–1966: ML MOM 573; 1942–1946: ML MOM 470

Correspondence of General Secretary of Methodist Overseas Missions, 1935–1943: ML MOM 314

McArthur, L.A., 'Educational Problems of the Methodist Mission in New Britain with special reference to the training of teachers', 1935: ML MOM 289(i)

Methodist Overseas Missions, Minutes of Board, 1939–1943: ML MOM 339

Methodist Overseas Missions, Minutes of Board, 1943–1947: ML MOM 340

Pacific Manuscripts Bureau, ANU, Canberra

Gordon Thomas, correspondence, diary, papers while prisoner in Rabaul, 1942–1945: PMB 600

Gordon Thomas, manuscript, Rabaul 1942–1945: PMB 36

VARIOUS LISTS OF THOSE PRESUMED TO BE LOST ON MON-TEVIDEO MARU AND DOCUMENTS GIVING EYEWITNESS REPORTS OF OTHER MISSING CIVILIANS IN NEW BRITAIN

Australian Archives, Canberra

Civilians reported lost on *Montevideo Maru*; nominal roll translated from Japanese Katakana language [No date: presumed to be made in

May 1942, located in Japan in August 1945, includes obscure spellings of personal and place names]; also, additional correspondence on the same subject with lists of names: A1066/1: IC45/55/3/19

Civilians seen at Kokopo, 25 February 1942 [List recorded by POW nurses in Manila, September 1945, also other eyewitness reports of other missing people by Rabaul survivors]: A1066/1: IC45/55/3/14/2/1

List of members of New Guinea Volunteer Rifles on full-time duty reported to be on board *Montevideo Maru* when torpedoed, 1/7/1942 [As recorded January 1942]: A7030/1: 13

Persons lost on *Montevideo Maru* [Listed in alphabetical order from various evidence in 1946]: A7030 6

Forms with information of death for civilians lost at sea on *Montevideo Maru* [Personal family details: forms completed by widows during 1945-1947]: A518/1: GR16/2/1

Persons lost on *Montevideo Maru* [Alphabetical order, with names and addresses of next-of-kin. No date, but no earlier than 1948 because it includes new names of widows who re-married in 1948]: A7030/1 6

Australian War Memorial
Documents regarding civilian population of New Ireland during 1941 with plans for evacuation: AWM54 831/3/93

'Left Rabaul' [Another typing with slight variations of AWM54 1010/1/30, no date]: AWM54 779/1/5

List of passengers believed to have left New Britain on the *Montevideo Maru* as compiled by Gordon Thomas and A. Cresswick from memory. List headed 'Left Rabaul', names only, not alphabetical order [List originally made in Rabaul late in 1942 and recorded officially in October 1945]: AWM54 1010/1/30

Nominal roll of civilians in Rabaul internment camp at the end of May 1942 [As recalled by four survivors in 1945]: AWM54 1010/9/78

Press releases of war correspondent Eric Thornton on entry into Rabaul in September 1945 following surrender: AWM54 73/4/22

Press releases of war correspondent Warren from Rabaul, September 1945: AWM773/4/12

Questionnaire of civilians captured in Rabaul, 23 January 1942 [Interviewed in Rabaul, 13 September 1945]: AWM54 1010/4/172

Rabaul — Report of civilians and prisoners-of-war [Correspondence, lists of civilian internees, reports on conditions of prisoners-of-war, 1945-1946]: AWM127 14

Records of interviews regarding war crimes during 1942 [Interviews in November 1945]: AWM54 1010/9/32

Statements by various Rabaul survivors [Interviews in September–November 1945]: AWM127 3; AWM127 13; AWM54 1010/4/177

Note:
A further series of material on the loss of the *Montevideo Maru* is held at Australian Archives, Melbourne.

INTERVIEWS

Jean Brawn, George and Edna Oakes: *taped* 4.2.92

Kath Brown, Elsie Wilson, Jessie March, Grace Young: *taped* 25.11.91

Rodger and Kath Brown: *taped* 25.11.91, 26.11.91, 11.7.92

Clem Christopher: *taped* 26.11.91

Mavis Green and Dora (Wilson) Dunn: *taped* 16–17 December 1991

Hazel Jones, Jean Chapple: *taped* October 1991

Jean (Poole) Mannering: *taped* October 1991

Malcolm McArthur, Bill Linggood: *taped* 26.11.91

Ping Hui: *taped* 27.9.92

Nellie (Simpson) Thirkettle: *taped* 26.11.91

Elsie Wilson: *taped* 27.11.91

Picture acknowledgements

**Numbers after name of person, organisation or magazine
indicate number of the picture in the text**

Australian War Memorial: **22** (AWM negative no. 19146), **23** (AWM
negative no. 19150), **24** (AWM negative no. 19149), **26** (AWM
negative no. 96810), **27** (AWM negative no. 96809) **28** (AWM
negative no. 96842)

Rodger Brown: **4, 33**

Mavis Green: **6**

Jessie March: **1**

Malcolm McArthur: **9, 10**

The Missionary Review, Uniting Church World Mission, Sydney,
15, 16, 17, 18, 19, 25, 29, 31

Jean Poole: **2, 3, 5, 8, 11, 12, 13, 14, 20, 21, 30, 32, 34**

Elsie Wilson: **7**